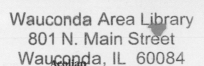

Aeolian
Islands

**NORTHEASTERN
SICILY**
Pages 158–191

Messina •

**NORTHEASTERN
SICILY**

CATANIA •

Enna
•

STERN
Y

•
Caltanissetta

**SOUTHERN
SICILY**

Syracuse •

**SOUTHERN
SICILY**
Pages 132–157

RAGUSA •

0 kilometres   250

0 miles   20

EYEWITNESS TRAVEL
SICILY

EYEWITNESS TRAVEL

SICILY

LONDON, NEW YORK,
MELBOURNE, MUNICH AND DELHI
www.dk.com

Produced by Fabio Ratti
Editoria Libraria e Multimediale, Milan, Italy

PROJECT EDITOR Giovanni Francesio
EDITOR Elena Marzorati
SECRETARY Emanuela Damiani
DESIGNERS STUDIO Matra–Silvia Tomasone, Lucia Tirabassi
MAPS Oriana Bianchetti

Dorling Kindersley Ltd
PROJECT EDITOR Fiona Wild
DTP DESIGNERS Maite Lantaron, Lee Redmond
PRODUCTION David Proffit
MANAGING EDITORS Fay Franklin, Louise Bostock Lang
MANAGING ART EDITOR Annette Jacobs
EDITORIAL DIRECTOR Vivien Crump
ART DIRECTOR Gillian Allan
PUBLISHER Douglas Amrine

CONTRIBUTORS
Fabrizio Ardito, Cristina Gambaro
Additional tourist information by Marco Scapagnini

ILLUSTRATORS
Giorgia Boli, Silvana Ghioni, Alberto Ipsilanti, Nadia Viganò

ENGLISH TRANSLATION Richard Pierce

Reproduced by Colourscan (Singapore)
Printed in Malaysia by Vivar Printing Sdn. Bhd

First American Edition, 2000
11 12 13 14 10 9 8 7 6 5 4 3 2 1

Published in the United States by DK Publishing,
375 Hudson Street, New York, New York 10014

Reprinted with revisions 2001, 2003, 2005, 2007, 2009, 2011

Copyright 2000, 2011 © Dorling Kindersley Limited, London

Published in Great Britain by Dorling Kindersley Limited.

A CATALOG RECORD FOR THIS BOOK IS AVAILABLE
FROM THE LIBRARY OF CONGRESS.

ISSN 1542-1554

ISBN 978-0-75667-023-8

THROUGHOUT THIS BOOK, FLOORS ARE REFERRED TO IN ACCORDANCE WITH
EUROPEAN USAGE, I.E., THE "FIRST FLOOR" IS THE FLOOR ABOVE GROUND LEVEL.

*Front cover main image: View of Giardini-Naxos
from the Greek Theatre, Taormina*

MIX
Paper from
responsible sources
FSC
www.fsc.org   FSC™ C018179

**The information in this
DK Eyewitness Travel Guide is checked regularly.**
Every effort has been made to ensure that this book is as up-to-date
as possible at the time of going to press. Some details, however,
such as telephone numbers, opening hours, prices, gallery hanging
arrangements and travel information are liable to change. The
Publishers cannot accept responsibility for any consequences arising
from the use of this book, nor for any material on third party websites,
and cannot guarantee that any website address in this book will be a
suitable source of travel information. We value the views and
suggestions of our readers very highly. Please write to: Publisher,
DK Eyewitness Travel Guides, Dorling Kindersley, 80 Strand,
London WC2R 0RL, Great Britain, or email: travelguides@dk.com.

◁ **The Temple of Hera in the Valle dei Templi at Agrigento**

CONTENTS

**Female bust sculpted in the
5th century BC** *(see pp30–31)*

INTRODUCING
SICILY

PALERMO
AREA BY AREA

**Backcloth, Museo delle Marionette
in Palermo** *(see pp50–51)*

Castellammare del Golfo *(see p96)*, one of many fishing villages on the Sicilian coast

Ancient theatre mask,
Museo Eoliano *(see p190)*

'TRAVELLERS' NEEDS

A cheese vendor at Catania's
open-air market *(see pp222–3)*

The medieval castle at Erice, in
Northwestern Sicily *(see p33 & p100)*

HOW TO USE THIS GUIDE

This guide will help you to get the most out of your visit to Sicily. It provides detailed practical information and expert recommendations. *Introducing Sicily* maps the island and sets Sicily in its historic, artistic, geographical and cultural context. *Palermo Area by Area* and the four regional sections describe the most important sights, with maps, floor plans, photographs and detailed illustrations. Restaurant and hotel recommendations are described in *Travellers' Needs* and the *Survival Guide* has tips on everything from transport to hiring a surfboard.

PALERMO AREA BY AREA

The historic centre of the city has been divided into two areas, East and West, each with its own chapter. *Further Afield* covers peripheral sights. All sights are numbered and plotted on the *Area Map*. The detailed information for each sight is easy to locate as it follows the numerical order on the map.

Sights at a Glance lists the chapter's sights by category: Churches and Cathedrals, Historic Buildings, Museums, Streets and Squares, Parks and Gardens.

All pages relating to Palermo have red thumb tabs.

A locator map shows where you are in relation to other areas of the city centre.

1 Area map
For easy reference, all the major sights are numbered and located on this map.

2 Street-by-Street Map
This gives a bird's-eye view of the key areas in each chapter.

A suggested route for a walk is shown in red.

Stars indicate the sights that no visitor should miss.

3 Detailed Information
The sights in Palermo are described individually. Addresses, telephone numbers, opening hours and admission charges are also provided. Map references refer to the Street Finder on pp78–9.

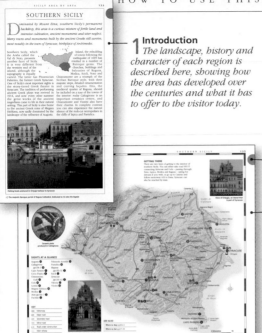

1 Introduction
The landscape, history and character of each region is described here, showing how the area has developed over the centuries and what it has to offer to the visitor today.

SICILY AREA BY AREA

Apart from Palermo, Sicily has been divided into four regions, each with a separate chapter. The most interesting towns, villages and sights to visit are numbered on a *Regional Map*.

Each area can be identified by its own colour coding.

2 Regional Map
This shows the road network and gives an illustrated overview of the whole region. All the interesting places to visit are numbered and there are also useful tips on getting to, and around, the region by car and by public transport.

For all top sights, a Visitors' Checklist provides the practical information you will need to plan your visit.

3 Sicily's top sights
These are given two or more full pages. Historic buildings are dissected to reveal their interiors. The most interesting towns or city centres are shown in a bird's-eye view, with sights picked out and described.

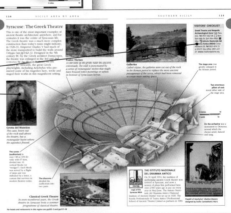

4 Places of Interest
All the important towns and other places to visit are described individually. They are listed in order, following the numbering on the Regional Map. Within each town or city, there is detailed information on important buildings and other sights. The Road Map *references refer to the inside back cover.*

INTRODUCING
SICILY

DISCOVERING SICILY

Off the toe of the Italian peninsula in the far south, the sun-baked island of Sicily has wonderful surprises in store for visitors. Active volcanoes light up the night sky, and windswept uplands punctuated by riots of wildflowers contrast with picture-postcard Mediterranean fishing villages. Imposing ancient temples and fortresses left by waves of occupiers vie for attention with glorious beaches on distant islands. Then there are the chaotic cities with their colourful markets, the museums crammed with priceless antiquities, and the joyous festivals that punctuate the Sicilian calendar year, creating memorable occasions for outsiders. These two pages detail the highlights of each region.

Preserved Roman mosaic

Olive stall at Vucciria market, Palermo

PALERMO

- Piazza della Vittoria area
- Colourful markets
- Monreale cathedral
- Cripta dei Cappuccini

The island's capital city is renowned for its fascinating blend of Arabic, Norman and Baroque architecture, as well as its unbelievably chaotic traffic. Visits are best on foot or by local transport. Off **Piazza della Vittoria** *(see pp60–1)* with its relaxing gardens is the 12th-century **Cappella Palatina** *(see pp62–3)*, an inspiring place to start before moving on to the lively **Vucciria** *(see p56)* and **Ballarò** *(see p69)* outdoor markets, feasts for all the senses. Well-stocked art galleries alternate with shady parks such as the wonderful **Orto Botanico** *(see p75)*, where beautiful tropical plants are clearly at home in the warm Sicilian climate. One unmissable highlight a short distance out of town is the cathedral at

Monreale *(see pp76–7)*, a unique masterpiece of Byzantine art with glittering mosaics and a cool Moorish-style courtyard. A rather different style of art, that of embalming, is on display at the **Catacombe dei Cappuccini** *(see p74)*. Intriguing, but definitely not for the faint-hearted, the catacombs host an army of the deceased, many in skeletal shape.

NORTHWESTERN SICILY

- Archaeological site of Selinunte
- Stunning Egadi islands
- Hilltop town of Erice
- Medieval Cefalù

Arguably Sicily's top archaeological site, the ancient port of **Selinunte** *(see pp104–7)* and its cluster of Hellenic temples occupies a beautiful seafront position

on the westernmost coast. The nearby port of **Trapani** *(see p102)* is the gateway to the divine **Egadi islands** *(see p108)* where islanders transport visitors by boat around the idyllic bays and isolated beaches.

Back on the mainland, the hilltop town of **Erice** *(see pp100–1)* boasts pretty paved streets, exquisite almond pastries and superb views. Nature lovers will appreciate the **Riserva dello Zingaro** *(see p97)*, a pristine stretch of mountainous coastline broken up by inviting coves and home to typical Mediterranean flora.

A hydrofoil trip north from Palermo takes you to the rocky volcanic island of **Ustica** *(see p109)*, its turquoise waters and underwater caves a haven for scuba divers. No visitor should miss the atmospheric medieval town of **Cefalù** *(see pp88–91)*, a warren of narrow streets and a landmark cathedral in the shadow of a limestone promontory.

A view of the dramatic coast from Riserva dello Zingaro

The rocky coastline of Lampedusa, Pelagie islands

SOUTHWESTERN SICILY

- **Roman mosaics at Piazza Armerina**
- **Agrigento's Valle dei Templi**
- **Volcanic Pelagie islands**

Any visit to this wild southwestern region of Sicily should begin with a visit to the ruined Roman villa at **Piazza Armerina** *(see pp129–31)*, which contains simply exquisite, beautifully preserved mosaics depicting scenes of hunting and the life of the well-to-do.

The Greek temple complex at **Agrigento** *(see pp114–15)* is also a highlight, though its proximity to busy roads detracts somewhat from its appeal. By contrast, the atmospheric archaeological site of **Morgantina** *(see p128)* is set in lovely rolling countryside, away from modern civilization. The town of **Sciacca** *(see pp118–19)* is worth a visit for its spa facilities and vast views from Monte San Calogero. To really get away from it all, take a ferry to the isolated, volcanically formed islands of **Pantelleria** *(see p124)* and **Lampedusa** *(see p125)*.

SOUTHERN SICILY

- **Baroque towns of Noto and Ragusa**
- **Majolica tiles at Caltagirone**
- **Greek theatre at Syracuse**

The ornate style of Sicilian Baroque architecture can be admired in a fascinating series of towns across the south of Sicily. Completely rebuilt in a new location after a devastating earthquake in the 1600s, **Noto** *(see pp144–7)* with its stone churches makes for a memorable visit, as does **Ragusa** *(see pp150–51)*.

Marvellous ceramics from a tradition that dates back to Arab times are the main draw in the hilly town of **Caltagirone** *(see pp154–5)*, which boasts a unique staircase studded with colourful majolica tiles. The lovely seafront city of **Syracuse** *(see pp136–43)* has many sightseeing attractions, not least its position on a high, rocky peninsula that juts out into the sea, and the intriguing maze of streets that make up the Ortygia district. Its archaeological site is also rewarding, with a Greek theatre carved into the hillside that continues to host live theatrical performances during the summer.

Adventurous visitors should make a point of visiting the Monti Iblei hinterland and the steep gorges at **Pantalica** *(see p157)*, accessible on foot or horseback.

The delightful town of Ragusa, famous for its Baroque architecture

NORTHEASTERN SICILY

- **Awesome Mount Etna**
- **Charming Taormina**
- **The Aeolian Islands**

This slice of Sicily is dominated by volcanoes of all shapes and sizes. **Mount Etna** *(see pp170–3)* towers to incredible heights and is visible from much of Sicily, often providing live firework shows from its summit craters.

Ruins of the Greek Theatre at Taormina, with imposing Mount Etna in the background

Accessible all year round (weather and geological conditions permitting) thanks to good roads and a high-altitude cable-car, it is always popular. At its feet is the bustling if rather run-down city of **Catania** *(see pp162–5)*, worth a visit for its lively fish market and Baroque cathedral.

No-one should miss the pretty town of **Taormina** *(see pp176–80)*, which spreads across steep flowered hillsides high above the sparkling Ionian coast. The town boasts a spectacular outdoor Greek theatre and perfect views of Etna.

The far-flung **Aeolian Islands** *(see p188–91)* offer countless delights to the hordes of visitors who arrive each summer. The largest island in this windswept archipelago is Lipari, which makes a good base for exploring its more remote neighbours. Stromboli, with its on-going minor eruptions, can be admired from a boat and the ruins of a prehistoric village can be found on Filicudi.

Putting Sicily on the Map

Sicily is the largest region in Italy (25,708 sq km, 9,923 sq miles) and the third most highly populated with more than five million inhabitants. The terrain is mostly hilly – the plains and plateaus make up only 14 per cent of the total land area. The most interesting features of the mountain zones are the volcanoes, especially Mount Etna, which is the largest active volcano in Europe. The longest river is the Salso, which is 144 km (89 miles) long. Besides Sicily itself, the Region of Sicily includes other smaller islands: the Aeolian Islands, Ustica, the Egadi Islands, Pantelleria and the Pelagie Islands. Palermo is the Sicilian regional capital, and with its population of almost 650,000 is the fifth largest city in Italy after Rome, Milan, Naples and Turin.

Palermo, Italy's fifth largest city

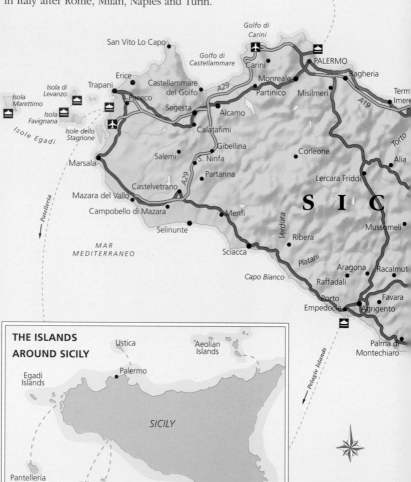

THE ISLANDS
AROUND SICILY

Ustica

Aeolian Islands

Egadi Islands

Palermo

Pantelleria

Pélagie Islands

SICILY

◁ The carnival at Acireale, one of the most colourful in Sicily

EUROPE

NORWAY FINLAND
SWEDEN ESTONIA
RUSSIAN FED.
LATVIA
DENMARK LITHUANIA
IRISH GREAT THE NETHERLANDS BELORUSSIA
REP. BRITAIN GERMANY POLAND
BELGIUM
LUXEMBOURG CZECH UKRAINE
REP. SLOVAKIA
FRANCE AUSTRIA HUNGARY
SWITZERLAND SLOVENIA
CROATIA ROMANIA
ITALY BOZNIA &
HERZEGOVINA SERBIA
BULGARIA
KOSOVO
MACEDONIA
PORTUGAL ALBANIA GREECE
SPAIN Palermo

ALGERIA TUNISIA

At the Heart of the Mediterranean

Sicily is the largest island in the Mediterranean, and in some respects is its focal point. Lampedusa, the largest of the Pelagie Islands, is, along with Crete, the southernmost point in Europe; being closer to Tunisia (113 km, 70 miles) than to Sicily (200 km, 124 miles). Pantelleria is only 70 km (43 miles) from Capo Mustafà, also in Tunisia.

Aeolian Islands

Golfo di
Milazzo Mortelle
Milazzo
Golfo di
Patti Barcellona Messina
Capo d'Orlando Tindari Pozza
Patti Castroreale di Gotto Stretto
Sant'Agata di Militello Terme di Messina
Torremuzzo Tortorici Ali Terme
Cefalù San Stefano di Camastra
Castelbuono Mistretta Randazzo Alcántara Taormina
Petralia Troina Bronte Monte Giarre
Gangi Nicosia Etna Riposto
Salso Acireale
Agira Adrano Belpasso
Leonforte Paternò
S. Caterina Enna Misterbianco Catania
Valguarnera MAR IONIO
Caltanissetta Caropepe
Pietraperzia Gomalunga Golfo di
Piazza Armerina Catania
Sommatino Palagonia
Mazzarino Mineo Lentini
Ravanusa Caltagirone Francofonte Augusta
Gela Grammichele Melilli Golfo di
Butera Niscemi Vizzini Sortino Augusta
Licata Pantalica Priolo Gargallo
Gela Floridia Siracusa
Golfo Palazzolo Canicattini
di Gela Vittoria Ragusa Acreide Bagni
Comiso Avola
Marina di Modica Noto Golfo
Ragusa Rosolini di Noto
Scicli Ispica
Pozzallo Pachino

L I A

KEY

⛴ Ferry service

✈ Airport

Motorway

= = Road under construction

Major road

0 kilometres   35

0 miles   25

A PORTRAIT OF SICILY

*S*icilian shores are washed by three different seas, and this is reflected in the island's ancient name for Sicily: "Trinacria", the three-cornered island. Each part of the island has its own history, its own character, creating a varied and complex whole. Yet over the centuries Sicily has acquired a sense of unity and identity.

Sicily's history can be traced back more than 3,000 years, during which time it has been dominated by many different rulers, from the Greeks to the Romans, Byzantines and Arabs, from the Normans to the Spanish. Each succeeding culture left a mark on the island and may perhaps help to explain aspects of the modern Sicilian character. This diverse inheritance manifests itself in a curious combination of dignified reserve and exuberant hospitality.

The western side of the island, which is centred upon Palermo, is historically considered to be of Punic-Arab influence. The eastern side was once the centre of Magna Graecia, with its coastal towns of Messina, Catania and Syracuse. This difference may be discerned in the speech of local people: the "sing-song" dialect of Palermo as opposed to the more clipped accent of Catania and Syracuse. Accent differences are still noticeable, although they have moderated to some degree over the centuries. There are east-west economic and social differences as well as linguistic ones.

However, the island's long, eventful and tortuous history has not been the only factor influencing its life and inhabitants. Few places have been so affected by their climate and topography: in Sicily the

The Easter Week procession in Enna

The rural landscape of the Sicilian interior, until recently characterized by its large estates

◁ Messina's Fontana del Nettuno (Fountain of Neptune), a traditional starting point for a tour of the island

Livestock raising, one of the mainstays of the economy in the Sicilian interior

temperature is 30°C (86°F) for six months of the year, and when the sun disappears, destructive torrential rains can take its place. The Sicilian climate is one of extremes and can sometimes even be cruel; it has shaped the island's extraordinary landscape which, as the Sicilian novelist Tomasi di Lampedusa described it, includes the hell of Randazzo and, just a few miles away, the paradise of Taormina. Then there are splendid verdant coasts everywhere, with the arid interior a stone's throw away, marvellous towns overlooking the sea and villages perched on hilltops surrounded by inhospitable, barren uplands. An aerial view of this unique island offers a spectacle that is at once both magnificent and awe-inspiring.

Villagers observing passers-by

A watermelon seller in Palermo

ECONOMY AND SOCIETY

The historic, geographic and climatic differences in Sicily have produced a complex and varied society. Yet Sicilians have a strong sense of identity and for centuries made their unique nature a point of honour (in a spirit of independence they used to call the rest of Italy "the continent"). Today this society is at a crossroads between tradition and modernity, much more so than other Mediterranean regions. Sicilian society is attempting to reconcile newer lifestyles and outlooks with deeply rooted age-old customs.

One of the poorest regions in Italy, Sicily has had to strive for a more streamlined and profitable economy against the resistance of the ancient *latifundia* (feudal estate) system, just as the fervent civic and democratic spirit of the Sicilian people clashes with what remains of Mafia mentality and practice.

The criminal organization known to all as the Mafia is one of Sicily's most notorious creations. Sociologists and criminologists both in Italy and abroad have tried to define the phenomenon without success. Is it a criminal structure that is simply stronger and more efficiently organized than others, partly

An outdoor café on the island of Lampedusa

ART AND CULTURE

For more than 3,000 years, Sicily has inspired the creation of artistic masterpieces, from the architecture of Magna Graecia to the great medieval cathedrals, from the paintings of Antonello da Messina to the music of Vincenzo Bellini, and from the birth of Italian literature under Frederick II to the poets and novelists of the 19th and 20th centuries. Sadly, this glorious artistic heritage is not always well cared for and appreciated, although attitudes are changing. Noto, near Syracuse, is a prime example of this. The town, one of the great achievements of Sicilian Baroque architecture, was subjected to neglect, leading to the collapse of the Cathedral dome in 1996. After repairs, UNESCO awarded the site World Heritage status in 2002, a prestigious honour that has made the inhabitants more aware of their surroundings. A mixture of splendour and decay, or as Gesualdo Bufalino, the acute observer of his land, once said, "light and lamentation", is typical of Sicily today. However, the creation of new nature reserves, renewed interest in preserving historic centres, and initiatives such as extended church opening hours, are all causes for cautious optimism in the future.

because of the massive emigration in the early 20th century, which took many Sicilians to the other side of the ocean? Or is it an anti-government movement whose leaders have played on the strong feelings of independence and diversity, which have always characterized Sicily? Is the Mafia the tool of the remaining large estate owners, who once dominated the island and are determined to retain power? Or is it perhaps a combination of all the above factors, which have found fertile soil in the innate scepticism and pessimism of the Sicilians? Whatever the answer may be, eliminating the Mafia is one of Sicily's greatest challenges. After the early 1990s, which saw the deaths of several anti-Mafia figures, the tide now seems to be turning in favour of the new Sicily, and many mafia dons have been caught and arrested after years on the run.

Renato Guttuso, View of Bagheria (1951)

Sicily's Geology, Landscape and Wildlife

Typical Sicilian landscape consists of coast and sun-baked hills. The irregular and varied coastline is over 1,000 km (620 miles) long, or 1,500 km (931 miles) if the smaller islands are included. The island's geological make-up is also quite varied, with sulphur mines in the centre and volcanic activity in the east. Sicily's many volcanoes, in particular Mount Etna (the largest in Europe), have created a landscape that is unique in the Mediterranean.

SICILIAN FAUNA

Painted frog

Sicily has preserved a variety of habitats in its large nature reserves, the most famous of which is the Mount Etna National Park. These parks are home to a wide range of species, some of which are endangered, including wildcats, martens and porcupines. The birdlife includes the rare golden eagle.

RUGGED COASTS AND STACKS

Vanessa butterfly

The Sicilian coastline is steep and rugged, particularly along the Tyrrhenian sea and the northern stretch of the Ionian, where there are many peninsulas, river mouths, bays and rocky headlands. It is also characterized by stacks, steep-sided pillars of rock separated from the coastal cliffs by erosion.

The sawwort *Serratula cichoriacea* *is a perennial found along these coastlines.*

Astroides calycularis *is an alga that thrives in the shaded cliff areas.*

SANDY COASTLINES

Flamingo

Around the Trapani area the Sicilian coast begins to slope down to the Mozia salt marshes, followed by uniform and sandy Mediterranean beaches. This type of coastline continues along the Ionian side of Sicily, where there are marshy areas populated by flamingoes. These birds can be seen nesting as far inland as the Plain of Catania.

The dwarf palm, *called* scupazzu *in Sicilian dialect, is a typical western Mediterranean plant.*

The prickly pear *is an example of an imported plant that was initially cultivated in gardens and then ended up crowding out the local flora.*

All kinds of coleoptera, *including this shiny-backed carabid beetle, can be found in Sicily. In the Mount Etna area alone, 354 different species have been identified.*

The reptile family *is represented by numerous species, ranging from various types of snake to smaller creatures such as this green lizard, which is well known for its shiny skin and sinuous body.*

Foxes
were at one time rare in Sicily, but in recent years they have been spotted near towns foraging for food among household refuse.

Martens
love to roam in the woods around Mount Etna. Weasels and ferrets can also be found in Sicily.

THE INTERIOR

Sicily's hinterland has not always looked the way it does today. Maquis once carpeted areas that, except for a few stretches far from the towns, are arid steppes today. As a result, apart from grain, which has always been the island's staple, the flora is not native, originating in North Africa or the Italian mainland. Birds like the woodpecker can be seen.

Green woodpecker

Orchids *come in a great number of varieties, but they are sadly becoming more and more rare. They can be seen in uncultivated areas or along screes.*

The vegetation *in the interior often looks like this: quite low-growing and with brightly coloured flowers.*

VOLCANIC AREAS

Volcanic zones, particularly around Mount Etna, are very fertile and yield rich vegetation: from olive trees growing on mountain slopes to the pines, birch and beech that thrive at 2,000 m (6,560 ft). Higher up grows the

A falcon, an Etna raptor

milk vetch, forming spiky racemes. Above 3,000 m (9,840 ft) nothing grows. Raptors can often be seen circling.

Moss and lichens *cover the walls of houses on the slopes of Mount Etna, which are built using volcanic sand.*

Cerastium *and Sicilian soapwort flourish on the Mediterranean uplands.*

Architecture in Sicily

Three periods have shaped much of Sicilian architecture. The first was the time of Greek occupation, when monumental works (especially temples and theatres) were built. Aesthetically they were often equal to, and in some cases superior to, those in Greece itself. The medieval period witnessed the fusion of the Byzantine, Arab and Norman styles in such buildings as the Duomo at Monreale near Palermo. Last came the flowering of Baroque architecture in the 17th–18th centuries. The style was so individual that it became known as Sicilian Baroque.

Hygeia, 3rd century BC

LOCATOR MAP

▢ Classical architecture
▨ Medieval architecture
▢ Baroque architecture

STYLES OF CLASSICAL GREEK TEMPLE

The earliest version of the Greek temple consisted of a rectangular chamber housing the statue of a god. Later, columns were added and the wooden elements were replaced by stone. There were three Greek architectural orders: the Doric, Ionic and Corinthian, in chronological order. They are easily distinguished by the column capitals. The temples built in Sicily displayed an experimental, innovative nature compared with those in Greece.

The Doric Temple *The Doric temple stood on a three-stepped base. The columns had no base, were thicker in the middle and tapered upwards, and the capital was a rectangular slab. Other elements were the frieze with its alternating metopes and triglyphs, and the triangular pediment.*

The Ionic Temple *The differences between the Ionic and Doric styles lay in the number of columns and in the fact that Ionic columns rest on a base and their capitals have two volutes, giving the appearance of rams' horns.*

The Corinthian Temple *The Corinthian temple featured columns that were more slender than in the Ionic temple, and the elaborate capitals were decorated with stylized acanthus leaves.*

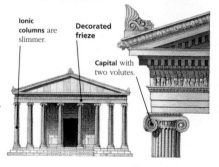

The column shafts were tapered upwards.

Triangular pediment

Doric capital

The metopes could be decorated.

Ionic columns are slimmer.

Decorated frieze

Capital with two volutes.

Acroterion with griffon motif.

Corinthian capital, decorated with acanthus leaves.

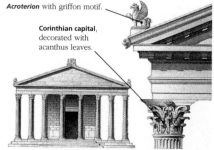

CLASSICAL ARCHITECTURE

① Segesta *p98*
② Selinunte *pp104–6*
③ Valle dei Templi (Agrigento) *pp116–17*
④ Morgantina *pp128–9*
⑤ Gela *p153*
⑥ Syracuse *pp136–43*
⑦ Taormina *pp176–80*
⑧ Tindari *p186*

MEDIEVAL CHURCHES

The drawings illustrate two of the greatest achievements of medieval architecture in Sicily. The Duomo of Monreale *(left)* is a masterpiece from the Norman period, with a splendid fusion of Byzantine, Arab and Norman figurative elements in the mosaics in the interior. A similar fusion of styles and cultures can be seen in the exterior architectural features. The Cathedral in Cefalù *(below)* also dates from the Norman period and, like Monreale, has beautiful mosaics. Its austere and stately quality is created by Romanesque elements such as the two lateral towers.

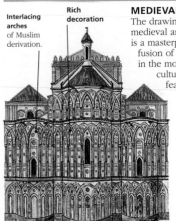

Interlacing arches of Muslim derivation.

Rich decoration

The windows, double and single lancet, make the towers look lighter.

Romanesque side towers

Interlacing arches

The Gothic portal is under a 15th-century narthex.

MEDIEVAL ARCHITECTURE

BAROQUE CHURCHES

After the 1693 earthquake the towns of eastern Sicily were almost totally rebuilt. Spanish-influenced Baroque was combined with Sicilian decorative and structural elements (convex church façades and impressive flights of steps), giving rise to an original, innovative style. Two great examples are shown here: the Cathedral in Syracuse *(left)* and the Basilica di San Giorgio in Ragusa *(below)*. The architect was GB Vaccarini (1702–1769), who also rebuilt Catania.

Curved decorative elements

Decorative elements include statues.

The façade has a typically convex shape.

The columns protrude from the façade.

Jutting cornices define the sections of the façade, adding a rhythmic element.

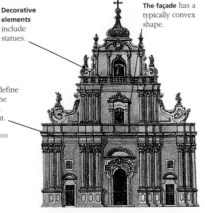

BAROQUE ARCHITECTURE

Sicilian Literature and Art

Luigi Pirandello, 1934 Nobel Prize winner

In the history of Sicilian art and literature there have been periods of tremendous creativity and others when little of note was produced. In the field of literature, the 13th-century Sicilian school of lyric poetry, 19th-century *verismo* or realism and Luigi Pirandello's novels and plays scale the heights of Italian and European literary production. In the field of art, Sicily has produced such great artists as Antonello da Messina, one of the great figures in 15th-century rationalism and portraiture, and the modern painter Renato Guttuso.

WRITERS

Metope from Temple E in Selinunte: Artemis and Acteon

Only fragments remain of Greek Sicilian literary works. Unlike other artistic fields such as architecture, Siceliot (ancient Greek-Sicilian) literature is indistinguishable from the local production, as both were the expression of the same religious, cultural and civic milieu. Apart from Pindar, who dedicated lyric poems to Syracuse and Agrigento, the names of two Siceliot poets have survived. Stesichorus, who lived in Catania in the 7th–6th century BC, "achieved great fame in all Hellas" according to Cicero, leaving a few fragments written in the Homeric style. Theocritus, a Syracusan who lived in the 4th–3rd centuries BC, created the genre of pastorals, short poems on bucolic or mythological subjects. Another important figure in the Greek context was the historian Diodorus Siculus (1st century BC).

The first known figure in medieval Sicilian literature is the Arab poet 'Ibn Hamdis, who was born in Syracuse in 1055 and was forced to leave the island while still young. He wrote moving verses filled with nostalgia for the land of his youth.

In the 13th century, the first school of lyric poetry in Italy developed at the court of Emperor Frederick II and his successor Manfred. It later became known as the Sicilian School. Among the key figures were Jacopo da Lentini, Pier della Vigna, Stefano Pronotaro, Rinaldo d'Aquino and Guido delle Colonne. Their love poetry took up the themes of Provençal lyric poetry but were written in vernacular Italian instead of Latin. Their psychological penetration and the stylistic and metric innovations led to the invention of the sonnet. After this period of splendour, Sicilian literature declined, as did conditions generally in Sicily. This literary "drought" lasted throughout the Renaissance and Baroque periods, and the only

author of note at this time is Antonio Veneziano (born in Monreale in 1543), a poet who wrote in the local dialect and left a collection of love poems. The 18th century was another fallow period for literary production, and it was not until the mid-1800s that there was a rebirth of Sicilian literature. The writers Giovanni Verga and Federico De Roberto became the mainspring of the realistic novel, *verismo*. This style of writing was an extreme and, to a certain extent, more refined version of French naturalism, as embodied in the work of Emile Zola. Giovanni Verga was born in Catania in 1840. After producing work in a late Romantic vein, in the 1870s he was drawn to French naturalism by creating his so-called "poetic of the defeated", in which he set out to depict the hardship of contemporary social reality. He began with short stories set in a rural context (the first was *Nedda*, 1873), which were followed by his masterpieces, the novels *I Malavoglia* (The House by the Medlar Tree, 1881) and *Mastro Don Gesualdo* (1889), which both depict the immutable Sicilian society of the time. The former – a truly innovative work from a stylistic and linguistic standpoint – is the story of a family of fishermen at Aci Trezza who, after a short-lived period of relative well-being, plunge into a life of poverty and suffering. *Mastro Don Gesualdo* narrates the rise on the social

Guidebook by Federico De Roberto

Giovanni Verga, author of *I Malavoglia* (1881)

scale and existential drama of a workman *(mastro)* who, thanks to his marriage, becomes a "Don". These two novels were part of Verga's planned *ciclo dei vinti* (cycle of the defeated), which was to have consisted of five novels; but the author left the project unfinished.

In the same vein as Verga were two other Sicilian writers, Luigi Capuana (1839–1915) and, more importantly, Federico De Roberto (1861–1927), who wrote *I Viceré* (The Viceroys, 1894), about a 19th-century aristocratic family in Catania.

The literature of Sicily continued to be at the forefront in the 20th century. The first half was dominated by Luigi Pirandello (1867–1936), who won the Nobel Prize for Literature in 1934. In his novels (such as *The Late Mattia Pascal,* 1904), nearly 300 short stories, plays *(see p25)* and essays he combines wit with a lucid and sometimes ruthless vision of reality.

One of Pirandello's earliest plays

Among the many noteworthy post-war Sicilian writers are the "hermetic" poet Salvatore Quasimodo (1901–68), author of the collection of poems *Ed è subito sera* (And Suddenly it's Evening, 1942). He won the Nobel Prize in 1959. Giuseppe Tomasi di Lampedusa (1896–1957), wrote *Il Gattopardo* (The Leopard, 1958; *see p122*), a vivid portrait of feudal Sicily, later made into a film, and Leonardo Sciascia (1921–89), wrote novels and essays painting a penetrating, lively portrait of post-war Sicily.

Leonardo Sciascia (1921–89)

Renato Guttuso, *Boogie-woogie* (1953 – 4)

ARTISTS

Until the Renaissance, Sicilian art was basically decorative. During the Greek period probably the best painting was produced in the 7th century BC, when Siceliot vase painters stopped imitating the mainland models and adopted a fresh, eclectic style that combined and elaborated upon the original Greek red-figure ware motifs. The only known artist was Zeuxis, and this only through literature, not his works. The Roman period distinguished itself for some fine wall paintings, in which wax-derived colours were applied, fused into a layer and then fixed onto the wall with heat. The decorative arts in the Middle Ages in Sicily were dominated by mosaics. Among earlier fine works in this medium are the mosaics of the late Roman period at Piazza Armerina and those in the Cappella Palatina in Palermo and Cefalù Cathedral, which are a magnificent combination of Byzantine, Arab and Norman motifs and stylistic elements. Sicilian art reached a peak during the Renaissance, thanks to artists such as Giuffrè (15th century), Quartararo (1484–1501), the unknown author of *Trionfo della morte* (The

Triumph of Death), and, last but by no means least, to the genius of Antonello da Messina (1430–79), one of the greatest Renaissance portraitists and exponents of figurative rationalism, who was active throughout Italy.

Although Sicily was one of the favourite subjects of the great European landscape artists, from the 17th to the 19th century the island produced only one important painter, Pietro Novelli, known as "the man from Monreale" (1603–47).

In the 20th century, the painter Renato Guttuso (1912–87) took up his artistic heritage in a realistic vein, becoming one of Italy's leading artists.

**Antonello da Messina,
St Sebastian (1476)**

Cinema and Theatre in Sicily

Anyone who witnesses the colour of Carnival in Sicily, the bustle of the Vucciria market in Palermo or the sombre pageantry of Easter week processions, will appreciate that Sicily is a theatrical place in its own right. The reasons perhaps lie in the turbulent history of the place. One thing is certain: the island has been a source of inspiration for both theatre and cinema, providing subjects from peasant life to the decadent aristocracy and the Mafia, and producing world-famous playwrights and award-winning films.

Burt Lancaster as the Prince of Salina in *Il Gattopardo* (1963)

SICILIAN CINEMA

The first Sicilian to forge a successful career in the seventh art was probably the playwright Nino Martoglio, who in 1914 directed *Sperduti nel Buio* (Lost in the Dark), a film set in Naples, and edited with a highly original technique. Shortly afterwards, in 1919, Pirandello also wrote two screenplays, *Pantera di Neve* (Snow Panther) and *La Rosa* (The Rose), followed by *Acciaio* (Steel) in 1933. The great playwright and the directors of the films experienced difficulties, however, and the results were not entirely successful. After World War II Sicilian cinema and films set in Sicily reached a peak. In 1948 Luchino Visconti produced *La Terra Trema*, a loose adaptation of Giovanni Verga's *I Malavoglia* (*see p169*). The Milanese director returned to the island in 1963 to film *Il Gattopardo* (The Leopard), based on the novel

of the same name by Tomasi di Lampedusa (*see p122*) and starring Burt Lancaster, Alain Delon and Claudia Cardinale.

In the same period, the Palermitan director Vittorio De Seta, following some fascinating documentaries on Sicily, directed a feature film set in Sardinia, *Banditi a Orgosolo* (Bandits at Orgosolo, 1961), and Neapolitan director Francesco Rosi made *Salvatore Giuliano* (1961), the story of the famous Sicilian bandit, acclaimed as "the greatest film on southern Italy". That same year Pietro Germi shot another famous film in Sicily: *Divorzio all'Italiana*, (Divorce – Italian Style), with Marcello Mastroianni and Stefania Sandrelli. Roman director Elio Petri made another important film about the island in the 1960s: *A Ciascuno il Suo* (To Each His Own, 1967), an adaptation of Leonardo Sciascia's novel of the same name (*see p23*).

The 1970s and 1980s produced a number of films about the Mafia, while Sicilian filmmaker Giuseppe Tornatore directed *Cinema Paradiso*, set in Palazzo Adriano (*see p120*), which won an Academy Award as the best foreign film of 1990.

Neon sign of the *Nuovo Cinema Paradiso* in Giuseppe Tornatore's award-winning film

CINEMA AND THE MAFIA

Marlon Brando as Don Corleone in *The Godfather*

Since the end of World War II the Mafia has been a favourite subject for film. (However, there is a distinction between Italian-made and Hollywood films.) The most distinguished Mafia films made in Italy are Francesco Rosi's *Salvatore Giuliano*; *Il Giorno della Civetta* (Mafia, 1968), adapted from Leonardo Sciascia's novel (*see p23*) directed by Damiano Damiani, who also made *Confessione di un Commissario di Polizia al Procuratore della Repubblica* (1971); and Elio Petri's *A Ciascuno il Suo* (To Each His Own, 1967). Last, the Mafia is also the subject of two films by Giuseppe Ferrara, *Il Sasso in Bocca* (1969) and more recently *Cento Giorni a Palermo* (A Hundred Days in Palermo, 1983), the tragic story of the Carabiniere general Dalla Chiesa, who was killed by the Mafia (*see p36*). Any number of Hollywood movies have been made about the Mafia, though they are almost always set in the US. The most famous is the Academy Award-winning film *The Godfather* (1972), directed by Francis Ford Coppola and starring Marlon Brando and Al Pacino.

SICILIAN THEATRE

The original script of *Il Berretto a Sonagli* **by Pirandello (1917)**

Sicilian theatre is most closely identified with Luigi Pirandello (1867–1936), but there is also a rich tradition of theatre in Sicilian dialect. This theatre form dates from the Middle Ages, but its greatest interpreters were active in the late 19th century. Popular actors included Giuseppe Rizzotto (*I Mafiusi de la Vicaria*, The Mafiosi of the Vicariate, 1863) and Giovanni Grasso, and playwright Nino Martoglio, who in 1903 founded the Grande Compagnia Drammatica Siciliana. Luigi Pirandello also began his theatre career with comedies in dialect such as *Il Berretto a Sonagli* (1917), but he gained international renown in the 1920s with his plays written in Italian. In 1921 he wrote *Six Characters in Search of an Author* and, the following year, *Henry IV*. In these plays, probably his greatest, Pirandello deals with the themes that made him world-famous: the relationship between illusion and reality, existential hypocrisy and the need to find a profound identity.

Sicilian puppets, now sought after by antique dealers

THE OPERA DEI PUPI

Pupi are large Sicilian rod puppets. They date from the 1600s but became a huge success only in the late 1800s. The traditional "puppet opera" stories narrate the adventures of Charlemagne and his paladins, but there are also more modern topics revolving around Garibaldi and King Vittorio Emanuele. Famous puppeteers included Greco, who was based in Palermo, and the Grasso family from Catania, renowned craftsmen in their own right.

CLASSICAL THEATRE IN SICILY

Sicilian playwright Nino Martoglio (1870–1921)

Ancient theatre in Sicily can boast a great genius as its adoptive father, since Aeschylus (525–456 BC), who is regarded as the inventor of Greek tragedy, spent long periods in Sicily and died here. A number of his works were first produced in Syracuse (*see pp138–9*). Sicily was therefore well acquainted with, and assimilated, the subject matter of Greek theatre: freedom versus destiny, the sense of divine power and human suffering, the anguish of the tragedies and excoriating, bitter satire of the comedies. Classical theatre declined with the fall of the western Roman Empire, and it was not until the 20th century that the great tragedies were again performed in Sicily. In 1913, Count Mario Tommaso Gargallo and his fellow Syracusans, including archaeologist Paolo Orsi (*see pp140–41*) decided to champion the production of Aeschylus' *Agamemnon*. The premiere was held on 16 April 1914 and since then, with the exception of war-time, the Greek Theatre in Syracuse, one of the most beautiful in the world, has remained a venue for ancient theatre – thanks to the efforts of the Istituto Nazionale del Dramma Antico (National Institute of Ancient Drama, *see p139*). Many famous theatre personalities have participated in these productions over the years, including poets Salvatore Quasimodo (*see p23*) and Pier Paolo Pasolini as translators, and the actors Giorgio Albertazzi and Vittorio Gassman.

Programme of the Istituto Nazionale del Dramma Antico, set up in 1925

THE HISTORY OF SICILY

Hercules killing a deer

The most striking aspect of Sicilian history is the enormous influence of all the different peoples who have colonized the island. Even the Sikanians, Elymians, Sicels and Ausonians, the first populations to leave traces of their cultures in Sicily, came from other parts of the Mediterranean. They were followed by the Carthaginians and then by the Greeks, under whom Sicily saw its first real period of great splendour. Greek domination ended in 212 BC with the siege of Syracuse, in which the great inventor Archimedes was killed. For the next six centuries, the island became the bread basket of the Roman Empire and during this period acquired a social system that was to be its distinguishing characteristic for centuries. After the fall of the Roman Empire and the barbarian invasions, Sicily was ruled by the Byzantines. The island was then conquered by the Arabs, under whom it became one of the most prosperous and tolerant lands in the Mediterranean. The next rulers were the Normans, who laid the foundations for the splendid court of Frederick II in Palermo. A long period of decadence coincided with the dwindling of the Middle Ages. The Angevins, Aragonese and Bourbons in turn took power in Sicily, but these dynasties exploited the island and treated it like a colony instead of improving life for the people there. Giuseppe Garibaldi's expedition in 1860 paved the way for the unification of Italy. Despite initial neglect by the central Italian government, Sicilians were finally given control of their own affairs. Yet many long-standing economic and social problems still need to be tackled and resolved, in particular, the continuing presence of the Mafia in Sicily.

Sicily in a 1692 print showing its three provinces: Val di Demona, Val di Noto, Val di Mazara

◁ Pietro Novelli, *St Benedict Offering the Book of the Order*, San Castrense Monreale (16th century)

The Conquerors of Sicily

Because of its strategic position in the middle of the Mediterranean, Sicily has always been fought over by leading powers. Its history is therefore one of successive waves of foreign domination: Greek tyrants, Roman proconsuls and barbarian chieftains, then the Byzantines, Arabs and Normans, the Hohenstaufen monarchs, the Angevin and Aragonese dynasties, the Spanish viceroys and then the Bourbons, the last foreign rulers in Sicily before Italy was unified.

Justinian I, the Byzantine emperor, annexes Sicily in AD 535

5th century BC Battles for supremacy in Sicily between the Greek and Punic colonies

Cleandros initiates the period of tyrannical rule in Gela

King Pyrrhus at Syracuse (280–275 BC)

Hippocrates succeeds Cleandros and extends Gela's dominion

Hieron II (265–215 BC)

Genseric, chief of the Vandals, conquers Sicily in AD 440

Verres becomes the Roman governor in 73–71 BC and is notorious for his corrupt rule

Agathocles, king of Syracuse (317–289 BC)

600 BC	400	200	AD 1	200	400	60
GREEKS		ROMANS			BARBARIANS AN	
600 BC	400	200	AD 1	200	400	60

Gelon conquers Syracuse in 490 BC

Theron tyrant in Agrigento in 488 BC

Ducetius, last king of the Siculi, dies in 440 BC

Timoleon restores democracy in Syracuse in 339 BC

The Romans conquer Sicily definitively in 212 BC

The Peloponnesian War (431–404 BC), brings an attack on Syracuse by the Athenian army, who are later defeated

Dionysius the Younger succeeds his father in 368 BC

Dionysius the Elder becomes tyrant of Syracuse in 405 BC and rules for 38 years

Odoacer and the Ostrogoths conquer Sicily in AD 491. He is succeeded by **Theodoric**

ARTISTS AND SCIENTISTS

In at least two significant periods, artists and scientists played a leading role in the long and eventful history of Sicily. The outstanding figure was Archimedes, born in Syracuse in 287 BC and on intimate terms with the ruler Hieron II. Thanks to the ingenious machines of war he invented, the city was able to resist Roman siege for three years (215–212 BC). Another great moment in Sicilian history came when the court of Frederick II in Palermo became known for its artists, poets and architects in the 1200s. Palermo became a leading centre for intellectuals.

Archimedes, the great Syracusan scientist

Diocletian divides the Roman Empire in AD 285. Sicily remains part of the Western Empire

Charles I of Anjou wrests the throne of Sicily from Manfred. He dies in 1285.

Charles II succeeds his father Charles I but in 1288 is forced to cede Sicily to **Peter III of Aragón**, who had occupied the island in 1282

Ferdinand II (1830–59) is the last Bourbon ruler in Sicily

Frederick II, emperor from 1216, is King of Sicily from 1197 to 1250, the year of his death. He moved his court to Palermo

James II of Aragón (1286–96)

The viceroys (above, Severino Filangieri) govern Sicily for the Spanish sovereigns until 1713

Tancred (1190–94)

Frederick II of Aragón (1296–1337)

William I (1154–66)

Peter II of Aragón (1337–41)

Ferdinand (1759–1825) unifies the kingdoms of Naples and Sicily in 1816

Roger I, the Norman lord, conquers Sicily in 1091 after a war lasting 30 years

Louis of Aragón (1341–55)

800	1000	1200	1400	1600	1800	
ES	ARABS		NORMANS	ANGEVINS AND ARAGONESE	BOURBONS	SAVOY
800	1000	1200	1400	1600	1800	

Roger II (1105–1154)

Manfred, the natural son of Frederick II, rules Sicily until 1266

Duke John of Pegnafiel, son of Ferdinand of Castille, begins the viceroyalty period in 1412. This system of rule lasts for three centuries

Vittorio Amedeo II of Savoy acquires Sicily in 1713 through the Peace of Utrecht, ceding it to the **Habsburgs of Austria** in 1718

Vittorio Emanuele II of Savoy becomes the first king of a unified Italy. Sicily forms a part of the new kingdom, having voted for annexation following Garibaldi's conquest of the island in 1860

Henry VI, emperor and son of Barbarossa, conquers Sicily in 1194. He dies in 1197

William II (1166–89)

Frederick III of Aragón (1355–77), whose death triggers a period of struggle and strife that brings about the end of the Kingdom of Sicily

The Arabs begin their invasion of Sicily in 827 and conquer the island in 902

Charles III of Spain acquires Sicily from Austria in 1735 and governs until 1759

Prehistoric and Ancient Sicily

Female bust (470–460 BC)

When Greek colonists arrived in Sicily in the 8th century BC, in the east they found the Sicels – a Mediterranean population that had been there since 2,000 BC – and the Phoenicians to the west. The former were soon assimilated, while the latter were ousted after the Battle of Himera (480 BC). This marked the beginning of Greek supremacy and the height of the Magna Graecia civilization, which ended in 212 BC with the Roman conquest of Syracuse. Roman Sicily saw the rise of large feudal estates and the imposition of taxes. Christianity began to spread in the 3rd–4th centuries AD.

GREEK COLONIZATION OF THE MEDITERRANEAN

MYTHS AND GODS

Magna Graecia adopted the religion of the mother country while adding local myths and legends. Mount Etna was seen as the home of Hephaestus, the god of fire, whom the Romans identified with Vulcan. Homer chose the island

Zeus, the supreme Greek deity

of Vulcano, in the Aeolians, as the workplace of this fiery god of blacksmiths. At Aci Trezza on the Ionian Sea, a group of stacks is known as "the islands of the Cyclops", since it was believed that they were the boulders Polyphemus hurled against Ulysses in the famous episode in Homer's *Odyssey*.

VOYAGE TO SICILY

The ships the Greeks used for the dangerous trip to Sicily were called triremes. These galleys were about 35 m (115 ft) long, were faster and more agile than the Phoenician vessels and travelled about 100 km (62 miles) per day. They were manned by a crew of 200 and were equipped for transport and battle.

The double oar on the stern was used as a rudder.

Stern

Mother Goddess
This intense limestone statue, an archetype of femininity, dates from the middle of the 6th century BC and is in the Museo Archeologico of Syracuse (see pp140–41).

TIMELINE

1600 BC	1300 BC	1000 BC	800 BC	600 BC
1500 BC Contacts between Aeolian and Cretan and Minoan cultures	**1000–850 BC** Second period of Siculan civilization	**730–650 BC** Fourth period of Siculan civilization **733 BC** Dorians from Corinth found Syracuse	**628 BC** Selinunte founded	**413 BC** Athenian invasion led by Nicias and Alcibiades a total failure
	1270–1000 BC First period of Siculan civilization	**850–730 BC** Third period of Siculan civilization **8th century BC** Greeks colonize east, Phoenicians west. *Panormos* (Palermo) founded	**729 BC** *Katane* (Catania) founded	**480 BC** Battle of Himera: Greeks defeat Carthaginians

The goddess Athena

The Roman Villas
Roman dominion in Sicily brought about the spread of latifundia *(large feudal estates) and landowners' villas such as the Villa del Casale (see pp130–31), whose mosaics were preserved thanks to a flood that buried them for centuries.*

WHERE TO SEE ANCIENT SICILY

Almost every Sicilian town of any size has an archaeological museum. The most interesting prehistoric ruins are to be found in the islands, particularly the Aeolians *(see pp188–91)*, while the few Punic remains are on display in the museums. The main Greek sites include Segesta *(see p98)*, Selinunte *(see pp104–6)*, Syracuse *(see pp136–43)*, the Valle dei Templi at Agrigento *(see pp116–17)* and Morgantina *(see pp128–9)*. One of the best preserved Roman sites is the ancient villa at Piazza Armerina *(see pp129–31).*

4th-century BC crater

A trireme drew only about 60 cm (24 in).

The spur was used to destroy the oars on enemy vessels.

The third rank of oars (hence "trireme" or three oars), was on an external deck jutting out from the hull. Everything was carefully calculated so that the 170 oar movements were synchronized.

Prehistoric Village
Remains of settlements dating from the beginning of the first millennium BC lie all over Sicily. However, the first populations who left traces in Sicily (Sikanians, Elymians and Sicels) were not native people.

Aeschylus, the great Greek tragedian who was also active in Syracuse

AD 293 The emperor Diocletian makes Sicily *regio suburbicaria*, or directly dependent on Rome

AD 325 Christianization of the Syracuse area

AD 535 Sicily becomes part of Justinian's Eastern Roman Empire

| 200 | AD 1 | AD 200 | 400 | 600 |

212 BC Syracuse conquered by Romans. Sicily loses its autonomy

Female clay bust

AD 440 During the barbarian invasions of Italy the Vandals led by Genseric conquer Sicily

AD 600 Christianization of all of Sicily

AD 491 The Ostrogoths under Odoacer take Sicily from the Vandals

Medieval Sicily

Coin with imperial coat of arms

The frequent Arab raids became in 827 a real campaign to conquer Sicily, which ended successfully in 902. Arab dominion coincided with the rebirth of the island after the decadence of the final years of Byzantine rule. In 1061 the Christian crusade began, the Normans conquering Sicily 30 years later. The Kingdom of Sicily was established in 1130 and reached its zenith with the splendour of Frederick II's court. In 1266 the Angevin dynasty took power, followed by the Aragonese, initiating a long period of decline in which powerful feudal landowners ruled the island.

THE ARAB REGIONS OF SICILY

- Val Demone
- Val di Noto
- Val di Mazara

Tancred
The natural son of Roger III of Puglia, Tancred was appointed king of Sicily by the feudal barons in 1190. He was the last Norman to rule Sicily. When he died, the emperor Henry VI, son of Barbarossa and father of Federico II, ascended the throne.

Sicily under Arab Rule
During the century of Arab dominion Sicily was the richest and most tolerant land in the Mediterranean. The governing administration was reorganized and the arts and culture flourished to an exceptional degree, as can be seen in this decorated coffer.

The poor and ill are spared.

The dog leads the man in the night of death.

TIMELINE

The Virgin of Odigitria, Lentini

Coin with Arab inscriptions

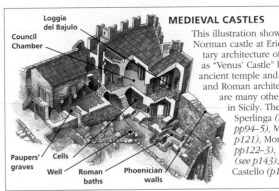

MEDIEVAL CASTLES

This illustration shows the 12th–13th-century Norman castle at Erice, an example of the military architecture of the time. It is also known as "Venus' Castle" because it was built near an ancient temple and incorporated Phoenician and Roman architectural elements. There are many other medieval fortifications in Sicily. The main ones are those at Sperlinga (see p93), Caccamo (see pp94–5), Mussomeli and Naro (see p121), Montechiaro and Falconara (see pp122–3), Enna (see p127), Syracuse (see p143), Catania (see p165), Aci Castello (p168) and Milazzo (see p187).

Loggia del Bajulo
Council Chamber
Paupers' graves
Cells
Well
Roman baths
Phoenician walls

Death strikes with bow and arrows, like a horseman of the Apocalypse.

A lady maintains her proud attitude.

Representation of the World
After the conquest of Sicily, the Normans and Hohenstaufens assimilated the culture of the Arabs, as can be seen in this representation of the world, executed in the Norman period by an Arab artist.

THE TRIUMPH OF DEATH

This mid-15th-century fresco, painted and kept in Palermo (see pp52–3), drew inspiration from the Apocalypse: Death is a horseman armed with bows and arrows who kills the rich and spares the poor. These symbolic "triumphs" were common in medieval iconography.

The rich and powerful are killed with arrows.

WHERE TO SEE MEDIEVAL SICILY

Besides the castles (see above), do not miss the Cappella Palatina in Palermo (see pp62–3), Monreale Cathedral (see pp76–7), and the towns of Cefalù (see pp88–91) and Erice (see pp100–1), including their cathedrals. Despite some rebuilding, the many villages that have preserved their Arab town planning layout are also interesting sites.

1194 Henry VI conquers Sicily and makes it part of his empire

The tiara of Constance of Aragón, Frederick II's wife

1282 The Sicilian Vespers revolt overthrows the Angevin rulers and Peter of Aragón becomes the new king

1415 Ferdinand of Castile sends his first viceroy, Giovanni di Pegnafiel, to Sicily

1100	1200	1300	1400

1130 Roger II is crowned King of Sicily. Palermo is the capital

1250 The death of the emperor Frederick II marks the end of Sicily's most glorious period

1302 The Peace of Caltabellotta sanctions the independence of the Kingdom of Sicily

1265 Charles of Anjou crowned King of Sicily by the Pope

1377 Under Maria of Aragón war breaks out among the feudal landowners, which leads to the union of the Kingdom of Sicily and the Kingdom of Aragón

From Spanish Rule to Unified Italy

Painter Pietro Novelli (1603–47)

In 1415 Sicily became an Aragonese province ruled by a viceroy. The island's economic and cultural decadence continued, and received the final blow when the Jews were driven away from Spanish territories in 1492. A series of revolts was subdued with the help of the Pope's Holy Office. There was a slight recovery after the devastating earthquake of 1693, which destroyed eastern Sicily. After brief periods of Savoyard and Austrian dominion, in 1735 Sicily passed to the Bourbons, in constant battles with the land barons. In 1814 the island became a province of the Kingdom of Naples; popular unrest led to Garibaldi's 1860 expedition and union with the burgeoning Kingdom of Italy. The late 1800s were marked by banditry and poverty in the rural areas.

THE STATES OF ITALY

- *Kingdom of Two Sicilies*
- *Papal States*
- *Grand Duchy of Tuscany*
- *Habsburg Empire*
- *Kingdom of Sardinia*
- *Duchy of Modena*
- *Duchy of Parma-Piacenza*

The 1693 Earthquake
On the night of 9 January 1693, Mount Etna burst into life. Two days later, "the Earth was rent from its bowels", as the historian Di Blasi said. The earthquake, seen above in a print of the time, levelled 23 towns, including Catania, Noto and Lentini.

Nino Bixio was immortalized in Giovanni Verga's short story Libertà *(see p174).*

Many volunteers joined Garibaldi's 1,000 Red Shirts.

Giuseppe Garibaldi, a socialist, set off for Sicily despite Cavour's initial opposition.

TIMELINE

1415 First year of the Viceroyalty, which ends in 1712

1458 Alfonso V dies and Sicily is again ruled by Spain

1442 Alfonso V unites the crowns of Sicily and Naples, thus founding the Kingdom of Two Sicilies

1535 Emperor Charles V visits Sicily

1571 The harbour in Messina houses the Christian fleet that later wins the Battle of Lepanto against the Ottomans

1649 Palermo rev

| 1450 | 1500 | 1550 | 1600 |

The Battle of Lepanto

The Revolt of Messina
This print depicts the 1848 insurrection at Messina. The city was bombarded by Ferdinand, afterwards known as "re Bomba", or "king Bomb".

The Sulphur Mines
After the unification of Italy, sulphur mining began in the Sicilian interior. Children were employed for their small size and agility.

The Baroque Period
This stucco work (c.1690) in Palermo (see pp56–7) by Giacomo Serpotta represents The Battle of Lepanto *and is a marvellous example of the style that became known as "Sicilian Baroque".*

GARIBALDI INVADES SICILY

On 11 May 1860, a thousand volunteers led by Giuseppe Garibaldi (1807–82) landed in Marsala to conquer the Kingdom of the Two Sicilies. They succeeded in this incredible feat, taking Palermo, then Messina and lastly Naples by storm.

Composers and Authors
In the 19th century, cultural life flourished in Sicily. The leading figures at this time were writer Giovanni Verga (1840–1922) and composer Vincenzo Bellini (1801–35), seen in this portrait.

The Sicilian Parliament

1674 Revolt in Messina

1759 Sicily taken over by the Kingdom of Naples

1812 The Sicilian Parliament sanctions an English-type constitution

1860 Garibaldi's Red Shirts invade in May. In October the people vote to merge with Kingdom of Italy

| 1650 | 1700 | 1750 | 1800 | 1850 |

1693 A disastrous earthquake destroys most of eastern Sicily

1735 The Spanish Bourbons become new rulers of Sicily

1713 With the Peace of Utrecht, Sicily is ceded first to Vittorio Amedeo II of Savoy and then (1720) to the Habsburgs

1820 First uprisings

1848 The entire island hit by revolts, especially Messina

Giovanni Verga

Modern Sicily

The new century began with the catastrophic 1908 quake in Messina. For the most part excluded from the process of modernization, Sicily was a living contradiction: its splendid cultural life as opposed to poverty, backwardness and the spread of the Mafia which, despite all attempts to curb its activities, had become a veritable state within a state. However, thanks to the perseverance and courage of public servants and growing public awareness of the problem, the Mafia seems to be less powerful than before.

1943 After heavy bombardment, the Allies land in Sicily on 10 July and take it in 38 days

1902
Heavy autumn rainfall triggers a tragic flood in southern Sicily, especially in Modica, in which 300 people lose their lives

1941 Syracusan novelist Elio Vittorini publishes *Conversation in Sicily*

1937 Popular Catanian actor Angelo Musco dies

1950
The bandit Giuliano is betrayed by his cousin Gaspare Pisciotta and killed

1908 The night of 28 December marks the greatest disaster in 20th-century Sicily: a quake totally destroys Messina and kills 100,000 persons

1936 Luigi Pirandello dies in Rome

1900	1910	1920	1930	1940	1950	196

1900	1910	1920	1930	1940	1950	196

1945
The founder of the the Sicilian Separatist Movement, Finocchiaro, is arrested

1934 Pirandello wins Nobel Prize for Literature

1957
Rebellion in Ucciardone prison in Palermo

1947
Salvatore Giuliano's bandits shoot demonstrators: 11 dead, 56 wounded

1919 Don Luigi Sturzo, from Caltagirone, founds the Partito Popolare and becomes its leader. After World War II the party is renamed Democrazia Cristiana

1930 Mussolini sends prefect Cesare Mori to try to suppress the Mafia

1959 Poet Salvatore Quasimodo, born in Modica, wins Nobel Prize for Literature, the second Sicilian to do so in less than 20 years

1921 At Rome, Luigi Pirandello directs the première of his famous play *Six Characters in Search of an Author*

1923 Mount Etna eruption in June destroys towns of Catena and Cerro, barely missing Linguaglossa and Castiglione. The king and Mussolini inspect the damage

1983 Thanks to a sophisticated system of controlled explosions, a lava flow from Mount Etna is deviated for the first time

1980 A DC9 crashes near Ustica, with 81 victims. The cause of the accident has never been explained

1984 The former mayor of Palermo, Vito Ciancimino, is arrested

1966 A landslide at Agrigento, perhaps caused by illegal building construction, leaves 10,000 people homeless

1987 In a trial in Palermo hundreds of Mafiosi are condemned to a total of 2,600 years in prison. The verdict is based on the confessions of Tommaso Buscetta

1995 After years in hiding, top Mafia boss Totò Riina is arrested

2009 A mudslide caused by torrential rain leaves 24 dead and 35 missing near Messina

1968 A huge quake in the Belice Valley claims over 400 victims

1970	1980	1990	2000	2010	2020

1970	1980	1990	2000	2010	2020

2006 After 43 years on the run, Mafia godfather Bernardo Provenzano is arrested in Sicily

1972 In May a plane crashes near Punta Raisi, the Palermo airport, and 115 persons are killed. In December, Mafia boss Tommaso Buscetta is arrested; he is the first Mafioso to cooperate with Italian justice

2002 The bronze Satiro Danzante is discovered by fishermen off the coast of Mazara del Vallo. Etna erupts again, completely destroying the cableway

1971 Another eruption of Mount Etna. In Palermo, the Mafia kills Public Prosecutor Pietro Scaglione

July 1992 Paolo Borsellino, the magistrate who worked with Falcone, is assassinated in Palermo

1968 Clashes between farm labourers and police at Avola cause 2 deaths

May 1992 Judge Giovanni Falcone, for years a huge thorn in the side of the Mafia, is killed in an ambush near Capaci

SICILY THROUGH THE YEAR

Sicilians say that Sicily has the most beautiful sky in the world; certainly the island enjoys more than 2,000 hours of sunshine per year, more than any other part of Europe. The climate is generally mild, but it can get hot in high summer. In 1885 the temperature rose to 49.6° C (121.3° F), the highest ever recorded in Italy. However, winters can be cold, especially inland, and Mount Etna remains snow-capped into the spring. A land of ancient customs and deep-rooted beliefs, Sicily has preserved most of its traditional celebrations, almost all of them religious in nature.

The Trinacria, ancient symbol of Sicily

SPRING

Spring generally begins early in Sicily, although the weather can be quite unpredictable and patterns vary from year to year. In areas with orchards the air is filled with the scent of spring blossoms, and early flowers make this a particularly lovely time for visiting ancient sites. This is also the season with the greatest number of feast-days, processions and festivals *(sagre)*. Almost all these events are linked with the celebration of Easter.

Festa della Crocifissione (Feast of the Crucifixion) procession, Calatafimi

The Sfilata dei Misteri, which takes place on Good Friday in Trapani

APRIL

Sagra della Ricotta e del Formaggio (cheeses), Vizzini. **Sagra del Carciofo** (artichokes), Cerda, Palermo.

EASTER WEEK

Celebrazione dei Misteri *(all week)*, Enna. The Stations of the Cross celebrations and processions all week long. **Festa del Pane** (bread) *(all week)*, San Biagio dei Platani and Agrigento. Bread sculpture and decoration. **Giorni della Pena** *(Wed, Thu, Fri)*, Caltanissetta. "Days of suffering and grief", with impressive processions. **Maundy Thursday Procession**, Marsala. A kilometre of masked figures. **Festa della Crocifissione** *(Fri)*, Calatafimi, Trapani. **Il Cristo Morto** *(Fri)*, Partanna, Trapani. The Crucifixion is re-enacted. **Processione dei Misteri** *(Fri)*, Trapani. Groups of statues and hooded men commemorate Christ's sacrifice in the Procession of Mysteries, which lasts for 20 hours. **Ballo dei Diavoli** *(Sun)*, Prizzi, Palermo. Masked men perform the "devils' dance", which symbolizes the struggle between good and evil.

MAY

International Windsurfing Championship, Mondello and Palermo. **Classic Theatre**, alternate years at Syracuse and Segesta. **Settimana delle Egadi**, island of Favignana. The traditional *mattanza* tuna fishing method is celebrated. **L'Infiorata**, Noto. The streets are filled with images and words created with flowers. **Sagra della Ricotta** *(24 May)*, Sicilian cheese, celebrated at Mussomeli near Caltanissetta.

Christ's crucifixion re-enacted at Partanna, Trapani

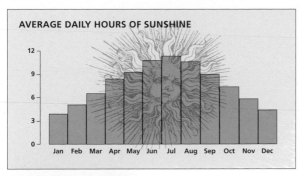

AVERAGE DAILY HOURS OF SUNSHINE

Jan Feb Mar Apr May Jun Jul Aug Sep Oct Nov Dec

Sunshine
Sicily has the highest average hours of sunshine in the whole of Europe. As the chart shows, the sunniest time is from May to September. In the autumn and winter months it may be cold and rainy.

The Pepper Festival at Sutera

SUMMER

Sports, summer vacations, many important musical events, folk celebrations and food festivals characterize the long summer in Sicily.

The weather does, however, get extremely hot in certain places on the island, particularly inland but occasionally even in coastal areas.

JUNE

Fiera Campionaria *(first two weeks)*, Palermo. A samples fair for the Mediterranean countries, with exhibitions and meetings.
Rappresentazioni Pirandelliane *(Jun–Aug)*, Agrigento. Luigi Pirandello's home town is the venue for theme theatre events.
Sagra delle Fragole e dei Frutti di Bosco (fruits), Maletto sull'Etna, Catania.
Taormina Arte *(Jun–Aug)*. Cultural events at the Greek Theatre, with leading figures from the entertainment world.

JULY

Festa di Santa Rosalia *(9–14 Jul)*, Palermo. Six days of festivities in honour of the city's patron saint, who, according to legend, saved

Palermo from the terrible plague of 1624.
Festa di San Giuseppe *(last week)*. Terrasini, Palermo. St Joseph is honoured with a procession of fishing boats bearing the saint's statue. Fried fish for everybody in the main square.
Festa di San Giacomo *(24 & 25 July)*, Caltagirone. The town's long ceramic stairway is decorated with lighted candles representing assorted figures and scenes.
International Cinema, Music, Theatre and Dance Festival *(Jul–Aug)*, Taormina. An important international festival that forms part of the Taormina Arte series of events.

AUGUST

Festa della Spiga *(1–10 Aug)*, Gangi, Palermo. An entire week of games, parades and spectacles.
Festa della Burgisi *(1–15 Aug)*, Palermo countryside. Festival dedicated to the goddess Demeter, symbolising man's labour and the fruits of the earth.
Festa della Castellana *(first Sun)*, Caccamo. An all-women feast that re-enacts the period when the lords – and grand ladies – of the castle ran the town.
Palio dei Normanni *(13–14 Aug)*, Piazza Armerina. Historical re-enactment in

period costume of various tests of courage on horseback, in honour of the great Norman king, Roger I.
Processione della Vara and Cavalcata dei Giganti *(15 Aug)*, Messina. Gigantic statues of the founders of Messina, Mata and Grifone, are paraded through the streets, followed by a float bearing a huge, elaborate triumphal cart and tableau called the "Vara".
Sagra della Mostarda (syruped and candied fruit), Regalbuto, Enna.
Sagra del Pane (bread) *(last Sun in Aug)*, Monterosso Almo, Ragusa.
Sagra del Pomodoro "Seccagno" (tomatoes), Villalba, Caltanissetta. Celebration of one of the island's most commonly and successfully grown products.

The statues of Mata and Grifone at Messina

AVERAGE MONTHLY RAINFALL

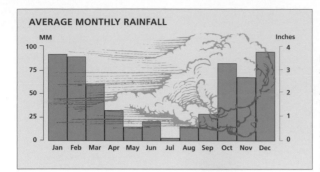

MM

Inches

Jan	Feb	Mar	Apr	May	Jun	Jul	Aug	Sep	Oct	Nov	Dec

Rainfall
As the chart shows, in the six months from April to September there is very little rain. In autumn, by contrast, violent storms are common throughout the island, raising the average rainfall.

AUTUMN

This season begins late in Sicily, as September and often October continue sunny and warm. In autumn you can see many of the characteristic festivals celebrating local produce, such as grapes, and the theatre, classical music, opera and the football (soccer) season all resume their annual cycle.

SEPTEMBER

International Medieval and Renaissance Music Week, Erice. A celebration of ancient music.
International Tennis Tournament, Palermo.
Sagra del Peperone (peppers), Sutera, Caltanissetta.
Sagra dell'Uva (grapes), Vallelunga, Caltanissetta; Roccazzo and Chiaramonte Gulfi, Ragusa.
Festa della Madonna della Luce *(17–18 Sep)*, Mistretta, Messina. The symbolic dance of two armed giants and the Madonna della Luce procession.
Festa di San Vincenzo Aragona, Agrigento. Masked

Statue for the Festa di San Vincenzo, at Aragona

revellers go in procession through the town.
Bellini Festival, Catania. Organized by the city opera company.
Vini dell'Etna, Milo sull'Etna, Catania. Exhibition and sale of the wines made from grapes grown on the slopes of Mount Etna.
Efebo d'Oro International Prize *(end Sep–early Oct)*, Agrigento. A prize is awarded to the best film adaptation of a novel.

OCTOBER

Coppa degli Assi, Palermo. Grand Prix of horsemanship at the Parco della Favorita.
Sagra del Miele (honey) *(first Sun in Oct)*, Sortino, Syracuse.
Sagra del Pesco (peaches), Leonforte, Enna.
Extempora, Palermo. An important and fascinating antiques fair.
Festival di Morgana *(Oct–Nov)*, Palermo. An international marionette workshop of the Opera dei Pupi, held at the Museo Internazionale delle Marionette, with plays and exhibits.
Festival sul Novecento, Palermo. First held in 1997, the 20th-Century Festival attracts media people, leading artists, writers and film directors.
Ottobrata, Zafferana Etnea, Catania. Every Sunday in October, in this village close to Mount Etna, the main square is filled with stalls selling produce and articles made by local craftsmen.

PUBLIC HOLIDAYS IN SICILY

New Year's Day (1 Jan)
Epiphany (6 Jan)
Easter Sunday and Monday
Liberation Day (25 Apr)
Labour Day (1 May)
Republic Day (2 Jun)
Ferragosto (15 Aug)
All Saints' Day (1 Nov)
Immaculate Conception (8 Dec)
Christmas (25 Dec)
Santo Stefano (26 Dec)

Ballet performances, staged at the theatres in Catania and Palermo

AVERAGE MONTHLY TEMPERATURE

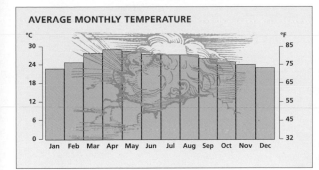

Temperature
From May to September the average temperature is rarely below 20° C (68° F), and, except for very unusual weather, it is seldom below 10° C (50° F) any other month. July and August may see peaks of more than 40° C (104° F).

NOVEMBER

Religious Music Week, Monreale. Another great musical event, which takes place in Monreale's splendid medieval abbey.

WINTER

Winter in Sicily is usually cool and often rainy, and may not be the ideal season to visit the interior and the larger towns. In February you might see one of the many Carnival festivities held throughout the island, which are famous for their originality and the enthusiastic participation of the local people. There are also a limited number of events in January.

The Madonna del Soccorso, celebrated at Sciacca in February

DECEMBER

Handicrafts Fair, Palermo. In Piazza Politeama, an exhibition of handicrafts from all over the island. **Rassegna di Studi Pirandelliani**, Agrigento. This workshop is important for all Pirandello scholars. It includes lectures and productions of his plays.

Festa di Santa Lucia *(13 Dec)*, Syracuse. On the saint's feast day, her statue is taken out in a public procession and is then placed on public exhibition for eight days.

Natale a Taormina *(Dec–Jan)*. Christmas fair with street theatre and gospel music.

JANUARY

Festa di San Sebastiano
Acireale, Catania. On 20 Jan

The Festa del Mandorlo in Fiore, Valle dei Templi at Agrigento

the saint's statue is taken from his church on an elaborately decorated wooden float and borne in a procession in front of a huge crowd.

FEBRUARY

Festa della Madonna del Soccorso, Sciacca.
Festa del Mandorlo in Fiore (Festival of the Almond Tree in Bloom), Agrigento. The arrival of spring is celebrated in the Valley of Temples. At the same time there is the **Folklore Festival**, which for more than 50 years has featured folk music and dance from all over the world.
Festa di Sant'Agata *(3–5 Feb)*, Catania. The city is filled with "strangers" who invoke the saint's protection, while Catanians, dressed only in "sackcloth", bear her statue in an impressive procession.
Carnival, Acireale. Allegorical floats, a colourful atmosphere and huge crowds.
Carnival, Sciacca. Together with Acireale, the most famous carnival in Sicily.
Sagra della Salsiccia, del Dolce e della Trota (sausage, pastries and trout), Palazzolo Acreide, Syracuse.

The carnival at Acireale, considered one of the most colourful in Sicily

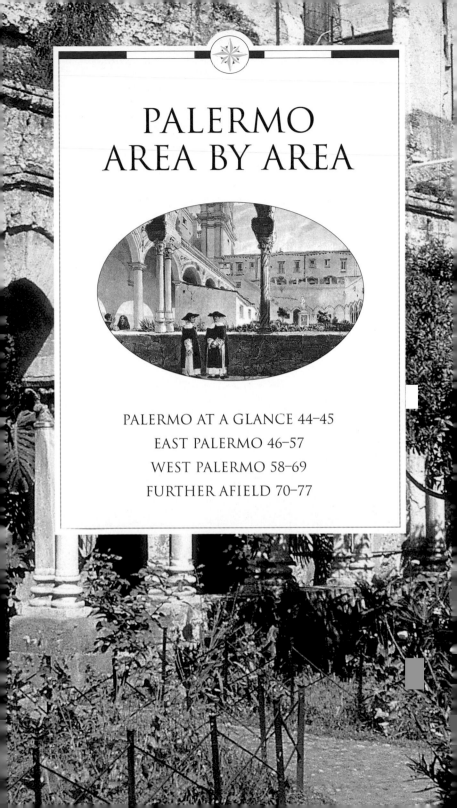

PALERMO
AREA BY AREA

Palermo at a Glance

The capital of Sicily is built along the bay at the foot of Monte Pellegrino. Palermo owes its name to the sea: it was originally called *Panormos*, or "port", in Phoenician times. The town prospered under the Romans, but its golden age was under Arab domination, when it rivalled Cordoba and Cairo in beauty. Later, Palermo became the capital of the Norman kingdom. Today very little remains of the fabulous city of bygone times, but the Middle Eastern influence can still be seen in the architecture of the churches, the many alleys in the old town and the markets. The other age of splendour, which left a lasting mark on the city's civic and religious buildings, was the Baroque period (17th–18th centuries). Palermo suffered badly in the massive bombardments of 1943 and was then rebuilt chaotically, the result of political corruption and the Mafia. Recently things have taken a turn for the better.

The Oratorio del Rosario di Santa Cita *(or Santa Zita), with its stuccoes by Giacomo Serpotta, is a splendid example of Baroque ornamentation (see pp56–7).*

The Palazzo dei Normanni, *built on Punic foundations, has superb mosaic and fresco decoration. It became the royal palace under the Normans (see p64).*

WEST PALERMO
(see pp58–69)

The Cappella Palatina, *a masterpiece of Norman art, is covered with Byzantine-influenced mosaics representing scenes from the Bible (see pp62–3).*

0 metres 350

0 yards 350

◁ **The cloister of San Giovanni degli Eremiti** *(pp64–5)*

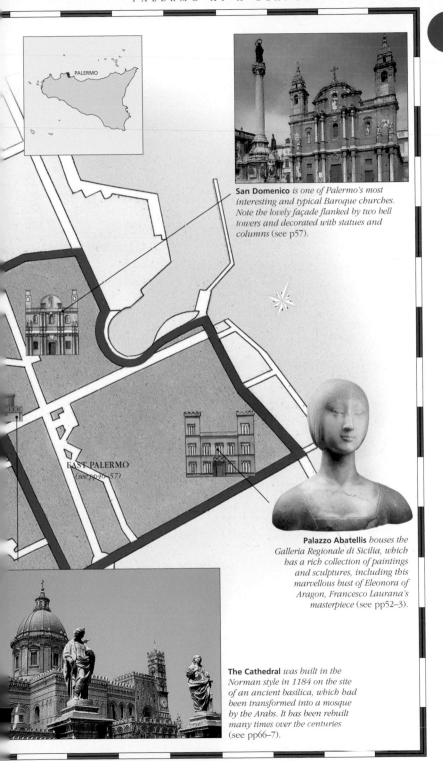

San Domenico *is one of Palermo's most interesting and typical Baroque churches. Note the lovely façade flanked by two bell towers and decorated with statues and columns* (see p57).

EAST PALERMO
(see pp46–57)

Palazzo Abatellis *houses the Galleria Regionale di Sicilia, which has a rich collection of paintings and sculptures, including this marvellous bust of Eleonora of Aragon, Francesco Laurana's masterpiece* (see pp52–3).

The Cathedral *was built in the Norman style in 1184 on the site of an ancient basilica, which had been transformed into a mosque by the Arabs. It has been rebuilt many times over the centuries* (see pp66–7).

EAST PALERMO

Between Via Maqueda and the sea lie the old Arab quarters of Palermo, with their maze of narrow streets and blind alleys. This area includes the Kalsa quarter (from the Arabic *al-Halisah*, or the Chosen), which was built by the Arabs in the first half of the 10th century as the seat of the Emirate, the government and the army. During the Norman era it became the sailors' and fishermen's quarter. It was badly damaged in World War II, and many parts are still being restored. Most of the Aragonese

Statue of the Fontana Pretoria

monuments, dating from the late Middle Ages and the Renaissance, are in the Kalsa. The focal point is Piazza Marina, for a long time the heart of city life and seat of the Aragonese court and the Inquisition courtroom. Via Maqueda opens onto Piazza Pretoria, the civic heart of Palermo, with Palazzo delle Aquile, Santa Caterina and San Giuseppe dei Teatini. West of Corso Vittorio Emanuele is Castellammare, with the Vucciria market and the Loggia quarter near the port, where Catalan, Pisan and Genoese communities once lived.

SIGHTS AT A GLANCE

Museums and Galleries
Galleria d'Arte Moderna Sant'Anna **8**
Museo Archeologico Regionale **14**
Museo Internazionale delle Marionette **4**
Palazzo Abatellis pp52–3 **2**

Historic Buildings
Palazzo Mirto **5**

Streets and Squares
Piazza Marina **1**

Churches
La Gancia **3**
La Magione **12**
La Martorana **10**
Oratorio del Rosario di San Domenico **18**
Oratorio del Rosario di Santa Cita **16**
San Cataldo **11**
San Domenico **17**

San Francesco d'Assisi **6**
Santa Caterina **9**
Santa Maria dello Spasimo **13**

Markets
Mercato della Vucciria **15**

Monuments
Fontana Pretoria **7**

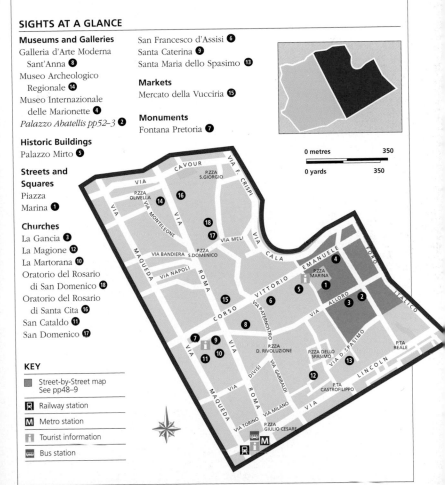

0 metres 350
0 yards 350

KEY

- Street-by-Street map See pp48–9
- **R** Railway station
- **M** Metro station
- **i** Tourist information
- Bus station

◁ **Christ Pantocrator in the mosaic decoration on the cupola of La Martorana (12th century)**

Street-by-Street: Around Piazza Marina

Poster for the Museo delle Marionette

The main square in Old Palermo lies at the edge of the Kalsa quarter. From the Middle Ages onwards it was used for knights' tournaments, theatre performances, markets and public executions. On the occasion of royal weddings, such as the marriage of Charles II and Marie Louise in 1679, impressive shows were put on in specially built wooden theatres. The square's irregular four sides are flanked by such monuments as Palazzo Steri-Chiaramonte, Palazzo del Castillo, Palazzo della Zecca, San Giovanni dei Napoletani, Palazzo della Gran Guardia, Santa Maria della Catena, Palazzo Galletti and Palazzo Villafiorita. In the middle is the Giardino Garibaldi, shaded by enormous fig trees.

LOCATOR MAP
See Street Finder map 1, 2

Santa Maria della Catena (early 16th century) owes its name to the chain (*catena*) across the mouth of the city harbour. A broad stairway leads to the beautiful three-arched porch of this Catalan Gothic church.

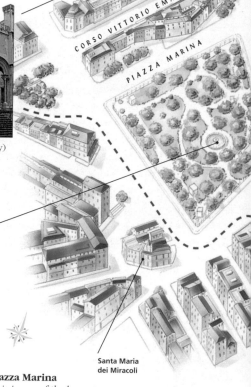

CORSO VITTORIO EMANUELE

PIAZZA MARINA

Santa Maria dei Miracoli

Piazza Marina
This is one of the largest squares in Palermo. Once part of the harbour, but long since silted up and reclaimed, its central garden is home to massive Ficus magnolioides *trees, with strange, exposed roots* ❶

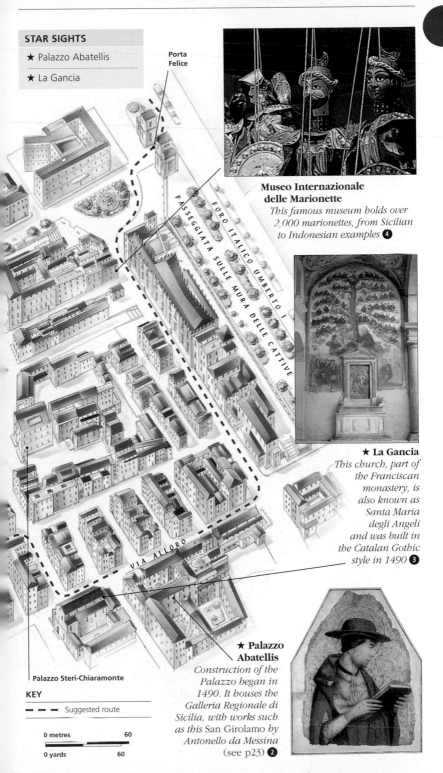

STAR SIGHTS

★ Palazzo Abatellis

★ La Gancia

Porta
Felice

PASSEGGIATA SULLE MURA DELLE CATTIVE

FORO ITALICO UMBERTO I

VIA ALLORO

**Museo Internazionale
delle Marionette**
*This famous museum holds over
2,000 marionettes, from Sicilian
to Indonesian examples* **4**

★ La Gancia
*This church, part of
the Franciscan
monastery, is
also known as
Santa Maria
degli Angeli
and was built in
the Catalan Gothic
style in 1490* **3**

Palazzo Steri-Chiaramonte

**★ Palazzo
Abatellis**
*Construction of the
Palazzo began in
1490. It houses the
Galleria Regionale di
Sicilia, with works such
as this* San Girolamo *by
Antonello da Messina*
(see p23) **2**

KEY

– – – Suggested route

0 metres   60

0 yards   60

The Giardino Garibaldi, in the middle of Piazza Marina

Piazza Marina ❶

Map 2 E3

This square is one of the largest in Palermo. It lies on what was once the southern side of the natural harbour. In the middle of Piazza Marina is the **Giardino Garibaldi**, designed in 1863 by GB Basile and planted with *Ficus magno-lioides*, a species of fig tree, which are now enormous. The garden is surrounded by a cast-iron fence decorated with bows and arrows, rabbits and birds. Inside are a fountain and busts of Risorgimento figures, including Benedetto De Lisi's monument to the Italian leader Garibaldi.

The most important building in Piazza Marina is **Palazzo Chiaramonte Steri**, built in 1307 by Manfredi Chiaramonte, a member of one of Sicily's most powerful families. In the Middle Ages the Chiaramonte family controlled most of the island. The name "Steri" comes from *Hosterium*, or fortified building, as most patrician mansions were just that during the turbulent period of Hohenstaufen rule. Built in the Gothic style with Arab and Norman influences, the palazzo has an austere façade. The portal is decorated with a double arched lintel of ashlars and a series of double and triple Gothic lancet windows with multicoloured inlay. When the new Aragonese rulers arrived in 1392, Andrea Chiara-monte was beheaded right in front of Palazzo Steri. It became the palace of the Aragonese

kings and then of the viceroys. In the 17th century it housed the Inquisition courtroom, or Holy Office, where suspected heretics were interrogated and often tortured. Later, the Palazzo became the city court of law and today it is the administrative headquarters of the University of Palermo. The courtyard is open to the public and tours of the palazzo are available.

Across the square is the Renaissance **Santa Maria dei Miracoli** (1547). On the corner of Via Vittorio Emanuele is the Baroque **Fontana del Garraffo**, a fountain with three shell-shaped basins supported by dolphins' heads. At the northeastern corner is the church of **San Giovanni dei Napoletani** (1526–1617), with a trapezoidal portico.

Palazzo Abatellis ❷

See pp52–3.

The Gothic portal of La Gancia, with bas-relief on the arch

La Gancia ❸

Via Alloro 27. **Map** 2 E3. *Tel 091-616 52 21.* ◯ *9:30am–noon, 3–6pm Mon–Sat, 10am–12:30pm Sun.*

This church was built in 1485 and dedicated to Santa Maria degli Angeli. The façade is decorated with two Spanish-Gothic portals. The aisleless nave in the interior has 16 side chapels, a multi-coloured marble floor and a wooden patterned ceiling. In the Baroque period, stucco decoration was added by the sculptor Giacomo Serpotta. The choir, in a separate room near the church's entrance, has a fine late-16th-century organ. The panels dating from 1697 show Franciscan saints painted by Antonio Grano.

Palermitan marionette from the theatre of Francesco Sclafani

Museo Internazionale delle Marionette ❹

Via Butera 1. **Map** 2 E3. *Tel 091-328 060.* ◯ *9am–1pm, 3:30–6:30pm Mon–Fri, 9am–1pm Sat.* **Shows** *5:30pm Tue & Fri (winter only).* 🖳 **www**.museomarionettepalermo.it

This museum boasts one of the world's main collections of puppets, marionettes and shadow puppets. In the first room are the great schools of marionettes, from the Catania style to those of Liège, Naples and Brussels. The second room has a collection of figures belonging to puppeteers from

Stage backdrop in the Museo delle Marionette depicting knights errant

Palermo, Castellammare del Golfo, Alcamo and Partinico. Among the stage scenery here is *Charlemagne's Council* and *Alcina's Garden*. The international section includes Chinese shadow theatre puppets, Thai *hun krabok*, Vietnamese, Burmese and Rajasthan marionettes, and Javanese *wayang* figures, as well as animated figures from Oceania and Africa. The theatre of puppeteer Gaspare Canino di Alcamo has back-cloths showing the feats of Orlando; most productions of the *Opera dei Pupi* (puppet opera) featured the exploits of Charlemagne's knights errant.

The museum also organizes the Festival di Morgana (usually in October) which features puppet operas from around the world, all performed in Italian.

Palazzo Mirto ❺

Via Merlo 2. **Map** 2 D3. **Tel** 091-616 75 41. ◯ Apr–Oct: 9am–6:30pm Mon–Sat, 9am–1pm Sun & hols.

This is a splendid example of a centuries-old nobleman's mansion that has miraculously preserved its original furnishings. Palazzo Mirto

Coat of arms of Palazzo Mirto

was built in the 18th century on to pre-existing 15th- and 16th-century architectural structures. The palazzo passed from the aristocratic De Spuches family to the equally noble Filangeri, who lived here until 1980, when the last heir donated it to the Region of Sicily. An 18th-century portal with the coat of arms of the Filangeri family leads to the courtyard, where a majestic marble stairway takes you to the piano nobile. Here there is a series of elegantly furnished drawing rooms. The first of these is the Sala degli Arazzi (Tapestry Hall), with mythological scenes painted by Giuseppe Velasco in 1804, then there is the "Chinese" room, and lastly the so-called Baldachin Salon with late 18th-century allegorical frescoes. The furniture and other furnishings date from the 18th and 19th centuries. Some rooms overlook a courtyard garden dominated by a theatrical Rococo fountain flanked by two aviaries.

San Francesco d'Assisi ❻

Piazza San Francesco d'Assisi. **Map** 2 D3. **Tel** 091-616 28 19. ◯ 8am–noon, 4–6:30pm daily.

This 13th-century church has retained its medieval aspect despite the numerous alterations it has undergone. Built in the early 13th century together with the Franciscan monastery, it was destroyed by Frederick II soon afterwards when he was excommunicated by the Pope. In 1255, work on the new church began, reaching completion only in 1277. The 15th and particularly the 16th centuries witnessed additions and alterations; for example, the wooden roof was replaced and the presbytery was enlarged.

After the 1943 bombardments the church was restored to its original state. The austere façade has a large rose window and Gothic portal, while the interior boasts many noteworthy works of art, including sculptures by Giacomo Serpotta *(see p35)* and Antonello Gagini. The side chapels house funerary stelae and sarcophagi.

The fourth chapel in the left-hand aisle is the Cappella Mastrantonio, with one of the first Renaissance works in Sicily, the portal by Francesco Laurana. Behind the high altar is a wooden choir built in 1520, as well as 17th-century paintings of the *Resurrection, Ascension* and *Mission*.

The drawing rooms in Palazzo Mirto, still with their original furniture

Palazzo Abatellis ❷

This Catalan Gothic building, which now houses the 16 rooms of the Galleria Regionale della Sicilia, has an austere air. The elegant doorway leads to the large courtyard, which has a portico on the right side and a stairway to the upper floors. On the ground floor is one of its most famous works, the *Triumph of Death* fresco (located in the former chapel) as well as a fine collection of statues by Antonello Gagini and Francesco Laurana. The first floor has noteworthy late medieval crucifixes including one by Pietro Ruzzolone (16th century), and paintings by Antonello da Messina. The most interesting work by a foreign artist is the *Malvagna Triptych* by Jan Gossaert (known as Mabuse). The museum is closed for restoration until 2010/11.

★ **Annunciation**
This is perhaps the best-known work by the great Antonello da Messina (1430–79). It is a master-ful and exquisite example of 15th-century figurative rationalism and the artist's fusion of Northern and Italian painting.

The "Laurana Room" houses the great sculptor's famous Bust of Eleonora of Aragon *(see p45).*

Ground floor

★ **The Triumph of Death**
Among the sculptures in this room, is a fine medieval fresco by an unknown artist, portraying Death in the guise of a knight shooting his bow (see pp32–3).

Virgin and Child
This sculpture group, attributed to Domenico Gagini (ca. 1420–1492) comes from the Basilica di San Francesco d'Assisi in Palermo (see p51). Note the delicate treatment of the Virgin's features.

Main entrance

Façade of the palazzo

The Malvagna Triptych
This work by the Flemish artist Mabuse (1478–1532) portrays the Virgin and Child among angels and saints.

VISITORS' CHECKLIST

Via Alloro 4. **Map** 2 E3.
Tel 091-623 00 11.
9am–1:30pm Tue–Sat.

Wooden Crucifix
Palermo artist Pietro Ruzzolone (15th–16th century) painted the Crucifixion (seen above) on the front and the risen Christ on the reverse.

First floor

KEY

- 12th-century carvings
- 14th–15th-century sculptures
  14th–16th-century majolicas
- 5th–16th-century sculptures and paintings
- 13th–16th-century paintings
- non-exhibition space

Ticket office

Portrait of a Youth
This work is attributed to Antonello Gagini (1478–1536), son of Domenico, and was once part of a statue of San Vito in the Palermo church of the same name. The facial features reveal the influence of Laurana.

HISTORY OF THE PALAZZO

Palazzo Abatellis was designed in 1490–95 by Matteo Carnalivari for Francesco Abatellis, the city's harbour-master and magistrate, who wanted to live in a luxurious mansion as befitted his social status. He died without leaving an heir, and the mansion was taken over by the Benedictine order and then by the Region of Sicily. It was damaged in the 1943 bombings and then restored by architect Carlo Scarpa.

The loggia

STAR SIGHTS

- ★ The Triumph of Death
- ★ Annunciation by Antonello da Messina

The Fontana Pretoria, once called "the fountain of shame" because of its statues of nude figures

Fontana Pretoria ❼

Piazza Pretoria. **Map** 1 C3.

Located in the middle of Palermo's most intriguing square, this fountain is on a slightly higher level than Via Maqueda. It was designed in 1552–5 by Tuscan sculptor Francesco Camilliani for the garden of a Florentine villa and was later installed in Piazza Pretoria. The concentric basins are arranged on three levels, with statues of mythological creatures, monsters, tritons, sirens and the four rivers of Palermo (Oreto, Papireto, Gabriele, Maredolce). Because of the nude statues it was known as "the fountain of shame".

A statue on the Fontana Pretoria

Palazzo delle Aquile ❽

Piazza Pretoria. **Map** 1 C3. **Tel** 091-740 2249. ⬜ 9am–1:30pm, 3–7pm Mon–Fri, 9am–1pm Sat.

Its proper name is Palazzo Senatorio, or Palazzo del Municipio, but it is commonly called "delle Aquile" because of the four eagles (*aquile*) decorating the exterior and the portal. Now the town hall, it is Palermo's major civic monument, although its original 16th-century structure was radically altered by 19th-century restoration. However, a statue of Santa Rosalia by Carlo Aprile (1661) still lies in a niche on the top of the façade. At the entrance, a grand staircase with a coffered ceiling takes you to the first floor and various public rooms: the Sala delle Lapidi, Sala dei Gonfaloni and Sala Rossa, which is also known as the Mayor's Hall.

Santa Caterina ❾

Piazza Bellini. **Map** 1 C3. ⬜ Nov–Mar: 9am–1:30pm Mon–Sun; Apr–Oct: 9:30am–1pm, 3–7pm Mon–Sat, 9am–1:30pm Sun. 📷

The church of the Dominican monastery of Santa Caterina is a splendid example of Sicilian Baroque art, despite the fact that both buildings originated in the 14th century.

The main features of the late Renaissance façade (the present church was built in 1580–96) are its double stairway and the statue of St Catherine (Caterina) in the middle of the portal. The large cupola was built in the mid-18th century. The interior has marble inlay, sculpture pieces, stuccoes and frescoes. In the chapel to the right of the transept is a fine statue of Santa Caterina, sculpted by Antonello Gagini in 1534.

La Martorana ❿

Piazza Bellini 3. **Map** 1 C4. **Tel** 091-616 16 92. ⬜ Apr–Oct: 9:15am–1pm, 3:30–7pm Mon–Sat, 8:30–9:45am, 11:45am–1pm Sun; Nov–Mar: 9:15am–1pm, 3:30–5:30pm Mon–Sat, 8:30–9:45am, 11:45am–1pm Sun.

Santa Maria dell'Ammiraglio is called La Martorana in memory of Eloisa della Martorana, who founded the nearby Benedictine convent. Built in 1143 on a Greek cross plan, it was partly altered and enlarged in the Baroque period. The 16th-century façade is also Baroque. This unique church combines Norman features and decor with those of later styles.

The portal on the Baroque façade of La Martorana

For hotels and restaurants in this area see p198 and p212

You enter the church by the bell tower, whose dome was destroyed in the 1726 earthquake. The Baroque interior is decorated with stuccoes and enamel. The bay vaulting has striking frescoes and the original church was decorated with 12th-century mosaics. The cupola shows *Christ Pantocrator Surrounded by Angels (see p46)*, on the tambour are *The Prophets* and *The Four Evangelists*, and on the walls are an *Annunciation, The Nativity* and *The Presentation at the Temple*. The most intriguing is of Roger II being crowned; it is the only known portrait of the king.

San Cataldo ⓫

Piazza Bellini 3. **Map** 1 C4. *Tel* 091-348 728. ◯ *Mar–Oct: 9am–2pm, 3:30–7pm Mon–Sat, 9am–2pm Sun; Nov–Feb: 9am–2pm daily.* 🎨

San Cataldo was the chapel of a palazzo built by Maio of Bari, William I's admiral, in the 12th century. It has kept the linear Arab-Norman style, with three red domes raised above the wall, the windows with pointed arches and the battlement decoration. Inscriptions with quotations from the Koran can still be seen. The interior has no decoration except for the mosaic-patterned floor. In the middle of the nave is a series of Arab arches supported by ancient columns.

Galleria d'arte Moderna Sant'Anna ⓬

Via Sant'Anna 21, Palermo. **Map** 2 D3. *Tel* 091-813 4605. ◯ *9:30am–6:30pm Tue–Sun.* 🎨

Housed in the restored 15th-century convent of Sant'Anna, this gallery features a range of works from the past 150 years. Many of the Italian and international artists on display have featured prominently in the Venice Biennale.

La Magione ⓭

Via Magione 44. **Map** 2 D4. *Tel* 091-617 05 96. ◯ *8:30am–noon, 4–6:30pm Mon–Sat; 8am–1pm Sun.* **Cloister & Chapels** ◯ *9:30am–7pm daily.* 🎨

Founded by Matteo d'Aiello in the mid-1100s, this church was frequently rebuilt and was then damaged in the bombings of 1943. Careful restoration has revived its original Norman features. A Baroque portico, with marble columns and statues, affords access to a garden. The façade has three doorways with double arched lintels and convex rustication, a series of blind arches and windows. Pointed arches run along the length of the nave.

Santa Maria dello Spasimo ⓮

Via dello Spasimo. **Map** 2 E4. *Tel* 091-616 14 86. ◯ *8am–8pm daily.*

The roofless interior of Santa Maria dello Spasimo

Santa Maria dello Spasimo lies in the heart of the Kalsa quarter. It was founded in 1506 by the monks of Santa Maria di Monte Oliveto and was dedicated to the Virgin Mary grieving before Christ on the Cross, subject of a painting by Raphael in 1516, which is now in the Prado Museum in Madrid. Santa Maria was the last example of Spanish Gothic architecture in the city. The cells and courtyards of the monastery were built around the church and in 1536 the complex, at that time outside the city walls, was incorporated into a rampart, so that it now looks like a watchtower.

The church was bought by the city and became, in turn, a theatre, warehouse, hospice and hospital, while all the time falling into a state of neglect. A few years ago, the Spasimo area was redeveloped and transformed into a cultural centre for exhibitions and concerts. Performances are held inside the church, part of which no longer has a roof.

San Cataldo, with its characteristic Arab architectural elements

One of the rooms in the Museo Archeologico Regionale

Museo Archeo-logico Regionale ⑮

Piazza Olivella 24. **Map** 1 C2.
Tel 091-611 67 05. ⬜ 8:30am–1:30pm, 2:30–6:30pm Tue–Fri, 8:30am–1:30pm Sat, Sun & hols. The Metopes room is closed until 2012 due to restoration works. 🖼

The Archaeological Museum is housed in a 17th-century monastery and holds treasures from excavations across the island. The entrance leads to a small cloister with a fountain bearing a statue of Triton. The former cells contain finds such as the large Phoenician sarcophagi in the shape of human beings (6th–5th centuries BC) and the *Pietra di Palermo*, a slab with a hieroglyphic inscription (2900 BC). On the first floor there is a display of Punic inscriptions and objects, as well as terracotta and bronze sculpture, including a fine 3rd-century BC ram's head. On the second floor is the Sala dei Mosaici, with mosaics and frescoes from digs at Palermo, Solunto and Marsala. The large cloister houses Roman statues, slabs and tombstones. At the end of the cloister are three rooms with the marvellous pieces taken from the temples at Selinunte; these include a lovely leonine head from the Temple of Victory and the valuable metopes from other temples. Those

Roman head, Museo Archeologico

from Temple C represent *Helios's Chariot, Perseus Helped by Athena while Killing the Gorgon* and *Heracles Punishing the Cercopes*; the metopes from Temple E are *Heracles Fighting the Amazons, Hera and Zeus on Mount Ida, Actaeon Attacked by Dogs in the Presence of Artemis* (see p22) and *Athena Slaying the Giant Enceladus.*

Mercato della Vucciria ⑯

Piazza Caracciolo and adjacent streets.
Map 1 C3.

This is Palermo's most famous market, immortalized by Renato Guttuso in his painting *La Vucciria (see p222)*. There are two theories as to the origin of the market's name. Some say it is a corruption of the French *boucherie*, or butcher, while others suggest the name

means "the place of loud voices", from when vendors called out their wares. Today, this outdoor market-place trades not only in vegetables, dried fruit and preserves, but also sells other foods such as cheese, fish and meat, amid a tumult of colours, sounds and smells reminiscent of the souks in North Africa. The Vucciria is especially impressive in the morning, when the fishmongers set up shop. There are stalls that serve sea urchin or will do skewered giblets for you on the spot. Another speciality is boiled spleen, also used for making *ca' meusa* bread, the locals' favourite snack. To get to the market, from Piazza San Domenico take Via Maccheronai, once the colourful pasta-producing area, where freshly made pasta was hung out to dry.

Oratorio del Rosario di Santa Cita ⑰

Via Valverde 3. **Map** 1 C2.
Tel 091-332 779. ⬜ 9am–1pm Mon–Sat (ring for admittance).

Founded in 1590 by the Society of the Rosary, this was one of the city's richest oratories. A marble staircase opens onto a cloister and then goes up to an upper loggia decorated with marble busts, and to the vestibule, with portraits of the Superiors of the Society. The Oratory (which was restored in 2005) is an example of Giacomo Serpotta's best work *(see p35)*,

The Mercato della Vucciria, Palermo's colourful open-air market

The Baroque façade of San Domenico

decorated walls. The altar in the transept is adorned with lateral volutes and bronze friezes, while the 18th-century high altar is made of marble and decorated with semi-precious stones.

Oratorio del Rosario di San Domenico ⑲

Via dei Bambinai. **Map** 1 C2.
◯ *9am–1pm Mon–Sat.*

Behind San Lorenzo, in the Vucciria market area, is the Oratory of San Domenico, founded at the end of the 16th century by the Society of the Holy Rosary. Two Society members were painter Pietro Novelli and sculptor Giacomo Serpotta, who left the marks of their genius on this elegant monument.

The black and white majolica floors fit in well with the tumult of figures of great ladies, knights and playful putti. These form a kind of frame for the statues of Christian virtues by Giacomo Serpotta and the paintings representing the mysteries of the Rosary. The latter were executed by Pietro Novelli and Flemish artists, while the altarpiece, *Madonna of the Rosary with St Dominic and the Patronesses of Palermo*, was painted by Anthony Van Dyck in 1628. In the middle of the vault is Novelli's *Coronation of the Virgin*.

a lavish display of Baroque decoration, its fusion of putti volutes, statues, floral elements and festoons creating an amazing theatrical atmosphere. The *Battle of Lepanto* sculpture group *(see p35)* is spectacular. On the sides of the tribune are statues of Esther and Judith, while the altarpiece is Carlo Maratta's *Madonna of the Rosary* (1695). Along the walls there are seats with mother-of-pearl inlay, and the floor is made of red, white and black marble.

Detail of stucco-work, Santa Cita

San Domenico ⑱

Piazza San Domenico. **Map** 1 C3.
Tel *091-589 172.* ◯ *9am–noon Tue–Sat, 5–7pm Sat & Sun.* **Cloister** ◯ *9am–1pm Tue–Sat, by appointment.*

This basilica, which belongs to the Dominican monastery, has been rebuilt many times over the past six centuries. The most drastic alteration

was in 1640, when Andrea Cirincione tore down part of the cloister to enlarge the church. In 1724, when Piazza San Domenico was remodelled, the façade was rebuilt and is now animated by the fusion of curves on the one hand, and jutting columns and statues, niches and twin bell towers on the other. The interior has a typical Latin cross plan with two aisles and a deep semicircular dome. The total lack of decoration serves to heighten the elegance of the architecture. In contrast, the chapels, used since the 19th century as the burial place for the city's most illustrious personages, are quite richly decorated. The third chapel is the tomb of the Oneto di Sperlinga family and has multicoloured marble funerary monuments, a statue of St Joseph by Antonello Gagini, and stucco- and putti-

Van Dyck's fine canvas stands behind the Oratorio altar

WEST PALERMO

The quarters south of Via Roma lie on the slopes occupied by the city's original Phoenician settlement, which was enlarged during the Roman era. In the 11th century the Arabs built a castle on the site where the Palazzo dei Normanni now stands. The Arab word *Al Qasar* (the castle) was used as the name of the quarter and the street that led to the castle, the present-day Corso Vittorio Emanuele, known as "Cassaro" to the people of Palermo. The area contains many impressive buildings and churches, including Palermo's

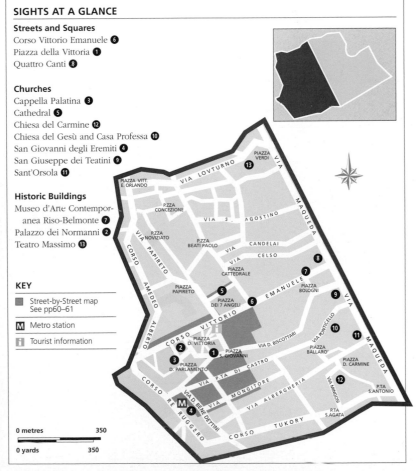

One of the statues on the Cathedral

Cathedral, as well as good shops and hotels. Between the Palazzo dei Normanni and Via Maqueda is the Albergheria quarter, the home of merchants and craftsmen in the Middle Ages. It is still enlivened by the daily market, the Mercato Ballarò, which is less famous but more authentic than the Vuccira market. The many oratories of the medieval brotherhoods demonstrate the wealth and industry of the inhabitants. In the first half of the 20th century parts were demolished, and the 1943 air raids dealt an additional blow to the area.

SIGHTS AT A GLANCE

Streets and Squares
Corso Vittorio Emanuele ⓺
Piazza della Vittoria ➊
Quattro Canti ➑

Churches
Cappella Palatina ➌
Cathedral ➎
Chiesa del Carmine ⓬
Chiesa del Gesù and Casa Professa ➓
San Giovanni degli Eremiti ➍
San Giuseppe dei Teatini ➒
Sant'Orsola ⓫

Historic Buildings
Museo d'Arte Contemporanea Riso-Belmonte ⓻
Palazzo dei Normanni ➋
Teatro Massimo ⓭

KEY

▦ Street-by-Street map
See pp60–61

Ⓜ Metro station

ℹ Tourist information

0 metres 350
0 yards 350

◁ The Atlantes at Porta Nuova, the city gate built in 1583 in honour of Emperor Charles V

Street-by-Street: Around Piazza della Vittoria

Mosaic lunette in the Stanza di
Ruggero, Palazzo dei Normanni

Piazza della Vittoria, opposite the Palazzo dei Normanni, is one of the city's major squares. Since the time of the Roman *castrum superius*, the Arab Alcazar and the Norman Palace, this area has been the military, political and administrative heart of Sicily, and religious prestige was added in the 12th century when the Cathedral was built nearby. In the 17th and 18th centuries the square was the venue for public festivities. It became a public garden in the early 1900s, surrounded by important monuments such as Porta Nuova, Palazzo Sclafani and Palazzo Arcivescovile.

The monument to Philip V, in the middle of Piazza della Vittoria, was built of marble in 1662.

The former hospital of San Giacomo

Porta Nuova was built in 1569 to commemorate Charles V's arrival in Palermo in 1535.

Palazzo dei Normanni
This has always been the palace of the city's rulers. Traces of the original Arab-Norman architecture can still be seen on the exterior ②

★ **Cappella Palatina**
Founded in 1130 by the Norman king Roger II, the chapel boasts an extraordinary cycle of mosaics ③

CORSO VITTOR

PIAZZA DEL PARLAMENTO

★ **San Giovanni degli Eremiti**
This church, surrounded by a luxuriant garden, is one of the most important monuments in Palermo, partly because of its unique Arab-Norman architecture ④

Palazzo Arcivescovile
and Museo Diocesano

Villa
Bonanno

PIAZZA

SETTEANGELI

ANUELE

PIAZZA DELLA VITTORIA

PIAZZA SAN
GIOVANNI
DECOLLATO

VIA DEL BASTIONE

Palazzo
Sclafani

LOCATOR MAP
See Street Finder map 1

WEST
PALERMO

EAST
PALERMO

★ **Cathedral**
*The history of the city can be
traced from the different
architectural styles* ❺

STAR SIGHTS

★ Cappella Palatina

★ San Giovanni degli
Eremiti

★ Cathedral

KEY

– – – Suggested route

Piazza della Vittoria
*This huge square
is entirely occupied
by the palm trees
and well-tended
gardens around
Villa Bonanno* ❶

0 metres   100

0 yards   100

Cappella Palatina ❸

Detail of a mosaic in the interior

Founded in 1132 by Roger II (*see pp28–9*), the Cappella Palatina with its splendid mosaics is a jewel of Arab-Norman art. The basilica has two side aisles and three apses, granite columns dividing the nave. The walls are decorated with Biblical scenes. On the cupola and the bowl of the central apse is the image of Christ Pantocrator surrounded by angels, while the niches house the Four Evangelists. Old Testament kings and prophets are on the arches, Christ blessing the faithful dominates the middle apse, and the transept walls bear scenes from the Gospel. Other important features are the wooden ceiling, a master-piece of Muslim art, and the marble pulpit and cande-labrum. The overall harmony of the design, and the perfection of the details, make this a unique monument.

★ **The Central Apse**
In the middle is the Christ Pan-tocrator; below him the Virgin Mary and the saints.

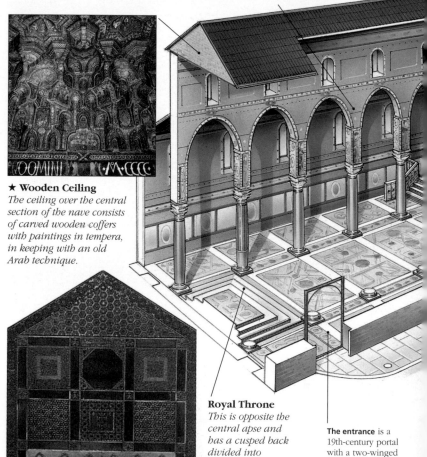

★ **Wooden Ceiling**
The ceiling over the central section of the nave consists of carved wooden coffers with paintings in tempera, in keeping with an old Arab technique.

Royal Throne
This is opposite the central apse and has a cusped back divided into squares bearing the Aragonese coat of arms.

The entrance is a 19th-century portal with a two-winged wooden door.

★ **Christ Pantocrator**
In the middle of the cupola is this glory of mosaic decoration, the figure of Christ Pantocrator, surrounded by angels and archangels dressed in Norman warrior garb.

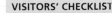

VISITORS' CHECKLIST

Piazza Indipendenza.
Map 1 A5. **Tel** 091-626 28 33.
◯ 8:15am–5:45pm Mon–Sat, 8:15am–1pm Sun & hols.

Candelabrum
Made entirely of white marble, this beautiful candelabrum is the oldest Romanesque work of art in Sicily. Four lions devouring animals decorate the base, while there are interlaced floral and human motifs along the shaft. On the top are three slender figures supporting the disc that held the Easter candle.

The side apse is decorated with images of St Paul and the Virgin Mary.

The Crypt
This lies under the presbytery. It is built on a square plan and was probably King Roger's original chapel. Sacred objects and works of art such as this Byzantine school Madonna and Child are now kept here.

STAR FEATURES

★ Wooden Ceiling

★ The Central Apse

★ Christ Pantocrator

Piazza della Vittoria, with Palazzo dei Normanni in the background

Piazza della Vittoria ❶

This square is completely occupied by the **Villa Bonanno** garden. In the middle is the **Teatro Marmoreo** fountain, built in honour of Philip V, with statues of the continents partly under this ruler's dominion (Europe, America, Asia and Africa). Archaeological digs have unearthed Roman villas and mosaics; the finds are in the Museo Archeologico Regionale *(see p56)* and the Sala dell'Orfeo pavilion. Among the palazzi and churches facing the square are the Baroque **Cappella della Soledad**, with multi-coloured marble and stucco decoration, and the former hospital of **San Giacomo** (now the Bonsignore barracks), with the lovely Norman **Santa Maria Maddalena** in the interior.

Palazzo dei Normanni ❷

Piazza Indipendenza. **Map** 1 A5. **Tel** 091-705 11 11. ◯ 8:15am–5:45pm Mon, Fri & Sat; 8:15am–1pm Sun & hols. ▨

The Arabs built this palace over the ruins of a Punic fortress in the 11th century. The following century it was enlarged and became the royal palace of the Norman king Roger II, with Arab architects and craftsmen building towers and pavilions for the king and his retinue.

Not much is left of the Norman age, partly because the palace was abandoned when Frederick II left his Palermo court. The Spanish viceroys preferred to use the more modern Palazzo Steri. The present-day appearance of the palace, now the seat of the Sicilian Regional Assembly, dates back to alterations made in the 16th and 17th centuries. The entrance is in Piazza Indipendenza. After a short walk uphill, you enter the Maqueda courtyard, built in 1600 with three rows of arcades and a large staircase leading to the first floor and the Cappella Palatina *(see pp62–3)*, one of the few parts remaining from the Norman period. The royal apartments, which now house the Sicilian Parliament, are on the second floor and can only be visited accompanied by a guard. The most interesting room is the Sala di Re Ruggero, the walls and arches of which are covered with 12th-century mosaics with animal and plant motifs in a naturalistic vein that probably reveals a Persian influence: centaurs, leopards, lions, deer and peacocks. The vault has geometric motifs and medallions with owls, deer, centaurs and lions. The tour ends with the Chinese Room, frescoed by Giovanni and Salvatore Patricolo, and the Sala Gialla, with tempera decoration on the vaults.

Cappella Palatina ❸

See pp62–3.

San Giovanni degli Eremiti ❹

Via dei Benedettini 18. **Map** 1 A5. **Tel** 091-651 50 19. ◯ 9am–7pm Tue–Sun. ▨

Built in 1132 for Roger II *(see pp28–9)* over the foundation of a Benedictine monastery that had been constructed in 581, San Giovanni degli Eremiti displays a clearly Oriental influence.

King Roger's Hall in Palazzo dei Normanni, showing the mosaics

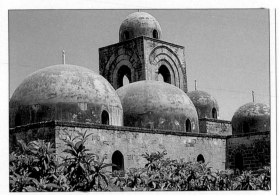

The five typically Arab domes on San Giovanni degli Eremiti

It was built by Arab-Norman craftsmen and labourers, and their work is at its most striking in the red domes and cubic forms.

The delightful garden of citrus trees, pomegranate, roses and jasmine leads to the ruins of the monastery, a small cloister with twin columns and pointed arches (see pp42–3).

The cross-plan interior has an aisleless nave ending in the presbytery with three apses. The right-hand apse is covered by one of the red domes, while above the left-hand one is a fine bell tower with pointed windows and a smaller red dome on top.

Cathedral **❺**

See pp66–7.

Corso Vittorio Emanuele **❻**

This is the main street in the heart of Palermo, which lies on the Phoenician road that connected the ancient city and the seaside. The locals call it "Cassaro", from the Arab al Qasar, or castle, to which the road led. In the Middle Ages it was the most important artery in the city, but in the 1500s it became an elegant street. In that period the street was extended to the sea, and two city gates were built: **Porta Felice** to the north and **Porta Nuova** to the south, next to Palazzo dei Normanni. It was called Via

Toledo during the Spanish period. The stretch between Porta Nuova and the Quattro Canti boasts several patrician mansions. On the western side is the former hospital of San Giacomo, now the Bonsignore barracks; the Baroque **Collegio Massimo dei Gesuiti**, the present Regional Library; **Palazzo Geraci**, a Baroque residence rebuilt in the Rococo style; the **Palazzo Belmonte-Riso**, which houses the Contemporary Art Museum; and the 18th-century **Palazzo Tarallo della Miraglia**, restored as the Hotel Centrale. On the eastern side are **San Salvatore**, a lovely Baroque church with lavish decoration and **San Giuseppe dei Teatini**. Just beyond Vicolo Castelbuono is **Piazza Bologni**, which has several Baroque buildings, among them the Palazzo Alliola di Villafranca.

Museo d'Arte Contemporaneo Riso-Belmonte **❼**

Corsa Vittorio Emanuele 365. ☐ 10am–8pm Tue–Sat (to 10pm Thu & Fri). 🎫

In a meticulously restored palazzo right in front of the Piazza Bologni, the Contemporary Art Gallery was conceived as a multi-functional centre, with a bookshop, café and multimedia room on the premises. The palazzo itself was

built in 1784 by Venanzio Marvuglia, who was one of the most prolific architects of the time. The collection has been laid out so that the whole building can be admired; works are placed both inside and outside the museum, taking visitors through old courtyards and hidden corners. Works by artists such as Pietro Consagra, Allesandro Bazan and Carla Accardi are part of the permanent collection. Guided tours are available.

Quattro Canti **❽**

Piazza Vigliena. **Map** 1 C3.

The intersection of Corso Vittorio Emanuele and Via Maqueda is Palermo's most fashionable square. Quattro Canti dates from 1600, when the new town plan was put into effect and the city was divided into four parts, called *Mandamenti*: the north-eastern *Kalsa* section, the southeastern one of Albergheria, Capo to the southwest and Castellammare or Loggia in the southeast. The piazza is rounded, shaped by the concave façades of the four corner buildings (hence the name) with superimposed architectural orders – Doric, Corinthian and Ionic. Each façade is decorated with a fountain and statues of the *Mandamenti* patron saints, of the seasons and of the Spanish kings.

One of the façades of the Quattro Canti

Cathedral ❺

Dedicated to Our Lady of the Assumption, the Cathedral stands on the site of an Early Christian basilica, later a mosque. It was built in 1179–85 but, because of frequent rebuilding and alterations, very little of the original structure remains. In the late 1700s the nave was widened and the central cupola was added. The original Norman structure can be seen under the small cupolas with majolica tiles, with the typical arched crenellation decoration on the wall tops. The exterior of the apses has maintained its original character with its interlaced arches and small columns. As a result of the mixture of styles, the right-hand side forms a kind of "carved history" of the city. Opposite the façade, on the other side of the street, is the medieval campanile. The tiara of Constance of Aragón (*see p3 and p33*) is kept here.

Statue of St Rosalie outside the Cathedral

Cupolas with Majolica Tiles
The small cupolas were built in 1781 over the side chapels, the addition of which drastically changed the Cathedral's original plan.

★ Catalan Gothic Portico
The work of Antonio Gambara (1430), the portico has three pointed arches and a Gothic tympanum with Biblical scenes and the city coat of arms in bas-relief.

Arab Inscription
Various parts of the former mosque were retained in the Cathedral, such as this passage from the Koran inscribed on the left-hand column of the southern portico.

The portal was built in the 1400s and is decorated with a two-winged wooden door with a mosaic of the Virgin Mary above.

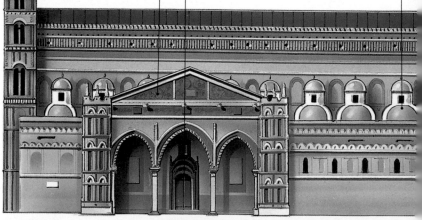

The Cappella di Santa Rosalia, patron saint of Palermo

Middle section of the nave, with statues by Antonello Gagini

VISITORS' CHECKLIST

Corso Vittorio Emanuele.
Map 1 B4. **Tel** 091-334 373.
104. 8am–7pm daily.
9:30am–5:30pm Mon–Sat.
www.cattedrale-palermo.it

THE INTERIOR OF THE CATHEDRAL

Alterations carried out in the 18th century gave the interior a Neo-Classical look. Of the many chapels, the most important are the first two on the right-hand side of the nave with the imperial tombs, and the chapel of Santa Rosalia, where the saint's remains are in a silver coffer on the altar.

★ **Towers with Gothic Double Lancet Windows**
The slender Gothic turrets with their lancet windows were added to the 12th-century Norman clock tower in the 14th–15th centuries.

The cupola, in Baroque style, was added in the late 1700s to a design by Ferdinando Fuga.

STAR SIGHTS

★ Catalan Gothic Portico

★ Towers with Double Lancet Windows

The arched crenellation motif characteristic of Norman architecture runs along the right side of the Cathedral.

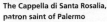

The exterior of the apses, decorated with interlaced arches, is the best preserved part of the original design.

The lavishly decorated Baroque interior of the Chiesa del Gesù

San Giuseppe dei Teatini ⑨

Piazza Pretoria. **Map** 1 C4.
Tel 091-331 239. ☐ Sep–Jul:
7:30am–noon, 5:30–8pm Mon–Sat,
8:30am–1pm, 6–8pm Sun; Aug–Jun:
7:30–11am, 6–8pm Mon–Sat,
8:30am–noon, 6–8pm Sun.

The Theatine congregation spared no expense in the construction of this church (1612–45). Despite the fact that the façade was finished in 1844 in Neo-Classical style, the church exudes a Baroque spirit, beginning with the cupola covered with majolica tiles. The two-aisle nave is flanked by huge columns, the ceiling is frescoed and the walls are covered with polychrome marble decoration. On either side of the entrance are two marble stoups held up by angels.

The chapels are richly decorated with stucco and frescoes, and the high altar is made of semiprecious stone.

Chiesa del Gesù and Casa Professa ⑩

Piazza Casa Professa. **Map** 1 C4.
Tel 091-606 71 11. ☐ 8–11:30am,
5–6:30pm daily.

This church perhaps represents the peak of Baroque art in Palermo. The late 16th-century façade was one of the sets for the film *Il Gattopardo (see p24)*. Work on the decoration began in 1597 and was interrupted permanently when the Jesuits were expelled in 1860. The grandiose interior is entirely covered with marble inlay – walls, columns and floor – in a profusion of forms and colours, blending in well with the fine stuccoes of Giacomo Serpotta *(see p35)*, the imitation bas-relief columns and the various decorative motifs. The pulpit in the middle of the nave was the work of the Genoese school (1646). To the right of the church is the western section of the Casa Professa, with a 1685 portal and an 18th-century cloister affording access to the City Library.

Sant'Orsola ⑪

Via Maqueda. **Map** 1 C4. ☐ 8:30–
11am. Oratory visits by request only.

Sant'Orsola was built in the early 17th century by the Society of St Ursula, known as "Dei Negri" because of the dark habits the members wore during processions. The late Renaissance façade is decorated with figures of souls in Purgatory and angels. Three skulls lie on the architrave. The aisleless interior is an example of a light-filled Baroque church, with deep semicircular chapels linked by galleries. The vault over the nave is decorated with the fresco *The Glory of St Ursula* and two medallions depicting Faith and Charity. The painting *The Martyrdom of St Ursula* by Pietro Novelli *(see p23)* is in the second chapel on the right, while frescoes of scenes of the saint's life are on the vault. Another work by Novelli, *Madonna with the Salvator Mundi*, is in the sacristy. From the sacristy there is access to the Oratorio di Sant'Orsola, decorated with 17th-century paintings and stucco sculpture.

The 18th-century cloister of the Casa Professa

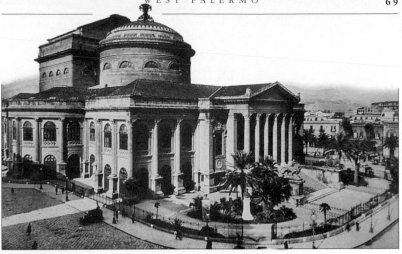

An old commemorative postcard of the Teatro Massimo, Palermo's opera house

Chiesa del Carmine ⑫

Via Giovanni Grasso 13a.
Map 1 C5. **Tel** 091-651 20 18.
☐ 9–10:30am. Outside these hours, ring bell for admittance.

This church, seat of the Carmelite friars, dates from the 1600s. It lies on a much higher level than the nearby Mercato del Ballarò and is topped by a cupola covered with multicoloured majolica tiles supported by four Atlantes. The interior is dominated by an altar resting on pairs of spiral columns decorated with stuccoes by Giuseppe and Giacomo Serpotta (1683) of scenes from the life of Mary. The painting by Pietro Novelli *(see p23)*, *The Vision of Sant'Andrea Corsini*, is also worth a look.

The cupola with polychrome majolica tiles, Chiesa del Carmine

Teatro Massimo ⑬

Piazza Giuseppe Verdi. **Map** 1 B2.
Tel 091-605 35 15. ☐ for visits: 10am–2:30pm Tue–Sun (not during rehearsals). 🎫 www.teatromassimo.it

The Teatro Massimo is one of the symbols of Palermo's rebirth. Designed in 1864 by Giovanni Battista Filippo Basile, it was finished in 1897. In order to make room for it, the city walls of Porta Maqueda, the Aragonese quarter, San Giuliano convent and church, and the Chiesa delle Stimmate di San Francesco and its monastery were all demolished. Its 7,700 sq m (9,200 sq yd) make it one of the largest opera houses in Europe. The theatre now boasts five rows of boxes, a lavishly decorated gallery and a ceiling frescoed by Ettore Maria Bergler and Rocco Lentini. The entrance, with its Corinthian columns, is also monumental in style.

GUIDED TOURS OF THE MERCATO BALLARÒ

The Albergheria is one of the poorest and most run-down quarters in the old town, but it is also one of the most intriguing. Guided tours are organized by the San Francesco Saverio parish church and by the agency **Albergheria Viaggi**. The neighbourhood children, accompanied by bilingual guides for foreigners, will take you on the same itinerary once used by those making the Grand Tour. The first stop is the bell tower of San Francesco Saverio, a typical example of Sicilian Baroque, with a view of the cupolas and rooftops of Palermo. Then you will be able to observe how the local carob sweets are made and to see one of the last remaining decorators of authentic Sicilian carts, Pippino La Targia, at work. This tour also allows you to see monuments normally closed to the public, such as the 17th-century Oratorio del Carminello. But the highlight is the Mercato di Ballarò, one of the best markets in the city, a vivid combination of colours, smells and lively atmosphere.

Detail of a mural in the Albergheria quarter

Albergheria Viaggi
Piazza San Francesco Saverio.
Map 1 B5. **Tel** 091-651 85 76.

FURTHER AFIELD

The destruction of the 16th-century defensive ramparts took place in the late 1700s, but it was only after the unification of Italy that Palermo expanded westwards past the city walls, which involved making new roads and demolishing old quarters. The heart of town shifted to Piazzas Verdi and Castelnuovo, where the Massimo and

Capital of a column at Monreale

Politeama theatres were built. This expansion also meant the disappearance of most of the lovely Arab-Norman gardens and parks the rulers had used for hunting and entertainment. Only a few, such as Castello della Zisa, have remained. At this time, "Greater Palermo" was created – an area that now includes Mondello and Monreale Cathedral.

SIGHTS AT A GLANCE

Galleries and Museums
Museo Etnografico Pitrè ❹

Historic Buildings
Castello della Zisa ❼
La Cuba ❽
Casina Cinese ❸
Ponte dell'Ammiraglio ⓭
Politeama ❺

Churches
Catacombe dei Cappuccini ❻
Monreale Cathedral
  pp76–7 ⓮
San Giovanni dei Lebbrosi ⓬
Santo Spirito ⓫

Parks and Gardens
Orto Botanico ❿
Parco della Favorita ❷
Villa Giulia ❾

Beaches
Mondello ❶

KEY

▨	Historic centre
▫	Urban area
▭	Motorway (Highway)
▬	Major road
═	Minor road
—	Railway line
🚉	Railway station
⚓	Ferry
Ⓜ	Metro station
🚌	Bus station

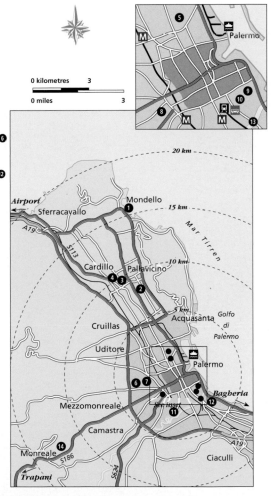

◁ **Cloister of the original Benedictine monastery next to Monreale Cathedral (12th century)**

The lively fishing harbour at Mondello, filled with boats

Mondello ❶

10 km (6 miles) north of Palermo.

A favourite with Palermitans, Mondello beach lies a short distance from the centre of the town, between the rocky promontories of Monte Pellegrino and Monte Gallo.

Mondello was once a small village of tuna fishermen, centred around a 15th-century square tower, but in the last 100 years it has become a residential area immersed in greenery. Mondello's golden age was at the turn of the 19th century, when a kind of garden-city was founded and well-to-do Palermitans had lovely Art Nouveau villas built here. The Kursaal bathhouse, built on piles in the sea a few yards from the beach, also dates from this period. Designed by Rudolph Stualket in the Art Nouveau style, it is decorated with mythological figures and sea monsters. Mondello is a popular town, perhaps even more so on

summer evenings, when the city dwellers come to escape from the heat and dine in one of the many fish and seafood restaurants lining the road in the old fishing quarter.

Parco della Favorita ❷

Viale Ercole, Viale Diana.

This large public park, which is unfortunately in a state of neglect, extends for almost 3 km (2 miles) behind Monte Pellegrino. It was originally a hunting reserve, but King Ferdinand I *(see p29)* turned it into a garden in 1799, when he fled to Palermo with his retinue after being forced into exile from Naples by Napoleon's troops. The park has two large roads. Viale Diana, which goes to Mondello, is intersected by Viale d'Ercole, at the end of which is a marble fountain with a statue of Hercules, a

copy of the famous *Farnese Hercules* that the king had wanted for himself in his court at Naples.

Most of the park is occupied by sports facilities (tennis courts, pools, stadium and racetrack). On the edge of the park there are many villas built in the 18th century as summer residences for the Sicilian nobility. The most interesting are the Villa Sofia, now a hospital; Villa Castelnuovo, an agricultural institute; and Villa Niscemi, mentioned in di Lampedusa's novel *The Leopard (see p23)*, now the venue for cultural activities.

Casina Cinese ❸

Via Duca degli Abruzzi. **Tel** 091-707 13 17. ☐ *by appointment only.*

The extravagant façade of the Casina Cinese

At the edge of the Parco della Favorita, the former hunting grounds of the Bourbons, is the "little Chinese palace", the summer residence of Ferdinand I and his wife

---

SANCTUARY OF SANTA ROSALIA ON MONTE PELLEGRINO

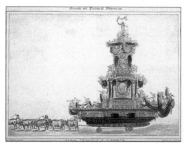

Period print of Santa Rosalia's float

On Monte Pellegrino, which dominates the city, is the Sanctuary dedicated to Santa Rosalia, the patron saint of Palermo. The daughter of the Duke of Sinibaldo, Rosalia decided to lead the life of a hermit in a cave. Five centuries after her death in 1166, the discovery of her remains coincided exactly with the end of the plague that had struck the city. Since then the saint has been venerated twice a year: on 11–15 July a triumphal float with her remains is taken in a procession through the city, and on 4 September the same procession goes to the Sanctuary. This was built in 1625; it consists of a convent and the saint's cave, filled with ex-votos.

For hotels and restaurants in this region see pp198–9 and pp213–14

Maria Carolina during their period of exile in Sicily. It was designed by Venanzio Marvuglia in 1799 and, it seems, the king himself had a hand in the palace's Oriental architecture, which was much in vogue at the time. Ferdinand I entertained such illustrious guests as Horatio Nelson and his wife, Lady Hamilton, here.

The Casina Cinese was the first example of eclectic architecture in Palermo, a combination of Chinese decorative motifs and Gothic, Egyptian and Arab elements. Overall it is an extravagant work, exemplified by details such as the repetition of bells in the shape of a pagoda on the fence, the cornices and the roof. The interior is equally flamboyant: Neo-Classical stuccoes and paintings are combined with 18th-century chinoiserie, scenes of Chinese life and Pompeiian painting. The building is undergoing an extensive renovation to bring it back to its original splendour.

Aerial view of the Neo-Classical Politeama

Museo Etnografico Pitré ❹

Via Duca degli Abruzzi. 🖼 *for restoration; a limited part of the collection can be seen at Palazzo Tarallo, via delle Pergole 74/A.* **Tel** *091-616 10 76.* ⬜ *9am–1pm Mon–Fri (3:30–5:30pm Wed).*

The Ethnographic Museum, next to the Casina Cinese, has a collection of about 4,000 exhibits, documenting Sicilian life, traditions and folk art. The museum was founded in honour of the Palermian ethnographer Giuseppe Pitré, who wrote the first bilingual Italian-Sicilian dictionary; the library houses over 26,000 volumes. Rooms feature local embroidery and weaving, along with sections on traditional costumes and rugs. A great many display cases contain ceramics and glassware, as well as a fine collection of oil lamps. A further section displays traditional Sicilian carts, late 19th-century glass painting, and carts and floats

dedicated to Santa Rosalia. The Sala del Teatrino dell' Opera dei Pupi has on display a number of rod puppets, which are traditional characters in Sicilian puppet opera, as well as playbills decorated with scenes taken from the puppeteers' works. The Sala dei Presepi features more than 300 nativity scenes, some by the 18th-century artist Giocanni Matera.

Politeama ❺

Piazza Ruggero Settimo. **Map** *1 B1.* **Tel** *091-605 32 49 (box office 091-588 001).*

This historic theatre is in the heart of modern-day Palermo, at the corner of Via Ruggero Settimo and tree-lined Viale della Libertà, the city's "outdoor living room". Giuseppe Damiani Almeyda designed the Neo-Classical building in 1867–74. The theatre's semi-circle shape resembles a horseshoe, while the two orders of colonnades are both in Doric and Ionian order. The exterior is frescoed in Pompeii red and gold, in tune with the Neo-Classical movement at the time. The façade is a triumphal arch whose attic level is decorated with sculpture crowned by a chariot. While the Teatro Massimo was closed, the Politeama was the centre of the city's cultural life. It still plays host to some operatic and theatrical performances (Nov–May).

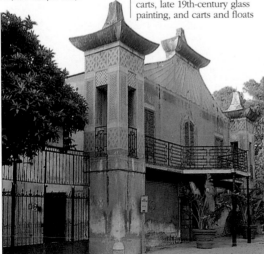

Entrance to the Museo Pitré, devoted to Sicilian folk art and customs

Catacombe dei Cappuccini ❼

Via Cappuccini. *Tel* 091-212 117.
◘ *9am–noon daily (3–6pm Apr–Oct).*

The catacombs of the Convento dei Cappuccini contain the bodies – some mummified, others skeletons – of the prelates and well-to-do citizens of Palermo. They are divided according to sex, profession and social standing, wearing their best clothes, some of which are moth-eaten. Visitors can see the cells where the corpses were put to dry. At the end of the stairway is the body of the first friar "buried" here, Fra' Silvestro da Gubbio, who died in 1599. In 1881, interment in the catacombs ceased, but on display in the Cappella dell' Addolorata is the body of a little girl who died in 1920 and was so skilfully embalmed that she seems asleep. In the outdoor cemetery behind the catacombs is the tomb of Giuseppe di Lampedusa.

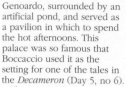

Embalmed body in the crypt

Castello della Zisa ❽

Piazza Zisa 1. *Tel* 091-652 02 69.
◘ *9am–7pm Tue–Sun.* **Museo d'Arte Islamica** ◘ *9am–7pm Tue–Sun.* 📷

This remarkable palace, built in 1165–7, once overlooked a pond and was surrounded by a large park with many streams and fish ponds. Sadly, the Zisa Castle now stands in the middle of an ugly fringe area of Palermo. After years of neglect, the castle has now been restored and once again merits the name given to it by the Arabs – *aziz*, or splendid. The handsome exterior gives the impression of a rectangular fortress; the blind arcades, which once enclosed small double lancet windows,

lend it elegance. Two square towers stand on the short sides of the castle. On the ground floor is the Sala della Fontana (Fountain Hall), one of the rooms with a cross plan and exedrae on three sides. The cross vault above is connected to the side recesses by means of a series of *muqarnas* (small stalactite vaults typical of Arab architecture). Along the walls is a fine mosaic frieze. Water gushing from the fountain runs along a gutter from the wall to the pavement and then pours into two square fish ponds. The air vents channelled the warm air towards the Sala della Fontana, where it then became cooler. The second floor of the palace is home to the Museo d'Arte Islamia.

La Cuba ❾

Corso Calatafimi 100. *Tel* 091-590 299. ◘ *9am–7pm Tue–Sat, 9am–1:30pm Sun & hols.*

William II ordered this magnificent Fatimite-style Norman palace to be built in 1180. It too stood in a large park, the Genoardo, surrounded by an artificial pond, and served as a pavilion in which to spend the hot afternoons. This palace was so famous that Boccaccio used it as the setting for one of the tales in the *Decameron* (Day 5, no 6).

The rectangular construction acquires rhythm and movement from the pointed blind arcading. The interior ran around an atrium that may have been open to the air. The recesses under the small towers originally would have housed fountains.

Villa Giulia ❿

Via Abramo Lincoln.

Despite its name, the Villa Giulia is not a house but an impressive Italianate garden designed in 1778 outside the city walls by Nicolò Palma and then enlarged in 1866. It was named after Giulia Avalos Guevara, wife of the viceroy, and was the city's first public park. Its square plan is divided by roads decorated with statues, such as the marble image of the "Genius of Palermo" and the statues representing *Glory Vanquishing Envy* and *Abundance Driving Out Famine*. The roads converge centrally in an area with four Pompeiian-style niches by Giuseppe Damiani Almeyda decorated with frescoes in great need of restoration.

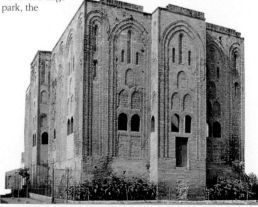

The distinctive Fatimite architecture of La Cuba, used by Boccaccio as the setting for one of the tales in the *Decameron*

San Giovanni dei Lebbrosi, built in the Arab-Norman style

Orto Botanico ⑪

Via Abramo Lincoln 2B. **Map** 2 E4.
Tel 091-623 82 41. ☐ Apr & Oct:
9am–6pm; May & Sep: 9am–7pm; Jun–
Aug: 9am–8pm; Nov–Mar: 9am–5pm.
🖳 www.ortobotanico.palermo.it

The Botanical Garden was
laid out in 1785 and has
attained international fame
thanks to the wealth and
range of its plant species: palm
trees, bamboo, dracaenas,
various cacti, euphorbias,
spiny kapok trees with bottle-
shaped trunks, pineapples and
huge tropical plants. One of
the marvels is a 150-year-old
Ficus magnolioides fig tree
with aerial roots. The Neo-
Classical *Gymnasium* (now a
museum), library and herbaria
are by the entrance, a pond
with waterlilies and papyrus
is in the centre, and glass-
houses line both sides.

Santo Spirito ⑫

Via Santo Spirito, Cimitero di
Sant'Orsola. **Tel** 091 422 691.
☐ 8am–noon daily. ● Wed, Aug.

Inside the Sant'Orsola
Cemetery, this Norman
church was founded by
Archbishop Gualtiero
Offamilio in 1178. It is also
known as the "Chiesa dei
Vespri" because, on 31 March
1282, at the hour of Vespers,
a Sicilian uprising against the
Angevin rulers *(see p33)*
began right in front of the
church. Simple and elegant,
like all Norman churches,
Santo Spirito has black
volcanic stone inlay on its
right side and on the apse.
The two-aisle nave with
three apses is bare but full
of atmosphere. The wooden
ceiling has floral ornamentation and there is a fine
wooden crucifix over the
high altar.

San Giovanni dei Lebbrosi ⑬

Via Cappello 38. **Tel** 091-475 024.
☐ 9:30–11am, 4–6pm Mon–Sat,
9–11am Tue.

One of the oldest Norman
churches in Sicily lies in the
middle of a luxuriant garden
of palms. San Giovanni dei
Lebbrosi was founded in 1071
by Roger I and, in 1119, a lep-
ers' hospital was built next to
it, hence its name. It was most
probably constructed by Arab
craftsmen and workers, as can
be seen in the pointed arches
crowned by arched lintels
(also visible in San Giovanni
degli Eremiti, *see pp64–5;*
and San Cataldo, *see p55*).
The façade has a small porch
with a bell tower above. Inside
the church there are three
apses and a ceiling with
trusses. Digs to the right of
the church have unearthed
remains of the Saracen Yahia
fortress, which once defended
southeastern Palermo.

Ponte dell'Ammiraglio ⑭

Via dei Mille.

The Admiral's Bridge used
to span the Oreto river before
the latter was diverted. It is
made of large cambered
blocks of limestone resting on
twelve pointed arches, five of
them no more than small
openings in the imposts. This
beautiful and amazingly well-
preserved bridge was built in
1113 by George of Antioch,
Roger II's High Admiral (the
ammiraglio of the name), but
is now a rather incongruous
sight, isolated without a river.

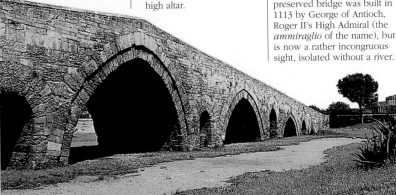

The impressive pointed arches of the 12th-century Ponte dell'Ammiraglio

Monreale Cathedral ⑮

Capital in the cloister

Dominating the Conca d'Oro, the Cathedral of Monreale is the pinnacle of achievement of Arab-Norman art. It was founded in 1172 by William II and a Benedictine monastery was built next to it. The cathedral is famous for its remarkable interior with the magnificent gold mosaics representing episodes from the Old Testament. The cloister *(see p70)* has pointed Arab arches with geometric motifs, and scenes from the Bible are sculpted on the capitals of the 228 white marble twin columns.

★ **Christ Pantocrator**
The church, with a Latin cross plan, is dominated by the 12th–13th-century mosaic of Christ in the middle apse.

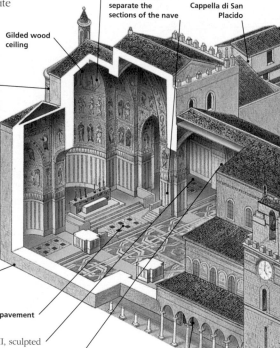

Roman columns separate the sections of the nave

Cappella di San Placido

Gilded wood ceiling

Exterior of the Apse
With its interlaced lava and tufa arches and its multicoloured motifs, the exterior of the apse is the apogee of Norman decoration.

Entrance to the Cappella del Crocifisso and the Treasury

Choir pavement

The royal tomb of William II, sculpted in white marble, is next to the tomb of William I in a corner of the transept.

The bronze door by Barisano da Trani (1179), on the northern side, is under the porch designed by Gian Domenico and Fazio Gagini (1547–69).

★ **The Mosaic Cycle**
The stupendous 12th–13th-century mosaics occupy the entire nave and the aisles, the choir and the transepts. They illustrate scenes from the New and Old Testaments.

★ Cloister
This masterpiece of Norman art has 228 small double columns with varied decoration culminating in the highly elaborate capitals supporting the arches of Arab inspiration.

VISITORS' CHECKLIST

AMAT 389 or AST from *Piazza Indipenza.* **Cathedral** (Piazza Duomo). *Tel* 091-640 44 13. ◯ 8am–1:30pm, 2:30–6pm *Mon–Sat, 8am–1pm Sun & hols.* 🅿 📷 ♿ 🖼 (tour of roof, north transept, treasury). **Cloister** (Piazza Guglielmo il Buono). *Tel* 091-640 44 03. ◯ 9am–7pm daily. 📷 🖼

A wing of the original monastery lies over the southern portico.

Arab-inspired fountain

Columns
The cloister columns were made by skilled craftsmen from throughout Southern Italy. This carved detail shows Adam and Eve.

18th-century portico, flanked by two bell towers.

Bronze Door on the Portal
This lovely door by Bonanno da Pisa (1185) has 42 elaborately framed Biblical scenes and other images. The lion and griffon were Norman symbols.

STAR FEATURES

★ The Mosaic Cycle

★ Christ Pantocrator

★ Cloister

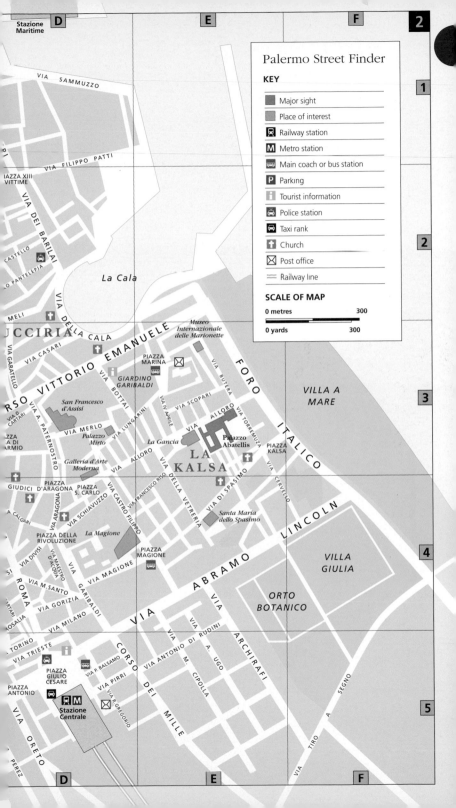

SICILY
AREA BY AREA

Sicily at a Glance

There are few places in the Mediterranean that can equal Sicily's striking landscapes and colourful history. There are noticeable differences between the eastern part of the island, culturally of Greek origin, and the Phoenician and Arab western side. However, Sicily is not simply an east and a west side – every village and town has its own unique story. Within a few kilometres of each other you may find splendid luxuriant coastline and arid, sun-parched hills, just as you can pick out different layers of civilization side by side or overlapping one another. It is not that unusual to see Greek, Arab, Norman and Baroque influences in the same site, sometimes even in the same building.

The Chiesa Madre in Erice (see pp100–1), *built in the 14th century, is a good example of Arab-Norman religious architecture.*

Egadi Islands

The Sciacca *thermae* (see pp118–19) *date back to the distant past. The oldest bathhouse in Sicily, it is said to be the work of the mythical architect Daedalus.*

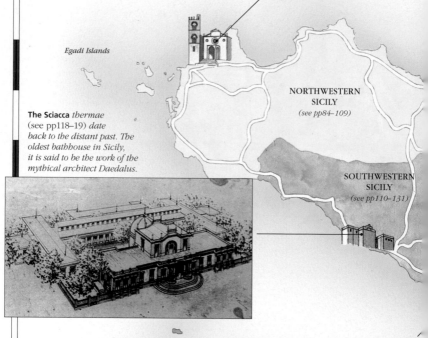

NORTHWESTERN SICILY *(see pp84–109)*

SOUTHWESTERN SICILY *(see pp110–131)*

Pelagic Islands

The Castello di Lombardia at Enna *(see p127) is one of the most important medieval fortifications in Sicily.*

◁ **Classical Greek theatre at Taormina, the second-largest of its kind in Sicily**

he 12th-century
Cathedral at Cefalù
(see pp88–91)
dominates Piazza
Duomo with its varied
architectural elements.

Aeolian Islands

Catania Cathedral
(see p162) *was
rebuilt in the
Baroque style
after the 1693
earthquake had
destroyed the
entire city.*

NORTHEASTERN
SICILY
(see pp158–191)

SOUTHERN
SICILY
(see pp132–157)

Ragusa *(see pp150–51) consists of two
cities in one: one area was built in the
18th century, while the ancient quarter of
Ibla dates back several thousand years.*

0 kilometres   20

0 miles   20

For additional map symbols see back flap

NORTHWESTERN SICILY

*O*ver the centuries, this area of Sicily has been particularly exposed to influences from different colonizing civilizations. The Phoenicians settled in Mozia and founded harbour towns at Palermo and Solunto. They were followed by the Greeks and then the Arabs, who began their conquest of the island at Marsala.

These cultures are still very much alive in the names of the towns and sights, in the architecture, and in the layout of the towns from Marsala to Mazara del Vallo. But, unfortunately, northwestern Sicily is also one of the areas most affected by the scourges of uncontrolled property development and lack of care for the environment. Examples of this are the huge area of unattractive houses between Palermo and Castellammare, which have disfigured what was one of the most fascinating coastlines in Sicily, and the squalidly reconstructed inhabited areas in the Valle del Belice, destroyed by the 1968 earthquake. However, there are other towns pursuing a policy of preserving and reassessing their history. Erice is one of these; its medieval architecture and town plan have been preserved, and many of the churches have been converted into art and culture centres, instead of being left in a state of neglect. The same holds true for Cefalù, Nicosia, Sperlinga and the two Petralias. There is also a good deal of unspoiled scenery besides the nature reserves. The areas around Trapani and Belice are fascinating, as are the rugged valleys in the interior, characterized by villages perched on the top of steep cliffs with breathtaking views. Other beautiful sights include the Egadi Islands and Ustica.

The Palazzina Pepoli at Erice, converted into a villa in the 19th century

◁ Typical Sicilian scenery: in the background is the Monte Cofano promontory near San Vito Lo Capo

Exploring Northwestern Sicily

With the magnificent ruins of Segesta, Selinunte, Soluto and Mozia, this area is full of archaeological fascination. The splendid medieval towns of Cefalù and Erice are also worth a visit in themselves. In the interior there are villages where time seems to have stood still, especially in the Madonie mountains. For those who prefer natural history, there are the crystal-clear waters of Ustica and the Egadi Islands, the Riserva Naturale Marina and the Riserva Naturale dello Zingaro between Scopello and San Vito Lo Capo.

27 USTICA

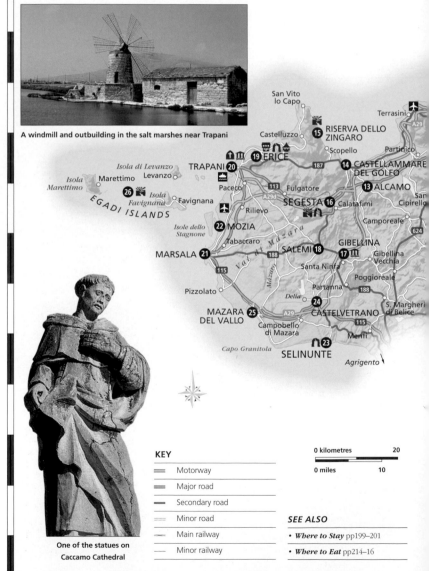

A windmill and outbuilding in the salt marshes near Trapani

San Vito
lo Capo

Terrasini

Castelluzzo   **15** RISERVA DELLO
ZINGARO

Scopello   Partinico

19 ERICE

Isola di Levanzo   TRAPANI **20**   **187**   **14** CASTELLAMMARE
DEL GOLFO

Isola   Marettimo   Levanzo   Paceco   **113**   Fulgatore   **13** ALCAMO

Marettimo   **26**   Isola   Favignana   **A29d**   San
Favignana   SEGESTA **16**   Calatafimi   Cipirello

EGADI ISLANDS   Rilievo   Camporeale   **624**

Isole dello   **22** MOZIA
Stagnone   Tabaccaro   GIBELLINA

MARSALA **21**   SALEMI **18**   **17**   Gibellina
Santa Ninfa   Vecchia

115   Poggioreale

Pizzolato   Partanna   **188**

Delia   **24**   S. Margheri
di Belice

MAZARA **25**   CASTELVETRANO
DEL VALLO   **A29**   Campobello   **115**
di Mazara   Menfi

Capo Granitola   **23**
SELINUNTE   Agrigento

One of the statues on
Caccamo Cathedral

KEY

━━━ Motorway

━━━ Major road

━━━ Secondary road

═══ Minor road

━━━ Main railway

──── Minor railway

0 kilometres   20
0 miles   10

SEE ALSO

• *Where to Stay* pp199–201

• *Where to Eat* pp214–16

For additional map symbols *see back flap*

SIGHTS AT A GLANCE

GETTING AROUND

Northwestern Sicily has a very good road network. Toll-free *autostrada* (motorway) A29 links Palermo with Mazara del Vallo, while a connecting road goes to Trapani. Travelling eastwards, A20 now goes to Messina, and a toll is charged. The main roads along the coast and in the Valle del Belice are good, while those leading to the villages at the foot of the mountains are winding and slow and, in the winter, may be covered with snow or ice. There are frequent trains between Messina and Palermo, less frequently to Trapani, Marsala and Mazara. The bus network connects the main towns and smaller and more remote villages.

The theatre at Segesta, on the top of Monte Barbaro, set in an extraordinary landscape. As with all Greek theatres, the scenery formed part of the stage set

Street-by-Street: Cefalù ➊

*Tonnaio Vase,
Museo
Mandralisca*

Founded on a steep promontory halfway between Palermo and Capo d'Orlando, Cefalù has retained its medieval appearance around the Norman cathedral, which was built by Roger II in the 12th century. The narrow streets of the city centre are lined with buildings featuring elaborate architectural decoration. There are also numerous churches, reflecting the town's status as a leading bishopric. The fishermen's quarter, with its old houses clustered along the seafront, is very appealing, as is the long beach with fine sand, considered to be one of the most beautiful stretches on the northern coast.

★ Cathedral
Oversized compared with the rest of the city, this masterpiece of Norman art contains magnificent mosaics in the presbytery.

Seventeenth-century fortifications

The Streets of Cefalù
The layout of the city is basically a grid plan crossed horizontally by Corso Ruggero and Via Vittorio Emanuele and intersected by alleys of medieval origin.

Capo Marchiafava rampart, 16th–17th centuries

Porta Marina
This striking city gate overlooking the sea is a Gothic arch. It is the only one remaining of the four that originally pierced the city wall, affording access to Cefalù.

KEY

━ ━ ━ Suggested route

Chiesa del Purgatorio
Most of Cefalù's many churches date from the 17th century. The Chiesa del Purgatorio (1668), on Corso Ruggero, has a richly decorated Baroque doorway at the top of a double stairway.

★ Museo Mandralisca
This museum was founded by Enrico Piraino, the Baron of Mandralisca, and has a wide range of precious works of art, such as this 4th-century BC tragic mask.

RUGGERO
VIA
VIA GIOENI
VIA MANDRALISCA
XXV NOVEMBRE
VIA PORTO SALVO
VIA VETERANI
VIA VITTORIO EMANUELE

| 0 metres | 40 |
| 0 yards | 40 |

Medieval Fountain
This recently restored medieval stone fountain was used for washing clothes until a few years ago.

STAR SIGHTS

★ Cathedral

★ Museo Mandralisca

Exploring Cefalù

Cefalù is mentioned for the first time in 396 BC in an account by Diodorus Siculus, but the city is more famous for its medieval monuments. Piazza Garibaldi (where you have to leave the car) is a good starting point for a walk around the town. Follow Corso Ruggero to reach the open space of Piazza Duomo, home to one of Sicily's most splendid cathedrals.

The medieval façade of the Cathedral of Cefalù

🚏 Piazza Duomo

This lively square, dominated by the sheer mass of the **Cathedral** and the steep **Rocca**, is the heart of Cefalù. It is surrounded by buildings constructed in different styles. On the southern side are the **Oratorio del Santissimo Sacramento; Palazzo Maria**, which was most probably Roger II's *Domus Regiae (see p29)*, decorated with an ogee portal and a Gothic window; and **Palazzo Piraino**, with its late 16th-century ashlar door. To the north, the square is bordered by the **Seminario** and the **Palazzo Vescovile**, while to the west is the **Palazzo del Municipio** (Town Hall), which incorporates the former **Santa Caterina monastery**.

🛈 Cathedral

Piazza Duomo. *Tel 0921-922 021.* 🕐 *9am–12:30pm, 2:30–6pm daily.* ✝ *9am–1pm, 3–7pm daily.* 📷 *(cloister).*
Cefalù Cathedral is one of Sicily's major Norman monuments. Building began in 1131 under Roger II. When he died work continued in fits and starts. The façade has two rows of blind arcades set over the three-arch outer narthex and is flanked by two massive bell towers with single and double lancet windows. On the right-hand side you can see the interlaced arch motifs of the three side apses. The nave is divided by arches supported by marble columns. The wooden ceiling, with its painted beams, bears an obvious Islamic influence, while the presbytery is covered with splendid mosaics.

Statue of a bishop, Cefalù Cathedral

On high in the apse is the figure of Christ Pantocrator with the Virgin Mary, Archangels and the apostles; on the choir walls are saints and prophets, while cherubs and seraphim decorate the vault. A door on the northern aisle leads to the entrance of the lovely cloister that has been extensively restored.

🚏 Corso Ruggero

This avenue goes all the way across the old town, starting from **Piazza Garibaldi**, where the **Porta di Terra** city gate once stood. A few steps on your left is **Palazzo Osterio Magno**, the residence of Roger II, built in the 13th and 14th centuries. Almost opposite, a modern building houses the remains of the ancient Roman road. Visits can be made from 9am to 4:30pm. Continuing to the right, you will come to **Piazzetta Spinola**, with **Santo Stefano** (or Delle Anime Purganti), the Baroque façade of which is complemented by an elegant double staircase.

🏛 Museo Mandralisca

Via Mandralisca 13. *Tel 0921-421 547.* 🕐 *9am–7pm daily.* 📷 www.museomandralisca.it
This museum was founded by Enrico Piraino, the Baron of Mandralisca, in the 19th century and includes fine archaeological, shell and coin collections. It also houses an art gallery and a library with over 9,000 historic and scientific works, including incunabulae, 16th-century books and nautical charts.
Among the most important paintings are the *Portrait of a Man* by Antonello da Messina, *View of Cefalù* by Francesco Bevilacqua, *Christ on Judgment Day* by Johannes De Matta (mid-1500s), and a series of icons on the second

Medieval fishermen's dwellings lining the seafront

Antonello da Messina, *Portrait of an Unknown Man* **(1465)**

floor. Archaeological jewels include a late Hellenistic mosaic and a 4th-century BC krater with a figure of a tuna fish cutter. A curiosity exhibit is the collection of patience (solitaire) playing cards made out of precious materials.

🏛 Via Vittorio Emanuele

This street runs along the seafront, separated by a row of medieval houses facing the bay. Under one of these is the famous **Lavatoio**, the stone fountain known as *U' Ciuni*, or river, which was mentioned by the writer Boccaccio and was used for washing clothes until a few years ago. A stairway leads to the basin where water gushes from holes on three walls. The lovely **Porta Marina** is the only remaining city gate

of the four that once afforded access to the town. It leads to the colourful fishermen's quarter, where scenes were shot for the film *Cinema Paradiso (see p120)*.

🏛 La Rocca

From Piazza Garibaldi a path halfway up the hill offers a fine view of the old town and the sea and leads to the ruins of the fortifications (most probably Byzantine) and the prehistoric sanctuary known as the **Tempio di Diana**, a megalithic construction with a portal dating from the 9th century BC. On the top of the Rocca are the ruins of a 12th–13th-century castle.

Environs

On the slopes of Pizzo Sant' Angelo is the **Santuario di Gibilmanna**, a sanctuary built in the 17th and 18th centuries and the most popular pilgrim-age site in Sicily. The former convent stables house the **Museo dell' Ordine**, the museum of the Capuchin friars with paintings, sculp-ture and vestments. The most interesting pieces are crèche figures, enamelled reliquaries, a 16th-century alabaster rosary, and a white marble Pietà by the local sculptor Jacopo Lo Duca, a pupil of Michelangelo.

A 16th-century statuette, Santuario di Gibilmanna

Castel di Tusa ❷

Road map D2. 🏠 *3,600.* FS *892021.* ℹ *0921-334 332.*

This beautiful swimming resort is dominated by the ruins of a 14th-century castle. The characteristic alleys with old stone houses and villas converge in the central square, which is paved with stone. To get to the little port you must go under the railway arches. The banks of the nearby Tusa River have been turned into an outdoor gallery with works by contemporary artists, inclu-ding sculptor Pietro Consagra. Only a few miles away are the **Ruins of Halaesa Arconidea**.

⋔ Ruins of Halaesa Arconidea

3 km (2 miles) on the road to Tusa. *Tel 0921-334 796.* ◯ *9am–2 hrs before sunset.*

On a hill covered with olive trees and asphodels are the ruins of the city of Halaesa Arconidea, a Greek colony founded in 403 BC, which prospered until it was sacked by the Roman praetor Verres. Excavations have started and you can see the Agora, remains of cyclopean walls and a Hellenistic temple. Near the archaeo-logical site is the **Monastery of Santa Maria della Balate**.

Ruins of the Hellenistic temple of Halaesa, amid olive trees and asphodels

Santo Stefano di Camastra ❸

Road map D2. 🏠 5,200.
FS Messina–Palermo.
ℹ️ Town hall (0921-331 127
or 331 181). 🎭 Easter Week.

This town facing the Tyr-
rhenian Sea is one of the
leading Sicilian centres for the
production of ceramics. All
the local craftsmen have their
wares on display: vases, jugs,
cornices and tiles with period
designs such as those used in
the **Villa Comunale**. In the
centre of town stands the
Chiesa Madre, or San Nicolò,
with a Renaissance doorway
and late 18th-century stucco
decoration in the interior.

Nicosia ❹

Road map D3. 🏠 15,100.
🚉 129 km (80 miles) from Catania,
44 km (27 miles) from Enna.
ℹ️ Town hall, Piazza Garibaldi
(0935-672 11 11). 🎭 Easter Week,
O' Scontro (Easter), Macaroni Festival
(May), Palio (2nd week Aug), Nicosia
da Vivere Festival (Jul–Sep).

Sprawled over four hills,
Nicosia is dominated by the
ruins of an Arab-Norman
castle. Originally a Byzantine
settlement, the town was re-
populated in the Norman era
by Lombard and Piedmontese
colonists, who have left traces
of their local dialects. The
many churches and patrician
mansions are a sign of the
town's former splendour.
Narrow streets and alleys run
up the hills, often providing
spectacular panoramic views.

The Villa Comunale, Santo Stefano
di Camastra, with a tiled altar

Piazza Garibaldi is the heart of
Nicosia, with the Gothic **San
Nicolò Cathedral** and old
buildings, including the
current Town Hall. The **Salita
Salomone** steps lead to
Romanesque **San
Salvatore**. There is
a fine view of the
old town from the
porch. The church
has a series of
sundials which,
according to
tradition, were
once used as the
town's "clocks".
Via Salomone,
lined with
aristocratic
palazzi, leads up
to **Santa Maria
Maggiore**, just under the
castle rock. The doorway is
decorated with pagan statues
of Jove, Venus and Ceres.
In the interior is Charles V's
throne, in memory of the
emperor's visit here in 1535,

Detail of the ceiling of the
Nicosia Cathedral

a gilded marble altarpiece
by Antonello Gagini and a
crucifix known as *Father of
Mercy*. From here you can
go up to the **Castle**, with its
Norman drawbridge and the
remains of the keep. At the
foot of the castle is the
Norman **Basilica of San
Michele**, with its austere
apses and majestic 15th-
century bell towers.

🏛️ Cathedral
Piazza Garibaldi.
◻️ Call 0935-638 139 for details.
The cathedral is dedicated to
the town's patron saint, San
Nicolò. It was founded in the
14th century and partially
rebuilt in the 19th century.
What remains of the original
structure are the 14th-century
façade with porticoes running
along the left-hand side and
the bell tower with three
sections, each distin-
guished by a different
style, from Arab to
Romanesque. The
rebuilt interior has
a crucifix attributed
to Fra Umile de
Petralia and a
font by Antonello
Gagini, while the
choir was carved
out of solid walnut
by local artists. The
vault, frescoed in
the 19th century,
conceals a fine
Norman truss
ceiling decorated in brilliant
colours with scenes from the
lives of the saints, hunting
scenes, images of wild
animals, a number of human
heads, stylized flowers and
geometric decorative motifs.

Nicosia, perched on a hill and once crucial to the area's defensive network

For hotels and restaurants in this region see pp199–201 and pp214–16

Panoramic view from the Norman castle at Sperlinga (c.1100)

Sperlinga ❺

Road map D3. 🏘 *1,100.* 🚌 *47 km (29 miles) from Enna.* ℹ️ *Town hall, Via Umberto I (0935-643 025 or 643 177).* 🎭 *Sagra del Tortone (16 Aug).*

Sperlinga seems to have been pushed against a spectacular rock face, its parallel streets on different levels connected by steps. In the eastern section, right up against the sandstone cliff, numerous troglodytic cave dwellings have been carved out. Until recently many of them were inhabited.

🏰 Norman Castle
Via Castello. **Tel** *0935-643 119.* 🕙 *10am–1pm, 2–5pm daily.* **Museum** 🕙 *10am–1pm, 3:30–8pm daily.* 🎨 🎫

Sperlinga's castle was built by the Normans under Roger I around the year 1100 on the top of an impregnable rock face. It was later reinforced by Frederick II. It is linked with the Sicilian Vespers revolt *(see pp32–3)*, when it was the last refuge of the Angevin rulers, who managed to resist attacks for a year. The events are commemorated by an inscription carved in the vestibule: *Quod Siculis placuit sola Sperlinga negavit* ("Sperlinga alone denied the Sicilians what they desired").

The numerous chambers in the castle make it a veritable stone labyrinth. The entrance hall, the Grotta delle Guardie (Guards' Grotto), is now an ethnographic museum with examples of cave dwellings and everyday work tools and objects. After passing through the second gate and crossing the Sala Riunioni, or assembly hall, you will find the stables, the prisons and the foundry (hewn entirely out of the rock). In the middle of the cliff is **San Domenico di Siria**, the nave of which has three side niches; next to this are the rooms used as a kitchen with the remains of two wood-burning ovens. Steep stairs lead to the top of the rock with magnificent views.

Gangi ❻

Road map D3. 🏘 *8,100.* 🚌 *51 km (32 miles) from Cefalù.* ℹ️ *Pro Loco, Cortile Ospedale 4.* 🎭 *Sagra della Spiga (2nd Sun Aug).*

This town lies on the southwestern slope of Monte Marone, facing the Nebrodi and Madonie mountains. The birthplace of painters Gaspare Vazano and Giuseppe Salerno has retained its medieval character, with winding streets and steps connecting the different levels. The towering **Chiesa Madre** has a 14th-century bell tower and a lovely *Last Judgment* by Salerno, inspired by Michelangelo's painting in the Sistine Chapel.

Petralia Sottana ❼

Road map D3. 🏘 *3,800.* 🚌 *98 km (61 miles) from Palermo.* ℹ️ *Town hall, Corso Agliata (0921-684 311).* 🎭 *Ballo della Cordella dance (1st Sun after 15 Aug).*

This village is perched on a rock 1,000 m (3,300 ft) up, and nestled at the foot of the tallest peaks in the Madonie mountains. Petralia Sottana is laid out around **Via Agliata**, which ends in **Piazza Umberto I**, opposite the **Chiesa Madre**. The late Gothic church was partially rebuilt in the 1600s. Inside is a fine wooden triptych, *The Virgin Mary and Child between Saints Peter and Paul*. An arch connects the bell tower with the **Santissima Trinità**, which has a marble altarpiece by Domenico Gagini.

Petralia Sottana, in the middle of the verdant Valle dell'Imera

Petralia Soprana, the highest village in the Madonie mountains

Petralia Soprana ⑧

Road map D3. 🏘 *3,900.* 🚍 *104 km (65 miles) from Palermo.*
🏛 *Town hall (0921-641 050).*

The highest village in the Madonie mountains lies on a plateau 1,147 m (3,760 ft) above sea level, where the panoramic view ranges from the Nebrodi hills to the volcanic cone of Mount Etna. Petralia Soprana was an extremely important Greek and Phoenician city. Under Roman dominion ancient "Petra" was one of the largest wheat-producing *civitates* in the Empire. The city became *Batraliah* after the Arab conquest and a powerful defensive stronghold under the Normans. Later, the two Petralias (Soprana and Sottana) were taken over by noble families.

The village has preserved its medieval layout, with narrow paved streets, old stone houses, patrician residences and churches. The old **Chiesa Madre**, dedicated to Saints Peter and Paul and rebuilt in the 14th century, stands in an attractive square with a 17th-century double-column colonnade designed by the Serpotta brothers. In the interior is the first crucifix by Fra' Umile Pintorno (1580–1639), who also painted many other crucifixes throughout the island. **Santa Maria di Loreto** was built in the 18th century over the remains of a castle; it has a cross plan and the façade is flanked by two decorated bell towers.

Polizzi Generosa ⑨

Road map D3. 🏘 *4,700.* 🚍 *93 km (58 miles) from Palermo.* 🏛
Pro Loco, Via Mistretta 18 (0921-649 018).

On the western slopes of the Madonie mountains, this village grew up around an ancient fortress rebuilt by the Normans. Among its many churches is the **Chiesa Madre**, with a fine 16th-century altarpiece, *Madonna and Child among Angels and Saints* by an unknown Flemish artist and a relief by Domenico Gagini (1482). A small museum shows the natural history of the area.

Coat of arms of a noble family of Caccamo

Environs
From Polizzi, ascend to Piano Battaglia, part of the nature reserve, with footpaths in summer and ski runs in winter.

Caccamo ⑩

Road map C2. 🏘 *8,700.*
🚍 *48 km (30 miles) from Palermo.*
🏛 *Town hall, Piazza Duomo (091-810 32 48).* 🚌 *Sat.* 🎪 *Agricultural and gastronomic show (Dec–Jan), Investiture of the Chatelaine (Aug).*

Caccamo lies under the castellated walls of its **Norman castle**, in a lovely setting of softly rolling hills only 10 km (6 miles) from the Palermo-Catania motorway. The town is laid out on different levels, with well maintained roads that open onto pretty squares. The most appealing of these is **Piazza Duomo**, with the **Chiesa Matrice** dedicated to San Giorgio, flanked by statues and two symmetrically arranged Baroque buildings: the **Oratorio della Compagnia del Sacramento** and the **Chiesa delle Anime Sante del Purgatorio**. The former was built by the Normans but was enlarged in the 17th century. Its richly decorated interior has a font by Gagini and his workshop. Not far away are the **Annunziata**, with twin bell towers, **San Marco** and **San Benedetto alla Badia**. The last is perhaps the loveliest of the three, with its Baroque stucco and majolica decoration, and a colourful floor depicting a ship sailing on the high seas, guarded by angels.

Interior of the impregnable Norman castle at Caccamo

The *Gymnasium* at Solunto, with its Doric columns intact

♣ Norman Castle

☐ *by appointment 9am–1pm, 4–8pm **Tel** 091-814 92 52 or 810-32 48.* ☑

This formidable Norman castle is truly impregnable. It was built on the top of a steep rock overlooking the valley and is protected by a series of walls. The first entranceway on the lower floor leads to a broad stairway flanked by castellated walls; this leads to the second entrance, where the guardhouse once stood. After crossing a drawbridge, you will find another door that leads to the inner courtyard. Through this you can reach the famous Sala della Congiura (Conspiracy Hall), so named because it was here in 1160 that the Norman barons hatched a plot against William I. The panoramic views from the large western terrace are breathtaking.

Solunto ⓫

Road map C2. 🚌 *Santa Flavia–Solunto–Porticello.* ⓘ *091-904 557.* ☐ *9am–4:30pm Tue–Sat (to 6:30pm in summer), 9am–1pm Sun & hols.* ● *Mon.* ☑

The ruins of the city of Solunto lie on the slopes of Monte Catalfano in a stupendous site with a beautiful panoramic view of the sea. Solunto was one of the first Phoenician colonies in Sicily and was mentioned, along with Palermo and Mozia, by the Greek historian Thucydides. In 254 BC it was conquered by the Romans. By the 2nd century AD the city had been largely abandoned, and it was later almost destroyed by the Saracens. At the entrance there is a temporary exhibition (the museum is closed for renovation) with finds from the various digs, which began in 1826 and are still under way.

Solunto follows a traditional layout. The path leading to the site takes you to Via dell'Agorà, with a fired-brick pavement and gutters for drainage. This street makes a right angle with the side stairs, which mark off the blocks of buildings (*insulae*). Six Doric columns and part of the roof of one of these, the *Gymnasium*, are still standing. Other *insulae* have mosaic floors and plastered or even painted walls. At the eastern end is the Agora, with workshops, cisterns to collect rainwater and a theatre with the stage area facing towards the sea.

Panoramic view of Solunto

THE VILLAS IN BAGHERIA

In the 18th century, Bagheria was the summer residence of Palermo's nobility, who built luxurious villas surrounded by orange groves as retreats from the torrid heat of the capital. Prince Ettore Branciforti built the first, Villa Barbera, in 1657, followed by other aristocrats such as the Valguarnera and Gravina families. The most famous is the Villa Palagonia (091-932 088; www.villapalagonia.it), restored in 2006 and decorated with hundreds of statues of monsters and mythological figures. Visitors can see the Salone degli Specchi (Hall of Mirrors), where balls were held, and the frescoed Room of the Labours of Hercules. The villas eventually proved too costly to keep and were either abandoned or put to other uses. When the gardens were destroyed to make room for ugly housing units, the villas lost most of their fascination.

Façade of Villa Palagonia, the most famous villa in Bagheria

"Monster" at the Villa Palagonia

Typical Piana degli Albanesi costumes

Piana degli Albanesi ⑫

Road map B2. 👥 6,200. ℹ️ Pro Loco, Via Kastrota 207 (091-856 10 59). 🎪 Sagra del Cannolo (Apr).

During the expansion of the Ottoman Empire in the Balkans, many groups of Albanians *(Albanesi)* fled to Italy. At the end of the 15th century, John II allowed an Albanian community to settle in this area, which originally took the name of Piana dei Greci, because the inhabitants belonged to the Greek Orthodox Church. The place was renamed Piana degli Albanesi in 1941. The town is famous for its colourful religious festivities, such as those during Epiphany and Easter, which are still celebrated according to the Orthodox calendar. The celebrations in honour of the patron saint Santa Maria Odigitria are followed by traditional folk festivities. **Piazza Vittorio Emanuele**, in the heart of town, is home to the Municipio (Town Hall) and the Orthodox church of **Santa Maria Odigitria**, which has a beautiful iconostasis in the interior. Opposite the parish church is the oldest church in Piana degli Albanesi, **San Giorgio**, which was altered in the mid-1700s. Along the avenue named after the Albanian national hero, Giorgio Kastriota Skanderbeg, is the cathedral, **San Demetrio**. As is customary in Orthodox churches, the apses are closed off by the iconostasis. On the vault is a fresco representing the Apostles, Christ and the four Orthodox patriarchs. Near the town is a large artificial **lake** that was created by a dam built in the 1920s.

Alcamo ⑬

Road map B2. 👥 44,000. 🚉 Palermo–Trapani line. ℹ️ Town hall, Piazza Ciullo (0924-590 111).

During the Arab period the fortress of *Manzil Alqamah* was built as part of this area's defensive network. The town of Alcamo developed later, and between the 13th and 14th centuries centred around the Chiesa Madre and the castle, which has been restored. In recent decades, population growth has led to the expansion of the town and the demolition of parts of the old city walls. In Piazza Ciullo is **Sant'Oliva**, built in 1723 over an earlier church, while the nearby **Chiesa del Rosario** boasts late 15th-century frescoes. Facing Piazza della Repubblica is **Santa Maria del Gesù**, with the so-called Greek Madonna altarpiece (1516), showing the Madonna with the Counts of Modica. But the most important church here is the **Chiesa Madre**, founded in 1332. Its Baroque façade, overlooking Piazza IV Novembre, has a 14th-century bell tower with double lancet windows, and many paintings and sculptures can be seen in the chapels.

Castellammare del Golfo ⑭

Road map B2. 👥 15,000. 🚉 Palermo–Trapani. ℹ️ Town hall, Via Alcide de Gasperi 6 (0924-30217).

This town was the Greek port for Segesta and Erice, and then an Arab fortress. It became an important trading and tuna-fishing centre in the Middle Ages. In the heart of the town, on an isthmus, is the **Norman-Swabian Castle**, and the old picturesque streets of the medieval quarter known as *castri di la terra*. On Via Garibaldi is the **Chiesa Madre**, frequently rebuilt in the 1700s and 1800s.

Castellammare del Golfo, on the Tyrrhenian Sea, a leading port town in the Arab-Norman period

Riserva dello Zingaro ⑮

Twenty kilometres (12 miles) from Erice, along the coast going towards Palermo, is the Riserva dello Zingaro, a nature reserve of about 1,600 ha (3,950 acres) sloping down to the sea. It is a paradise for birds, especially for raptors such as Bonelli's eagles, peregrine falcons and kites, and even, in recent years, golden eagles.

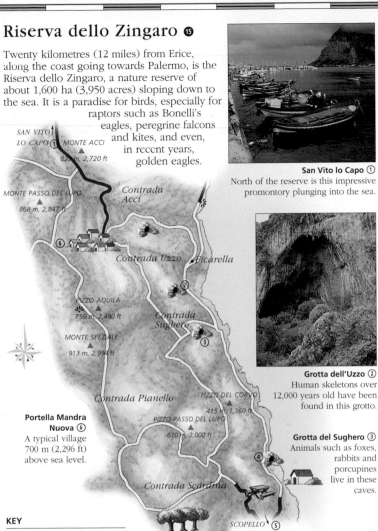

SAN VITO
LO CAPO ①   MONTE ACCI
▲
829 m, 2,720 ft

MONTE PASSO DEL LUPO
▲
868 m, 2,847 ft

Contrada
Acci

⑥ 🏠

Contrada Uzzo   Ficarella

②

PIZZO AQUILA
🌿 ▲
759 m, 2,490 ft

Contrada
Sughero

③

MONTE SPEZIALE
▲
913 m, 2,994 ft

Contrada Pianello

PIZZO DEL CORVO
▲
415 m, 1,360 ft

PIZZO PASSO DEL LUPO
▲
610 m, 2,000 ft

④

Contrada Scardina

SCOPELLO ⑤

MONTE SCARDINA
▲
680 m, 2,230 ft

San Vito lo Capo ①
North of the reserve is this impressive promontory plunging into the sea.

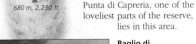

Grotta dell'Uzzo ②
Human skeletons over 12,000 years old have been found in this grotto.

Grotta del Sughero ③
Animals such as foxes, rabbits and porcupines live in these caves.

Portella Mandra Nuova ⑥
A typical village 700 m (2,296 ft) above sea level.

Contrada Capreria ④
Punta di Capreria, one of the loveliest parts of the reserve, lies in this area.

Baglio di Scopello ⑤
Scopello is a farming hamlet that grew up around an 18th-century fort.

KEY

▬ Negotiable road

▬ Path

🌿 Viewpoint

TIPS FOR WALKERS

Road map C2.
Tour length: there are four marked footpaths. The shortest one (6 km/4 miles) goes from Scopello to Tonarella dell'Uzzo, taking about 2 hrs 20 mins. The longest is 19 km (12 miles) and takes about 9 hrs. The reserve can also be explored on horseback.
www.riservazingaro.it

| 0 kilometres | | 2 |
| 0 miles | 1 | |

Segesta ⑯

According to legend, the ancient capital of the Elymians was founded on the rolling green hills of the Castellammare del Golfo area by exiles from Troy. Segesta was constantly at war with Selinunte and was frequently attacked. Yet the majestic Doric temple has miraculously survived sacking and the ravages of time, and stands in splendid and solemn isolation on the hill facing Monte Barbaro. The city of Segesta was built above the temple on the top of the mountain. Here lie the ruins of some buildings and the well-preserved 3rd-century BC theatre, where ancient Greek plays are performed every other summer.

VISITORS' CHECKLIST

Road map B2. ⚑ 0924-952 356. 🚌 32 km (20 miles) from Trapani. 🚉 Trapani-Palermo (coach to theatre). ◯ Apr–Oct: 9am–7pm; Nov–Mar: 9am–4pm. 🎭 Classical theatre (Jul & Aug).

Panorama
Ancient Segesta and the beautiful setting create an atmospheric scene.

The Temple
Built in the 5th century BC, the temple is still well preserved; 36 Doric columns support the pediments and entablatures.

Ruins of the city

Monte Barbaro (431 m, 1,414 ft)

| 0 metres | 350 |
| 0 yards | 350 |

Interior of the Temple
The lack of architectural elements in the interior has led scholars to believe that the construction was interrupted by the war with Selinunte.

The Theatre
The Segesta theatre is a semicircle with a diameter of 63 m (207 ft) hewn out of the top of Monte Barbaro. A curious feature is that the stage area faces north, probably to allow a view of the hills and sea.

Gibellina ⑰

Road map B3. 🏘 *5,000.*
🚌 *89 km (55 miles) from Trapani.*
ℹ️ *Town hall, Piazza XV Gennaio (0924-67877).* 🎭 *Oresteia (classical theatre, biennial, summer).*

In 1968 a terrible earthquake destroyed all the towns in the Valle del Belice and the vicinity, including Gibellina. The new town was rebuilt, after years of bureaucratic delay, in the Salinella zone about 20 km (12 miles) from the original village. Over 40 years after the event, the new Gibellina already seems old and rather sad. However, it is worth visiting because, thanks to the cooperation of contemporary architects and artists, the area has been enriched with many works of art, including a huge sculpture, *Stella* (Star) by Pietro Consagra, the city gate and symbol of Gibellina Nuova. Other attractions are the **Torre Civica Carillon**, a tower in Piazza del Municipio, and the **Centro Culturale**, the cultural centre built over the remains of the 17th-century **Palazzo Di Lorenzo**.

Lastly, be sure to visit the **Museo Antropologico-Etnologico**, with everyday objects and tools illustrating local folk customs, and, above all, the **Museo Civico d'Arte Contemporanea**.

The town of Salemi, dominated by its impressive medieval castle

🏛 **Museo Civico d'Arte Contemporanea**
Via Segesta. *Tel 0924-67428.*
⏰ *8.30am–1.30pm daily.*
This museum contains works by artists such as Fausto Pirandello, Renato Guttuso, Antonio Sanfilippo and Mario Schifano.

The Star of Gibellina, by Pietro Consagra

Environs
Eighteen kilometres (11 miles) from the new town are the ruins of old Gibellina. Here you will see a disturbing and gigantic work of land art by Alberto Burri, who covered the ruins with a layer of white cement. The cracks cutting through this white expanse, known as *Burri's Crevice*, follow the course of the old streets, creating a labyrinth.

Salemi ⑱

Road map B3. 🏘 *12,500.* 🚌 *95 km (59 miles) from Palermo.* ℹ️ *Town hall, Piazza Lampiasi Ignazio (0924-982 233).* 🚌 *Sat.* 🎭 *San Giuseppe (Mar).*

This agricultural town in the Valle del Delia dates from ancient times (it was probably the Halicyae mentioned by Diodorus Siculus). Despite the 1968 earthquake, the Arab town plan has remained, with a jumble of narrow streets at the foot of the three towers of the **Castle**. Here, on 14 May 1860, Garibaldi proclaimed himself ruler of Sicily in the name of King Vittorio Emanuele II *(see pp34–5)*. The castle was built in the 12th century by Frederick II and rebuilt in 1210.

In the old town, interesting sights are **Sant'Agostino** with its large cloister and the 17th-century **Collegio dei Gesuiti**, which houses the **Chiesa dei Gesuiti**, the **Oratorio del Ritiro** and the city museums, in particular the **Museo Civico d'Arte Sacra**.

🏛 **Museo Civico d'Arte Sacra**
Collegio dei Gesuiti. *Tel 0924-982 376.*
⏰ *9am–1pm, 4–6pm Tue–Fri, 9am–1pm, 3–7pm Sat.*
This museum of religious art has sculptures by Domenico Laurana and Antonello Gagini *(see p21)*, 17th-century paintings and wooden Baroque sculpture. The Risorgimento section features objects commemorating Garibaldi's feats.

The so-called *Burri's Crevice* covering part of the ruins of old Gibellina

Erice ⑲

Sign for an art gallery in Erice

The splendid town of Erice, perched on top of Monte San Giuliano, has very ancient origins, as is shown by the cult of the goddess of fertility, Venus Erycina. Laid out on a triangular plan, the town has preserved its medieval character, with fine city walls, beautifully paved streets, stone houses with decorated doorways, small squares and open spaces with numerous churches – including the medieval Chiesa Madre – many of which have recently become venues for scientific and cultural activities.

Cyclopean walls

These extend for 700 m (2,296 ft) on the northern side of the town, from Porta Spada to Porta Trapani. The lower part of the wall, with its megalithic blocks of stone, dates back to the Phoenician period; the letters *beth, ain, phe* of the Phoenician alphabet are carved in it. The upper part and the gates were built by the Normans. The **Porta Spada** gate owes its name to the massacre of the local Angevin rulers during the Sicilian Vespers (*spada* means sword) (*see pp32–3*). Nearby are **Sant'Antonio Abate** and **Sant'Orsola**. The latter houses the 18th-century "Mysteries", sculptures borne in procession on Good Friday.

Castello Pepoli e Venere

Via Conte Pepoli. **Tel** 0923-869 388.
⏰ 9am–1 hour before sunset daily. 📷

This Norman castle was built on an isolated rock over the ruins of the **Temple of Venus Erycina**. Entrance is gained via a tower, the only remaining original part of the castle, with Ghibelline castellation. It was used as a prison and watchtower. Above the entrance, with its pointed arch, is a plaque with the coat of arms of the Spanish Habsburgs, surmounted by a 14th-century double lancet window. Inside are a sacred well and the ruins of the Temple of Venus Erycina, a Phoenician house and a Roman bath. The castle is the starting point of a system of fortifications including the **Torri del Balio**, formerly the headquarters of the Norman governor. Further down, on a ledge over the Pineta dei Runzi pine forest, is the **Torretta Pepoli** (*see p85*), built as a hunting lodge in 1872–80 and one of the symbols of Erice. In front of the castle are the 19th-century public gardens, **Giardini del Balio**, which link this zone with the eastern side of Erice.

The Norman castle, built on the site dedicated to Venus Erycina in ancient times

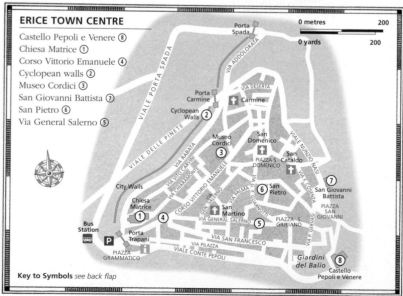

ERICE TOWN CENTRE

0 metres   200
0 yards   200

Key to Symbols *see back flap*

The austere exterior of the Chiesa Madre in Erice

🏠 Chiesa Matrice

Piazza Matrice. **Tel** 0923-869 123.
🕐 10am–1pm, 3–6pm. 🎥
This church is dedicated to Our Lady of the Assumption. It was built in 1314. The austere façade has a portico with pointed arches surmounted by a beautiful rose window; it faces the detached campanile with double lancet windows, which was built in 1312 as a lookout tower. The interior was drastically restored in 1865, and little remains of its original look.

Plaque commemorating the Sicilian scientist Ettore Majorana

🏛 Corso Vittorio Emanuele

The Corso, the main street in Erice, begins at **Porta Trapani**, one of the three gates through the massive city walls, and goes uphill. The street is lined with Baroque patrician residences and tempting pastry shops selling local specialities. To the left is **San Salvatore**, which once had a monastery annexe and boasts a 15th-century portal. At the end of the Corso, formerly called Via Regia, is **Piazza Umberto I**, redesigned in the 19th century, and the **Palazzo del Municipio** (town hall), which houses the **Museo Comunale Cordici**.

🏛 Museo Cordici

Piazza Umberto I. **Tel** 0923-502 148.
🕐 8am–2pm Mon–Fri (also 2:30–5:30pm Mon & Thu).
This museum features finds from the necropolis, coins, terracotta items and a small head of Venus. Some rooms also exhibit vestments and old paintings and sculpture such as the *Annunciation*, a marble group by the artist Antonello Gagini.

🏠 San Pietro

Via Filippo Guarnotti.
Founded in the 14th century in the middle of Erice, this church was rebuilt in 1745, and a fine Baroque portal added. The nearby convent is now one of the bases for the **Centro di Cultura Scientifica Ettore Majorana**. This centre, founded in the early 1960s to honour the brilliant Sicilian scientist who disappeared in mysterious circumstances before World War II, runs courses and conferences on various subjects, from medicine to mathematical logic. The centre makes use of abandoned buildings such as the former convents of San Domenico, San Francesco and San Rocco.

🏛 Via General Salerno

This street, with its noble palazzi, connects **Corso Vittorio Emanuele** with the castle area. Immediately to the left is **San Martino**, a Norman church with a Baroque portal and interior, where there is a fine 17th-century wooden choir. The sacristy takes you to the **Oratorio dei Confrati del Purgatorio**, built in Rococo style, with a carved altar decorated with gilded stucco. Further along the street is **San Giuliano**, which looks over a square made more spectacular by the pink colour of the façade. The church was begun in 1080 by Roger I but was radically altered in the 1600s. It was closed when the vault caved in on the central section of the nave; now restored, it is used as a cultural and artistic centre.

An example of the lovely paved streets in Erice

🏠 San Giovanni Battista

Piazzale San Giovanni.
Tel 0923-869 171.
🕐 only for events.
This white-domed church is probably the oldest in Erice, despite the many alterations that have changed its appearance. The last refurbishing phase took place in the 1600s, when the nave was totally rebuilt. The church is now used only as an auditorium, but interesting works of art remain. These include the statue of St John the Baptist by Antonino Gagini and the 14th-century frescoes moved here from the deconsecrated church of Santa Maria Maddalena.

Environs

On the slopes of Monte San Giuliano, in the restored Baglio Cusenza, is the **Museo Agroforestale**, with an exhibition of farm equipment. Old ploughs, presses, barrows and a limestone millstone are on display in the courtyard.

🏛 Museo Agroforestale

Località San Matteo.
Tel 0923-869 532. 🕐 8:30am–2pm Mon–Sat, 9am–5pm Sun.

Boats anchored in the large port of Trapani

Trapani ⑳

Road map A2. 👥 70,000.
✈ Vincenzo Florio a Birgi (0923-842
502). ⒇ 892021. 🚌 0923-871 922.
ℹ Via San Francesco d'Assisi (0923-
545 511). ◢ Thu. ✦ Processione
dei Misteri (Good Friday).

The town was built on a
narrow, curved promontory
(hence the name, which
derives from the Greek word
drepanon, or sickle) that juts
out into the sea opposite the
Egadi Islands. In ancient
times Trapani was the port
town for Erice *(see pp100–1)*.
It flourished under the Carthaginians and languished under
the Vandals, Byzantines and
Saracens. The economy has
always been linked to the sea
and reached its peak in the
1600s and 1700s with ship-
yards and tuna fishing. The
town now extends beyond
the promontory to the foot of
Monte San Giuliano and the
edge of the salt marshes.

🏛 Museo Pepoli
Via Conte Agostino Pepoli 200.
Tel 0923-553 269. ◗ 9am–
1:30pm Mon–Sat, 9am–12:30pm
Sun & hols. 🖼
This museum was opened in
1906 in the former Carmelite
monastery, thanks to Count
Agostino Pepoli, who donated
his private collection. A broad
polychrome marble staircase
leads to the first floor, which
has archaeological finds,
12th–18th century Sicilian
painting, jewellery and ceramics. The art produced in
Trapani is interesting: wooden
16th-century angels, an 18th-
century coral and alabaster
nativity scene, jewellery, clocks
with painted dials, tapestries
with coral and majolica from
Santa Maria delle Grazie.

▥ Via Garibaldi
This is the street that leads
to the old town. It begins in
Piazza Vittorio Veneto, the
heart of the city with **Palazzo
d'Ali**, now the Town Hall.

The street is lined with
18th-century patrician
residences such as **Palazzo
Riccio di Morana** and **Palazzo
Fardella Fontana**. Almost
directly opposite the 1621
Baroque façade of **Santa
Maria d'Itria** are the steps
leading to **San Domenico**,
built in the 14th century and
restructured in the 18th. In
the interior is the sarcophagus
of Manfred, natural son of
Frederick II *(see p29)*.

▥ Corso Vittorio Emanuele
This is the main street in the
old town, lined with late
Baroque buildings and **San
Lorenzo Cathedral**, which
has a fine portico. The main
features of the interior are
the painted ceiling, stucco
decoration and, in the right-
hand altar, a *Crucifixion*
attributed to Van Dyck.

⛪ Santuario di Maria
Santissima Annunziata
Via Conte Agostino Pepoli. **Tel**
0923-539 184. ◗ winter: 7am–
noon, 4–7pm including hols; summer:
7am–noon, 4–8pm (7am–1pm,
4–8pm hols). ✝ 8am, 9am, 6pm.
www.madonnaditrapani.com
Known as the Madonna di
Trapani, this church was built
by the Carmelite fathers in
1224. The portal and part of
the rose window are the only
original elements remaining,
as the rest of the church is
Baroque, thanks to the
restoration effected in 1714.
Inside are the Cappella dei
Pescatori, the Cappella dei
Marinai, and

THE SALT MARSHES

The Stagno and Trapani salt
marshes were exploited in
antiquity and reached the height
of their importance in the 19th
century, when salt was exported
as far away as Norway. The
long periods of sunshine (five
or six months a year) and the
impermeable nature of the land

Windmills, used for draining
water from the basins

A workman at the Stagnone
salt marsh

made these marshes very productive, although activity has
declined in the last 20 years. At one time, windmills supplied
energy for the Archimedes screws used to take water from
basin to basin; some of them have now been restored. At
Nubia the Museo delle Saline (Salt Marsh Museum) is now
open, and the Stagnone area is a fully fledged nature reserve.
The seawater will be protected from pollution, and the age-old
tradition of salt extraction will survive.

Bell tower of the Santuario dell'Annunziata in Trapani

the Cappella della Madonna di Trapani with the *Madonna and Child* by Nino Pisano, one of the most important Gothic sculptures in Sicily.

🔒 Chiesa del Purgatorio

Via San Francesco d'Assisi. *Tel 0923-21321.* ⬜ *10am–noon Tue, 10am–noon, 5–7pm Fri (10am–noon, 4–7pm daily in Lent; 9am–midnight Jul & Aug).*
This church is well known because it houses unusual 18th-century wooden statues with precious silver decoration representing the Stations of the Cross *(Misteri)*. At 2pm on Good Friday, they are carried in a 24-hour procession, a ritual dating from the 1700s.

🏛 Museo di Preistoria

Torre di Ligny. *Tel 0923-223 00.*
⬜ *9:30am–12:30pm (also 4–6:30pm Nov–Mar; 9am–midnight Jul & Aug).*
At the tip of the peninsula, the **Torre di Ligny** (1671) affords a fine view of the city and its port. The tower is now used as an archaeological museum, with objects from the Punic Wars and from the shipwrecks that occurred on the ancient trade routes, and amphoras used to carry wine, dates and garum, a prized fish sauce.

🏛 Museo del Sale

Via delle Saline, Contrada Nubia, Paceco. *Tel 0923-867 442.*
⬜ *9am–7pm daily.* **WWF Reserve**
Tel 0923-867 700.
From Trapani to Marsala the coast is lined with salt marshes. The area is now a

WWF nature reserve, a unique habitat for migratory birds. The landscape, with its salt marshes and windmills (three of which can be visited), is striking. A museum illustrates the practice of salt extraction.

Marsala ㉑

Road map *A3.* 🏙 *85,000.*
🚉 *124 km (77 miles) from Marsala and 31 km (19 miles) from Trapani.*
ℹ *0923-714 097.* 🚌 *Tue.*
🎭 *Maundy Thursday procession.*

Sicily's largest wine-producing centre was founded by the colonists from Mozia who survived the destruction of the island by Dionysius of Syracuse in 397 BC. It then became a major Carthaginian city, but in the first Punic War it was conquered by the Romans, who made it their main Mediterranean naval base. The city plan is basically Roman, other quarters being added by the Arabs, who conquered the city in 830 and made it a flourishing trade centre. **Piazza della Repubblica**, bounded by **Palazzo Senatorio** and the **Cathedral**, dedicated to St Thomas of Canterbury, is the heart of town. The Cathedral was founded by the Normans and completed in the 1900s. It boasts sculptures by the Gaginis and their school. Behind the apse is the **Museo degli Arazzi Fiamminghi**, with eight 16th-century Flemish tapestries depicting Titus' war against the Hebrews. They were donated by Philip II of Spain to the Archbishop of Messina and later taken to Marsala Cathedral.

🏛 Museo degli Arazzi Fiamminghi

Chiesa Madre, Via G Garaffa 57.
Tel 0923-216 295. ⬜ *9am–1pm, 4–6pm.* ⬤ *Mon.* 🎫

🏛 Museo Archeologico

Via Capo Lilibeo 34. *Tel 0923-952 535.* ⬜ *9am–7pm Mon–Sat, 9am–1pm Sun & hols.*
This archaeological museum features prehistoric and ancient finds from local digs, including the mosaics from the Roman ruins at Capo Boeo and a 3rd-century-BC Punic shipwreck.

Mozia ㉒

Road map *A2–3.* 🚤 *from Trapani and Marsala (dawn to sunset).* ℹ *APT di Trapani (0923-712 598).* **Museum** ⬜ *9am–1:30pm, 2:30–6pm daily.* 🎫

The prosperous Phoenician city of Mozia was built on the island of San Pantaleo, a very short distance from the shores of Sicily. The ancient site is linked with Joseph Whitaker, the son of an English wine merchant who made his fortune from Marsala wine. He became owner of the island in the early 1900s, began archaeological digs in 1913, and founded a museum that houses the statue of the "young man from Mozia". You can also visit the dry docks, which, together with those in Carthage, are the most ancient in the Mediterranean.

Punic head, Mozia museum

Ruins of the northern gate on the island of Mozia, destroyed in 397 BC

Selinunte ㉓

The ruins of Selinunte, overlooking the sea, are among the most striking archaeological sites in the Mediterranean and a supreme example of the fusion of Phoenician and Greek culture. Founded in the 7th century BC by colonists from Megara Hyblaea, Selinunte soon became a powerful city with flourishing trade and artistic activity. A rival to Segesta and Mozia, it was destroyed by Carthage in 409 BC and largely forgotten. Excavations (still under way in the oldest parts of the Selinunte ruins) have brought to light eight temples with colossal Doric columns, as well as a fortification system.

Attic vase found in Selinunte

★ Temple C (580–550 BC)
Decorated with metopes now kept in Palermo, this was the largest and oldest temple on the acropolis, dedicated to Heracles or Apollo.

Temple A (480–470 BC), perhaps dedicated to Leto.

Sanctuary of Malophoros

Ruins of ancient city

Temple D (570–550 BC) was perhaps dedicated to Aphrodite.

Temple O (480–470 BC)

Car park

Temple B (c.250 BC) was probably the only one built in the Hellenistic age.

★ Acropolis
This was the hub of public life. It centred around two main streets that divided it into four quarters protected by a wall 1,260 m (4,132 ft) long.

Temple F (560–530 BC) was dedicated to Athena and is the most ancient temple on the eastern hill. Sadly it is totally in ruins.

★ Temple E (490–480 BC)

This temple, located at the top of an eight-stepped base (crepidoma), was partly rebuilt in the 1960s. It was probably sacred to Hera and is considered one of the finest examples of Doric architecture in Sicily.

The harbour area lay at the junction of the Cotone river and the road connecting the Acropolis to the eastern hill.

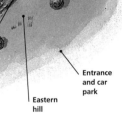

Entrance and car park

Eastern hill

Temple G (540–480 BC)

This temple is also completely in ruins but is still an important monument because, at 6,120 sq m (65,850 sq ft), it was one of the largest temples in antiquity. It reached a height of 30 m (98 ft) when complete.

STAR FEATURES

★ Acropolis

★ Temple

★ Temple E

0 metres	130
0 yards	130

Exploring Selinunte

You will need at least two hours to visit the archaeological site of Selinunte. The excavated area is divided into four zones, starting off from the east: the eastern hill with its group of temples; the Acropolis; the ancient city; and the Sanctuary of Malophoros. Besides its great cultural interest, the surrounding landscape is very beautiful, and there are lovely views of the sea.

The metopes of Temple C are now in Palermo museum *(see p56)*

Acropolis

This lies on a bluff right over the sea, between the Modione river to the west and the Gorgo Cottone river to the east. Their mouths once formed the city harbour, now silted up. The Acropolis was surrounded by colossal stone walls 3 m (10 ft) high, with two gates, the larger one on the northern side. This area contained the public buildings and temples, all facing east. From the southern end, the first places are the sparse ruins of **Temples O and A**, close together and much alike. There were originally six columns along the short

Hellenistic vases, Museo Archeologico, Palermo *(see p56)*

sides and 14 on the longer ones. Further on you come to the small **Temple B**, which was thought to have been brightly coloured. **Temple C** is the most ancient on the Acropolis. It was dedicated to Apollo and had six columns on the short sides and 17 on the long ones. The pediment was decorated with superb metopes, three of which are now kept in the Museo Archeologico in Palermo *(see p56)*.

In 1925–6, 14 columns on the northern side and on part of the architrave were reconstructed. Seeing these among the other blocks of

massive columns placed here and there around the ancient sacred precinct is quite an impressive sight.

Temple D is also reduced to a state of fragmentary ruins. The Acropolis area was divided by two main perpendicular streets, which can be reached by means of stone steps.

The eastern hill

The sacred precinct has remains of three temples set parallel to one another at the entrance to the archaeological zone. In ancient times it was surrounded by an enclosure. The partially reconstructed **Temple E** was built in the pure Doric style. An inscription on a votive stele found in 1865 shows that it was dedicated to Hera (Juno). Its 68 columns still support part of the trabeation.

An eight-step stairway leads to **Temple F**, dedicated to either Athena or Dionysus, the smallest and most badly damaged of the three. It was built in the archaic style, surrounded by 36 columns which were more than 9 m (29 ft) high. The vestibule had a second row of columns, and

The bronze ephebus, Selinunte

Temple E, one of the best examples of Doric architecture in Sicily

The Collegio dei Gesuiti at Mazara del Vallo, home to the Museo Civico

the lower part of the peristyle was enclosed by a wall.

The size of **Temple G** was 110.36 by 50.10 m (362 by 164 ft). It was begun in the 6th century BC and took another 100 years to complete. It was considered the town's main religious building. Today it is only a huge mass of stones, in the middle of which stands a column, which was restored in 1832. It was probably dedicated to Zeus, but its construction was never completed.

⋔ The Ancient City

On the Collina di Manuzza hill north of the Acropolis, the ancient city only became the subject of archaeological excavations late in the 20th century. After the destruction of the city in 409 BC, this ancient part was used as a necropolis by those inhabitants who remained.

⌂ Malophoros Sanctuary

Situated west of the Modione river, about a kilometre (half a mile) away from the Acropolis, the Malophoros Sanctuary is extremely old and perhaps was founded even before the city itself.

The main building in this sanctuary is enclosed by walls and was dedicated to a female divinity, Malophoros (meaning "bearer of pomegranate"), the goddess of fertility, many statuettes of whom have been found in the vicinity. According to experts, the sanctuary was a stopping point on the long, impressive funeral processions making their way to the Manicalunga necropolis.

Castelvetrano ㉔

Road map B3. 👥 *30,300.* 🚌 *73 km (45 miles) from Trapani, 110 km (68 miles) from Palermo.* ℹ *APT, c/o Museo Civico (0924-904 932).* 🚌 *Tue.* 🎭 *Funzione dell'Aurora (Easter).*

The centre consists of three linked squares. The main one is **Piazza Garibaldi**, where the mainly 16th-century **Chiesa Madre** has an interesting medieval portal. Inside are stuccoes by Ferraro and Serpotta, and a *Madonna* by the Gagini school. By the church are the **Municipio** (Town Hall), the **Campanile** and the Mannerist **Fontana della Ninfa**. Close by is the **Chiesa del Purgatorio**, built in 1624–64, its façade filled with statues, and the neo-Doric **Teatro Selinus** (1873).

Environs

At **Delia**, 3.5 km (2 miles) from town, is Santa Trinità, a church built in the Norman period.

Mazara del Vallo ㉕

Road map A3. 👥 *50,000.* 🚌 *50 km (31 miles) from Trapani, 124 km (77 miles) from Palermo.* ℹ *Piazza Santa Veneranda 2 (0923-941 727).* 🚌 *Wed.* 🎭 *Festino di San Vito (Aug).*

Facing the Canale di Sicilia, at the mouth of the Mazarò river, the town, a colony of Selinunte, was destroyed in 409 BC by the Carthaginians, passed to the Romans and then became a prosperous city under the Arabs, who made it the capital of one of the three "valleys" into which they split Sicily *(see p32).* In 1073 Mazara was conquered by Roger I; he convened the first Norman Parliament of Sicily here.

In **Piazza Mokarta** remains of the castle can be seen. Behind this is the **Cathedral**, of medieval origin but rebuilt in 1694. It houses the *Transfiguration*, a sculpture group by Antonello Gagini. The left side of the Cathedral closes off Piazza della Repubblica, with the façade of the **Seminario dei Chierici** and the **Palazzo Vescovile**. On Lungomare Mazzini you will see the **Collegio dei Gesuiti**, seat of the **Museo Civico** and can enter the old Arab town.

🏛 Museo Civico

Via Garibaldi 50. **Tel** *0923-940 266.* ◯ *8:30am–2pm Mon–Sat.* The former Collegio dei Gesuiti, with its Baroque door with four telamons, contains archaeological finds, sculpture and medieval paintings.

Mazara del Vallo, one of the most important fishing harbours in Italy

Egadi Islands 26

Road map A2. 4,700. *from Trapani (Siremar: 0923-545 455).* Consorzio Turistico Egadi, Largo Marina 14, Favignana (0923-922 121); APT Trapani (0923-545 511). www.isoleegadi.it

The Sicilian islands of Favignana, Levanzo and Marettimo were connected to mainland Sicily 600,000 years ago. As the sea level gradually rose, the links were submerged, slowly changing the islands into an archipelago in the centre of the Mediterranean. The islands are now popular as places for vacations and swimming as they are easily reached from Trapani.

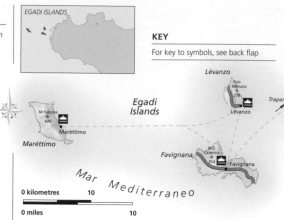

KEY

For key to symbols, see back flap

A stretch of the Favignana coastline

Favignana

This island has two distinct parts. The eastern side is flat, with pastureland and farmland, while the other half is craggy and barren. In the middle is the small town of **Favignana**, which was rebuilt in the 1600s over its original medieval layout. Sights worth visiting are the **Chiesa Matrice** (dedicated to the Immaculate Conception), the buildings constructed during the height of the tuna fishing industry and the 19th-century **Villino Florio**, which is now the Town Hall. The so-called **Bagno delle Donne** (Ladies' Bath), a Roman bath with traces of mosaics, is worth a look.

The boat tour of the island is to be recommended. It departs from the port and visits **Punta Faraglione, Punta Ferro** and **Punta Sottile**, where there is a lighthouse.

It continues to the small islands of **Galera** and **Galeotta, Punta Fanfalo** and **Punta Calarossa**, where there are heaps of tufa from the island quarries. The tour ends here, taking you back to the port.

Levanzo

The smallest of the Egadi Islands has a wilder aspect than Favignana: the tall, rocky coastline is dominated by a cultivated plateau. There is only one small village, **Cala Dogana**, and the landscape is barren and desolate, interrupted here and there by the green maquis vegetation. A series of footpaths crosses the island and provides very pleasant walks to the beautiful **Cala Tramontana** bay.

Northwest of Cala Dogana is the **Grotta del Genovese**, which can be reached on foot in about two hours or by boat. The grotto has a series

of carved Palaeolithic drawings of human figures, animals and idols, some in a rather naturalistic style, others rendered more schematically.

Marettimo

The rugged, mountainous and varied landscape of Marettimo, the first island in the group to break off from the mainland, is very striking. The paths crossing the island – there are no roads or hotels here – will introduce you to a world of limestone pinnacles and caves leading up to Monte Falcone (686 m, 2,250 ft). The island has many rare plant species that grow only here – caused by the long isolation of Marettimo – as well as some introduced moufflon and boar. The **Punta Troia fort** housed a Bourbon penal colony where the Risorgimento hero, Guglielmo Pepe, was held for three years. Not far from the tiny village of Marettimo there are some ancient Roman buildings and, in the vicinity, a small Byzantine church.

The little harbour at Cala Dogana, the only village in Levanzo

For hotels and restaurants in this region see pp199–201 and pp214–16

The Grotta Azzurra, a major attraction on boat tours around Ustica

Ustica ㉗

Road map B1. 👥 *1,200.* ⚓ *from Palermo (Siremar: 091-582 403); in summer from Naples (Ustica Lines: 081-251 4721).* ✈ *Palermo Punta Raisi 091-591 663.* ℹ *Pro Loco di Ustica (091-844 91 90; open Jun–Sep); APT Palermo (091-583 847).*

Ustica is the result of ancient volcanic eruptions: its name derives from the word *ustum* (burned) and the land is made up of sharp black volcanic rock, which lends it its unique appearance. The emerged part of the gigantic submerged volcano, about 49 km (30 miles) from the Sicilian coast, is only 8.6 sq km (3.32 sq miles), but its extremely fertile lava terrain is ideal for the cultivation of capers and lentils. The steep and rocky coasts and the landscape of the island make it an ideal spot for underwater sports. Because of the importance of the sea beds, the first **Marine Reserve** in Italy was established here on 12 November 1986; it is run by the local authorities. The park is divided into three sections, and the degree of protection ranges from total (from Caletta to Cala Sidoti) to partial. Guided tours are organized by the Marine Reserve itself, and in July the island plays host to a series of international skin- and scuba-diving programmes. A particularly interesting underwater excursion is the one that starts off at **Punta Gavazzi**, with what could be described as an archaeological

diving tour of the ancient Roman amphorae, old anchors, and traces of the passage of sailors since the beginning of human history in this part of the sea.

The village of **Ustica** is dominated by the **Capo Falconara** promontory, where the Bourbon rulers built a little fort offering a splendid view as far as the Sicilian coast. Ustica was founded in the mid-1700s and is still inhabited. Local life revolves around Piazza Umberto I, where there is a whitewashed parish church. Age-old human presence on the island is visible in a number of interesting sites,

such as the prehistoric village of **Faraglioni** and the Phoenician tombs at **Falconara**, which were used at different times by the Greeks, the Romans and the Byzantines.

The main feature of a boat tour of the island is the great number of underwater caves in the rocky coastline: the **Grotta Azzurra**, whose large caverns are preceded by an imposing natural arch, the **Grotta delle Colonne**, with a cliff of the same name, and the **Grotta Blasi, Grotta dell'Oro** and **Grotta delle Barche** (where fishermen used to moor their boats during storms), are only a few of the many caves to be seen.

Underwater exploration around the island of Ustica

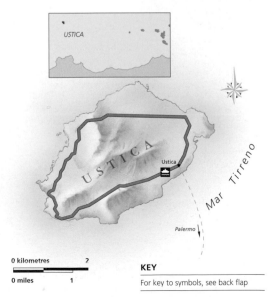

USTICA

USTICA

Ustica ⚓

Mar Tirreno

Palermo

0 kilometres 2

0 miles 1

KEY

For key to symbols, see back flap

SOUTHWESTERN SICILY

Τ*his corner of Sicily is only a stone's throw from North Africa. The landscape is varied, much of it hilly or mountainous, with rugged cliffs along parts of the coast and arid, barren plateaus inland. The Greeks built classically beautiful temples at Agrigento, and the Romans left an extensive villa at Piazza Armerina, saved for posterity by being buried under mud for centuries.*

Along the coast, steep craggy cliffs alternate with flatter stretches of sand. This southern shore was a favourite landing place for travellers plying the Mediterranean, with their ships putting in at places like Agrigento, Eraclea and Sciacca.

Agrigento became an important Greek centre, and an entire valley of temples still remains as evidence of their skills. Some are still in good condition 2,000 years later. The mud-preserved Roman mosaics at the Villa del Casale at Piazza Armerina are in marvellous condition and provide an excellent picture of Roman life.

The land rises away from the sea to become soft, rolling hills and then, quite abruptly, rugged mountains. Rivers may emerge for only a few weeks each year. Around the towns of Enna and Caltanissetta lies the stony heart of the island, exploited for its sulphur mines and quarries for centuries. Inland, Southwestern Sicily is a totally different world from the coast. Towns like Enna seem to perch precariously on hilltops. Many of the people of these rather isolated towns have retained a deep-seated religious faith, which is expressed in the colourful processions held during Easter Week *(see p126).* The flatter land and slopes nearer to the sea were once the domain of ancient feudal estates with their olive and orange groves, vividly described in Giuseppe di Lampedusa's novel *The Leopard*. This, perhaps the most truly "Sicilian" part of Sicily, was also the birthplace of the great Italian writer Pirandello.

A boar being captured in one of the fine hunting scene mosaics in the Villa del Casale, at Piazza Armerina

◁ **The beautifully preserved Temple of Concord (c.430 BC) in the valley of the Temples at Agrigento**

Exploring Southwestern Sicily

A good starting point for a visit to this corner of Sicily is Agrigento, as it is within easy reach of the eastern coast, with Palma di Montechiaro and Licata, and the western coast, moving towards Eraclea Minoa and Sciacca. Major communications routes travel into the interior towards Caltanissetta and Enna on the one hand and, westwards, into the hinterland towards Palermo. From the port at Agrigento there is a regular boat service to the islands of Lampedusa and Linosa.

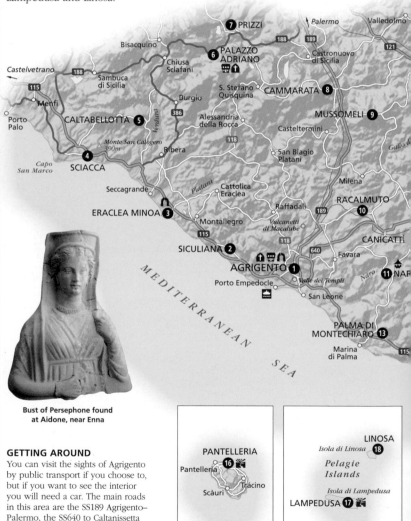

Bust of Persephone found
at Aidone, near Enna

GETTING AROUND

You can visit the sights of Agrigento by public transport if you choose to, but if you want to see the interior you will need a car. The main roads in this area are the SS189 Agrigento–Palermo, the SS640 to Caltanissetta (from Caltanissetta to Enna it becomes the SS117b and returns to the coast via Piazza Armerina and Gela) and lastly the SS115, which runs along the entire southwestern coastline of Sicily.

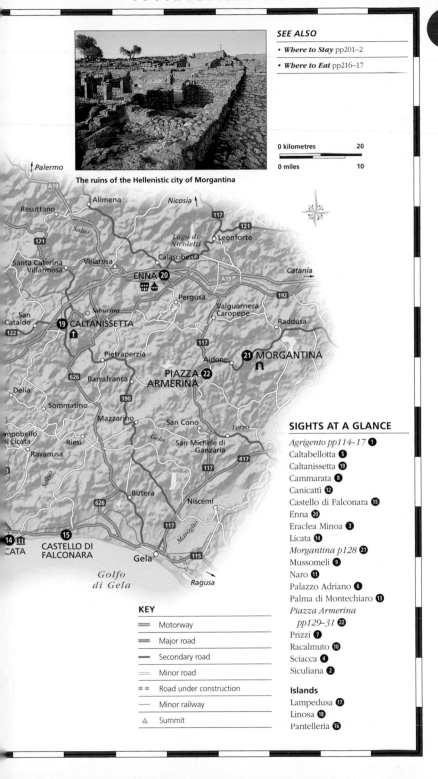

SEE ALSO

• *Where to Stay* pp201–2

• *Where to Eat* pp216–17

0 kilometres   20

0 miles   10

The ruins of the Hellenistic city of Morgantina

SIGHTS AT A GLANCE

KEY

═══ Motorway

═══ Major road

─── Secondary road

═══ Minor road

═ ═ Road under construction

─── Minor railway

△ Summit

Agrigento ●

There are two main sights in Agrigento: the magnificent remains of the Greek colony in the Valle dei Templi (see pp116–17) and the rocky hill where the medieval town was built. The city of Akragas was founded by the Greeks, then conquered by the Romans in 210 BC, who gave it the name of Agrigentum. During a period of barbarian invasions the town moved from the valley to the rock. It was then ruled by the Byzantines and for some time by the Arabs, whose dominion came to an end with the Normans in 1087.

Detail of San Nicola, Museo Archeologico

in the 1600s. The two-stage façade has an interesting portal flanked by two large spiral columns and a large bell tower. Both interior and exterior have a series of allegorical statues representing the Christian Virtues, executed in the early 1700s by Giuseppe and Giacomo Serpotta, and a Madonna of the Pomegranate attributed to Antonello Gagini.

Near the church, under a stone lion, is the Ipogeo del Purgatorio (Hypogeum of Purgatory), a network of underground conduits built

Façade of Agrigento Cathedral (11th century)

⛪ Cathedral and Museo Diocesano
Piazza Don Minzoni.
Museo Diocesano Tel 0922-401 352. ◯ daily.
Agrigento's cathedral was founded in the 12th century and subsequently enlarged and altered, as can be seen in some of the exterior details. For example, the bell tower has a series of Catalan-Gothic single lancet windows, while others are in the original style.

Inside is the Cappella di San Gerlando, named after the bishop who founded the church, with an elegant Gothic portal. The ceiling features both painted and coffered sections, dating from the 16th and 17th centuries respectively. A curious acoustic phenomenon, known as the portavoce, takes place in the chapel: if you stand under the apse, you can clearly hear the whispering of people at the other end of the nave, 80 m (262 ft) away.

The **Museum** has some Roman sarcophagi and a series of frescoes taken from the Cathedral walls in 1951.

🎭 Teatro Pirandello
Piazza Pirandello. Tel 0922-203 91.
www.teatropirandello.it
Founded in 1870 and originally called Teatro Regina Margherita, the Teatro Pirandello was renamed after the Agrigento-born playwright (see p22 & p25). Part of the Town Hall, it was designed by Dionisio Sciascia, and the decoration was executed by Palermo architect Giovanni Basile.

🏛 Museo Civico
Piazza Pirandello. Tel 0922-597 198. ● Mon. 📷
The city museum, which is located in the old Convento degli Agostiniani, opposite the Municipio (Town Hall), contains a collection of paintings from the 14th to the 18th century and medieval sculpture.

⛪ San Lorenzo
Piazza del Purgatorio. ◯ daily.
Little remains of this church (also known as Chiesa del Purgatorio), which was rebuilt in the Baroque style

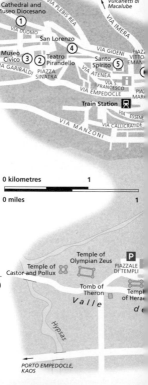

AGRIGENTO

Cathedral and Museo Diocesano ①
Convento di Santo Spirito ⑤
Museo Archeologico Nazionale ⑦
Museo Civico ③
Piazza Vittorio Emanuele ⑥
San Lorenzo ④
Teatro Pirandello ②
Valle dei Templi
　(see pp116–17) ⑧

The arched coupled windows in the Convento di Santo Spirito (1295)

in the 5th century BC by the Greek architects to supply water to the various quarters of the city.

🏛 Convento di Santo Spirito

Salita Santo Spirito. ☐ *daily.*
This abbey complex is of ancient origin. The church and adjacent Cistercian monastery were founded in the 13th century by the Countess Prefoglio of the powerful Chiaramonte family. They were altered several times, particularly the façade, which, however, still maintains a Gothic portal and rose window. For many centuries the church was the most important in the Agrigento area and was known as the Badia Grande. In the 18th century the nave was decorated with lavish and fantastic stuccowork that mirrors the shapes of the church; the motif is also developed in sculpted panels.

Next to the church is the monastery, now city property, where the cloister is well worth a visit. The impressive chapterhouse is lined with Gothic arcades.

🏛 Piazza Vittorio Emanuele

This large, lively, traffic-filled square connects the old town of Agrigento with the more recently built part, which developed during the 19th century. The two areas, Girgenti to the west and Rupe Atenea to the east, were once separated by a valley that was filled in during the late 19th century, blocking what was traditionally known as "Empedocles' opening", through which the north wind passed, cooling the valley below.

Environs

Towards the sea is the parish of Kaos, near Villaseta, worth visiting to see the **Birthplace of Luigi Pirandello**, the house of the great dramatist and novelist (*see pp22–5*). The winner of the 1934 Nobel Prize for Literature once lived here; it is now a museum. The urn containing Pirandello's ashes can be found in a crack in a rock next to an old fallen pine, facing the sea.

Nearby, **Porto Empedocle** was once an important outlet for the mining activity in the interior. In the old harbour is the Bastione di Carlo V (Rampart of Charles V), while there is a constant bustle of fishing boats around the more industrialized area.

Heading north from Agrigento and turning off SS189 at the Comitini crossroads, two kilometres (one mile) of dirt road to the south takes you to a place famous for a curious geological phenomenon: little volcano-shaped cones known as the **Vulcanetti di Macalube** emit methane gas bubbles and brackish mud in a lunar landscape made sterile by this pseudo-volcanic activity.

🏛 Museo Archeologico Regionale

Contrada San Nicola. **Tel** 0922-401 565. ☐ 9am–7:30pm Tue–Sat, 9am–1:30pm Mon, Sun & hols. 🖼
Part of the Convento di San Nicola and located in a panoramic spot that affords beautiful views over the Valley of the Temples (*see pp116–17*), this interesting archaeological museum shows material recovered from several excavations around Agrigento.

Among the items on display are a remarkable Attic vase, the Crater of Dionysus, and the marble statue of a young athlete known as the Ephebus of Agrigento.

🏛 Birthplace of Pirandello

Contrada Kaos, SS 115. **Tel** 0922-511 826. ☐ 9am–1pm, 2:30–7pm daily. 🖼

The eerie landscape of the Vulcanetti di Macalube

Key to Symbols *see back flap*

[Map labels:]
VIA CICERONE
VIA MINERVA
VIA GIOVANNI XXIII
VIALE DELLA VITTORIA
VIA F. CRISPI
...A U. LA MALFA
...RARCA
VIA DEMETRA
San Biagio
Museo Archeologico Nazionale ⑦
San Nicola
Hellenistic Roman Quarter
VIA DEI TEMPLI
Temple of Concord
...SACRA
Temple of Hera
⑧
SS 115
Templi
Temple of Asclepius

Valle dei Templi

The Ephebus of Agrigento

Agrigento was founded in 581 BC by colonists from Gela, who named the town Akragas *(see p30)*. Yet only a century later the population had grown to 200,000 and the Greek poet Pindar described it as "the fairest city inhabited by mortals". It was ruled briefly by the Carthaginians. The Valley of Temples is the site of the main temples (dedicated to Olympian Zeus, Heracles, Concord and Hera), minor shrines (Sanctuary of the Chthonic Divinities) and the Archaeological Museum.

Sanctuary of the Chthonic Divinities (6th–5th century BC)
A shrine dedicated to Demeter and Persephone (also known as Kore), with altars and sacred precincts.

**Temple of Hephaistos
(5th century BC)**

**Temple of Olympian Zeus
(5th century BC)**
Only fragmentary ruins remain of this temple, except for this Telamon now on display in the Museo Archeologico.

Porta Aurea

Entrance

Tomb of Theron
(1st century BC)

Villa Igea
(see inset)

**Temple of Castor and Pollux
(5th century BC)**
The four surviving columns, a symbol of the Valley of Temples, were restored in the 19th century.

Temple of Heracles (6th century BC)
These eight columns, put back in place in 1924, belonged to the oldest temple dedicated to the hero worshipped by both the Greeks and Romans (as Hercules). The archaic Doric structure has an elongated rectangle plan.

★ Museo Archeologico
The Archaeological Museum was opened to the public in 1967. The 13 rooms display objects ranging from prehistoric times to the early Christian period, including pieces from the Classical era.

EARLY CHRISTIAN CATACOMBS

The niches, hewn along the floors and walls

The Valle dei Templi is famous for its splendid monuments of the Magna Graecia civilization, but it also has Early Christian ruins. The Ipogei of Villa Igea (also known as the Grotta di Frangipane), between the Temple of Heracles and the Temple of Concord, were cut out of the rock to house the bodies of the first Christians here. A series of niches, closed off by stone slabs, alternated with chapels that still bear traces of wall paintings.

The Hellenistic-Roman quarter is all that remains of the large post-Classical age settlement.

Rock sanctuary of Demeter

★ Temple of Hera (5th century BC)
This well-preserved temple was restored in Roman times. Note the northern colonnade with its architrave.

Line of fortifications

★ Temple of Concord (5th century BC)
With its 34 columns, this is one of the best preserved Doric temples in the world, partly thanks to alterations made in the 4th century AD, when it became a Christian basilica. It was restored to its original classical form in 1748.

| 0 metres | 200 |
| 0 yards | 200 |

STAR FEATURES

★ Museo Archeologico

★ Temple of Concord

★ Temple of Hera

Siculiana ❷

Road map C4. 🏘 *5,100.* **FS** *from Palermo and Trapani to Castelvetrano, then* 🚌 ℹ️ *Town hall, Piazza Kennedy (0922-815 105).*

The present-day town of Siculiana was built on the site of an Arab fort destroyed by the Normans in the late 11th century. The new lords – the Chiaramonte family from Agrigento – rebuilt the fortress in the 1300s and it was altered several times afterwards. Despite all the changes, Siculiana has retained some Arab features.

In central Piazza Umberto I is the Baroque **Chiesa Madre**, dedicated to San Leonardo Abate, dominating the square at the top of a flight of steps. In the old centre, divided into large blocks, you can glimpse entrances to courtyards and alleys, which were once part of the covered Arab town.

The archaeological site at Eraclea Minoa, close to the rocky shore

Siculiana, built on a hill during Arab rule

Eraclea Minoa ❸

Road map B4.
Digs *Cattolica Eraclea.* **Tel** *0922-846 005.* ⭕ *9am–1 hr before sunset.* 📷

This ancient settlement was founded during the Mycenaean age and then developed by Spartan colonists who arrived in the 6th century BC and gave it its present name. After being fought over by Agrigento and Carthage, Eraclea became a Roman colony. Today it is a stone's throw from the craggy coast jutting out into the sea. Eraclea is a wonderful combination of a lovely setting and atmospheric ruins. The **theatre** is well preserved – excavations began in the 1950s – and hosts special performances of Greek theatre, although the overall impression is marred somewhat by the plastic used to protect it in bad weather. All around the theatre are the ruins of the ancient city with its defence system, as well as some necropolises.

Sciacca ❹

Road map B3. 🏘 *40,000.* **FS** *from Palermo and Trapani.* ℹ️ *AAST, Corso Vittorio Emanuele 84 (0925-21182 or 22744); AAR Terme di Sciacca, Via Agatocle 2 (0925-961 111).* **www**.*aziendaturismosciacca.it*

From a distance, Sciacca seems to be overwhelmed by Monte San Calogero, with its thermal waters and steam vapours, which have made the town famous over the centuries. Although the hot springs had been used since prehistoric times, Sciacca was founded as a mere military outpost for Selinunte during the interminable warfare with the city of Agrigento, and was called *Thermae Selinuntinae* (Selinunte baths) by the Romans. It developed rapidly under Arab rule (Sciacca derives from *as-saqah*) and many traces of their culture can be seen in the old Rabato and Giudecca-Cadda quarters, with their blind alleys and maze of roofed courtyards.

THE ORANGES OF RIBERA

Orange decoration for the festival

The real home of orange-growing is the plain around Mount Etna, but oranges play an important role in the southwestern corner of Sicily, too. At Ribera, an agricultural town where the statesman Francesco Crispi was born *(see p36)*, they grow a special type of navel orange that was brought to Sicily from America by emigrants returning home. These enormous and delicious oranges are celebrated in an annual orange festival during which the public gardens are filled with sculptures made of fruit. A short distance from Ribera, the impressive ruins of the Poggio Diana castle tower above the wooded gullies of the Verdura river.

Locally grown oranges, still harvested by hand in this area

The rusticated façade of the Catalan-Gothic Palazzo Steripinto

The town was further fortified by the Normans, who quickly recognized its strategic importance in controlling the trade routes. Much fought over in the years that followed, the town was fortified again and again, in particular against the assault of Charles I of Valois.

In the middle of town is **Palazzo Steripinto**, built in Catalan-Gothic style in 1501 with a rusticated façade. The church of **Santa Margherita** has a splendid Gothic portal; note the bas-relief sculpture in the lunette representing Santa Margherita, the Archangel Gabriel, Our Lady of the Assumption and saints Calogero and Maddalena. Do not miss the cloister of the former **Convent of San Francesco** and the unfinished Baroque façade of the **Chiesa del Carmine**, with its 14th-century rose window. In central Piazza Don Minzoni stands the **Cathedral**, dedicated to Santa Maria Maddalena. It was rebuilt in 1656, but retains three Norman apses.

However, the main attractions in Sciacca are Monte San Calogero and its thermal pools. From the large square at the summit, with the sanctuary dedicated to the evangelist San Calogero, who in the 5th century eliminated pagan rites in the mountain caves, the panorama is breathtaking. The summit is almost 400 m (1,312 ft) high, and on a clear day there is a commanding view from Capo

Bianco to Capo Lilibeo, with the limestone ridge of Caltabellotta in the background and Pantelleria island before you. The older spas are on the slopes of the mountain, while new ones have been built closer to the seaside.

Sciacca is also known for its ceramics, which were mentioned in antiquity by Diodorus Siculus. Local production thrived during the period of Arab rule, and another golden age came in the 16th century. The tradition is being maintained today by the local craftsmen.

Sculpture at the Hermitage of San Pellegrino

Caltabellotta ⑤

Road map B3. 🏠 *5,300.*
🛈 *Town hall, Piazza Umberto I 1 (0925-951 013).*

Visible from most of the hilly area of Sciacca, the rocky crest of Caltabellotta (950 m, 3,116 ft) has been inhabited for millennia, as can be seen in the many ancient necropolises and hypogea. The site was fortified at different stages until the arrival of the Arabs, who gave the castle its definitive form, calling it *Kal'at-at-al ballut* (rock of the oak trees). The county capital, Caltabellotta witnessed the signing of peace between Charles I of Valois and Frederick II of Aragon in 1302 *(see pp28–9)*, who took over the whole of Sicily. Perched on the ridge above the houses of the Torrevecchia quarter are the ruins of the **Norman castle** and **San Salvatore**, while on the other side of the rock is the **Chiesa Madre**, now being restored, founded by Roger I to celebrate his victory over the Arabs. On the western slope, the **Hermitage of San Pellegrino**, which consists of a monastery and a chapel, dominates the city.

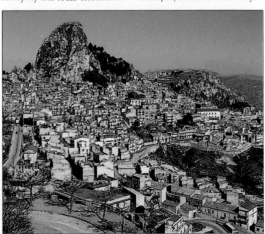

The town of Caltabellotta at the foot of Monte Castello

The façade of San Nicolò, in the upper part of Palazzo Adriano

Palazzo Adriano ❻

Road map C3. 🏛 *2,800.*
🛈 *Pro Loco, Piazza Umberto I
(091-834 9911).*

Almost 700 m (2,296 ft)
above sea level, on the
ridge of Cozzo Braduscia, is
Palazzo Adriano, founded in
the mid-15th century by
Albanian refugees who fled
from the Turkish conquerors.
Central Piazza Umberto I
boasts two important
churches: Greek Orthodox
Santa Maria Assunta, built
in the 16th century and
then rebuilt (the interior

has a lovely iconostasis and
an icon of Our Lady of the
Assumption); and **Santa Maria
del Lume**, which is Catholic
and was founded in the 18th
century. In the middle of the
square, bordered by **Palazzo
Dara**, now the Town Hall,
and **Palazzo Mancuso**, there
is a lovely octagonal fountain
sculpted in 1607. Further up
the hill, in the oldest part of
Palazzo Adriano, the red
dome of the 15th-century
San Nicolò overlooks the
alleyways of this quarter,
which were built around the
castle that stood here before
the town was founded.

Prizzi ❼

Road map C3. 🏛 *6,900.*
🛈 *Town hall, Piazza Francesco Crispi
(091-834 50 45).*

The slopes of wind-blown
Mount Prizzi overlooking the
surrounding valleys have
been inhabited since ancient
times. There was once a
fortified Arab town here,
but present-day Prizzi mostly
reflects the influence of the
Middle Ages. The maze of
alleys winding up the slopes
to the summit (960 m, 3,149
ft) is crowned by the ruins of
the medieval castle. Along the
narrow streets you will see
San Rocco, a large stretch
of open space with **Santa
Maria delle Grazie**, and the
18th-century **Chiesa Madre**
dedicated to St George and
bearing a fine statue of the
Archangel Michael.

Cammarata ❽

Road map C3. 🏛 *7,000.*
🚆 *from Palermo & Agrigento.*
🛈 *Town hall (0922-907 211).*

The earliest historic records
for this town date from the
Norman period, when Roger I
donated the fief to Lucia de
Cammarata. The **Chiesa
Madre**, San Nicolò di Bari,
and the **Dominican monastery**, whose church was
rebuilt in the 1930s, are
all worth a visit. But the
fascination of Cammarata lies
in the overall layout: a
labyrinth of alleys and steps –
narrow or wide, depending
on the natural slope of the
rock – offering an unforgettable view of the valleys
below this medieval hill town.

CINEMA PARADISO

In 1990 the film *Cinema Paradiso* by the Sicilian director
Giuseppe Tornatore *(see p24)* won an Oscar for the best
foreign film. The film tells the story of the arrival of cinema
(the "Nuovo Cinema Paradiso") in an isolated village in
Sicily and the effect the big screen has on the main
character, a young boy. *Cinema Paradiso* was filmed in
the streets and squares of Palazzo Adriano and used many
of the locals as extras, conferring fame on the village. The
weeks the film unit and the inhabitants of Palazzo Adriano
spent working together are commemorated on a majolica
plaque on a corner of Piazza Umberto I.

The plaque commemorating the
filming of *Cinema Paradiso*

The characteristic stone trough at Piazza Fontana, in Racalmuto

Mussomeli ❾

Road map C3. 🏘 *11,700.* 🚹
0934-961 111 or 951 192. **Castello**
Manfredano ☐ *Summer: 9:30am–*
noon, 3:30–6pm Tue–Sun; winter:
9:30am–noon Sat & Sun.

In the 14th century, Manfredi
III Chiaramonte founded the
town of Mussomeli and the
large fortress that still towers
over what has since become a
large agricultural centre. The
castle, called Manfredano or
Chiaramontano in honour of its
founder and built over the
remains of a Hohenstaufen fortification, was altered in the
15th century by the Castellar
family. It has a second walled
enclosure in the interior as well
as the Sala dei Baroni, with
noteworthy portals. From the
outer walls there are panoramic
views of the valleys and hills of
the interior of the island.

Racalmuto ❿

Road map C4. 🏘 *10,300.*
🚆 *from Catania and Palermo*
(via Caltanissetta). 🚹 *Comune*
di Racalmuto (0922-948111).

The town of Racalmuto
(the name derives from the
Arab *rahalmut*, or destroyed
hamlet) was founded by
Federico Chiaramonte (head
of the powerful Sicilian Chiaramonte family) over an existing
fortification. For centuries the

growth of the town went hand
in hand with the development
of various monastic orders
(Carmelite, Franciscan, Minor
and Augustines), but the
place still bears traces of the
typical Arab layout marked
by courtyards and alleys. For
centuries Racalmuto thrived
on the mining of rock salt
and sulphur. The town is
also the birthplace of author
Leonardo Sciascia *(see p23)* .
Today it is a famous agricultural centre, especially
known for its dessert grapes.

In the middle of town,
in Piazza Umberto I, is the
17th-century **Chiesa Madre**
dell'Annunziata, its interior
decorated with lavish stucco,
as well as **San Giuseppe** and
the ruins of the 13th-century
Chiaramonte castle (closed
to the public). Steps lead to
Piazza del Municipio, with the

Santa Chiara Convent, now
the Town Hall, and the **Teatro**
Regina Margherita, founded
in 1879 by Dionisio Sciascia.
Further up the hill, at the far
end of the steps is the **Sanc-**
tuary of Santa Maria del
Monte, where an important
annual festival is held on 11–14
July. Inside the sanctuary is a
statue of the Virgin Mary from
1503. Other churches worth
visiting are the Carmelites'
(with canvases by Pietro
D'Asaro), the Itria and San
Giuliano, which was once the
chapel of the **Sant'Agostino**
Convent A short walk from
the centre takes you to **Piazza**
Fontana, with a stone
drinking trough, and, further
along, Piazza San Francesco,
where there is the monastery
complex of the Conventual
friars, rebuilt in the 1600s.

Naro ⓫

Road map C4. 🏘 *8,800.*
🚹 *Pro Loco (0922-953 011).*

Naro lies on a hill in the
middle of a water-rich area.
Its name derives from ancient
Greek and Arab origins – the
Greek word for river is
naron, and *nahr* is the Arab
translation of the same.

A "resplendent" royal city
during the reign of Frederick
II Hohenstaufen, it was fortified at different times. Besides
the Baroque churches and the
remains of monasteries, there
are the ruins of the medieval
Chiaramonte castle, which is
always closed, 14th-century
Santa Caterina and the 16th-
century Chiesa Madre.

The Chiaramonte castle at Naro, built in the 14th century

The 15th-century Castello di Montechiaro, overlooking the sea

Canicattì

Road map C4. 🏛 *32,000.*
ℹ *Town hall (0922-856 738).*

The large agricultural town of Canicattì owes its fame to the production of dessert grapes (a festival in celebration is held each autumn). Known to Arab geographers as *al-Qattà*, this town became a part of documented Sicilian history in the 14th century, when it was registered as the fief of the Palmieri family from Naro. The late 18th century marked a period of prosperity and growth under the Bonanno family, who commissioned numerous buildings and public works.

In the centre of town are the ruins of the **Castello Bonanno** and the **Torre dell'Orologio**, rebuilt in the 1930s. Economic prosperity is confirmed by the many churches – **San Diego**, rebuilt in the Baroque period with stucco decoration; the **Chiesa del Purgatorio**, with a statue of the Sacred Heart; the **Chiesa del Carmelo**, rebuilt in the early 20th century with funds donated by the local sulphur mine workers – and civic works such as the **Fountain of Neptune** and the recent **Teatro Sociale**. The **Chiesa Madre** is dedicated to San Pancrazio. It was rebuilt in the early 20th century. The new façade is the work of Francesco Basile and among its many interesting sculptures and paintings is the *Madonna delle Grazie*, sculpted in the 16th century in Byzantine style. Along the main street in the upper town there are three monasteries.

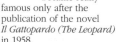

Baroque decoration on a building in Licata

Palma di Montechiaro

Road map C4. 🏛 *21,500.*
ℹ *Town hall (0922-799 111).*

Founded in 1637 by Carlo Tomasi, the Prince of Lampedusa, Palma owes its name to the palm tree on the coat of arms of the De Caro family, relatives of the Tomasi. The town was the property of the Tomasi di Lampedusa family up to the early 19th century, but the family name became really famous only after the publication of the novel *Il Gattopardo (The Leopard)* in 1958.

Palma was created with a town plan, partly the inspiration of the 17th-century astronomer Giovanni Battista Odierna, and loosely based on that of Jerusalem. The layout revolves around **Piazza Provenzani**, with the church of **Santissimo Rosario** and a Benedictine monastery. Further up is the monumental stairway leading to Piazza Santa Rosalia, with the **Chiesa Madre**, built in the late 1600s with an impressive two-stage façade flanked by twin bell towers. On Sundays and holidays this square is the hub of city life.

A walk through town reveals a number of interesting Baroque buildings.

IL GATTOPARDO

Giuseppe Tomasi di Lampedusa (1896–1957)

Tomasi di Lampedusa's famous novel *(see pp23–4)* was a great success when it was published posthumously in 1958, selling over 100,000 copies. It was later made into a highly acclaimed film by Luchino Visconti. The novel was published thanks to the efforts of novelist Giorgio Bassani, who met Tomasi di Lampe-dusa in 1954, three years before he died. Most of the novel is set in Palermo, but there are recognizable descriptions of the villages and landscape in this part of Sicily, with which the author had strong bonds.

A typical square in Licata

A few miles away, not far from the sea, are the evocative ruins of **Castello di Montechiaro**, founded, according to tradition, by Federico III Chiaramonte. Although it is now closed for restoration, it is worthwhile visiting the site of this 15th-century castle because of the wonderful views of the coastline from its walls.

Licata ⑭

Road map C4. 🏙 35,000.
FS from Syracuse, Palermo & Catania, via Caltanissetta (0922-774 122). ℹ️ Town hall (0922-868 111).

Licata is one of the chief-market garden towns in southern Sicily. It was built in the Greek period – according to tradition it was founded by the tyrant of Agrigento, Phintias, in 280 BC and was named after him – and under Roman dominion became the port for the shipment of local produce. Evidence of the town's former wealth can be seen in the many rock-hewn Byzantine churches. After the period of Arab rule, in 1234 Frederick II made it part of the public domain, building fortresses which over the centuries have disappeared (Castel Nuovo was destroyed by the Turks at the end of the 1561 siege). Licata again became a part of history on 10 July 1943, when Allied troops landed nearby and advanced northwards in their conquest of Italian territory.

The centre of town life is Piazza Progresso, where there is the art deco **Municipio** or Town Hall, designed in 1935 by Ernesto Basile, which houses some interesting art works, including a statue of the *Madonna and Child* and a 15th-century triptych. Also worth visiting is the **Museo Archeologico**, which has exhibits of prehistoric artifacts from the Palaeolithic to the Bronze Age, archaic Greek (particularly funerary objects) and Hellenistic archaeological finds, and a series of medieval statues representing the Christian virtues. Along Corso Vittorio Emanuele, which leads towards the coast, there are some patrician mansions such as **Palazzo Frangipane**, which has an 18th-century façade decorated with reliefs. On the Corso you can also see the **Chiesa Matrice di Santa Maria la Nova**, which, according to local legend, the Turks tried to burn down in 1553. Founded in the 1500s, it houses a 16th-century crucifix and a 17th-century Flemish Nativity scene. The harbour is almost exclusively given over to fishing boats since the decline of sulphur mining drastically decreased its industrial importance.

🏛 **Museo Archeologico**
Via Dante, Badia di Licata. **Tel** 0922-772 602 ⏰ 8am–8pm Mon–Sat, 8am–1pm Sun.

Castello di Falconara ⑮

Road map D4. ⏰ by appt only.
Tel 0934-347 929.
www.castellodifalconara.it

Not far from Licata, on the road towards Gela, is the village of Falconara, famous most of all for the impressive castle towering above the sea from the top of a rocky bluff. The Castello di Falconara was built in the 15th century. It is usually closed, but you can make an appointment to view with the custodian.

Towards Licata is the Salso river, the second largest in Sicily. Its name derives from the many outcrops of rock salt that make its waters salty (*salso* means saline). The river flows through the Sommatino plateau and down a series of gullies before meandering across the coastal plains.

Castello di Falconara, constructed in the 15th century, set among greenery at the water's edge

Pantelleria 🔟

Road map A5. 👥 *7,800.* 🚢 ✈
ℹ️ *Town hall (0923-695 011); Pro
Loco (0923-911 838).*
www.pantelleria.it

Pantelleria, the largest
island off the Sicilian
coastline, is also closer
to the Tunisian coast
(Capo Mustafà is 70 km
or 44 miles away) than
to Capo Granitola in
Sicily (100 km, 62 miles).
Despite this isolation,
Pantelleria was colonized by
the Phoenicians and then by
the Greeks. It was controlled
by the Arabs for almost 400
years (in fact, its name
derives from *Bent el-Rhia*,
"daughter of the wind") and
was then conquered and
fortified in 1123 by Roger I.
Since that time its history
has run in parallel to the
vicissitudes of Sicily.

The strong wind that blows
here all year round has forced
the inhabitants to protect their
plants and kitchen gardens
with enclosures and walls,
and to prune the olive trees
so that they grow almost horizontally, close to the ground.
Wind is also responsible for
a typical style of building
called *dammuso*, a square,
whitewashed peasant's house
with walls almost 2 m (6 ft)
thick and tiny windows in
order to provide the best
insulation. Water is scarce
on the island, so the roofs of
these homes are shaped to
collect rainwater. The coastal
road is 45 km (28 miles) in
length; it starts at the town of

KEY

🚢 Ferry port

✈ Airport

💢 Viewpoint

▬ Scenic route

═ Major road

Pantelleria and goes
past the **archaeolo-
gical zone of Mursia**
(with a series of
megalithic struc-
tures called *sesi* in
local dialect) and
then goes up to
high ground. The
main sights here are
**Punta Fram, Cala
dell'Altura** and
Punta Tre Pietre, where
another road takes you to the
village of **Scauri**. The coast is
steep and craggy with some
inlets (like the **Balata dei
Turchi,** a favourite landing
place for Saracen pirates,

Walled gardens on Pantelleria

or the lovely **Cala Rotonda**)
up to the **Punta Tracino**
promontory– with a striking
rock formation in front of it –
which separates the **Tramontana** and **Levante inlets**. After
the village of Gadir and the
lighthouse at Punta Spasdillo
the road descends to the **Cala
Cinque Denti** inlet or the
Bagno dell'Acqua hot springs
and then back to its starting
point. The town of **Pantelleria**,
at the foot of the **Barbacane
Castle**, was almost destroyed
by Allied bombings in World
War II. Life revolves around
Piazza Cavour and the new
Chiesa Madre, both facing the
sea. Renting a bicycle is a very
pleasant way of getting to
know the island and the local
way of life, as well as the
handicrafts, the famous *Moscato passito* dessert wine and
the locally grown capers.

Arco dell'Elefante, one of the most beautiful spots in Pantelleria

Map labels: Trapani, PANTELLERIA, Pantelleria, S.Vito, M. Grande 836, Khamma, PANTELLERIA, M. Gibelé 700, Scauri, Cuddia Attalora 560, 0 kilometres 3, 0 miles 3

Baia dei Conigli in Lampedusa, where the rare sea turtle still survives

Lampedusa 🕖

Road map B5. 🏞 *(with Linosa)*
5,200. ⛴ ✈ *0922-970 588.* ℹ
APT Agrigento (0922-401 352);
Consorzio Albergatori 35° Parallelo
(0922-971 906); Pro Loco (0922-971
390). 🎏 *22 Sep.* www.lampedusa.it

The largest island in the
Pelagie (the archipelago that
includes Linosa and the small
island of Lampione), Lam-
pedusa is 200 km (124 miles)
from Sicily and 150 km (93
miles) from Malta. The Greek
name *Pelaghiè* reflects their
chief characteristic – isolation
in the middle of the sea.
Inhabited for a little more
than a century – from the time
Ferdinand II of Bourbon sent
a group of colonists and prisoners there – Lampedusa was
soon deforested, which in turn

brought about the almost total
degradation of the soil and
any possibility of cultivating it.
Human settlements have also
led to a dramatic decrease in
local fauna, and the Baia dei
Conigli nature reserve was set
up to create a safe refuge for
sea turtles *(Caretta caretta)*.
The island's main beaches are
**Cala Maluk, Cala
Croce, Baia dei
Conigli, Cala Galera**
and **Cala Greca**, and
diving is one of the
many popular sports.
Near the town of
Lampedusa (almost
completely destroy-
ed in 1943) is the
**Madonna di Lam-
pedusa Sanctuary,**
where on 22
September the
Bourbon takeover
is commemorated.

Entrance to a
house in Linosa

Linosa 🕗

Road map B5.
🏞 *(with Lampedusa) 5,200.* ⛴
ℹ *APT Agrigento (0922-401 352);*
Consorzio Albergatori 35° Parallelo
(0922-971 906).

Ancient Aethusa, 40 km
(25 miles) from Lampedusa,
is a small volcanic
island where life
centres around the
village of Linosa,
with its brightly
coloured houses.
Thanks to the natur-
ally fertile volcanic
soil, agriculture
thrives on the island.
One of the best ways
of exploring Linosa
is by leaving the
road behind and
rambling around the craters
and the fenced-in fields.

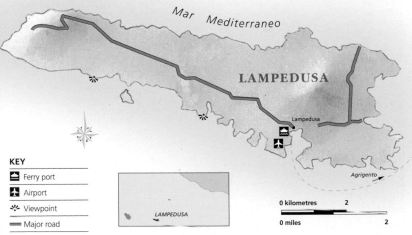

Mar Mediterraneo

LAMPEDUSA

Lampedusa

Agrigento

KEY

⛴ Ferry port

✈ Airport

🔆 Viewpoint

▬ Major road

LAMPEDUSA

0 kilometres   2

0 miles   2

Caltanissetta ⑲

Road map D3. 🏛 *61,000.* 🚉 *from Catania & Palermo (095-532 719).* 🛈 *Corso Vittorio Emanuele 109 (0934-530 403).* **www.**aapit.cl.it

One of the earliest traces of a settlement in this area is the **Badia di Santo Spirito**, a Norman abbey commissioned by Roger I and his wife Adelasia in the late 11th century and consecrated in 1153. It is still one of the most interesting sights in Caltanissetta and its immediate vicinity. In common with other hill towns in the interior, Caltanissetta was surrounded by medieval walls and then expanded towards the monasteries, built around the city from the 15th century on. The centre of a thriving mineral-rich area, it became prosperous after the unification of Italy thanks to the **sulphur and rock salt mines**. It was during this period that the look of the town changed with the construction of buildings and public works. In the heart of town, in Piazza Garibaldi, are the Baroque **San Sebastiano** and the **Cathedral** (dedicated to Santa Maria la Nova and San Michele). A brief walk down

The Baroque façade of San Sebastiano, completed in the 1800s

Corso Umberto I will take you to **Sant'Agata** – or Chiesa del Collegio – built in 1605 for the Jesuits of Caltanissetta, next to their seminary. The rich decoration inside includes a marble statue of *St Ignatius in Glory* on the left-hand transept altar, the altarpiece *San Francesco Saverio* in a side chapel and a canvas of the *Martyrdom of Sant'Agata*. Not far from the **Castello di Pietrarossa**, probably a former Arab fortress, is the **Museo Archeologico**, where the sections are given over exclusively to archaeology and modern art.

The **Museo Mineralogico, Paleontologico e della Zolfara**, established by the local Mineralogy School, has a fine and extensive collection of minerals and fossils.

🔒 Badia di Santo Spirito
Tel 0934-566 596.
◯ 9am–12:30pm, 4–7pm daily.

🏛 Museo Archeologico
Contrada Santo Spirito. *Tel* 0934-567 062. ◯ 9am–1pm, 3:30–7pm daily. ◯ last Mon of month. 📷

🏛 Museo Mineralogico
Tel 0934-591 280.
◯ 9am–1pm Mon–Sat.

Environs

About 5 km (3 miles) along the main road to Enna is the site of the ancient city of **Sabucina**, where you can see a prehistoric village and cave tombs dating from the 12th–10th centuries BC. The city became a Greek colony, but subsequently declined and was later abandoned.

The Badia di Santo Spirito, one of the major Norman churches in Sicily

EASTER WEEK

In the interior of Sicily the celebrations of the *Misteri*, or statues of the Stations of the Cross, during Easter Week, are of the greatest importance. At Enna they begin on Palm Sunday. For four days, the 15 city confraternities take part in processions through the streets to the Cathedral; on Good Friday a huge torchlit procession bears the statue of the Madonna of the Seven Griefs, the Reliquary of Christ's Thorn and the Dead Christ's Urn through the city; then on Easter Sunday the Resurrected Christ and the Virgin Mary statues meet in Piazza Duomo. At Caltanissetta, celebrations begin on Wednesday with the Procession of the Holy Sacrament, followed by the representatives of the 11 city confraternities. On Maundy Thursday the large statues of the Passion of Christ are taken through the city and on Good Friday the Passion of the Black Christ ends the celebrations.

Part of the colourful
Easter Week celebrations

⋔ Sabucina
Tel 0934-566 982. ◯ *9am–1pm, 4:30–7pm daily.* ● *last Mon of the month.* 🎟

⛏ The Sulphur Mines
ℹ *Ente Parco Minerario Floristella, Grottacalda (0935-958 105).*

For centuries the Floristella sulphur field was one of the most important sources of wealth in the Sicilian hinterland. Mining activity ceased in 1988 and the mines are closed to the public, but now work is under way to turn this yellow-stained land into a mining park. Extraction reached its height during the 19th century – when Palazzo Pennisi, the residence of the mine owners, was built.

Enna ⑳

Road map D3. 🏠 *30,000.* **FS** *from Catania and Palermo (0935-500 91 10).* ℹ *AAPIT, Via Roma 411 (0935-528 288); AST, Piazza Colaianni 6 (0935-500 875).* **www**.apt-enna.com

A mountain town – at 931 m (3,054 ft) the highest provincial capital in Italy – in antiquity Enna was first Greek, then Carthaginian and finally Roman. It remained a Byzantine stronghold even after the Arab conquest of Palermo, and was then conquered by general Al-Abbas Ibn Fadhl in 859 and was wrested from the Muslims only in 1087. From that time it was repeatedly fortified around the strongholds of Castello di

Enna Cathedral, built in the 15th century and rebuilt after a fire

The Castello di Lombardia, built over an Arab fortification

Lombardia and Castello Vecchio (present-day Torre di Federico). The defensive walls, no longer visible, were the basis of the city's plan, while all the principal sites of religious and civic power were constructed on what is now Via Roma. Because of its altitude, Enna has a climate unique in the interior of Sicily and even during summer the temperature is pleasant. The town's exceptional position means splendid views. Going up Via Roma, you first come to Piazza Vittorio Emanuele, site of **San Francesco d'Assisi**, the only original part of which is the fine 15th-century bell tower. In Piazza Colajanni you will see the façade of **Palazzo Pollicarini**, which has many Catalan Gothic features on the side next to the stairway, as well as the former church of **Santa Chiara**.

In 1307 Eleonora, wife of Frederick II of Aragon, founded the **Cathedral** of Enna. The building was destroyed by fire in the mid-1400s and subsequently rebuilt. A fine 16th-century doorway – with a bas-relief depicting *St Martin and the Beggar* – leads to the Latin cross interior with two aisles. The cathedral is richly decorated with an assortment of statues and paintings.

The "Madonna's Crown", Museo Alessi in Enna

Just past the Gothic apse are the rooms housing the **Museo Alessi**, which includes the Cathedral Treasury with its candelabra and vestments, a fine collection of coins and an art gallery featuring *St John the Baptist*, part of a 16th-century wooden triptych.

Almost directly opposite the entrance of the Museo Alessi is the **Museo Archeologico**, with a fine display of prehistoric, Greek and Roman archaeological items found in the city, in the area around and near Lake Pergusa. But the pride and joy of Enna are its two fortresses. The **Castello di Lombardia**, built by the Hohenstaufens and altered in the Aragonese era, is one of the grandest in Sicily. A tour here includes the three courtyards, the Torre Pisana and the Rocca di Cerere. In the public gardens is the octagonal **Torre di Federico II**, the only remaining part of the original defences.

🏛 Museo Alessi
Tel 0935-503 165. ◯ *8am–8pm.* 🎟
🏛 Museo Archeologico
Tel 0935-507 611. ◯ *9am–1 hr before sunset.* 🎟
♜ Castello di Lombardia
Tel 0935-500 962. ◯ *8am–8pm.*
♜ Torre di Federico II
◯ *9am–7pm.*

Morgantina ㉑

Situated about 4 km (2 miles) from Aidone, the ancient city of Morgantina was founded by the Morgeti, a population from Latium who settled here around 1000 BC. The city was then occupied by Greek colonists. Its golden age, when the city was a strategic trade centre between the north and south of Sicily, was in the Hellenistic and Roman periods. From the top of the hill visitors have a fine view of what remains of the theatre, the city streets and the agora. The coins of Morgantina and the Venus of Morgantina, which were looted and sold to US museums, will finally be returned in 2012.

The Gymnasium
This was a large area for athletic exercises, with baths (in the photo), dressing rooms and rooms with equipment for the athletes.

RECONSTRUCTION OF MORGANTINA

This drawing shows the city as it appeared around 300 BC. The reconstruction is based on studies made by archaeologists from Princeton University in the United States.

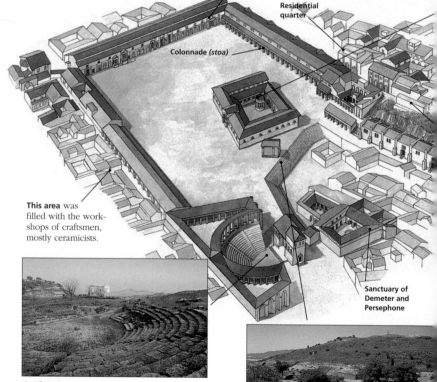

Residential quarter

Colonnade *(stoa)*

This area was filled with the workshops of craftsmen, mostly ceramicists.

Sanctuary of Demeter and Persephone

★ **Theatre**
Constructed at the end of the 4th century BC, the theatre at Morgantina was carved out of the slope of a hill and could seat about a thousand spectators.

0 metres   50

0 yards   50

★ **Agora**
Unusually, the agora, or forum, was divided into two parts, one above the other linked by a trapezoidal, 14-step stairway.

For hotels and restaurants in this region see pp201–2 and pp216–17

The Market
*This lay in the middle of the
upper agora. Above is the
tholos, a round structure
which had a number of
different functions.*

Street Paving
*In the eastern residential
quarter, the remains of the
paved street leading out of
the city walls are still visible.*

Piazza Armerina ㉒

Road map D4. 🏛 21,000. ⓘ AAST,
Piazza Armerina, Via Muscara
Generale. **Tel** 0935-680 201.
🎪 Palio dei Normanni (13–14 Aug).

In the middle of an area
inhabited since the 8th
century BC, Piazza Armerina
developed in the Middle
Ages, a period marked by
frequent clashes between the
local population – strongly
influenced by the centuries of
Arab domination – and the
Latin conquerors. After the
huge devastation wrought in
the 12th century by battles
between these two factions,
Piazza Armerina was
recreated around the Colle
Mira hill (in the middle of the
present-day Monte quarter)
and was populated by a
colony of Lombards from
Piacenza. A new, massive
defensive wall system was
built in the late 14th century,
but the city soon spread
well beyond this into the
surrounding hills and slopes.

In the heart of town is
a large **Aragonese Castle**,
built by King Martin I in
the late 14th century, whose
massive towers dominate the
Cathedral. Dedicated to Our
Lady of the Assumption, the
Cathedral is flanked by the
campanile of another church
which had been built on the
same site in the 14th century.
Inside, look out for the choir,
built in 1627, and a wooden
crucifix painted in the late
15th century. The Cathedral
also affords access to the
small **Museo Diocesano**,

**The Cathedral at Piazza Armerina,
with its 14th-century bell tower**

which has vestments,
monstrances and reliquaries
on display. Elsewhere in
the town are many other
interesting attractions. **Piazza
Garibaldi** is the heart of town
life, boasting the Baroque
Palazzo del Senato and two
palatial mansions belonging
to the barons of Capodarso.
The whole of the historic
centre deserves further
exploration on foot, through
charming medieval alleys,
steps and lanes.

Not far from town, at the
end of Via Tasso, is the
**Chiesa del Priorato di
Sant'Andrea**, founded in
1096 and then acquired by
the Knights of the Order of
the Holy Sepulchre. This
magnificent example of
Sicilian Romanesque architecture has a commanding
view over a valley. Do not
miss seeing the series of
12th- to 14th-century frescoes
in the interior (visits are
allowed only on Sundays,
when mass is celebrated).

View of Piazza Armerina, which developed around the Colle Mira hill

Piazza Armerina: Villa del Casale

This famous villa was part of a 3rd-4th century AD estate, and is one of the most fascinating attractions in archaeologically rich Sicily. The exceptionally beautiful mosaics that decorated every one of the rooms of the landowner's apartments have been preserved through the centuries, thanks to a flood that buried them in mud in the 12th century. The villa was discovered in the late 19th century. A logical sequence for a visit to the site is as follows: the thermae, the large peristyle, the long corridor with hunting scenes and, lastly, the owners' private apartments.

Autumn, from the Hall of the Seasons

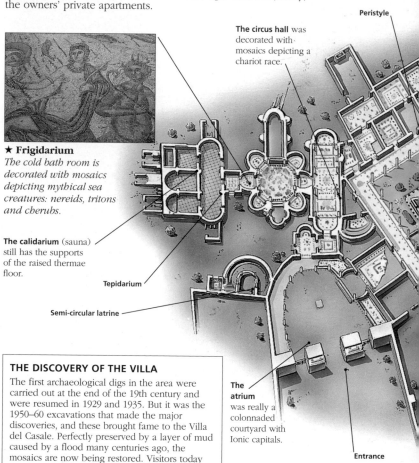

Peristyle

The circus hall was decorated with mosaics depicting a chariot race.

★ Frigidarium
The cold bath room is decorated with mosaics depicting mythical sea creatures: nereids, tritons and cherubs.

The calidarium (sauna) still has the supports of the raised thermae floor.

Tepidarium

Semi-circular latrine

The atrium was really a colonnaded courtyard with Ionic capitals.

Entrance

THE DISCOVERY OF THE VILLA

The first archaeological digs in the area were carried out at the end of the 19th century and were resumed in 1929 and 1935. But it was the 1950–60 excavations that made the major discoveries, and these brought fame to the Villa del Casale. Perfectly preserved by a layer of mud caused by a flood many centuries ago, the mosaics are now being restored. Visitors today may come across expert archaeologists working on the tesserae of what have been called "the most exceptional Roman mosaics in the world".

The exterior of the Villa del Casale

STAR FEATURES

* ★ Frigidarium

* ★ Hall of the Female Gymnasts in Bikinis

* ★ Corridor with Hunting Scenes

* ★ The Myth of Arion

★ **Corridor with Hunting Scenes**
This passageway contains splendid mosaics representing wild game hunting. Ferocious beasts such as boar and lions are being loaded onto ships after capture.

Northern Area
The vestibule in the private apartments of the villa has a large mosaic depicting Ulysses and Polyphemus.

0 metres	10
0 yards	10

★ **The Myth of Arion**
In the colonnaded semicircular atrium the mosaic shows Arion saved by a dolphin and surrounding him are female figures, sea creatures and cupids.

Aqueduct

★ **Hall of the Female Gymnasts in Bikinis**
The ten gymnasts seen in the mosaics in this hall are a rare and precious record of the Roman fashions of the time.

Triclinium
The mosaics in the dining room feature the Labours of Hercules and other mythological subjects.

SOUTHERN SICILY

ominated by Mount Etna, southern Sicily's permanent backdrop, this area is a curious mixture of fertile land and intensive cultivation, ancient monuments and utter neglect. Many towns and monuments built by the ancient Greeks still survive, most notably in the town of Syracuse, birthplace of Archimedes.

Southern Sicily, which the Arabs called the Val di Noto, presents another facet of Sicily. It is very different from the western end of the island, although the topography is equally varied. The latter has Phoenician Palermo, the former Greek Syracuse. One of Sicily's most important sights is the stony-tiered Greek theatre in Syracuse. The tradition of performing ancient Greek plays was revived in 1914, and now every other summer the great works of the ancient tragedians come to life in their natural setting. This part of Sicily is also home to the ancient Greek ruins of Megara Hyblaea, now sadly dominated by the landscape of the refineries of Augusta.

Inland, the rebuilding of towns following the earthquake of 1693 has resulted in a number of Baroque gems. The churches, buildings and balconies of Ragusa, Modica, Scicli, Noto and Chiaramonte are a triumph of the Sicilian Baroque style, with their majestic steps, detailed ornamentation and curving façades. Ibla, the medieval quarter of Ragusa, should be included on a tour of the towns of the interior: rocky Caltagirone is an important ceramics centre, and Chiaramonte and Vizzini also have their charms. In complete contrast you can also experience the natural silence of the rock-cut necropolises in the cliffs of Ispica and Pantalica.

Fishing boats anchored in Ortygia harbour in Syracuse

◁ The majestic Baroque portal of Ragusa Cathedral, dedicated to St John the Baptist

Exploring Southern Sicily

An excellent starting point for any visit to Sicily's southern tip is Syracuse, with its exceptional artistic and cultural heritage. It lies about 60 km (37 miles) from Catania airport and is a two-hour drive from Messina, along a scenic route with the Ionian Sea to your left and Mount Etna to your right. Other popular sights in this area are the old cities in the interior – those in Val di Noto (Caltagirone, Modica, Noto, Palazzolo Acreide, Ragusa and Scicli, along with Militello Val di Catania and Catania itself) have all been named UNESCO World Heritage sites. The mountains conceal an impressive testimony to the ancient history of southern Sicily in the crevices of Pantalica, Ispica and Lentini.

Ceramic plate produced in Caltagirone

SIGHTS AT A GLANCE

Augusta ⑰
Caltagirone pp154–5 ⑭
Capo Passero ④
Cava d'Ispica ⑤
Chiaramonte Gulfi ⑪
Gela ⑩
Lentini ⑮
Megara Hyblaea ⑯
Modica ⑧
Noto pp144–7 ②
Pachino ③

Palazzolo Acreide ⑬
Pantalica ⑱
Ragusa pp150–51 ⑦
Scicli ⑥
Syracuse pp136–43 ①
Vittoria ⑨
Vizzini ⑫

KEY

===	Motorway
===	Major road
—	Secondary road
===	Minor road
= =	Road under construction
—·—	Main railway
—	Minor railway

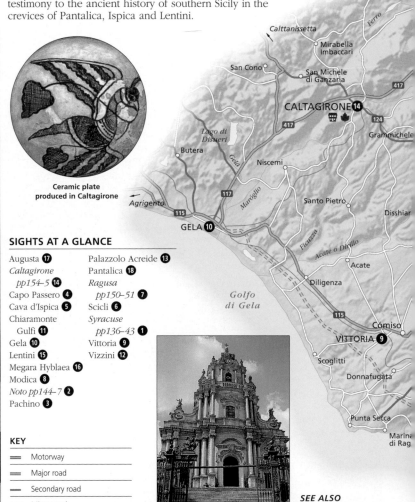

Calttanissetta

○ Mirabella Imbaccari

San Cono ○

San Michele di Ganzaria

CALTAGIRONE ⑭

417

124

Grammichele

Lago di Disueri

Butera ○

Niscemi ○

Santo Pietro ○

Disshiar

Agrigento

117

115

GELA ⑩

Acate o Dirillo

Acate ○

Diligenza ○

Golfo di Gela

115

Cómiso ○

VITTORIA ⑨

Scoglitti ○

Donnafugata ○

Punta Secca ○

Marina di Rag

The Baroque façade of the Basilica di San Giorgio in Ragusa

SEE ALSO

• *Where to Stay* pp202–3
• *Where to Eat* pp217–18

GETTING THERE

There are two ways of getting to the interior of southern Sicily. You can either take road SS115 connecting Syracuse and Gela – passing through Noto, Ispica, Modica and Ragusa – opting for detours if you wish, or go up to Catania and follow motorway A19 to Enna, or A18 to Syracuse. Syracuse can also be reached by train.

View of Ortygia, an island that is part of Syracuse

Gornalunga
Ramacca — 417
Piana di Catania
Catania
194
Palagonia
385
Scordia
Militello
Mineo
Francofonte
Licodia Eubea
Lago di Diriillo
194
12 VIZZINI
124
Buccheri
Ferla
Monterosso Almo
Buscemi
Giarratana
11 CHIARAMONTE GULFI
194
Lago di Rosalia
Casa Nobile
7 RAGUSA
MODICA 8
115
5 CAVA D'ISPICA
Grande
Rosolini
6 SCICLI
Ispica
onnalucata
Sampieri
Pozzallo
Punta Religione
15 LENTINI
Carlentini
Agnone Bagni
114
Golfo di Catania
Capo Campolato
Capo Santa Croce
193
17 AUGUSTA
MEGARA HYBLAEA 16
Golfo di Augusta
Sortino
Melilli
Penisola Magnisi
18 PANTALICA
Anapo
Solarino
124
Floridia
Castello Euríalo
1 SYRACUSE
Ortygia
13 PALAZZOLO ACREIDE
Canicattini Bagni
287
Cassibile
115
Ognina
Noto Antica
Avola
NOTO 2
Calabernardo
Tellaro
Golfo di Noto
Marzamemi
PACHINO 3
Portopalo di Capo Passero
Isola Capo Passero
CAPO PASSERO 4
Capo delle Correnti
Isola delle Correnti

0 kilometres   10
0 miles   10

Syracuse ●

Goddess, Museo Archeologico

For 27 centuries the city of Syracuse, in modern Italian, Siracusa, has been of great economic and cultural importance. From the prehistoric populations to the Corinthians who founded the Greek city, to the introduction of Baroque architecture, the history of Syracuse is an open book, clearly visible in many streets and buildings. The Greek theatre survives in good condition, and you can still see the stone quarries, or Latomie, which provided stone for many of the ancient monuments, but also served as prisons.

Entrance to the Orecchio di Dioniso, in the Latomie area

⛩ The Neapolis Archaeological Zone

Viale Paradiso. **Tel** 0931-66206.
⬜ 9am–6pm daily. ⬛ Mon. 📷

The Neapolis Archaeological Zone was established in 1955 with the aim of grouping the antiquities of Syracuse within one site, enabling visitors to make an uninterrupted tour of the city's most remote past. Not far from the ticket office for the park is medieval **San Nicolò dei Cordari**, built over a reservoir (*piscina*) cut out of the rock, which was used for cleaning the nearby Roman amphitheatre.

⛩ Greek Theatre

See pp138–9.

🎭 Latomie

A huge hollow separates the theatre area and the southern section of the archaeological site. This is the area of the Latomie – stone quarries – from which Syracuse architects extracted millions of cubic metres of stone for building. The enormous caves were also used as prisons for centuries. The Ear of Dionysius (**Orecchio di Dioniso**), is one of the most impressive

quarries. According to legend, thanks to the extraordinary acoustics of this cave, the local tyrant Dionysius could hear the whispers of his most dangerous prisoners and take

SYRACUSE

Key to Symbols see back flap

0 metres 600
0 yards 600

The large Grotta dei Cordari, the most interesting of the Latomie caves

due precautions. There are other huge adjacent caves, such as the **Grotta dei Cordari**, which until recently was used by local rope makers *(cordari)*, the **Latomia Intagliatella** and the **Latomia Santa Venera**.

🏛 Tomb of Archimedes

In the northwestern corner of the Neapolis site there is an area that was used as a burial ground until the Hellenistic era. This is known as the **Necropoli Grotticelli**. One of the largest tombs here is traditionally called the **Tomb of Archimedes**. Archimedes was a native of Syracuse and one of the greatest scientists in antiquity *(see p28)*.

🏛 Altar of Hieron II and Roman Amphitheatre

These lie on the other side of the road that cuts the Neapolis area in two. Although only the foundations remain of the **Altar of Hieron II**, its impressive size (198 x 23 m, 649 x 75 ft) is clear. This monument was dedicated to Zeus and was used for public sacrifices, in which as many as 400 bulls were put to death at one time.

A huge public work undertaken in the early years of the Empire, the **Roman Amphitheatre** (outer diameter, 140 x 119 m, 459 x 390 ft) is only slightly smaller than the Arena in Verona. The walls in the interior were part of the underground section, used to house the stage scenery. Beneath the tiers were corridors through which the gladiators and wild beasts entered the arena.

🏛 Museo Archeologico Regionale
See pp140–41.

🏛 Catacombs of San Giovanni Evangelista
Viadi San Giovanni. **Tel** *0931-646 94.*
⏱ *Apr–Oct: 9.30am noon, 2:30–
4:30pm; May–Jun: 9:30am–1pm,
2:30–5:30pm; Jul–Aug: 9:30am–
1:30pm, 2:30-6pm.*

This underground complex – which dates back to 360–315 BC – housed hundreds of loculi, or rooms, which were used to bury the followers of the new Christian religion in Roman times.

The main gallery of the catacombs leads to a series of round chapels that still bear traces of frescoes.

🏛 Museo del Papiro
Viale Teocrito 66. **Tel** *0931-616 16.*
⏱ *9am–2pm.* ⬤ *Mon.*

This museum is devoted to the *Cyperus papyrus* plant. The largest European colony of the papyrus plant thrives on the banks of the Ciane river near Syracuse.

The stepped base of the Altar of Hieron II, giving an idea of the impressive size of the original sacrificial site

Syracuse:The Greek Theatre

This is one of the most important examples of
ancient theatre architecture anywhere, and for
centuries it was the centre of Syracusan life.
The Greek theatre was a much more complex
construction than today's ruins might indicate;
in 1520–31, Emperor Charles V had much of
the stone transported to build the walls around
Ortygia *(see pp142–3)*. Designed in the 5th
century BC by the Greek architect Damacopos,
the theatre was enlarged in the 3rd and 2nd
centuries BC by Hieron II. From the 5th
century BC onwards, the great Greek
playwrights, including Aeschylus who pre-
miered some of his tragedies here, wrote and
staged their works in this magnificent setting.

Votive Niches
*To the west of the grotto near the ancient
colonnade, the wall is punctuated by
a series of rectangular niches that might
have housed votive paintings or tablets
in honour of Syracusan heroes.*

Grotta del Museion
*This cave, hewn out
of the rock wall above
the theatre, has a
rectangular basin where
the aqueduct flowed.*

**The *cavea*
(auditorium) is**
over 138 m (453 ft)
wide with 67 tiers,
divided into 10
vertical blocks (or
"wedges"). Each block
was served by a flight
of steps and was
indicated by a letter, a
custom that survives in
modern theatres today.

The diazoma
divided the
auditorium into
two parts.

Classical Greek Theatre
*In even-numbered years, the Greek
theatre in Syracuse hosts a summer
programme of classical theatre.*

Galleries
Called criptae, *the galleries were cut out of the rock in the Roman period to replace the more ancient passageways of the* cavea, *which had been removed to create more seating space.*

The stage area was greatly enlarged in the Roman period.

Two enormous pillars of rock stood either side of the stage area.

| 0 metres | 10 |
| 0 yards | 10 |

On the orchestra was a monument to Dionysus, around which the chorus acted, danced and sang.

Logo of the Syracuse INDA

THE ISTITUTO NAZIONALE DEL DRAMMA ANTICO

On 16 April 1914, the tradition of performing ancient Greek theatre was revived at Syracuse, and now a season of plays first performed here over 2,500 years ago is put on every year in May/June. The Istituto Nazionale del Dramma Antico (National Institute of Ancient Drama) was set up in 1925. The Scuola Professionale di Teatro Antico (Professional School of Ancient Theatre) joined as partners in 1983.

Playbill of Aeschylus' *Libation Bearers* **designed by Duilio Cambellotti (1921)**

Syracuse: Museo Archeologico Regionale

6th–5th-century BC theatre mask

Founded in 1967 (and opened to the public in 1988), in order to establish a proper home for the enormous quantity of material excavated from digs throughout southeastern Sicily, the Regional Archaeological Museum is divided into three main sections with over 18,000 pieces on display. The museum is named after the eminent archaeologist Paolo Orsi, head of the Antiquities Department of Sicily from 1888, who was instrumental in fostering interest in the island's past and was personally responsible for many important excavations and discoveries. The collections named after him have been reorganized since the museum moved from its Ortygia site.

Syracuse

Megara
Hyblaea

★ **Funerary Statue**
*This came from the digs
at Megara Hyblaea,
dating from 560–550
BC. The inscription on
the right thigh shows it
was dedicated to the
physician Sambroditas.*

Chalcidian
colonies

Protohistory

Prehistory

Prehistory

GUIDE TO THE MUSEUM
*The museum is divided into three sections.
Section A features the geological history of
Sicily and then the prehistoric, protohistoric
and Siculan cultures. Section B is given over to
the Greek colonies, and includes the Landolina
Venus and the friezes from the Temple of
Apollo. Last, Section C has material from the
subcolonies founded by the Syracusans in
663–598 BC and from digs in the Hellenized
towns in the interior. Finds from Gela and
Agrigento complete the exhibition.*

Prehistory

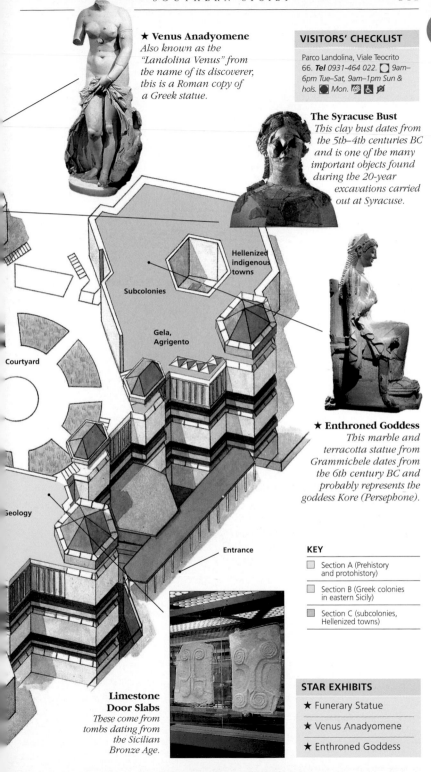

★ **Venus Anadyomene**
*Also known as the
"Landolina Venus" from
the name of its discoverer,
this is a Roman copy of
a Greek statue.*

VISITORS' CHECKLIST

Parco Landolina, Viale Teocrito
66. *Tel* 0931-464 022. ⬜ 9am–
6pm Tue–Sat, 9am–1pm Sun &
hols. ⬤ Mon. 📷 ♿ 🚫

The Syracuse Bust
*This clay bust dates from
the 5th–4th centuries BC
and is one of the many
important objects found
during the 20-year
excavations carried
out at Syracuse.*

Hellenized
indigenous
towns

Subcolonies

Gela,
Agrigento

Courtyard

Geology

★ **Enthroned Goddess**
*This marble and
terracotta statue from
Grammichele dates from
the 6th century BC and
probably represents the
goddess Kore (Persephone).*

Entrance

KEY

⬜ Section A (Prehistory
and protohistory)

⬜ Section B (Greek colonies
in eastern Sicily)

⬜ Section C (subcolonies,
Hellenized towns)

**Limestone
Door Slabs**
*These come from
tombs dating from
the Sicilian
Bronze Age.*

STAR EXHIBITS

★ Funerary Statue

★ Venus Anadyomene

★ Enthroned Goddess

Syracuse: Exploring Ortygia

The island of Ortygia has always been the focal point
of Syracuse. A stronghold until the end of the 19th
century, it separates the city's two harbours (connected
by the dock canal). Ortygia (in Italian, Ortigia) is now
linked to the mainland by the Umbertino bridge. The
town's long history is visible in many buildings, going
back as far the 6th-century BC Temple of Apollo.

Façade of Palazzo Beneventano del
Bosco, opposite the Cathedral

🗺 Lungomare di Levante

This is the promenade that
overlooks the **Porto Piccolo**,
or small port, and is still the
maritime heart of town. By
going southwards along the
promenade you reach **Spirito
Santo**, with an 18th-century
façade dramatically facing the
sea. This church was the seat
of the Holy Spirit Confra-
ternity, hence its name.

⌂ Temple of Apollo

A good part of Piazza Pancali,
as you enter Ortygia, consists
of the ruins of the Temple of
Apollo, which were
discovered in 1860 inside the
old Spanish barracks. The
temple was built in the early
6th century BC, which makes
it the oldest extant Doric
temple in Western Europe.
It is of an imposing size –
58 x 24 m (190 x 79 ft). On
the top step of the base, an
inscription to Apollo provides
proof that the building was
dedicated to the god. Over
the centuries the temple has
served as a Byzantine church,
a mosque, again a Christian
church under the Normans,
and a military stronghold.

🏛 Palazzo Greco

On Corso Matteotti, an avenue
created by demolition during
the Fascist era, only one old
building has survived: Palazzo
Greco, founded in the mid-
14th century and now serving
as the home of the Istituto
Nazionale del Dramma
Antico *(see p139)*. It has a
lovely Gothic double lancet
window and a loggia.

🏛 Palazzo Beneventano
del Bosco

Piazza Duomo is home to
Palazzo Beneventano del
Bosco, built in 1779 by
architect Luciano Alì. The
façade, with
its doorway
supporting
a lovely
balcony, is
an impressive
sight. The interior
is also interesting;
a broad staircase
leads up to the
private apartments
filled with
Venetian furniture, where
Admiral Horatio Nelson
and King Ferdinand III of
Bourbon once stayed.

Decorative coat of arms
on the Duomo façade

⚲ Duomo

Piazza Duomo. **Tel** *0931-65328.*
⧗ *7:30am–8pm.*

In Piazza Duomo, next to the
Palazzo del Senato, now the
Town Hall, is the city's
Cathedral, built in 1728–53.
It was designed by Andrea
Palma, and incorporates an
ancient Temple of Minerva,
which in turn had been built
over the site
of a 6th-
century BC
monument,
which Gelon
had dedicated to
Athena. The intact
ancient structures
can be best seen
by skirting the
outer northern
side of the church,
where a series of massive
columns from the temple
are clearly visible. Initially a
temple, and then a Christian

The ruins of the Temple of Apollo, in the heart of Ortygia

The Baroque façade of the Duomo, designed by Andrea Palma (1728–53)

church, the building became a Muslim mosque and finally a glorious example of Sicilian Baroque religious architecture. The Duomo contains a 13th-century font, Norman era mosaics, and many fine paintings and sculptures. The sacristy has 16 wooden choir stalls carved in 1489.

🏛 Galleria Regionale di Palazzo Bellomo
Via Capodieci. *Tel* 0931-695 11 or 653 43. ◯ 9am–7pm Tue–Sat, 9am–1:30pm Sun. 📷
This museum, housed in the **Parisio** and **Bellomo** palazzi, has both interesting architecture (much of the original Hohenstaufen construction still stands) and artworks on display. The first rooms contain medieval and Renaissance sculpture. The courtyard, decorated with coats of arms, leads to the first floor, with the jewel of the collection, Antonello da Messina's *Annunciation* (1474, see p23). In the next room is a display of Christmas cribs. The exhibition ends with Arab and Sicilian ceramics and jewels.

🏛 Fonte Aretusa
On Largo Aretusa, facing the **Porto Grande**, the waters of this spring still gush just as they did in Greek times. According to the myth made famous by Pindar and Virgil, Arethusa was a nymph transformed into a spring by the goddess Artemis.

🔒 San Filippo Apostolo
In the heart of the Giudecca – the Jewish quarter of Syracuse – is **San Filippo Apostolo**, which was built over the old synagogue. In the crypt you can still see the basin of holy water in which the Jewish women purified themselves.

🏛 Palazzo Margulensi-Montalto
A stone's throw from central **Piazza Archimede**, with the 19th-century **Fountain of Artemis**, a walk along Via Montalto takes you to Palazzo Margulensi-Montalto, one of the most interesting medieval buildings in Syracuse. Built in 1397, this palazzo still features some original elements: the Gothic windows of the façade supported by spiral columns, the staircase and the arcade.

♟ Castello Maniace
Tel 0931-464 420
◯ 9:30am–1:30pm Tue–Sat. 📷
This castle is on the southern tip of Ortygia, where tradition says the temple of Hera and the villa of the Roman governor once stood. It was built by Frederick II in the 1200s and over the centuries had various functions: royal residence, fortress and even storehouse. The name derives from the Byzantine general Maniakes, who took the city from the Arabs.

Environs
On the hill overlooking the city is the main work of military architecture in the Greek world, the **Castello Eurialo** (currently being restored), built by Dionysius the Elder in 402 BC to protect Syracuse. Two rock-cut moats and a tower protected the fortress on the eastern side, a 15-m (49-ft) keep was built in the middle of the fortification, and the towers overlooked the sea.

🏰 Castello Eurialo
Frazione Belvedere, 8 km (5 miles) from Syracuse. *Tel* 0931-711 773. ◯ 9am–6pm daily (to 5pm in winter, to 7pm in summer).

The ruins of the extensive Castello Eurialo

Street-by-Street: Noto ❷

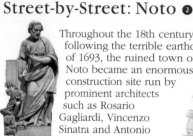

Throughout the 18th century, following the terrible earthquake of 1693, the ruined town of Noto became an enormous construction site run by prominent architects such as Rosario Gagliardi, Vincenzo Sinatra and Antonio Mazza. Today Noto's

Sculpture in the Cathedral

magnificent Baroque architecture is unique in Sicily, despite an unmistakable air of decay. However, substantial restoration work started after the town was named a UNESCO World Heritage site. Soon, Noto's Baroque buildings will be revealed in all their glory.

Palazzo Nicolaci

Montevergine church

Palazzo Astuto lies behind the Cathedral.

VIA CAVOUR

VIA ROCCO PIRRI

VIA CORRADO NICOLACI

VIA A. DE BRESCIA

VIA SILVIO SPAVENT

CO

VIA DUCEZIO

★ **Cathedral**
Dedicated to San Nicolò, the Cathedral looks down on three flights of steps. The cupola collapsed in 1996.

Palazzo Landolina (Sant'Alfano)

★ **San Carlo al Corso**
Formally called San Carlo Borromeo, this church contains paintings and frescoes attributed to Carasi.

Palazzo Ducezio
This building, now the Town Hall, stands opposite the Cathedral. The façade, with its lovely round arches, has been described as "a triumph of columns".

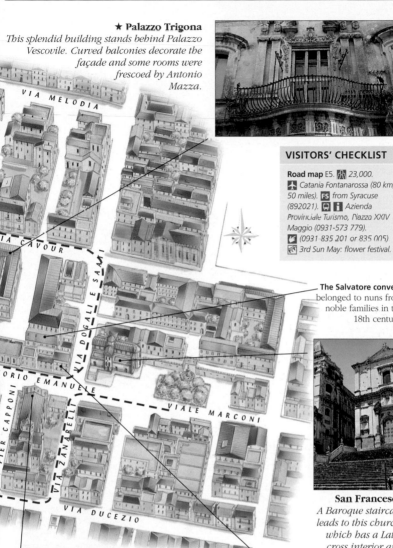

★ Palazzo Trigona
This splendid building stands behind Palazzo Vescovile. Curved balconies decorate the façade and some rooms were frescoed by Antonio Mazza.

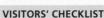

The Salvatore convent
belonged to nuns from noble families in the 18th century.

San Francesco
A Baroque staircase leads to this church, which has a Latin cross interior and an aisleless nave.

Museo Civico

Santa Chiara
The church was designed by Rosario Gagliardi. It is built on an oval plan and is richly decorated. This 19th-century altarpiece of San Benedetto and Santa Scolastica is by the Palermo artist Lo Forte.

KEY

– – – Suggested route

STAR SIGHTS

★ Cathedral

★ San Carlo al Corso

★ Palazzo Trigona

0 metres		70
0 yards		70

Exploring Noto

The heart of the town is the main avenue, modern Viale Marconi, which becomes Corso Vittorio Emanuele at the monumental Porta Reale (or Ferdinandea) city gate, and passes through Piazza XXIV Maggio, Piazza Municipio (a good starting point for a visit) and Piazza XXX Ottobre. Steps lead to the upper town, with marvellous views of the landscape around.

The Cathedral prior to 1996

The Cathedral after the collapse

🔒 Cathedral

In the winter of 1996, a loud rumble signalled the collapse of the Cathedral cupola, leaving a noticeable scar in the heart of Noto. It was a great loss to Sicilian Baroque art. The church was originally completed in 1776, and dedicated to San Nicolò. It stands at the end of a spectacular three-flight staircase designed by Paolo Labisi, the façade bearing twin bell towers and a bronze portal. The interior has a wealth of frescoes and other decoration, especially in the side chapels. The Cathedral has now been brought back to its former splendour following restoration.

🏛 Palazzo Ducezio

Tue–Sun.
This palazzo, which stands opposite the Cathedral, was built in 1746 by Vincenzo Sinatra. The façade is decorated with an impressive series of columns. In the interior, which now houses the town hall offices, there is a huge drawing room decorated in the French Louis XV style, with gold and stucco decorative elements and a fine fresco on the vault by Antonio Mazza.

🏛 Museo Civico

Corso Vittorio Emanuele 34. **Tel** 0931-836 462. ◯ 9am–1pm, 3:30–7:30pm Tue–Sun.
The Civic Museum (some rooms of which are closed for restoration) features ancient and medieval material from the old town, Noto Antica, and from many nearby places.

🔒 San Francesco

◯ 8:30am–12:30pm, 4:30–6:30pm.
On the wide stretch of Piazza XXX Ottobre, a monumental stairway leads to San Francesco, which was once part of a convent, and is now a high school. The church, with fine stucco decoration, was built in the mid-18th century and has some paintings of interest as well as a wooden statue of the Virgin Mary (1564), which probably came from one of the churches in the old town, Noto Antica.

Statue on the Cathedral façade

🏛 Palazzo Trigona

◉ *to the public.*
This palazzo is perhaps the most "classically" Baroque building in Noto. The façade with its curved balconies blends in with the adjacent religious and civic buildings, in line with the schemes of the architects who rebuilt Noto. The drawing rooms of the palazzo were frescoed by Antonio Mazza.

BAROQUE ARCHITECTURE AND ART IN NOTO

After the devastating 1693 earthquake, a programme of reconstruction was introduced throughout eastern Sicily in the early 18th century. The architects entrusted with this task elaborated upon the achievements of 17th-century Baroque architecture and adopted recurrent features that can still be seen in the streets of Noto. The façades of both churches and civic buildings became of fundamental importance in the hands of these men. Some of them, like Rosario Gagliardi, who designed the churches of Santa Chiara, Santissimo Crocefisso and San Domenico in Noto, were originally craftsmen themselves. Their skills can be seen in the great attention paid to decorative detail in façades and balconies. Rebuilding made the large monastery complexes – which together with the mansions of the landed gentry were the economic and social backbone of 18th- and 19th-century Noto – even more grandiose than before. In 2002 Noto and other Baroque towns were named World Heritage sites by UNESCO.

An 18th-century Baroque balcony on Palazzo Nicolaci in Noto

San Carlo

Along Corso Vittorio Emanuele, San Carlo (also called
Chiesa del Collegio because
of the attached former Jesuit
monastery) has a slightly
convex façade with three
levels – Doric, Ionic and
Corinthian. The impressive
Latin cross plan interior is
decorated with frescoes.

San Domenico

Looking over Piazza XXIV
Maggio, the church of San
Domenico is part of a group
of buildings that includes the
Dominican Convent, worth
visiting because of its
splendid entrance with a host
of friezes. Like other buildings
of this kind, the convent
was abandoned after the elimina-
tion of all congregational
orders, decreed by the Italian
government in 1866. The
lovely façade of the church,
with its convex central part,
was designed by the architect
Rosario Gagliardi. The portal
gives way to a rounded
church interior, which is
crowned by five cupolas
with fine stucco decoration.

The convex façade of San
Domenico, designed by Gagliardi

🏛 Palazzo Nicolaci
Villadorata

◻ *10am–1pm, 3pm–1 hr before
sunset.*

On nearby Via Nicolaci, one of
Noto's most striking streets, is
Palazzo Nicolaci del Principe
di Villadorata. The façade has
six balconies supported by
corbels which are decorated –
in keeping with the pure

Palazzo Landolina, former residence of the Norman Sant'Alfano family

Baroque style – with complex
wrought-iron work and
grotesque and mythological
figures: lions, sirens, griffons
and cherubs. The interior is
interesting because of the
fresco decoration in the
lavish rooms, the most
striking of which is the
Salone delle Feste
(Hall of Festivities).
The palazzo will
soon house the
**Biblioteca
Comunale**, or
City Library
(currently on Via
Cavour), founded
in the mid-19th
century, with many
old volumes and
the architects'
original designs for Noto.

Detail of Baroque
decoration

🏛 Palazzo Landolina

To the right of the Cathedral
is the 19th-century **Palazzo
Vescovile** (Bishop's Palace),
while to the left is Palazzo
Landolina, residence of the
marquises of Sant'
Alfano, an old and
powerful family of
the Norman aristo-
cracy. Once past the
elegant Baroque
façade you enter
a courtyard where
two sphinxes flank
the stairway leading
to the main floor
and frescoed rooms.

🏛 Chiesa del
Crocefisso

In the heart of Noto
Alta, at the end of a
stairway that begins
at Piazza Mazzini, is
this church, built at

the end of the street that leads
upwards from Piazza Muni-
cipio and the Cathedral. The
façade – designed by Gagliardi
but never finished – has a
large Baroque door. The
Latin cross plan interior
boasts a magnificent
Renaissance statue by
Francesco Laurana,
known as the
*Madonna della
Neve* (Madonna
of the Snow,
1471) which
miraculously
survived the earth-
quake. At the end of
the left-hand aisle is
Cappella Landolina.
The Romanesque
statues of lions also
come from the old town. The
church is surrounded by
palazzi, convents and churches.
Among others, the façades of
Sant'Agata, the **Badia della
Santissima Annunziata** and
Santa Maria del Gesù are
well worth a longer look.

The unfinished façade of the Chiesa del
Crocefisso in the upper town, Noto Alta

The road leading to Pachino, one of the most important agricultural towns in southern Sicily

Pachino ❸

Road map E5. 🏘 22,000. ℹ️
Pachino Town Hall (0931-803 111).

The town of Pachino, founded in 1758 by the princes of Giardineli and populated by a few dozen families, has evolved into a large agricultural and wine-producing centre. Despite inroads made by modern architecture, there are still some traces of the original town plan: a series of courtyards and alleys reveals an Arab influence.

Pachino is also synonymous with a variety of small red tomato used for sauces and salads, which has become familiar throughout the country (it has even acquired DOC status). Besides the *pachini* tomatoes, the area – close to the sea and seaside resorts – is famous for the production of red wine.

Capo Passero ❹

Road map E5.

Fishing boats on the beach at Capo Passero

At the southern tip of Sicily, on the Capo Passero headland, lies the small town of **Portopalo di Capo Passero**, a centre for agricultural produce and fishing. Portopalo, together with the nearby town of **Marzamemi**, has become a popular summer tourist spot. Just off

the coast is the small island of **Capo Passero**, which, because of its strategic position, has always been considered an excellent observation point. Proof is provided by the 17th-century watchtower, which replaced a series of military installations and fortifications, some of which were of ancient origin.

The southernmost point on the headland is **Capo delle Correnti**. Opposite the point a lighthouse stands on an island called **Isola delle Correnti**. Near here – or more precisely, close to Portopalo – Allied troops landed on 10 July 1943 with the aim of establishing a bridgehead on Sicily.

North of Portopalo you can see a tuna fishery *(tonnara)* and a fish processing plant. In nearby Marzamemi the town also grew up around a tuna fishery and the residence of the noble Villadorata family, who are still the proprietors of the local *tonnara*.

The waters of the central Mediterranean are still populated by large schools of tuna fish which migrate annually. Enticed towards the *tonnara*, the fish become trapped in a complicated network of tuna fishing nets. Tuna caught using this traditional method is prized and considered highly superior to tuna caught out on the open sea, because the method of killing (which involves very rapid loss of blood) seems to enhance the flavour of the meat.

Portopalo di Capo Passero, a fairly recent tourist attraction

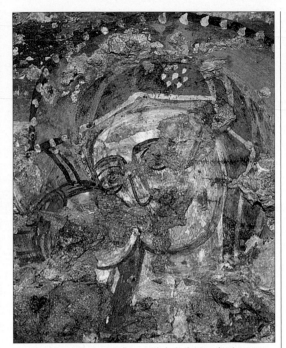

Byzantine fresco in the Ipogeo di San Michele, in the Cava d'Ispica gorge

Cava d'Ispica ❺

Road map E5. *Access from SS115 from Ispica to Modica, right-hand turn-off at Bettola del Capitano, follow the branch for 5.5 km (3.5 miles) as far as the Cavallo d'Ispica mill.*
FS *Syracuse–Ispica (0931-464 467).*
Tel *0932-771 667.* ⬜ *Apr–Oct: 9am–7pm Mon–Sat, varies Sun; Nov–Mar: 9am–1:30pm Mon–Sat*

An ancient river carved the Cava d'Ispica out of the rock and the gorge has developed into an open-air monument. The sides of the canyon are perforated with the tombs of a necropolis, places of worship and cave dwellings where religious hermits went through mystical experiences. It was an Egyptian hermit, Sant'Ilarione, who initiated the monasticism in the canyon, which was used only as a burial site in antiquity.

Improved access has made it possible to visit the **Larderia Necropolis**, although since the establishment of a new enclosure, it is much more difficult to gain an overall idea of the complex of caves that have made Cava d'Ispica such a world-famous attraction for decades. While the Larderia necropolis is an impressive network of catacombs (there is also a small museum), not far from the entrance you can visit – on request – the **Ipogeo di San Michele**, a cave with a Byzantine fresco of the Madonna, or the small Byzantine church of **San Pancrazio**, set in a claustrophobically narrow enclosure. Despite the difficult terrain, the unfenced part of the gorge is also well worth visiting. Every step of the way you will be well rewarded for the strenuous climb.

Scicli ❻

Road map E5. 🏛 *25,200.*
FS *from Syracuse (0931-464 467).*
🚌 *from Noto.* ℹ️ *Pro Loco, Via Castellana 2 (0932-932 782).*
🎭 *Festa delle Milizie: last Sun in Jun.*

The town lies at the point where the Modica river converges with the valleys of Bartolomeo and Santa Maria la Nova. Scicli, a UNESCO World Heritage site, once played a major role in controlling communications between the coast and the uplands. It was an Arab stronghold and then became a royal city under the Normans. It was totally rebuilt after the 1693 earthquake, and Baroque streets, façades and churches emerged from the devastated town.

For visitors arriving from Modica along the panoramic San Bartolomeo valley, the first stop is San Bartolomeo followed by the new town centre, built on the plain after the old hill town was abandoned. In the centre is the church of **Santa Maria la Nova**, rebuilt several times and now with Neo-Classical features, **Palazzo Beneventano** with its Baroque motifs, the former **Convent of the Carmelites** and the adjoining **Chiesa del Carmine**. Lastly is the **Chiesa Madre**, in Piazza Italia. This has a papier mâché statue – the Madonna dei Milici – depicting the Virgin Mary on horseback subduing two Turks, which represents the famous 1091 battle between Christians and Arabs. Higher up are the ruins of **San Matteo**, the old cathedral, at the foot of the ruined **castle** built by the Arabs.

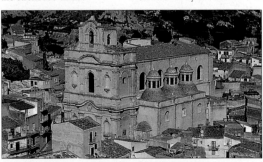

Santa Maria la Nova, at Scicli, rebuilt in the Neo-Classical style

Ragusa ❼

Baroque decoration, Duomo

This ancient city was founded as Hybla Heraia when the Sicels moved into the interior to escape from the Greek colonists. Ragusa, a UNESCO World Heritage site, is divided into two communities: new Baroque Ragusa, built on the plateau after the 1693 earthquake, and quiet, atmospheric Ibla, which is linked to the modern town by a rocky crest. A visit to Ragusa therefore involves two stages.

The Duomo of Ibla in the heart of the old town

Exploring Ragusa
The new town was designed to suit the needs of the emerging 17th-century landed gentry as opposed to the old feudal nobles, who preferred to stay entrenched in old Ibla. It was laid out on an octagonal plan, the result of detailed planning following the earthquake of 1693.

🏛 Cathedral
Piazza San Giovanni. ⬜ 8am–noon, 4–7pm daily.
This splendid cathedral was built between 1706 and 1760 in the middle of the new town. It replaced a smaller building that had been hastily erected after the earthquake of 1693.

The low and broad façade is an excellent example of Sicilian Baroque, with a lovely monumental portal *(see p132)* and fine sculptures of St John the Baptist, to whom the cathedral is dedicated, the Virgin Mary and St John the Evangelist. There is also an impressive porticoed terrace and a massive cusped bell tower.

The ornate Baroque interior has a Latin cross plan with two side aisles and fine stucco decoration.

🏛 Museo Archeologico Ibleo
Via Natalelli. **Tel** 0932-622 963.
⬜ 9am–1:30pm, 4–7:30pm daily. 🎫
The Archaeological Museum is divided into six sections and is devoted to the cultures that have dominated the province of Ragusa. The first section has prehistoric finds from Modica, Pantalica and Cava d'Ispica. The second one is given over to Kamarina, the Syracusan subcolony founded on the banks of the Ippari river on a

coastal site not far from present-day Vittoria. Kamarina once enjoyed important trade links with ancient Ibla. Among the displays here are the statue of a warrior, the bronzes of Kamarina and Attic vases, all recovered during the excavations at Kamarina, organized and sponsored by the Syracuse Archaeological Office. The third section of the museum features the Siculi cultures, followed by an exhibit of Hellenistic finds – especially from Scornavacche, a very important trade and caravan centre – including an interesting reconstruction of a potter's oven. The fifth

section focuses on the Roman epoch, while the last one illustrates the growth of this area in the Byzantine age, with finds from the ancient port of Caucana.

🏛 Santa Maria delle Scale
This church stands at the top of a flight of 340 steps connecting Ibla and Ragusa, hence the name, *scale* meaning stairs. Santa Maria delle Scale was built in the

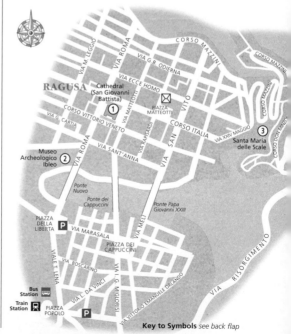

14th century over a Norman convent and was rebuilt after the 1693 earthquake. The original Gothic doorway and external pulpit of the campanileare still intact.

Exploring Ibla

The hill of Ibla has probably been inhabited since the 3rd millennium BC and is rich in history. However, its economic importance has waned, particularly compared with the "new" town of Ragusa.

Duomo (San Giorgio)

The Cathedral stands at the top of a stairway that begins at **Piazza Duomo**, the real centre of Ibla. It was built over the foundations of San Nicolò, which was destroyed by the 1693 earthquake. The new church was designed by Rosario Gagliardi and built in 1738–75. The huge façade is immediately striking, with its three tiers of columns which, together with the vertical lines of the monumental stairway leading to the church, accentuate the vertical thrust of the building. An impressive Neo-Classical

cupola dominates the nave. The interior contains a series of paintings from different periods (including a 16th-century *Enthroned Madonna and Child*) and 13 stained-glass windows.

Circolo di Conversazione

If you go down Corso XXV Aprile, you will see the Neo-Classical Circolo di Conversazione (Conversation Club), on your left. This private club has a plush Neo-Classical interior, steeped in the atmosphere of 19th-century Ibla.

San Giuseppe

Also along Corso XXV Aprile, at Piazza Pola, is the Baroque **San Giuseppe**, which is in many ways similar to the Duomo, San Giorgio, and for this reason is also attributed to the architect Gagliardi. The oval-shaped interior has a large cupola decorated with Sebastiano Lo Monaco's fresco *Glory of St Benedict*. After leaving this church, turn down Corso XXV Aprile and you will come to a fascinating series of monuments. First

Statue of San Giuseppe

VISITORS' CHECKLIST

Road map E5. 67,500.
from Syracuse (892021).
Piazza Stazione (0932-623 440). AAPIT, Via Bocchieri 33 (0932-221 511 or 663 094).
www.ragusaturismo.it

The façade of San Giuseppe, with its Corinthian columns

there are the ruins of the Norman church of Santa Maria la Nova. Then there is San Francesco all'Immacolata, built over Palazzo Chiaramonte and incorporating its Gothic portal. Last is **San Giorgio Vecchio**, for the most part destroyed by the 1693 earthquake. A splendid Catalan-Gothic portal survives – its lunette has a bas-relief of St George killing the dragon and, above, the eagles from the House of Aragon coat of arms.

Giardino Ibleo

This delightful 19th-century public garden has a fine view of the area. It also contains a number of churches, such as San Giacomo and the Chiesa dei Cappuccini. The former was built in the 14th century and restructured in the 1600s, when it was given a Baroque slant. The Chiesa dei Cappuccini has a simple aisleless nave and contains some interesting 15th-century altarpieces, including one by Pietro Novelli.

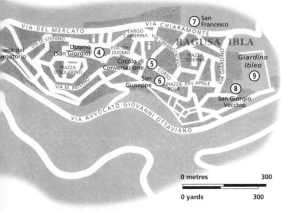

RAGUSA AND IBLA

The Duomo at Modica, a remarkable example of Sicilian Baroque

Modica ⑧

Road map E5. ▨ *52,500.* **FS** *from Syracuse (0931-464 467).* **ℹ** *Pro Loco, Via Maccalle' (0932-763 459).*

Inhabited since the era of the Siculi culture, Modica (a UNESCO World Heritage site) rebelled against Roman rule in 212 BC and, thanks to its strategic position, became one of the most important towns in medieval and Renaissance Sicily. Peter I of Aragon made it capital of an area that roughly corresponds to the present-day province of Ragusa, and it was later ruled by the Chiaramonte and Cabrera families. Perched on the rocky spurs dominating the large "Y" formed by the confluence of the Janni Mauru and Pozzo dei Pruni rivers, Modica grew, occupying the valley where the rivers were filled in after a disastrous series of floods.

Modica Alta is built on the hill and is connected to the lower town, Modica Bassa, via flights of steps. Some of these are monumental, such as the 250-step flight built in the 19th century which descends from San Giorgio. Alleys and lanes evoke the walled town, which from 844 to 1091 was an important Arab city known as *Mohac*.

Sculpture on Corso Umberto I

🏛 Duomo (San Giorgio)

It is worthwhile making the effort to climb up the hill to see the Cathedral. It is dedicated to St George and was built by Count Alfonso Henriquez Cabrera on the site of a 13th-century church which had been destroyed by an earthquake. The magnificent façade (which, because of its similarity to several churches in Noto, is attributed to the architect Rosario Gagliardi) rises upwards elegantly with three ranks of columns. In the interior are ten 16th-century wooden panels with scenes from the New Testament.

Corso Regina Margherita, the main street in Modica Alta, has many fine 19th-century palazzi.

🏛 Santa Maria di Betlem

By going up the road following one branch of the confluence of the valley rivers, now called Via Marchesa Tedeschi, you will come across the façade of Santa Maria di Betlem, a 16th-century church which was rebuilt after the 1693 earthquake. At the end of the right-hand aisle is the beautiful Cappella del Sacramento, a splendid example of late Gothic-Renaissance architecture. It was commissioned by the Cabrera family.

🏛 Corso Umberto I

The many interesting churches and buildings along the city's main street include the former **Monastero delle Benedettine** (a convent for Benedictine nuns now used as a courthouse), the 19th-century **Teatro Garibaldi**, the 18th-century **Palazzo Tedeschi**, **Santa Maria del Soccorso** and **Palazzo Manenti**, whose corbels are decorated with figures of all kinds: knights with plumes in their hats, lovely girls and grotesque monsters.

🏛 San Pietro

Also on Corso Umberto I is a flight of Baroque **monumental steps**, flanked by statues of the Apostles, which leads to the entrance of **San Pietro**. This church was built after the 1693 earthquake on the site of a 14th-century church. The two-aisle interior has a number of paintings and statues. The *Madonna dell'Ausilio*, a Gagini-school statue, stands in the second chapel in the right-hand aisle.

San Pietro stands at the top of a monumental Baroque staircase

🏛 Museo Civico

Largo Mercè. *Tel 0932-945 081.* ◻ *9am–1pm Mon–Sat.* ▨

Craftsmen and their tools are featured in this ethnographic museum, with workshops reconstructed in the cells of the former monastery of the Mercedarian friars. You can make an appointment to see the various local artisans (saddle-makers, smiths, basket weavers, shoemakers and stone-cutters) demonstrating their ancient skills.

The ruins of the Greek walls at the Capo Soprano headland, Gela

Vittoria ⑨

Road map D5. 🏘 *54,300.*
🛈 *Pro Loco (0932-992 953).*

Founded by Vittoria Colonna in 1603, this agricultural town lies on the plain between the Ippari and Dirillo rivers. In the central Piazza del Popolo are the **Teatro Comunale** (1877) and **Santa Maria delle Grazie**, a Baroque church built after the disastrous 1693 earthquake.

Gela ⑩

Road map D4. 🏘 *72,000.* 🚉 *from Syracuse (0931-464 467).* 🛈 *AAST (0931-911 423).* **Fortifications at Capo Soprano** *Tel 0933-554 964.* ◯ *9am–1 hr before sunset.* **Museo Archeologico Comunale** *Tel 0933-912 626.* ◯ *9am–1pm, 3–7:30pm.* ⬤ *last Mon of month.* 🎟 *(combined with excavations.)* **Acropolis excavations** ◯ *9am–1 hr before sunset.* 🎟

According to Greek historian Thucydides, Gela was founded in 688 BC. In the 6th century BC its inhabitants founded Agrigento. Extending over two slopes – the present-day **Acropolis** and the **Capo Soprano** area – the town was revived,

after a long period of abandonment, by Frederick II. Today Gela is marred by ugly buildings, industrial plants and a strong anti-Mafia military presence. However, there are the archaeological sites: a long stretch of Greek fortifications built by Timoleon at Capo Soprano and the sacred precinct and ancient Temple of Athena on the **Acropolis**, all good introductions to a visit to the **Museo Archeologico**.

Chiaramonte Gulfi ⑪

Road map E4. 🏘 *8,100.*

This town was founded by Manfredi Chiaramonte, the Count of Modica, on the steep slopes of a rise and then developed towards the valley. The **Chiesa del Salvatore** and **Matrice Santa Maria la Nova** are in the centre, while the **Madonna delle Grazie Sanctuary** is on the outskirts.

Vizzini ⑫

Road map E4. 🏘 *7,000.*
🛈 *Town hall (0933-968 211).*

The fascination of Vizzini lies in the small streets and alleys of the old town, which has preserved its atmosphere and town plan – increasingly rare in Sicily because of modern urban growth. Also worth a look is the fine architecture of the **Chiesa Madre di San Gregorio** with its Gothic portal, taken from the destroyed Palazzo di Città.

Palazzolo Acreide ⑬

Road map E4. 🏘 *9,000.*
🛈 *Town hall (0931-875 841).*

Originally named Akrai, this town, a UNESCO World Heritage site, has some important Baroque churches and buildings – the **Chiesa Madre di San Nicolò, Palazzo Zocco** and the 18th-century **Chiesa dell'Annunziata**. However, the most interesting sight is the peaceful plain with the **excavations of Akrai**.

A Baroque balcony in the centre of Palazzolo Acreide

♫ Excavations at Akrai

2 km (1.2 miles) from the centre. *Tel 0931-881 499.* ◯ *9am–1 hr before sunset (Nov–Apr: 9–1pm, 3:30–5pm).* This area was inhabited in 664 BC, when the city was founded by the Syracusans. A small **theatre** stands by the entrance. The **acropolis** contains an **agora**, two **latomie** (the Intagliata and Intagliatella quarries, *see p136*), the ruins of the **Temple of Aphrodite** and the so-called **Santoni**, 12 rock-hewn statues representing the goddess Cybele.

The theatre at Palazzolo Acreide: the colony dates back to the early 7th century BC

Caltagirone ⑭

Ceramic tile on Ponte San Francesco

In the history of this city (a UNESCO World Heritage site), built between the Erei and Iblei hills, there is one element of continuity – ceramics production. Prehistoric pottery has been found on the hills around the Arab *Cal'at Ghiran* ("castle of vases"). The local potters were world famous in the Middle Ages, and the tradition is maintained today.

San Giuliano, displaying some 20th-century architectural features

Exploring Caltagirone
It is pleasant exploring Caltagirone on foot, walking around the streets and squares, pausing at the local craftsmen's workshops. There is quite a difference in altitude between the lower part and the hill of Santa Maria del Monte, so plan your visit with this in mind.

🏛 Piazza Municipio
The former Piano della Loggia – now Piazza Municipio – is the heart of the city, where the main streets converge. In the piazza are the **Town Hall** and **Palazzo Senatorio**, formerly the city theatre, now home to the Galleria Sturzo.

🏛 Duomo di San Giuliano
The Cathedral is in Piazza Umberto I. The exterior of the church, dedicated to San Giuliano, has a long history: first it was Norman, then Baroque, and was rebuilt in the 20th century (the façade in 1909, the bell tower in 1954). In the interior is a 16th-century wooden crucifix. By going down Via Roma towards the **San Francesco bridge** – you will come to an open space with the old Bourbon prison and the church of **Sant'Agata**.

🏛 Museo Civico
Via Roma. **Tel** 0933-31590.
⏺ 9:30am–1:30pm, 4–7pm Tue & Fri–Sun.
This museum in the former 17th-century Bourbon prison has prehistoric, Greek and Roman material, sculptures and ceramics from the 1500s to the present.

🏛 San Francesco d'Assisi
The Ponte San Francesco, decorated with typical coloured tiles, leads to the church of San Francesco d'Assisi, which was founded in the 12th century and rebuilt in Baroque style after the 1693 earthquake.

🏛 Giardino della Villa
The public gardens can be reached by going down Via Roma. The park was designed in the mid-1800s by Giovanni Battista Basile, and the long balustrade and the bandstand are richly decorated with coverings of ceramic tiles.

🏛 Museo della Ceramica
Viale Giardini Pubblici. **Tel** 0933-58418. ⏺ 9am–6:30pm. 🎫
From the Belvedere del Teatrino, in Giardino della Villa, you can visit the Ceramics Museum. There are Bronze Age pots and Greek, Hellenistic and Roman kraters and figurines. The Middle Ages are represented by Arab vases and Sicilian pieces. The collection also has more recent pharmacy jars and glazed vases with religious figures.

🏛 Santa Maria del Monte Stairway
Once back in the centre of town, one of the most impressive sights is the monumental Santa Maria del Monte

Ponte San Francesco in Caltagirone

Coloured majolica tiles, decorating every step of this staircase

staircase, with its 142 steps decorated with majolica tiles. The flight of steps was built in 1608 to link the seat of religious power – the Cathedral – with that of civic power, the **Palazzo Senatorio**.

During the feast day of San Giacomo (24 July) *(see p39)* the entire flight of stairs is illuminated with thousands of lamps, skilfully arranged to create interesting patterns of lighting effects.

VISITORS' CHECKLIST

Road map D4. 37,500.
FS *from Catania and Gela (095-532 719).* AAST, Volta L Libertini 3 (0933-538 09). *24 Jul, Festa di San Giacomo.*

Santa Maria del Monte

At the top of the stairway is the former Cathedral of Caltagirone, built in the mid-1500s and then rebuilt after the 1693 earthquake. A slender bell tower, designed by Natale Bonaiuto, was also added. A castle once stood at the top of the hill. Today, in an area that was once heavily fortified, can be found the **Sant'Agostino Convent** and **San Nicola**, both constructed in the 18th century.

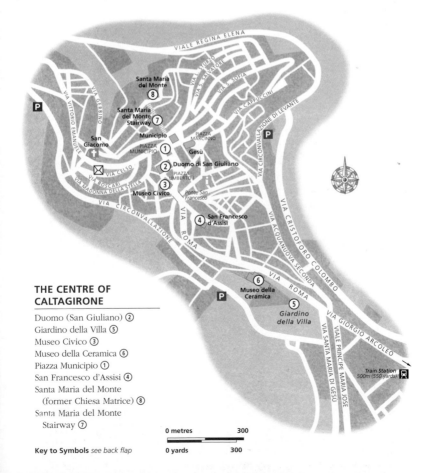

THE CENTRE OF CALTAGIRONE

Duomo (San Giuliano) ②
Giardino della Villa ⑤
Museo Civico ③
Museo della Ceramica ⑥
Piazza Municipio ①
San Francesco d'Assisi ④
Santa Maria del Monte (former Chiesa Matrice) ⑧
Santa Maria del Monte Stairway ⑦

Key to Symbols *see back flap*

0 metres   300
0 yards   300

The Cathedral of Lentini, dedicated to Sant'Alfio, in Piazza Duomo

Lentini ⑮

Road map E4. 🏠 23,700. 🚈 from Catania, Syracuse & Messina (095-532 719). 🚹 APT Siracusa (0931-481 200 or 464 255); Pro Loco Lentini, Piazza Duomo (095-941 433).
Museo Archeologico: Via Museo **Tel** 095-832 962 ⬛ for restoration; call ahead for up-to-date information.
Digs at Leontinoi: ⬤ 9am–1 hr before sunset, daily. 🎭 Good Friday "Scesa e Cruci"; 1st week of May: Festival of orange trees in bloom.

An ancient Siculan city originally named *Xuthia*, Lentini was conquered by the Chalcidians in 729 BC and fought against neighbouring Syracuse with the support of Athens. Defeated and then occupied by the Romans, the city went into a period of decline. In the Middle Ages it became an important agricultural centre. The local museum has finds from the ancient city, especially from the Siculan and Greek epochs. The digs at ancient Leontinoi, at the edge of town in the Colle Castellaccio area, can be reached via the ancient Porta Siracusana city gate. The various walls testify to the city's battle-worn history, and there are a number of ancient burial grounds inside the archaeological precinct.

Megara Hyblaea ⑯

Road map F4. 🚈 Augusta station. 🚹 APT Siracusa (0931-481 200 or 464 255). ⬤ 9am–6pm daily. 📷

One of the first Greek colonies in Sicily was founded in 728 BC here at Megara. According to legend, the founders were the followers of Daedalus, who had escaped from Crete. Unfortunately, today the site is surrounded by the oil refineries of Augusta and in such squalid surroundings it is difficult to visit the ruins of the ancient city with a sense of atmosphere. The Megara colonists who founded Megara Hyblaea were soon at war with Syracuse and Leontinoi, and a century later founded the city of Selinunte, in western Sicily (*see pp104–5*). You should be able to see the ruins of the Hellenistic walls, the Agora quarter, and the remains of some temples, baths and colonnades. The excavations were led by the eminent archaeologist Paolo Orsi and the École Française of Rome. Information display boards will help you to get orientated.

Find from Megara Hyblaea, now in the Museo Archeologico in Syracuse

Ruined foundations in the ancient Greek colony of Megara Hyblaea, founded in the 8th century BC

The Porta Spagnola in Augusta (1681), the old city gate

Augusta ⑰

Road map F4. 🏛 *34,000.*
FS *from Catania, Syracuse,
Messina (0931-994 100).* ℹ️ *APT
Siracusa (0931-481 200 or 464 255);
Augusta town hall (0931-521 269).*

Augusta was founded on an
island by Frederick II as
a port protected by a castle.
Under the Aragonese the city
was constantly at war with
Turkish and North African
pirates. It was almost totally
destroyed by the 1693 earthquake. In the early 1900s the
city expanded and became a
major petrochemical port, and
this drastically changed the
landscape. You enter the old
town through the **Porta
Spagnola** city gate, built by
the viceroy Benavides in

1681, next to which are the
ruins of the old walls. In the
centre, the Baroque **Chiesa
delle Anime Sante**, the **Chiesa
Madre** (1769) and the **Museo
delle Armi** (Arms Museum)
are worth a look.

Pantalica ⑱

Road map E4 (19 km, 12 miles from
Ferla, 45 km, 28 miles from Syracuse).

Rock-cut tombs, dwellings
and temples line the steep
walls of the limestone gorges
at the confluence of the
Bottiglieria and Anapo rivers.
Pantalica was the heart of the
ancient kingdom of Hybla
which, in its heyday, used
Syracuse as its port. The city
was conquered by the Greeks
when the coastal colonies
became powerful in the 8th
century BC, and Pan-talica
became important again
during the early Middle Ages,
when Arab invasions and
constant wars led the locals to
seek refuge in its inaccessible
canyons. The cave-dwellings
and hermitages date from this
period, as do the ruins of a
settlement known as the
"Byzantine village".

View of the steep gorges surrounding the necropolis of Pantalica

A WALK THROUGH PANTALICA

This archaeological site – the largest necropolis in Sicily – covers a large area, but the steep
gorges mean there are few roads, and the only practical way of getting around is on foot.
About 9 km (5 miles) from Ferla stands the Filiporto Necropolis, with more than 1,000
tombs cut out of the cliffs. Next is the North Necropolis; the last place to park is near the

Anaktoron, the megalithic palace of the
prince of ancient Hybla dating from the
12th century BC. The road ends 1 km
(half a mile) further on. From this
point, one path goes down to the
Bottiglieria river, where steep walls are
filled with rock-cut caves, and another
takes you to the so-called "Byzantine
village", the rock-hewn church of San
Micidiario and the other necropolises in
this area. It is not advisable to try to go
to Pantalica from Sortino (the northern
slope); it is an extremely long walk.

The North Necropolis at Pantalica

NORTHEASTERN SICILY

T*hanks to the presence of Mount Etna, the Ionian coast of Sicily has often had to deal with violent volcanic eruptions. One of the most devastating was in 1669, when the molten lava even reached Catania and the sea. The lava flows have formed Etna's distinctive landscape, and flowers and festoons of black lava now adorn many churches and buildings in Catania and the surrounding towns.*

In 734 BC the first colonists from Greece landed on this coast and founded Naxos, the first of a series of powerful colonies in Sicily that gave rise to a period of prosperity and cultural sophistication. However, volcanic eruptions and devastating earthquakes have destroyed almost all traces of the splendid Greek cities in this area, with the exception of the ancient theatre in Taormina, which was rebuilt in the Roman era. The panoramic position, mild climate and wealth of architectural beauty have made this coast a favourite with visitors. The first of these were people who undertook the Grand Tour in the 1700s and made their first stop at Messina, just as many modern travellers do. In summer, the Ionian coast is crowded because of the beauty of its beaches and sea. But it is also fascinating in the winter, when the top of Mount Etna is covered with snow and the citrus orchards are heavy with fruit, or in spring, when the air is filled with the scent of orange blossoms and flower gardens in bloom. Another part of northeastern Sicily worth visiting is the archipelago of the unique Aeolian Islands, of volcanic origin.

The old harbour at Catania, still crowded with fishing boats

◁ The awe-inspiring sight of an erupting Mount Etna at night

Exploring Northeastern Sicily

The pearl of the Ionian coast is Taormina, famous for its stupendous panoramic views, but this area has many other fascinating sights too – from the fishing villages of Aci Trezza and Aci Castello to the Baroque splendour of Catania, as well as Mount Etna, the largest active volcano in Europe. You can go up to the edge of its awesome crater by jeep or on foot, or visit the villages on its black lava slopes with the quaint Ferrovia Circumetnea trains. Those who prefer the seaside can visit the beaches of the Aeolian Islands, which also offer unique scenery with volcanic soil and maquis vegetation.

The ravine of the Alcantara River near Taormina

SIGHTS AT A GLANCE

Aci Castello ⑨
Acireale ⑪
Aci Trezza ⑩
Adrano ⑦
Agira ⑥
Bronte ⑭
Capo d'Orlando ㉔
Castiglione di Sicilia ⑳
Catania pp162–5 ①
Centuripe ④
Giardini Naxos ⑲
Giarre ⑰
Linguaglossa ⑯
Mascalucia ⑧
Messina pp182–5 ㉑
Milazzo ㉕
Motta Sant'Anastasia ②
Mount Etna pp170–73 ⑬
Paternò ③
Patti ㉓
Randazzo ⑮
Regalbuto ⑤
Taormina pp176–80 ⑱
Tyndaris ㉒
Zafferana Etnea ⑫

Islands

The Aeolian Islands pp188–91 ㉖

The Monastery of Santa Lucia at Adrano, on the slopes of Etna

KEY

▬▬	Motorway
▬▬	Major road
—	Secondary road
═ ═	Minor road
—	Main railway
—	Minor railway
△	Summit

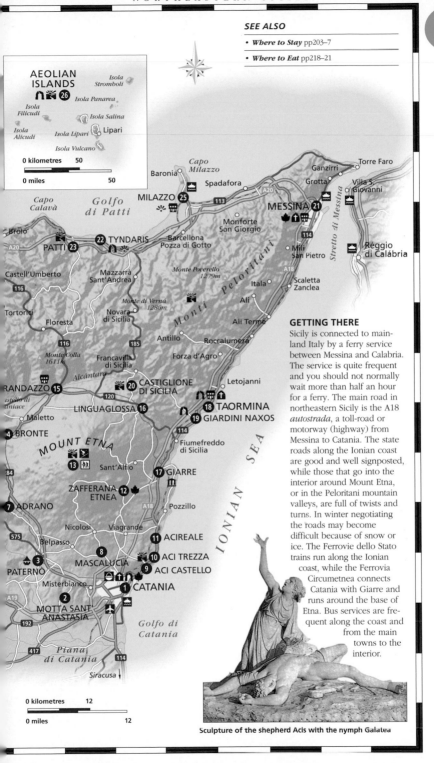

SEE ALSO

- *Where to Stay* pp203–7

- *Where to Eat* pp218–21

AEOLIAN ISLANDS

Isola Stromboli

Isola Panarea

Isola Filicudi

Isola Salina

Isola Alicudi

Isola Lipari — Lipari

Isola Vulcano

26

0 kilometres   50

0 miles   50

Capo Calavà

Golfo di Patti

Brolo

PATTI **23**

22 TYNDARIS

Castell'Umberto

Mazzarrà Sant'Andrea

Tortorici

Floresta

Novara di Sicilia

Monte Colla 1611m

Antillo

Francavilla di Sicilia

Alcántara

RANDAZZO **15**

istello di aniace

Maletto

CASTIGLIONE DI SICILIA **20**

LINGUAGLOSSA **16**

BRONTE

MOUNT ETNA

13

Sant'Altio

ZAFFERANA ETNEA **12**

ADRANO

Nicolosi   Viagrande

Belpasso

8

MASCALUCIA

PATERNÒ

3

Misterbianco

MOTTA SANT'ANASTASIA **2**

Piana di Catania

Capo Milazzo

Baronia

Spadafora

MILAZZO **25**

Monforte San Giorgio

Barcellona Pozza di Gotto

Monte Poverello 1279m

Monte di Vernà 1286m

Monti Peloritani

Itala

Roccalumera

Forza d'Agro

Letojanni

TAORMINA **18**

GIARDINI NAXOS **19**

Fiumefreddo di Sicilia

GIARRE **17**

Pozzillo

ACIREALE **11**

ACI TREZZA **10**

ACI CASTELLO **9**

CATANIA **1**

Golfo di Catania

Siracusa

Ganzirri   Torre Faro

Grotta   Villa S. Giovanni

MESSINA **21**

Stretto di Messina

114

Réggio di Calábria

Mili San Pietro

Scaletta Zanclea

Alì

Alì Terme

IONIAN SEA

0 kilometres   12

0 miles   12

GETTING THERE

Sicily is connected to mainland Italy by a ferry service between Messina and Calabria. The service is quite frequent and you should not normally wait more than half an hour for a ferry. The main road in northeastern Sicily is the A18 *autostrada*, a toll-road or motorway (highway) from Messina to Catania. The state roads along the Ionian coast are good and well signposted, while those that go into the interior around Mount Etna, or in the Peloritani mountain valleys, are full of twists and turns. In winter negotiating the roads may become difficult because of snow or ice. The Ferrovie dello Stato trains run along the Ionian coast, while the Ferrovia Circumetnea connects Catania with Giarre and runs around the base of Etna. Bus services are frequent along the coast and from the main towns to the interior.

Sculpture of the shepherd Acis with the nymph Galatea

Catania ❶

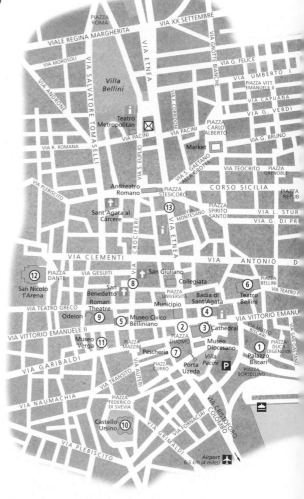

Situated between the Ionian Sea and the slopes of Mount Etna, Sicily's second city (a UNESCO World Heritage site) has always had a close relationship with the volcano, and most of the city's buildings are made from black lava. According to the historian Thucydides, the city was founded in 729 BC by Greek colonists from Chalcis (*see p156*). Since then it has been flooded with lava and shaken by earthquakes, most radically in 1693, when it was razed to the ground. Catania today is the result of 18th-century rebuilding: broad, straight streets and large, unevenly shaped squares, a precaution against earthquakes.

The Fontana dell'Elefante

🏛 Palazzo Biscari

Via Museo Biscari, Via Dusmet. **Tel** *095-715 2508 or 321 818.* ⬚ *by appt.* **www**.palazzobiscari.com
This is the largest private palazzo in 18th-century Catania. Construction was begun by Prince Paternò Castello on an embankment of the 16th-century city walls. Work continued for nearly a century and involved some of the leading architects of the time. The most interesting side of the building faces Via Dusmet, with a large terrace decorated with putti, telamons and garlands sculpted by Antonino Amato. The building is partly private and partly used as city administrative offices.

🏛 Piazza Duomo

The heart of city life lies at the crossing of Via Etnea and Via Vittorio Emanuele. The square boasts many fine Baroque buildings: **Palazzo del Municipio** (the Town Hall), the former **Chierici Seminary**, the **Cathedral** and **Porta Uzeda**, the city gate built in 1696 to connect Via Etnea with the port area. In the middle is the **Fontana dell'Elefante**, a well-known fountain sculpted in 1736 by Giovanni Battista Vaccarini. On a pedestal in the basin is an elephant made of lava, on the back of which is an Egyptian obelisk

Key to Symbols *see back flap*

Entrance to the lovely 18th-century Palazzo Biscari

with a globe on top. The latter, a late Roman sculpture, has become the city's symbol.

🏛 Cathedral
Piazza Duomo. *Tel 095-320 044.*
◻ *9am–1pm, 4:30–7:30pm daily.*
✝ *8, 10, 11:30am & 6pm.*
The principal church in Catania is dedicated to the city's patron saint, Sant'Agata. It still has its three original Norman apses and transept. The façade, with two tiers of columns, is fully Baroque thanks to the design of GB Vaccarini, who also designed the left-hand side of the Cathedral.

The majestic interior has a cupola, a tall transept and three apses with lovely columns. On the second pilaster to the right is the **Tomb of Vincenzo Bellini**; on the first one to the left, a 15th-century stoup. A door in the right-hand transept leads to the Norman Cappella della Madonna, with the remains of various Aragonese rulers.

🏛 Badia di Sant'Agata
Via Vittorio Emanuele II. ◻ *7:30am– noon Mon–Sat, 4–7:30pm Sun.*
This masterpiece of Catanian Baroque architecture was built in 1735–67 and designed by Giovanni Battista Vaccarini. The façade is a play of convex and concave surfaces. The octagonal interior, a triumph of Rococo decoration, is equally impressive.

🏛 Museo Civico Belliniano
Piazza San Francesco 9. *Tel 095-715 05 35.* ◻ *9am–1:30pm Tue–Sat, 9am–1pm Sun.* ● *1 Jan, 1 May, 25 Dec.* 📷
Vincenzo Bellini's birthplace *(see p35)* is now a museum with mementos, autographed scores, musical instruments and models of scenes from some of his operas.

🎭 Teatro Bellini
Via Perrotta 12. *Tel 095-730 61 11.*
◻ *Oct–Jun.*
Named after the Catania-born composer Vincenzo Bellini, this theatre attracts praise from both critics and the public for its high-quality performances.

Detail of the façade of Teatro Bellini

The Baroque façade of Catania Cathedral, dedicated to Sant'Agata

The lively Mercato della Pescheria (fish market) in Catania

Pescheria

Situated at the beginning of Via Garibaldi, the **Fontana dell'Amenano** fountain is fed by the waters of the underground Amenano river, which also forms a pool in the Roman theatre. Sculpted in 1867, the fountain is the focal point of a colourful fish market, the **Mercato della Pescheria**, which occupies the nearby streets and small squares every morning. The smells and atmosphere of the market are reminiscent of North Africa and the Middle East. At the end of Via Garibaldi is the monumental **Porta Garibaldi** city gate, built of limestone and lava in 1768 to celebrate the wedding of Ferdinand IV of Sicily.

Via Cruciferi

This street is lined with lavishly decorated Baroque palazzi and churches. The road begins at **Piazza San Francesco**, with the Baroque **San Francesco d'Assisi**. In the interior are the so-called *candelore*, carved and gilded wooden constructions which symbolize the various artisans' guilds in the city. Every February the *candelore* are carried in procession as part of the impressive celebrations honouring Sant'Agata, the city's patron saint. Outside the church is the **Arco di San Benedetto**, an arch connecting the fine **Badia Grande** abbey, designed by Francesco Battaglia, and the **Badia Piccola**, attributed to Giovanni Battista Vaccarini. To the left is **San Benedetto**, where the wooden portal carries scenes of the life of St Benedict, and **San Francesco Borgia**, at the top of a double flight of steps flanked by the former **Jesuit College**. Opposite stands **San Giuliano**, a masterpiece of Catanian Baroque architecture designed by Vaccarini.

Roman Theatre

Via Vittorio Emanuele 226. **Tel** 095-715 05 08. ◯ 9am–1:30pm, 2:30–5pm daily.

Built of limestone and lava on the southern slope of the acropolis, the theatre had a diameter of 87 m (285 ft) and could seat 7,000 people. Although there was probably a Greek theatre on this site once, the present ruins are all Roman. The theatre was badly damaged in the 11th century, when Roger I authorized the removal of the marble facing and limestone blocks for use as building material for the cathedral. What remains of the theatre today are the cavea, the edge of the orchestra and part of the backstage area of the theatre. Next to the theatre is the small semicircular **Odeion**, made of lava and used mainly for competitions in music and rhetoric. It had a seating capacity of 1,500. The entrance to the Odeion is near the top tiers of seats in the Roman theatre.

Castello Ursino

Piazza Federico di Svevia. **Tel** 095-345 830. ◯ 9am–1pm, 3–7pm Mon–Sat. ● Sun & hols.

This castle was built in 1239–50 by Riccardo da Lentini for Frederick II and is one of the few vestiges of medieval Catania. The Castello Ursino originally

The Roman theatre in Catania, now completely surrounded by buildings

For hotels and restaurants in this region see pp203–7 and pp218–21

Castello Ursino, one of the rare medieval buildings in Catania

stood on a promontory overlooking the sea and was part of a massive defence system that once included the Motta, Anastasia, Paternò and Adrano castles. Castello Ursino is square, with four corner towers, and was rebuilt in the mid-1500s. On the eastern side of its exterior, above a large window, a five-pointed star with a cabalistic meaning is visible. In a niche on the façade, the Swabian eagle seizing a lamb with its claws is the symbol of Hohenstaufen imperial power. In the inner courtyard, where the kings of Aragon administered justice, there is a display of sarcophagi, columns and other pieces.

The upper rooms house the interesting **Museo Civico**, which has a fine art gallery with important works such as *The Last Judgement* by Beato Angelico, *The Last Supper* by the Spanish painter Luis de Morales, *St John the Baptist* by Pietro Novelli (*see p23*) and a dismantled polyptych by Antonello Saliba of the *Madonna and Child* taken from Santa Maria del Gesù.

🏛 Home and Museum of Giovanni Verga

Via Sant'Anna 8. **Tel** 095-315 630.
🕐 9am–12:45pm, 3–5:30pm
Tue–Fri, 9am–1pm Sat & Sun. 📷
The apartment where the great Sicilian author Giovanni Verga lived for many years and died in 1922 is on the second floor of a 19th-century building. The house contains period furniture and personal mementos. At the entrance are displayed reproductions of manuscripts, the originals of which are at the Biblioteca Universitaria Regionale di

Catania. The library in Verga's house boasts over 2,500 books from the author's collection, ranging from works by the Italian Futurist Marinetti to the Russian author Dostoevsky. The bedroom is quite simple, with a bed, a dressing table, a wardrobe and portraits of Verga painted by his grandson Michele Grita.

San Nicolò, intended to be the largest church in Sicily

🔒 San Nicolò l'Arena

Piazza Dante. **Tel** 095 312 366.
🕐 9am–1pm daily (3–6pm Tue & Thu).
San Nicolò was built on the site of a Benedictine monastery

damaged in the 1669 eruption. After collapsing in the 1693 earthquake, the church was rebuilt in the 1700s. It now houses the faculty of letters of the University of Catania.

The nave has two aisles, separated from the central section by huge piers. In the transept is one of the largest sundials in Europe, restored in 1996. It was built in the mid-1800s by the German baron Wolfgang Sartorius von Waltershausen and is extremely precise. Twenty-four slabs of inlaid marble show the signs of the zodiac, days of the year and the seasons. At noon, sunlight falls on the spot from an opening in the roof, marking the day and month.

🚋 Via Etnea

Catania's main street goes up a slight incline and connects the most important parts of the city. Partly closed to traffic, Via Etnea has the most elegant shops and cafés in town. Halfway along it lies **Piazza Stesicoro**, with the ruins of the Roman amphitheatre, built in the 2nd century AD. Nearby is the vast **Piazza Carlo Alberto**, where a bustling antiques market is held every Sunday morning. Back on Via Etnea is the **Collegiata**, a chapel built in the early 1700s and one of the most important late Baroque works in the city. The concave façade, designed by Stefano Ittar, is enlivened by columns, statues and niches. Near the end of Via Etnea is the **Villa Bellini**, a public garden with subtropical plants and busts of famous Sicilians.

The University building on Via Etnea, the most elegant street in Catania

Motta Sant'Anastasia, with its medieval tower dwarfed by Mount Etna

Motta Sant'Anastasia ❷

Road map E3. 🏛 7,600.
🚆 Ferrovia Circumetnea
(095-541 250). 🛈 Pro Loco,
Piazza Umberto 42 (095-308 161).

Mount Etna forms a constant backdrop to Motta. From the top of the village, with the massive tower of the 12th-century **Norman Castle**, the snow-capped volcano gleams through the winter, gradually darkening in spring and summer. Not far away is the **Chiesa Madre** (Cathedral), also built in Norman times. At the foot of the old town is the heart of Motta Sant'Anastasia with its *pasticcerie* (pastry shops), Baroque churches and bustling atmosphere, placed as it is on a major route through the Catania region.

Paternò ❸

Road map E3. 🏛 46,000.
🚆 Ferrovia Circumetnea (095-541 250). 🛈 095-797 01 11.
🎭 Carnival (before Lent).

Surrounded by orchards of citrus fruit, this town lies at the foot of a **castle**, which has a stunning view of Mount

The 12th-century Norman castle, dominating Paternò from above, with its wide-ranging views taking in the Simeto valley and Etna

Etna and the Simeto Valley. The massive square castle was built by Roger I in 1073, totally rebuilt in the 14th century and then restored twice in the 1900s. To get to the castle, go up Via Matrice, which will also take you to the **Chiesa Madre**, the Cathedral dedicated to Santa Maria dell'Alto. The church was originally Norman, but it was rebuilt in 1342.

Centuripe ❹

Road map E3. 🏛 6,600. 🚆 from
Catania or Enna, Romano (0935-73114). 🛈 0935-74755. 🚌 Mon.

Known as "the balcony of Sicily" because of the wide views, Centuripe is especially pretty in February and March, when snow-capped Mount Etna forms a striking contrast with the blossoms of orange and almond trees. An impor-

---

THE CIRCUMETNEA RAILWAY

The picturesque carriages of the Ferrovia Circumetnea climb up the slopes of Mount Etna, passing through barren stretches of black lava alternating with luxuriant vegetation. This delightful route will take you back to the dawn of tourism, when the pace of travel was much slower than today. It takes about five hours to cover the 90 km (56 miles) or so between Catania and Riposto, the two termini, plus another hour to get back to Catania from Riposto via state rail. However, the rewards are magnificent views of terraced vineyards and almond and hazelnut groves, as well as the awe-inspiring volcano itself.

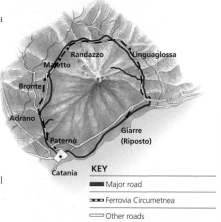

Randazzo   Linguaglossa
Maletto
Bronte
Adrano
Giarre
(Riposto)
Paternò
Catania

KEY
▬▬ Major road
➤•➤ Ferrovia Circumetnea
▭▭ Other roads
▬▬ River

🚆 **Ferrovia Circumetnea**
Corso delle Provincie 13, Catania.
Tel 095-541 250. **www**.circumetnea.it

For hotels and restaurants in this region see pp203–7 and pp218–21

Agira, perched on a sloping hillside, has preserved its fascinating Arab town plan

tant Greek-Roman town, it was destroyed by Frederick II and rebuilt in the 16th century. A long tree-lined avenue leads to a viewing terrace called **Castello di Corradino**, with ruins of an Imperial Roman mausoleum.

Regalbuto ❺

Road map E3. 🧍 8,200. 🚌 from Catania. 🛈 Pro Loco (0935-710 99).

This town was destroyed in 1261 by the inhabitants of Centuripe and rebuilt by Manfredi. The heart of Regalbuto is **Piazza della Repubblica**, with its multicoloured paving and **San Rocco**. **San Basilio** and **Santa Maria del Carmine** are also worth a look. Nearby is the **Lake Pozzillo dam**, the largest artificial basin in Sicily, and a **Canadian military cemetery** with the graves of 490 soldiers who were killed in 1943.

The Saracen bridge on the Simeto river, near Adrano

Agira ❻

Road map D3. 🧍 9,200. 🚌 from Enna. 🛈 Pro Loco, Largo Fiera 40 (0935-692 793).

Because of its elevated position, Agira is clearly visible from a distance, with Mount Etna rising behind it. The ancient Siculan town of *Agyron* was colonized by the Greeks in 339 BC, and the ancient historian Diodorus Siculus was born here *(see p22)*. The most interesting aspect of Agyron's modern-day counterpart is its Arab layout, with Norman churches and patrician residences with Arab-style portals. Centrally located **Piazza Garibaldi** boasts **Sant'Antonio**, with a 16th-century wooden statue of San Silvestro and a painting on marble of *The Adoration of the Magi*. In the vicinity is **Santa Maria del Gesù**, with a crucifix by Fra' Umile da Petralia. In Piazza Roma is the lovely 16th-century façade of **San Salvatore**, with its bell tower covered with majolica tiles.

Adrano ❼

Road map E3. 🧍 35,500. 🚉 Ferrovia Circumetnea (095-541 250). 🛈 Pro Loco, Via Roma 56 (095-769 94 23). 🎭 Easter: the "Diavolata".

A sanctuary dedicated to the local deity Adranos stood on a lava plateau facing the Valle del Simeto, where Sicilian hounds *(cirnecos)* were trained as hunting dogs *(see p170)*. The city was founded in the Greek period by Dionysius the Elder, who chose this natural balcony to build a military stronghold.

The centre of town is Piazza Umberto I, site of the **Norman Castle**, a massive, quadrilateral 11th-century construction. It houses the **Museo Archeologico**, with a collection of Neolithic pottery, Greek amphoras and millstones. A narrow stair, cut out of the Hohenstaufen wall in the Middle Ages, leads to the upper floors. Two have displays of archaeological items while the third houses the **Art Gallery**. The **Chiesa Madre**, built by the Normans and reconstructed in the 1600s, also stands in the same square.

Environs
A byroad below the town leads to a dirt road that passes through citrus orchards for 1 km (half a mile) to the **Ponte dei Saraceni**, a 14th-century bridge on the Simeto river, with an **archaeological zone** nearby.

Mascalucia ❽

Road map E3. 🏠 *24,500.* 🚌 *from Catania.* ℹ️ *Pro Loco, Via Etnea 145 (095-727 77 90).*

On the eastern slopes of the volcano, just above Catania, to which it is connected by an uninterrupted series of villages and hamlets, is Mascalucia, a town of largish houses and villas. It is worth stopping here to visit the **Giardino Lavico**, at the Azienda Trinità farmstead, a small "oasis" surrounded by modern building development on the slopes of Etna. The "lava garden" consists of an organically cultivated citrus grove, a 17th-century house and a garden filled with prickly pears, yuccas and other plants that thrive in the lava soil. The orchard's irrigation canals were inspired by Arab gardens. For helicopter trips over Mount Etna, make inquiries at the Azienda.

🌿 Giardino Lavico
Azienda Agricola Trinità, Via Trinità 34. **Tel** *095-727 21 56.* 📷 *by appt.*

Aci Castello ❾

Road map E3. 🏠 *18,000.* ℹ️ *Corso Italia 302 (095-373 084).* 🚌 *AST (095-746 10 96 or 840-000 323).* 📷 *15 Jan: Festa di San Mauro.*

The name of this fishermen's village, a few kilometres from Catania, derives from the Norman **Castle** built on the

The castle at Aci Castello, destroyed by Frederick II of Aragon

top of a basalt rock jutting into the sea. It was built in 1076 from black lava and in 1299 was the base for the rebel Roger of Luria. The castle was subsequently destroyed by Frederick II of Aragón *(see p29)* after a long siege. Some rooms in the surviving parts are occupied by the **Museo Civico**, with archaeological and natural history collections relating to the Etna region (temporarily closed). There is also a small **Botanical Garden**. The town, with straight streets and low-rise houses, marks the beginning of the **Riviera dei Ciclopi**: according to Greek mythology, Polyphemus and his friends lived on Etna.

Aci Trezza ❿

Road map E3.
📷 *24 Jun: San Giovanni Battista.*

This picturesque fishing village, part of Aci Castello, was the setting for Giovanni Verga's novel *I Malavoglia* and for Luchino Visconti's film adaptation, *La Terra Trema (see p22 and p24)*. The small harbour faces a pile of basalt rocks, the **Isole dei Ciclopi**, now a nature reserve. On the largest island there is a biology and oceanography station. According to Homer, Polyphemus hurled the rocks at the sea in an attempt to strike the fleeing Ulysses, who had blinded him.

The Aci Trezza stacks, hurled by Polyphemus at Ulysses, according to Greek myth

Acireale ⓫

Road map E3. 🏛 48,500. 🚋
Stazione FS (095-606 914 or 532 719).
🚌 Messina–Catania. 🛈 Via Scionti
15 (095-891 999). 🎭 Carnival; Good
Friday: Procession with traditional
costumes; Jul: Santa Venere.

Acireale stands on a lava
terrace overlooking the
Ionian Sea in the midst of
citrus orchards. Since Roman
times it has been famous as a
spa town with sulphur baths.
It is the largest town on the
eastern side of Mount Etna
and has been destroyed time
and again by eruptions and
earthquakes. It was finally
rebuilt after the 1693 earthquake, emerging as a jewel of
Sicilian Baroque architecture.
The heart of town is **Piazza
Duomo**, with its crowded
cafés and ice-cream parlours.
Acireale is dominated by its
Cathedral, built in the late
1500s. The façade has two
cusped bell towers covered
with multicoloured majolica
tiles. The Baroque portal
leads to the vast interior with
its frescoed vaults. In the
right-hand transept
is the Cappella di
Santa Venera, the
patron saint of the
town. On the tran-
sept floor is a meri-
dian marked out in
1843 by a Danish
astronomer. Piazza
Duomo also boasts
the **Palazzo Comu-
nale**, with a Gothic
door and a fine
wrought-iron bal-
cony, and **Santi
Pietro e Paolo**, built
in the 17th century
but with an 18th-
century façade.

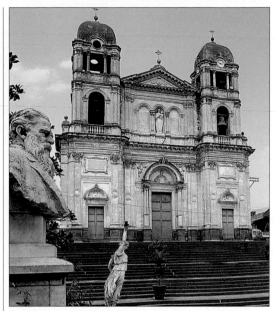

The Chiesa Madre at Zafferana Etnea, on the eastern slopes of Etna

Baroque detail,
Acireale

Close by is the **Teatro dei
Pupi**, known for its puppet
shows, and the **Pinacoteca
dell'Accademia Zelantea**,
with works by local painter
Pietro Vasta, whose paintings
also appear in the town's
churches. The main street,
Corso Vittorio Emanuele,
has elegant shops and cafés
and crosses squares such as
Piazza Vigo, with **Palazzo
Pennisi di Floristella** and **San
Sebastiano**, decorated with
a balustrade and statues.

Zafferana Etnea ⓬

Road map E3. 🏛 8,000. 🚌 22 km
(14 miles) from Catania. 🛈 Pro Loco,
Piazza L Sturzo 1 (095-708 28 25).

Zafferana Etnea lies on the
eastern slopes of Mount Etna
and is one of the towns most
frequently affected by recent
lava flows. The most
destructive eruptions occurred
in 1852, when the lava reached the edge of town, and in
1992. The heart of Zafferana
is its large tree-lined main
square, dominated by the
Baroque **Chiesa Madre**. The
square is also the home of a
permanent agricultural fair
which, besides selling local
wine and produce, has old
farm implements on display.

Environs
Down the road towards
Linguaglossa is **Sant'Alfio**, a
town surrounded by vineyards
and known for the huge 2,000
year-old tree called "Castagno
dei cento cavalli" (Chestnut
tree of 100 horses). According
to legend, the leaves of this
famous tree once protected
Queen Jeanne d'Anjou and
her retinue of 100 knights.

I MALAVOGLIA

Published in 1881 in Milan,
I Malavoglia (The House by
the Medlar Tree) is a masterpiece by novelist Giovanni
Verga (*see p22*) and of Italian
verismo. Set on the Riviera
dei Ciclopi at Aci Trezza, it
describes the harsh life of
fishermen and their constant
struggle with the sea. The
Toscano family, "I Mala-
voglia", are "all good
seafaring people, just the
opposite of their nickname"
(*malavoglia* means ill-will). In 1947 Luchino Visconti made
a film inspired by the book, *La Terra Trema*.

The beach at Aci Trezza, the
setting for *I Malavoglia* (1881)

Mount Etna ⓭

Mount Etna is fundamental to Sicily's
nature and landscape. The Italian writer
Leonardo Sciascia *(see p23)* called it "a
huge house cat, that purrs quietly and
awakens every so often". Etna is Europe's
largest active volcano and dominates the
whole of eastern Sicily. Feared and loved,
Etna is both snow and fire, lush vegetation
and black lava. Around the crater you can
still see the remnants of numbers of ancient
vents. Further down is the eerie, barren
landscape of the
Valle del Bove.

Valle del Bove
*Many recent lava flows have ended here.
The craters Calanna and Trifoglietto I are
of very ancient date. This is one of the
most fascinating places in the Etna area.*

Rifug
Sapie

The Sicilian Hound
*The Sicilian hound or
cirneco is a breed of dog
native to the Etna area.
In ancient times it was
a hunting dog.*

Ragalna

The 1983 eruption
was the first that man
was able to divert.

Nicolosi

Paternò

Catania

Acireale

THE LARGEST VOLCANO IN EUROPE

Etna, or Mongibello (from the Italian *monte* and the
Arab *gebel*, both meaning "mountain"), is a relatively "recent"
volcano that emerged two million years ago. It has erupted frequently in
known history. Some of the most devastating eruptions were in 1381 and
1669, when the lava reached Catania. The most recent ones took place in
2001 and 2002. On these occasions the lava flow caused extensive damage
to Rifugio Sapienza, destroyed the ski facilities and the cable-car apparatus
and came within 4 km (2.5 miles) of the village of
Nicolosi. Eruptions that have occurred in
the last 20 years are shown here.

**2001 and 2002
eruptions**

Zafferana Etn

Lowland Landscape
*The breakdown of volcanic material in the valley below Mount Etna has resulted in very fertile land
which supports almonds, olives, grapes, citrus fruit and vegetables below 1,000 m (3,280 ft).*

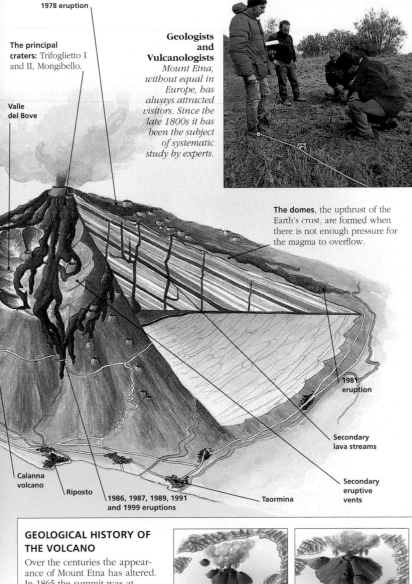

1978 eruption

The principal craters: Trifoglietto I and II, Mongibello.

Valle del Bove

Geologists and Vulcanologists
Mount Etna, without equal in Europe, has always attracted visitors. Since the late 1800s it has been the subject of systematic study by experts.

The domes, the upthrust of the Earth's crust, are formed when there is not enough pressure for the magma to overflow.

1981 eruption

Secondary lava streams

Calanna volcano

Riposto

1986, 1987, 1989, 1991 and 1999 eruptions

Taormina

Secondary eruptive vents

GEOLOGICAL HISTORY OF THE VOLCANO

Over the centuries the appearance of Mount Etna has altered. In 1865 the summit was at 3,313 m (10,867 ft); in 1932 it was 3,263 m (10,703 ft); and today it is 3,320 m (10,892 ft) high. Eruptions in the central crater are rare, but they are frequent in the side vents, and here they create smaller secondary cones.

On the eastern slope of Mount Etna is a huge chasm known as the Valle del Bove, the result of an immense explosion.

First stage, 200,000–100,000 years ago (Monte Calanna)

Second stage, 80,000 years ago (Vulcano Trifoglietto)

Third stage, 64,000 years ago (the cone collapses)

Fourth, current stage (the Mongibello cone)

Exploring Mount Etna

A protected area 58,000 ha (143,260 acres) in size, Mount Etna offers many opportunities for excursions, and attracts thousands of visitors every year. A popular excursion is from Zafferana to the Valle del Bove, the spectacular hollow whose shape was changed by the 1992 eruptions. The hike up to the large craters at the summit is not to be missed. Start off at the Rifugio Sapienza and Rifugio Citelli hostels and Piano Provenzana (after suffering eruption damage, these hiker centres are now being rebuilt). A trip around the mountain is also thrilling: from the Sapienza to the Monte Scavo camp, Piano Provenzana and the former Menza camp. There are also several lava grottoes.

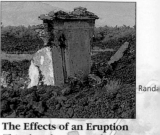

The Effects of an Eruption
This chapel was one of many buildings destroyed in the massive lava flows caused by the 1983 eruptions.

Skiing on Etna
Although there are few chair lifts, skiing on Mount Etna is a unique experience. Besides the regular ski runs you can do cross-country skiing or mountain climbing in the snow.

• Maletto

MONTE SF
1,547 m,
Grotta del
Burò

• Bronte

Rifugio Monte Sca
MO
NUN
1,803 m

MONTE RUVOLO
Grotta della 1,410 m, 4,624 ft
Neve

MONTE TURCHIO
1,295 m, 4,248 ft

Randa

Torrente Milia

• Adrano

• Biancavilla

0 kilometres   3

0 miles   3

NATURE ON MOUNT ETNA

Despite the many eruptions and the bitter cold that freezes the terrain in winter, many species of plants have succeeded in colonizing the lava soil. At high altitudes you can see small lichens, camomile and soapwort on the slopes. Poplars thrive in the more humid areas. Further down are woods of beech, birch, larch and Corsican pine. Centuries of hunting have reduced the animal population, though there are still rabbits, weasels, wildcats and foxes, while the main bird species are the Sicilian partridge and the *Dendrocopus* woodpecker.

Pine forest on the slopes of Etna

Rifugio Sapienza

At over 1,800 m (5,904 ft), the Sapienza hostel is a base for hikers in the summer and for skiers in winter.

VISITORS' CHECKLIST

Road map E2, E3, F3. ✈ *Catani or V. Bellini 095-723 91 11.* 🚌 *AST (095-746 10 96); SAIS (095-536 168).* 🚆 *Catania (892021).* 🚆 *Ferrovia Circumetnea (095-541 111).* **Parco dell'Etna** *(095-821 111).* **Italian Alpine Club (CAI)** *(095-715 35 15).* **Etna Alpine Guides** *(095-914 141).* **Rifugio Sapienza** *(hostel) (095-915 321).* **www**.parcoetna.ct.it

SS120

MONTE SANTA MARIA
1,632 m, 5,353 ft

Grotta dei Lamponi

MONTE COLARANDAZZO
967 m, 3,172 ft

MONTE ROSSO
1,756 m, 5,760 ft

MONTE CORRUCCIO
1,361 m, 4,464 ft

MONTE NERO
2,049 m, 6,721 ft

Lave cordate

Grotta del gelo

MONTE PIZZILLO
2,414 m, 7,918 ft

Piano Provenzana

I DUE MONTI
1,662 m, 5,451 ft

NTE FRUMENTO NETTO
2,299 m, 7,541 ft

MONTE DAGALOTTO
2,623 m, 8,603 ft

MONTE ZAPPINAZZO
1905 m, 6,248 ft

Grotta dei Ladroni

PUNTA LUCIA
2,934 m, 9,623 ft

Rifugio Citelli

MOUNT ETNA (MONGIBELLO)
3,320 m, 10,892 ft

Lava tunnels

MONTE FRUMENTO SUPINO
2,845 m, 9,332 ft

Valle del Bove

Casa Pietracannone

Ex Rifugio Menza

Rifugio Sapienza

Zafferana Etnea

Grotta delle Palombe

Nicolosi

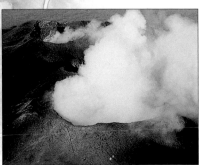

Eruptions and Lava Flows

The volcano can be visited even when it is active, provided you scrupulously follow instructions. Above, the 1991 eruption.

KEY

ℹ	Tourist information
═	Major road
🚆	Ferrovia Circumetnea
🚠	Cable car
※	Area of natural beauty, interest
🍴	Restaurant
🎿	Ski run
🎿	Cross-country skiing
※	Viewpoint
▪▪	Footpath (Trail)

Craters and Eruptions

At this stage in the history of Mount Etna, most of the eruptions occur in the side vents, while on the summit craters the occasional explosive eruption may take place.

Bronte ⑭

Road map E3. 🚉 *18,500.* 🚆
Ferrovia Circumetnea. **ℹ** *Pro Loco,*
Via D'Annunzio 8 (095-774 71 11).
📅 *Oct: Pistachio festival.*

Situated on a terraced lava
slope, Bronte was founded by
Charles V. In 1799 Ferdinand
IV of Bourbon gave the town
and surrounding estates to
Admiral Horatio Nelson, who
had helped him suppress the
revolts in Naples in 1799.
In 1860, after the success
of Garibaldi's Red Shirts in
Sicily, the peasants of Bronte
rebelled, demanding that
Nelson's land be split up
among them, but their revolt
was put down by Garibaldi's
men. The episode was
immortalized in a short story
by Verga *(see pp22–3)*. The
eruptions of 1651, 1832 and
1843 struck the centre of
Bronte, which has however
managed to retain its original
character, with stone houses
and steeply rising alleyways.
The 16th-century **Annunziata**
has a sandstone portal and,
inside, an *Annunciation*
(1541) attributed to
Antonello Gagini
(see p53) as well as
some 17th-century
canvases. In the
village of Piana
Cuntarati, the
Masseria Lombardo
farm has been
converted into
an Ethnographic
Museum which,
among many
interesting objects, has an
Arab paper mill dating from
the year 1000. Today Bronte
is famous for the production
of pistachios.

Environs
Around 12 km (7 miles) from
Bronte is **Castello di Maniace**,
a Benedictine monastery
founded by Margaret of
Navarre in 1174, on the spot
where the Byzantine general
Maniakes had defeated the
Arabs. Destroyed by the 1693
earthquake, the site became
the property of Horatio Nelson.
Today it looks like a fortified
farm, with a garden of exotic
plants. Nearby is the medieval
Santa Maria, with scenes from
the Book of Genesis sculpted
on the capitals of the columns.

🏛 **Castello di Maniace**
Tel *095-690 018.* ⏱ *9am–1pm,*
2:30–7pm (2:30–5pm Nov–Mar).

Randazzo ⑮

Road map E3. 🚉 *11,500.*
🚆 *Ferrovia Circumetnea.* **ℹ** *Pro*
Loco, Piazza Municipio 17 (095-799
14 31). 📅 *Easter Week, 15 Aug:*
Processione della "Vara", Jul–Aug:
medieval festival. 🚌 *Sun.*

Built of lava stone 765 m
(2,509 ft) above sea level,
Randazzo is the town closest
to the craters of
Mount Etna, but
it has never been
inundated with lava.
In the Middle Ages
it was surrounded
by a 3-km (2-mile)
city wall, some
parts of which have
survived, such as the
Porta Aragonese
gate, on the old
road to Messina.
The major monument and
symbol of the town is **Santa**
Maria, a basilica built in
1217–39: the towered apses
with the characteristic ribbing

Medieval window in
central Randazzo

The restored Via degli Archi with its
cobbled lava paving

are all that is left of the original
Norman construction, while
the double lancet windows
and portals are Catalan. The
nave with its black lava
columns has multicoloured
marble altars and a marble
basin sculpted by the Gagini
school. **Corso Umberto**, the
main street in Randazzo, leads
to **Piazza San Francesco**
d'Assisi, dominated by the
Palazzo Comunale, once
the monastery of the Minor
Order, which has an elegant
cloister with a cistern.

The narrow side streets
have many examples of
medieval architecture. The
most characteristic of these
is **Via degli Archi**, which
has a lovely pointed arch
and black lava cobblestone
paving. In **Piazza San Nicolò** is
the church of the same name,
with a late Renaissance façade
made of lava stone. In the
interior there is a fine statue
of San Nicola of Bari sculpted
in 1523 by Antonello Gagini.
The bell tower was damaged
by an earthquake in 1783. Its
reconstruction replaced the
original cusp with a wrought-
iron balcony. After a turn to
the left, Corso Umberto
crosses a square where **San**
Martino stands. It has a
beautiful bell tower with
single lancet windows with
two-coloured borders, and
a polygonal spire.

The Castello di Maniace, the property of Lord Nelson's heirs until 1981

The Randazzo skyline, dominated by the bell tower of San Martino

Opposite is the **Castle**, which was a prison in the 1500s, and is now the home of the **Museo Archeologico Vagliasindi**, with interesting Greek finds from Tissa, such as the famous vase depicting the punishment of the Harpies.

Linguaglossa ⑯

Road map E3. 🚶 6,000. 🚆 Ferrovia Circumetnea. 🛈 095-643 094; APT Piano Provenzana (095-647 352); Pro Loco (095-643 094). 🎉 Last Sun in Aug: Mount Etna festival.

Linguaglossa is the largest village on the northeastern slopes of Etna as well as the starting point for excursions to the volcano summit and for the ski runs. Its name derives from a 17th-century lava flow that was called *lingua glossa* (big tongue). The town streets are paved with black lava and the houses have small wrought-iron balconies. The **Chiesa Madre**, dedicated to Santa Maria delle Grazie, is worth a visit for its Baroque decoration and fine coffered ceiling. Linguaglossa also boasts the **Museo delle Genti dell'Etna**, a museum with geological and natural history exhibits as well as everyday objects and craftsmen's tools.

🏛 **Museo delle Genti dell'Etna**
Piazza Annunziata. **Tel** 095-643 094. 🕐 9am–1pm, 4–8pm Mon–Sat, 9:30am–12:30pm Sun. 📷

Giarre ⑰

Road map F3. 🚶 27,200. 🚆 Ferrovia Circumetnea. 🚌 from Catania. 🛈 095-963 111.

This town lies in the middle of citrus groves extending down to the sea. Giarre is famous for its handmade wrought-iron products. The heart of town is **Piazza Duomo**, dominated by the impressive Neo-Classical **Duomo**, built in 1794 and dedicated to Sant'Isidoro Agricola. The façade has two square bell towers with windows and a tambour. There are many delightful patrician residences made of lava stone in the old town. In the nearby village of Macchia is the **Museo degli Usi e dei Costumi delle Genti dell'Etna**, an ethnographic museum. One interesting exhibit here is a reproduction of a typical Etna farmhouse, with its old kitchen and bread oven, well and washtub. Also on display are farm implements, looms, and period photographs and daguerreotypes.

🏛 **Museo degli Usi e dei Costumi delle Genti dell'Etna**
Tel 095-963 111. 🕐 By appt only; 9am–1pm Mon–Fri (also 4:30–6pm Mon & Thu).

The rusticated façade of the late 18th-century Neo-Classical Duomo in Giarre

Street-by-Street:Taormina ⑱

Byzantine mosaic

On a bluff above the Ionian Sea, at the foot of Monte Tauro, Taormina is Sicily's most famous tourist resort. Immersed in luxuriant subtropical vegetation, it was a favourite stop for those on the Grand Tour and the preferred summer residence of aristocrats and bankers, from Wilhelm II of Germany to the Rothschilds. In its time the town has been Siculan, Greek and Roman, but its medieval layout gives it today's look.

Piazza IX Aprile
The second largest square in Taormina is home to the churches of San Giorgio and San Giuseppe, the Torre dell'Orologio and the Wünderbar Café.

Porta Catania

Chiesa del Carmine

Badia Vecchia

Convento di San Domenico

Palazzo dei Duchi di Santo Stefano was built in the Norman period with Arab motifs.

Chiesa della Visitazione

San Giorgio

★ **Piazza del Duomo**
This is the heart of town, at the western end of Corso Umberto I. In the middle of the square is a Baroque fountain, facing the Cathedral of San Nicolò and the Palazzo Comunale (Town Hall).

Villa Comunale
Located on a cliff with a stunning view, this lovely garden was donated to the town by a rich Englishwoman, an aristocrat who had fallen in love with Taormina.

★ **Palazzo Corvaja**
The Norman structure, with a castellated façade with double lancet windows, was built over an Arab tower. It houses the Museo di Arte e Tradizione Popolari.

VISITORS' CHECKLIST

Road map F2. 10,500.
Catania Fontanarossa 70 km
(43 miles). 5 km (3 miles)
from Giardini-Naxos. SAIS
(0942-625 301). AAST (0942-
232 43). Wed. Jun: Film
Festival; Jul–Sep: Taormina Arte.

| 0 metres | 100 |
| 0 yards | 100 |

Chiesa dei Cappuccini

San Pancrazio

Naumachie

Roman Odeion

Santa Caterina was constructed in the mid-17th century over the ruins of the Odeion.

★ **Greek Theatre**
This is the second largest ancient theatre in Sicily after the one in Syracuse. It was originally built in the Hellenistic age (3rd century BC) and was almost entirely rebuilt by the Romans in the 2nd century AD. The theatre has a magnificent view of the sea and Mount Etna.

STAR SIGHTS

★ Piazza del Duomo

★ Palazzo Corvaja

★ Greek Theatre

Exploring Taormina

From Easter to October and during Christmas, Taormina is inundated with visitors, so if you prefer peace and quiet it is a good idea to go out of season. The climate is mild here even in the winter. The town is especially delightful in the spring, when the air is filled with the scent of orange and lemon blossoms, the gardens are in bloom and Mount Etna is still snow-capped. A regular shuttle bus links the car park to the centre of town, or you can park at Mazzarò and take the cable car to town.

Corso Umberto I, running the length of the town

🏛 Corso Umberto I

The main street in Taormina begins at **Porta Messina** and ends at **Porta Catania**, a gate crowned by a building showing the municipal coat of arms. The street is lined with shops, *pasticcerie* and cafés famous for their glamorous clientele, like the **Wünderbar**, where you can try the cocktails that Liz Taylor and Richard Burton were so fond of. Halfway down the Corso is **Piazza IX Aprile**, a panoramic terrace with **Sant'Agostino** (now the Municipal Library) and **San Giuseppe**. A short distance away is the **Porta di**

The Wünderbar has always been a favourite with film stars

Mezzo gate with the 17th-century Torre dell' Orologio, or clock tower. Above and below Corso Umberto I there are stepped alleyways and lanes passing through quiet, characterful areas. One such alley leads to the **Naumachie**, a massive Roman brick wall dating back to the Imperial Age with 18 arched niches, which once supported a huge cistern.

🏛 Palazzo Corvaja

Piazza Vittorio Emanuele. **Tel** 0942-23243. ⏱ 9am–1pm, 4–6pm Tue–Sun.
Taormina's grandest building dates from the 15th century, although it was originally an Arab tower. The austere façade topped by crenellation is made elegant by the three-mullioned windows and the limestone and black lava decorative motifs. The courtyard stairway decorated with reliefs of the *Birth of Eve* and *The Original Sin* takes you to the *piano nobile*, where the Sicilian parliament met in 1411 and where Queen Blanche of Navarre and her retinue lived for a short period. Some of the rooms are open to visitors. On the ground floor is the

local tourist information bureau. Next to the palazzo are the Baroque **Santa Caterina** and the ruins of the **Odeion**, a small Roman theatre.

🎭 Greek Theatre

Via Teatro Greco. **Tel** 0942-23220. ⏱ 9am–1 hr before sunset daily. 🎫 🎟
Set in a spectacular position, this theatre is one of the most famous Sicilian monuments in the world. It was built in the Hellenistic age and then almost completely rebuilt in the Roman period, when it became an arena for gladiatorial combat.

From the cavea, carved from the side of a hill, the view takes in Giardini-Naxos *(see p180)* and Mount Etna. The upper part of the nine-section theatre is surrounded by a double portico. The theatre originally had a diameter of 109 m (358 ft) and a seating capacity of 5,000. Behind the stage area stood a wall with niches and a colonnade. Some of the Corinthian columns are still standing.

The Greek Theatre in Taormina, capable of seating 5,000 spectators

🏛 Villa Comunale

Via Bagnoli Croci. ⏱ 9am–1 hr before sunset in summer; 8am–sunset in winter.
Dedicated to Duke Colonna di Cesarò, this public garden was bequeathed to Taormina by an English aristocrat, Florence Trevelyan, who fell in love with the town. Situated on a cliff with a magnificent view of Etna and the coast, the garden is filled with Mediterranean and tropical plants. A characteristic part of the garden is the arabesque-decorated tower, similar to a Chinese pagoda, that the owner used for bird-watching.

A view of Piazza del Duomo: in the foreground, the Baroque fountain, which faces the Cathedral

🏠 Cathedral

Piazza Duomo. **Tel** *0942-23123.*
🕐 *8am–1pm, 4–7pm.* 🔺 *May–Sep: 7pm (Sun also 10am, 11:30am, 6pm); Oct–Apr: 6pm (Sun also 10am, 11:30am).*

The Cathedral (San Nicolò) was built in the 13th century and has been altered over the centuries. The austere façade is crowned by crenellation. The 17th-century portal is decorated with a medallion pattern, and over this are a small rose window and two windows with pointed arches. The nave has two side aisles and a wooden ceiling, as well as some interesting works of art: *The Visitation* by Antonio Giuffrè (15th century), a polyptych by Antonello Saliba of the *Virgin Mary and Child*, and an alabaster statue of the Virgin Mary by the Gagini school. In Piazza Duomo, in the middle of which is a lovely Baroque fountain, is the Town Hall, **Palazzo del Municipio**, with a storey lined with Baroque windows.

🏛 Palazzo dei Duchi di Santo Stefano

Via De Spuches.
🕐 *8am–noon, 3–6pm.*
This 13th-century building near Porta Catania was the residence of the De Spuches, the Spanish dukes of Santo Stefano di Brita and princes of Galati, two towns on the Ionian coast near Messina. In this masterpiece of Sicilian Gothic architecture the influence of Arab masons is clearly seen in the wide black lava frieze alternating with rhomboidal white Syracusan stone inlay. Note the tri-lobated arches and double lancet windows on the façade. The interior has a permanent exhibition of the works of sculptor Giuseppe Marzullo.

🏛 Castelmola

A winding road of 5 km (3 miles) leads to this village perched on a rock. Today you only see the ruins of a medieval castle, but in antiquity this may have been the site of the ancient acropolis of Tauromenion. From Castelmola you can enjoy one of the most famous panoramic views in the world, especially fine at sunset.

Palazzo dei Duchi di Santo Stefano, influenced by Arab masons

View of Isola Bella from the steps that go from Taormina to the beach at Mazzarò

🌴 Mazzarò

This small town is virtually Taormina's beach. It can be reached easily by cable car from Taormina or via the road leading to the Catania–Messina state road N144. An alternative is the steps which descend from the centre of Taormina through gardens of bougainvillea in bloom. From the **Bay of Mazzarò**, with its crystal clear water, you can go on excursions to other sights along the coast: **Capo Sant'Andrea**, with the **Grotta Azzurra**, a spectacular marine grotto, can be visited by boat; to the south are the stacks of **Capo Taormina** and the beach at **Villagonia**; and to the north are **Isola Bella**, one of the most exclusive places in the area, partly because of

its clear waters, and the beaches at the **Baia delle Sirene** and the **Lido di Spisone**. Further on is the beach at **Mazzeo**, a long stretch of sand that leads as far as Letojanni and continues up to **Lido Silemi**.

Letojanni

This small seaside resort is 5 km (3 miles) from Taormina. Busy and bustling in the summer, it is perhaps best seen in the spring or autumn. Locals and visitors alike come here to dine out in one of the many good fish restaurants by the water.

The sea at Giardini-Naxos, the first Greek colony in Sicily

Ancient Silenic mask

Giardini-Naxos ⑲

Road map F3. 🏘 9,000. ✈ Catania Fontanarossa 66 km (41 miles). 🚆 095-532 719. 🚌 Autolinee SAIS (0942-625 179). ℹ AAST, Via Tysandros 54 (0942-510 10).

Between Capo Taormina and Capo Schisò, Giardini-Naxos is a seaside resort near what was once the first Greek colony in Sicily. Thucydides relates that Naxos was founded in 735 BC by Chalcidians led by the Athenian Thucles, and Naxos became the base for all further colonization of the island. Naxos was destroyed by Dionysius of Syracuse in 403 BC. On the headland of Capo Schisò, amid lemon trees and prickly pears, is the **Museo Archaeologico**.

Of the two phases in the life of the city, the one which yielded the most important (if scarce) archaeological finds dates from the 6th and 5th centuries BC, with remains of the city walls and houses as well as stones from a temple that may have been dedicated to Aphrodite. In the village of **Giardini**, by the beach, there are still some fine mansions on the oldest streets.

🏛 **Museo Archaeologico**
Tel 09425-1001. ⬛ 9am–7pm. 🖼

Castiglione di Sicilia ⑳

Road map F3. ⟨⟨⟨ *4,000*.
🚃 *Ferrovia Circumetnea.*
🚢 *Giardini di Naxos.* 🏛 *Town hall
(0942-980 211 or 800-010 552).*

This pretty village lies on a crag dominating the **Alcantara Valley**. It was founded by the Greeks, then, many years later, it became a royal city under the Normans and the Hohenstaufens, and the fief of Roger of Lauria at the end of the 13th century.

Castiglione still retains its medieval layout, the narrow streets converging in central **Piazza Lauria**. From this point, moving up the hill, you will see many churches. The first is the **Chiesa Madre**, or San Pietro *(see p185)*, which still has a Norman apse; then there are the 17th-century **Chiesa delle Benedettine** and the Baroque **Sant'Antonio** and **Chiesa Della Catena**. At the top of the village is the medieval **Castel Leone**, built by the Normans over the Arab fortifications, where you have a view of the **medieval bridge** on the Alcantara River.

Environs
The **Alcantara ravine**, 20 m (66 ft) deep, cut out of black basalt by the rushing waters of the Alcantara river, is a marvellously compelling sight. If the weather is good, it is worth following the gorge for about 150 m (490 ft), but only if you can manage without raincoats and weatherproof gear. There is also a lift (elevator) that you can take to avoid the long flight of steps that leads from the parking area to the entrance of the ravine.

The Alcantara River flowing between basalt cliffs

Forza d'Agrò, a medieval village with a
16th-century castle at the summit

THE PELORITANI MOUNTAINS

The Monti Peloritani form a ridge between two seas peaking in **Monte Poverello** (1,279 m, 4,195 ft) and the **Pizzo di Vernà** (1,286 m, 4,218 ft). It is a marvellous area for excursions, often with stunning views of the sea and Mount Etna, in a landscape of knife-edge ridges and woods. On 4 August a major pilgrimage is made to the **Antennamare Sanctuary**, while 7 September is the day for festivities at the **Sanctuary of the Madonna del Crispino**, above the village of **Monforte San Giorgio**. Many of the mountain villages are interesting from a historical and artistic point of view. **Forza d'Agrò**, dominated by a 16th-century castle; **Casalvecchio I Siculo**, with the Arab-Norman Basilica dei Santi Pietro e Paolo; **Savoca**, with Capuchin catacombs and embalmed bodies; **Ali**, which has a strong Arab flavour; **Itala**, overlooking the Ionian Sea, with San Pietro e Paolo, built by Roger I as a thanks offering for a victory over the Arabs; and lastly **Mili San Pietro**, with the basilica-monastery of Santa Maria, which was founded in 1082 by Roger I.

Messina ㉑

The position of this ancient city, founded by the Sicels, who named it Zancle, has always been the key to its importance. Situated between the eastern and western Mediterranean, and between the two vice-royalties of Naples and Sicily, Messina has always been influenced by its role as a meeting point. Over the centuries it has been populated by Greek Armenians, Arabs, Jews and other communities from the large maritime cities of Europe, becoming increasingly important up to the anti-Spanish revolt of 1674–8, after which the city fell into decline. Already damaged by the 1783 earthquake, Messina was almost totally razed in 1908.

The votive column at the entrance to the port of Messina

Exploring Messina

The city developed around the harbour and its layout is quite easy to understand if you arrive by sea. The defences of the **Forte San Salvatore** and the **Lanterna di Raineri**, on the peninsula of the same name that protects the harbour to the east, are your introduction to Messina, which lies on the gently sloping sides of the Peloritani Mountains. The main streets are **Via Garibaldi** (which skirts the seafront by the harbour) and **Via I Settembre**, which leads from the sea to the centre of town around **Piazza Duomo**. Interesting attractions such as the **Botanic Garden** and the **Montalto Sanctuary** are located on the hillside above the city.

⌂ Santissima Annunziata dei Catalani

Piazza dei Catalani. *Tel* 090-661 691 or 360 585. ☐ *by appointment only.* Paradoxically, the devastating 1908 earthquake helped to "restore" the original 12th–13th-century structure of this Norman period church, as it destroyed almost all the later additions and alterations. The nave has two side aisles and leads to the apse with its austere brick cupola.

THE CENTRE OF MESSINA

Key to Symbols *see back flap*

The Orion Fountain, with the Duomo and the Torre dell'Orologio in the background

VISITORS' CHECKLIST

Road map F2. 236,000.
SNAV (090-364 044).
FS (090-532 719).
AAST, Piazza Cairoli 45 (090-293 5292);
AAPT, Via Calabria 301b (090-674 236).
Carnival: procession of floats with tableaux; Aug: Cavalcata dei Giganti.
www.aptmessina.it

Monument to John of Austria

In the square in front of the Annunziata church is a statue of John of Austria, the admiral who won the famous Battle of Lepanto, with his foot on the head of the defeated Ottoman commander Alì Pasha. The work was sculpted in 1572 by Andrea Calamech.

The pedestal celebrates the formation of the Holy League and the defeat of the Turks in this historic naval battle. One of the sailors taking part was the great Miguel de Cervantes, author of *Don Quixote*, who recovered from his wounds in a Messina hospital.

Duomo

The Cathedral is in Piazza Duomo, in the heart of town. Although it was reconstructed after the 1908 earthquake and the 1943 bombings, it has preserved its medieval aspect. It was built by Henry VI Hohenstaufen in 1197. The façade was totally rebuilt but you can still see the original central portal built in the early Middle Ages, decorated with two lions and a statue of the Virgin Mary and Infant Jesus. The side doors are decorated with statues of the Apostles and lovely inlay and reliefs. On the left-hand side of the façade is the large campanile, almost 60 m (197 ft) high, built to house

a unique object – the largest astronomical clock in the world, built by a Strasbourg firm in 1933. Noon is the signal for a number of mechanical figures to move in elaborate patterns, geared by huge cogwheels. Almost all of the impressive interior is the result of fine post-war reconstruction. Some sculptures on the trusses in the central section of the two-aisle nave, a 15th-century basin and the 1525 statue of St John the Baptist by Gagini are part of the original decoration. The doorways in the right-hand vestibule leading to the Treasury are of note, as is the tomb of Archbishop Palmieri, sculpted in 1195. In the transept is an organ, built after World War II, with five keyboards and 170 stops. The side aisles house many works of art, especially Gothic funerary monuments, most of which have been reconstructed.

Orion Fountain

This lovely 15th-century fountain stands next to the Duomo. It

One of the two lions on the portal of the Duomo

incorporates statues representing four rivers: the Tiber, Nile, Ebro and Camaro (the last of which was channelled into Messina via the first aqueduct in the city specifically to supply the fountain with water).

University

The University is in **Piazza Carducci**. It was founded in 1548, closed by the Spanish in 1679 and reconstructed at last in 1927. Besides the university faculties, the complex also includes the small **Museo Zoologico Cambria** (tel: 090-392 721), with its fine collections of vertebrates, shells and insects. Follow Viale Principe Umberto, and you come to the **Botanic Garden** and the **Montalto Sanctuary**, with the *Madonna of Victory*, built after the Battle of Lepanto, standing out against the sky.

THE 1908 EARTHQUAKE

At 5:20am on 28 December 1908, it seemed that nature was intent upon destroying Messina: an earthquake and a tidal wave struck at the same time, bringing over 91 per cent of the buildings to the ground and killing 60,000 people. Reggio Calabria, on the other side of the Straits of Messina, was also destroyed. Reconstruction began immediately. Some of the remains of the old town were salvaged by being incorporated into a new urban plan, designed by Luigi Borzi. His scheme gives Messina its present-day appearance.

Messina the day after the earthquake

🏛 Marina

After walking along the Marina in 1789, the author Frances Elliot wrote: "There is nothing in the world like the Messina seafront. It is longer and more elegant than Via Chiaia in Naples, more vigorous and picturesque than the Promenade in Nice…". Not far away is another focal point in Messina, **Piazza dell'Unità d'Italia**. The buildings that lined the marina before the earthquake were part of the "Palazzata" complex, also known as the **Teatro Marittimo**. The Teatro was a series of buildings that extended for more than a kilometre in the heart of the port area – the centre of commercial transactions – which also included the homes of the most powerful families in Messina.

🏛 Acquario Comunale

The garden of the **Villa Mazzini** is decorated with busts and statues, and is also home to the Municipal Aquarium. Next door is the **Palazzo della Prefettura**, in front of which is the **Fountain of Neptune**, sculpted in the mid-1500s by Giovanni Angelo Montorsoli. The statues are 19th-century copies and the originals are on display in the Museo Regionale.

🏛 Forte San Salvatore

Beyond the busy harbour area, at the very tip of the curved peninsula that protects the harbour, is Forte San Salvatore, built in the 17th century to block access to the Messina marina. On top of one of the tall towers in this impressive fort is a statue of the *Madonna della Lettera*: according to tradition, the Virgin Mary sent a letter of benediction to the inhabitants of Messina in AD 42.

On **Via Garibaldi** is the bustling **Stazione Marittima**, the boarding point for the ferry boats that connect Messina to Calabria on the mainland of Italy.

One of the five panels of Antonello da Messina's *St Gregory Polyptych* (1473)

Madonna and Child,
Francesco Laurana

🏛 Museo Regionale

Viale della Libertà. **Tel** 090-361292. ◯ 9am–1:30pm Mon–Sat (also Apr–Oct: 4–6:30pm Tue, Thu, Sat; Nov–Mar: 3–5:30pm Tue, Thu, Sat); 9am–12:30pm Sun & hols. 🖼

This fascinating museum is close to Piazza dell'Unità d'Italia. It boasts a major collection of art works salvaged after the catastrophic 1908 earthquake. In fact, most of the works come from the Civico Museo Peloritano, which was in the now destroyed Monastery of St Gregory. The museum has 12 rooms that present an overview of the artistic splendour of old Messina and include a number of famous paintings. At the entrance there are 12 18th-century bronze panels depicting the *Legend of the Sacred Letter*. Some of the most important works include paintings from the Byzantine period and fragments from the Duomo ceiling (room 1); the Gothic art in room 2; the examples of Renaissance Messina in room 3; the *Polyptych* that Antonello da Messina *(see p23)* painted for the Monastery of St Gregory

---

BRIDGING THE STRAITS OF MESSINA

Communications with the mainland have always been a fundamental issue for Sicily, and for over 30 years the question of building a bridge over the Straits of Messina has been debated. There has even been a proposal to build a tunnel anchored to the sea bed. This idea now seems to have been discarded, and work on the design of a bridge is under way. In 1981 the Società Stretto di Messina was established with the aim of designing a single-span suspension bridge over the straits to connect Torre Faro and Punta Pezzo – a distance of 3 km (2 miles). A multitude of problems still needs to be tackled, however, one of which is the constant danger of earthquakes.

A 1997 design for the planned bridge over the Straits of Messina

---

(room 4) and, in the same room, a *Madonna and Child* sculpture attributed to Francesco Laurana and a 15th-century oil on panel by an unknown Flemish artist.

Room 9 has two of the "pearls" of the museum, two masterpieces by Caravaggio, executed in 1608–1609: *The Raising of Lazarus* and *The Nativity*. This great artist's sojourn in Messina exerted an influence on other artists, giving rise to a local Caravaggesque school, as can be seen in the canvases by Alonso Rodriguez, *Supper at Emmaus and Doubting Thomas*, on view in room 10.

Environs

By proceeding northwards along the coastline of the Straits, past the Museo Regionale, you will come to **Grotta** and then, about 7 km (4 miles) from Messina, the turn-off to **Ganzirri**. A short drive along the coastal road takes you to the **Pantano Grande** (or Lago Grande), a lagoon that measures 30 ha (74 acres) and is at most 7 m (23 ft) deep. One side of the lagoon consists of a long sandbar and it is connected to the sea by an artificial canal. The Pantano Grande is supplied with fresh water from underground streams and it is used for shellfish farming on a large scale. This point is quite close to the easternmost tip of Sicily: 3 km (2 miles) away is **Torre Faro**, a fishing village known for its excellent swordfish, facing the coast of Calabria. The panorama here is dominated by the pylon

The Pantano Grande lake at Ganzirri, used for shellfish farming

and electric power cable that crosses the Straits of Messina for 3,646 m (11,959 ft) in a single span, from the power stations in Calabria. **Capo Peloro**, a short distance from Torre Faro, is crowned by a 16th-century tower that has been used for centuries as a lighthouse. Further along the coastal road you will come to the second, smaller lagoon of Ganzirri, known as the **Pantano Piccolo**. The lake is a stone's throw away from the Tyrrhenian Sea and is linked to the Pantano Grande.

🔒 Santa Maria di Mili

If you head southwards from Messina for about 12 km (7 miles), you will reach the villages of **Mili San Marco** and, higher up in the Peloritani Mountains, **Mili San Pietro**. Not far from the latter, in an area of wild landscape characterized by the deep **Forra di Mili** (ravine), is the **Santa Maria di Mili Sanctuary**. The church is in a convent. It has been rebuilt several times and now has a 17th-century appearance. It was founded in 1090 by Roger I as proof of his recovered religious faith after taking Sicily from the Arabs. The Norman king later chose it as the burial site for his son.

The splendid 16th-century marble portal is crowned by a sculpture of the Madonna and Child. Above the two-aisle nave is a finely wrought wooden ceiling that dates from 1411. Once past the three arches marking off the apse area, this ceiling becomes a series of small domes, a characteristic feature of religious architecture of the Norman period.

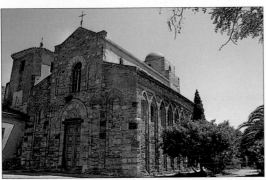

The church of San Pietro e Paolo in Itala *(see p181)*

Tyndaris ㉒

Road map E2. 🚌 *from Messina
(090-675 184 or 662 244).* 🚌 *0941-
369 184.* ☐ *9am–1 hr before sunset
daily.* 🎫 *combined ticket with Roman
House, Patti.* 📅 *8 Sep: Pilgrimage of
the Madonna Nera.*

Ancient Tyndaris was one
of the last Greek colonies
in Sicily, founded by the
Syracusans in 396 BC, when
the Romans were beginning
to expand their territory in the
Mediterranean. The town also
prospered under Roman rule
and became a diocese during
the early Christian period,
after which time it was
destroyed by the Arabs. A
visit to the archaeological site
is fascinating, partly because
of the monuments but also
because of the many details,
which give you an idea of
everyday life in the ancient
city. The town is laid out in a
classical grid plan consisting
of two straight and parallel
streets *(decumani)* intersected
by other streets *(cardines)*.

Past the walls through the
main city gate, not far from
the **Madonna di Tindari
Sanctuary** (which houses the
famous Byzantine *Madonna
Nera* or Black Madonna,
honoured in a pilgrimage
held every 8 September) is
the **Greek Theatre**, situated on
the slope of a rise and facing
the sea; it has a diameter of
more than 60 m (197 ft).
Nearby is the **Agora**, which
has, unhappily, been obs-
cured by modern buildings.

In the theatre area are the
remains of a **Roman villa** and
baths. If you stroll through the
streets of the ancient city you
will see storehouses for food
and the Greek-era drainage
system. A large building
known as **Ginnasio** or **Basilica**
was probably used for public
meetings during the Imperial
Age. Next to the theatre is the
Museo Archeologico, which
has a large model of the
Greek theatre stage, as well
as Greek statues and vases, a
colossal head of the Emperor
Augustus and prehistoric finds.
One unmissable sight is the
splendid scenery under the
Promontory of Tyndaris: the
Laguna di Oliveri, the place
celebrated by the poet and
Nobel Prize winner Quasi-
modo *(see p23)*.

THE NEBRODI MOUNTAINS

The Arabs occupied the Nebrodi Mountains for centuries and
referred to them as "an island on an island". The name comes
from the Greek word *nebros*, or "roe deer", because of the
rich wildlife found in this mountain range, which separates
the Madonie Mountains to the west from the Peloritani
Mountains to the east. The Parco Regionale dei Monti Nebrodi
is a nature reserve with extensive forests and some pastureland, which is covered with snow in the winter. In the middle
of the park is the Biviere di Cesarò lake, a stopover point
for migratory birds and
an ideal habitat for the
Testudo hermanni marsh
turtle. The tallest peak
is Monte Soro (1,850 m,
6,068 ft). Higher up, the
maquis is replaced by
oak and beech woods.

🦌 **Parco Regionale dei
Monti Nebrodi**
Tel 0941-705 934.
www.parcodeinebrodi.it

**Horses grazing in the Parco
Regionale dei Monti Nebrodi**

The unusual natural scenery at the Laguna di Oliveri, seen from the Promontory of Tyndaris

The sarcophagus of Roger I's wife Adelaide in Patti Cathedral

Patti ㉓

Road map E2. 🏠 13,100.
🚆 from Messina and Palermo (0941-361 081). 🛈 AAST (0941-241 136).
www.pattietindari.it

On one of the stretches where the coastal scenery is most fascinating, just past the rocky promontory of **Capo Calavà** on the slopes overlooking the sea, is the town of Patti. Initially a fief of the Norman ruler Roger I, it was later destroyed during the wars with the Angevins and then frequently pillaged by pirates from North Africa.

Patti boasts an 18th-century **Cathedral** built over the foundations of the former Norman church. Inside is a sarcophagus with the remains of Queen Adelaide, Roger I's wife, who died here in 1118.

Along the road down to **Marina di Patti** are the ruins of a **Roman villa** which were brought to light during the construction of the Messina–Palermo motorway. This Imperial Age building measures 20,000 sq m (215,200 sq ft) and comprises a peristyle, an apse-like room, thermal baths and many well-preserved mosaics. The villa was destroyed by an earthquake; on the basis of various archaeological finds, historians have been able to date this event at the second half of the 4th century AD.

🏛 **Roman Villa**
Via Papa Giovanni XXIII, Marina di Patti. **Tel** 0941-361 593. ⌚ hours vary; call ahead. 📷 combined with Tyndaris.

Capo d'Orlando ㉔

Road map E2. 🏠 11,300.
🛈 AAST (0941-912 784).

Forming part of a region known for the intensive cultivation of citrus fruits, the Nebrodi Mountains jut out into the sea at intervals. The coastal town of Capo d'Orlando lies at the foot of the **Rupe del Semaforo** cliff and the rocky hill after which the town was named.

A climb of about 100 m (328 ft) will take you to the top of the cliff. There, in a large open space, stand the remains of a 14th-century fortress and **Maria Santissima**, a church built in the late 1500s and now home to a number of interesting paintings. However, the main reward for climbing up the hill is the panoramic view of the sea and of the fishing boats moving about in the pretty harbour below.

Milazzo ㉕

Road map F2. 🏠 30,000.
🚆 from Messina & Palermo (091-616 18 06). 🛈 AAST (090-922 28 65 or 922 27 90).

Milazzo began to take its place in written history when *Mylai* was colonized by the Greeks in 716 BC. The Normans later chose it as their main coastal stronghold. Frederick II personally designed the castle built here in 1239. The town was divided into three distinct zones in the Middle Ages – the **walled town**, the **Borgo** and the **lower town** – and it was expanded in the 1700s. The **Salita Castello** leads up to the **ancient rock**, which affords access to the walled town via a covered passageway. A doorway opens into **Frederick II's Castle**, surrounded by a wall with five round towers and the great hall of the **Sala del Parlamento** (Parliament Hall). On the same rise are the remains of the old **Duomo**, the original 17th-century cathedral, now in a state of disrepair. Do not miss the chance of an excursion to **Capo Milazzo**, where you will be rewarded with towers, villas and, at the foot of the 18th-century lighthouse, a marvellous view of the Aeolian Islands, with Calabria beyond. This was the site of the 260 BC naval battle in which the Romans routed the Carthaginian fleet. Steps lead to the place where St Anthony is said to have taken refuge from a storm in 1221.

The castle at Milazzo, strengthened structurally by Alfonso of Aragon

The Aeolian Islands ㉖

Three-colour clay vase, 4th century BC

Consisting of Strikingly beautiful volcanic cliffs separated by inlets, sometimes quite deep, the Aeolian Islands (in Italian, Isole Eolie) are unique for their extraordinary rock formations and volcanoes, and for their history. The islands attract hordes of visitors every summer who come to bathe and dive, yet despite the crowds, each island somehow manages to preserve its own individual character. Dominating the islands, especially in the winter, is the sea, with migratory birds nesting on the cliffs and frequent storms, which can reinforce a sense of isolation, even in this age of rapid communications.

Filicudi
There are three villages on this island: Val di Chiesa, Pecorini and Filicudi Porto. On the Capo Graziano promontory are the ruins of a prehistoric village.

M a r

Pecorini

Alicudi
The 5 sq km (2 sq miles) of Alicudi do not leave room for many inhabitants. The highest peak is the Filo dell'Arpa – 675 m (2,214 ft).

Lipari
The main island in the archipelago, Lipari has many hot springs and fumaroles, evidence of its volcanic origin. The old town, with a castle and cathedral, is built within walls. There is an important Museo Archeologico Eoliano here, with an excellent collection.

Stromboli
The main attraction on this island is the climb up the volcano and the fine view from the "Sciara del Fuoco".

VISITORS' CHECKLIST

FS *Milazzo.* from Catania airport, SAIS (090-771 914); from Messina to Milazzo Giunta (090-673 782). Siremar, all year from Milazzo (892123), summer only from Naples (081-551 90 96); SNAV, all year from Milazzo (090-9287821 and Naples (081-4285 555). In summer: connections from Messina, Palermo, Reggio Calabria, Sant'Agata di Militello, Cefalù, Maratea, Riposto/ Giardini and Salerno.* **Lipari** (090-988 00 95). **Vulcano** *Jul–Sep* (090-985 20 28). **Salina** *at Malfa (090-984 43 26), at Leni (090-980 92 25).* **Stromboli** *Jul–Sep (090-986 023).*

KEY

 Ferry port

Tirreno

Napoli

Ginostra   Stromboli

Messina

S. Pietro

Malfa

S. Marina Salina

Acquacalda

Canneto

Lipari

Messina

Porto Levante

0 kilometres   12

0 miles   12

Milazzo

Panarea
This is the smallest Aeolian island, surrounded by rocks and small islands. It was inhabited in prehistoric times.

Vulcano
According to ancient mythology, the fabulous island of Vulcano was the workplace of the god of fire and blacksmiths, Hephaestus.

Salina
The island, consisting of two volcanic cones, is the second largest in the group and was named after the ancient salt mine (salina) at Lingua, now closed.

Exploring the Aeolian Islands

Gold ring, 4th
century BC

The best starting point for a visit to the
varied Aeolian Islands is Lipari, because
it is the largest of the islands and the boat
service is good. Here you can decide what
type of holiday you want – natural history
excursions, including Vulcano and
Stromboli, the exclusive tourist resort at Panarea among
villas and yachts, or the timeless tranquillity of Alicudi.

The summit of the Vulcano crater,
an hour's climb from the base

Lipari

Road map E1. 🏠 *11,000 (the
municipality of Lipari includes all the
other islands, except for Salina).*
The main Aeolian island is
not large – a little less than 10
km (6 miles) long and barely
5 km (3 miles) wide, cul-
minating in **Monte Chirica**,
602 m (1,974 ft) high. The
volcanic activity of the
past can be noted here
and there in the hot
springs and fumaroles.
The town of Lipari
has two landing
places: **Sotto-
monastero** for ferry
boats and **Marina
Corta** for hydrofoils.
Inevitably, this is the
busiest stretch of
the seafront.

The old
Cathedral is worth
a visit. Built by the
Normans in the
11th century, it was
rebuilt after a barbarous
pirate raid completely
destroyed the town in 1544.
Next door to the Cathedral
is the **Museo Archeologico
Eoliano**, which takes up part
of the **old castle**, built by the
Spanish (who incorporated
the ancient towers and walls)
in order to put an end to the
constant pirate raids.

The first rooms in the
museum are devoted to
prehistoric finds in Lipari.
The adjoining rooms have
objects from the same period,
but from the other islands.
Then there is a large section
featuring classical archaeological finds, some discovered
under water. Part of the
museum has volcano-related
exhibits, with interesting
detailed descriptions
of the geological
configuration of
each island. Three
further sights are
the **Belvedere
Quattrocchi** view-
point, the ancient
**San Calogero
thermal baths and
Acquacalda beach**,
which was once
used as a harbour
for the ships that
came to load the
local pumice
stone. The best way to get
about is by scooter or bicycle,
both of which can be rented
in the town of Lipari.

Ancient theatre mask,
**Museo Archeologico
Eoliano**

🏛 **Museo Archeologico
Eoliano**
Via Castello 2. **Tel** 090-988 01 74.
🕐 9am–1pm, 3–6pm Mon–Sat,
   9am–1pm Sun & hols.

Vulcano

Road map E1.
Close to Lipari is the aptly
named island of Vulcano.
Dedicated to Vulcan, the
Roman god of fire and metal-
working, Homer described
the island as the workshop of
Hephaestus, the Greek god
of fire. The only landing
place is the **Porto di Levante**,
from which a paved road
leads to the **Faro Nuovo** (new
lighthouse). Vulcano consists
of three old craters. The first,
in the south between **Monte
Aria** and **Monte Saraceno**,
has been extinct for centuries;
the **Gran Cratere**, on the other
hand, is still active, the last
eruption occurring in 1890.
Vulcanello, the third crater,
is a promontory on the
northeastern tip of the island
created almost 2,000 years
ago by an eruption. The
climb up to the middle crater
is particularly interesting, and
you can reach the top in less
than an hour. Once there,
it is worthwhile going down
the crater to the Piano delle
Fumarole. Bathing and mud
baths are available all year
round at the spas near Porto
di Levante, while hot springs
heat the sea around the
stack (*faraglione*).

Salina

Road map E1. 🏠 *800.*
The second largest Aeolian
island is 7 km (4 miles) long,
5.5 km (3 miles) wide, and
962 m (3,155 ft) high at its
highest point, **Monte Fossa
delle Felci**. There are three
villages: **Santa Maria di Salina,
Leni** and **Malfa**. Santa Maria
overlooks the sea and
is not far from a beach; it
is connected to the other
villages by an efficient mini-
bus service which runs until
late in the evening in the
summer. Salina is also the site

The archaeological zone at Lipari, home to many different cultures

of a nature reserve, created to protect the two ancient volcanoes of **Monte dei Porri** and **Fossa delle Felci**. The dominant vegetation here is maquis, as the inhabitants have almost exterminated the forests that grew here in antiquity. The starting point for a visit to the reserve is the **Madonna del Terzito Sanctuary**, the object of colourful pilgrimages. Salina, and, in particular, the steep walls of the Pizzo di Corvo is also a regular nesting ground for colonies of the rare Eleonora's falcon, which migrate to this spot every year from Madagascar.

Among the best-known local products is a highly prized sweet Malvasia wine.

Santa Maria di Salina, one of the three villages on the island

🏝 Panarea
Road map E1.
The smallest Aeolian island is surrounded by cliffs and stacks. Visitors land at the small harbour of **San Pietro** (the other villages are **Drauto** and **Ditella**). At **Capo Milazzese**, in one of the most fascinating spots in the Aeolian Islands, archaeologists have un-

covered the ruins of a Neolithic village, founded at **Cala Junco**. Interesting finds such as Mycenaean pottery, tools and other items are on display in the local museum. A half-hour walk will take you to the village, starting off from **San Pietro** and passing through **Drauto** and the **Spiaggia degli Zimmari** beach. This island now has luxury tourist facilities.

🏝 Stromboli
Road map F1.
The still-active crater of the northeasternmost island in the archipelago has been described by travellers for more than 20 centuries. Italian volcanoes have always been both famous and feared. The ancient Greeks believed that Hephaestus, the god of fire (known as Vulcan to the Romans), lived in the depths of Mount Etna. Boats call either at **Scari** or **Ginostra**, but the island has other villages: **San Vincenzo, Ficogrande** and **Piscità**. The characteristic features of Stromboli are its stunning craggy coast (the deep waters are a favourite with swimmers and divers) and its famous volcano. For an excursion to the crater, start off from **Piscità**; you first come to the old **Vulcanological Observatory** and then the top of the **crater**. The best time to go is

The Stromboli volcano, active for 2,000 years

around evening, as the eruptions are best seen in the dark. The climb is not always accessible, and the volcano can be dangerous. It is best to go with a guide and to wear heavy shoes (or hiking boots) and suitable clothing. There are also boats offering evening excursions to take visitors close to the **Sciara del Fuoco** lava field for the unforgettable spectacle of lava flowing into the sea.

Filicudi
Road map E1.
Halfway between Salina and Alicudi, this extremely quiet island has three villages: **Porto, Pecorini a Mare** and **Val di Chiesa**. You can make excursions into the interior or, even better, take a boat trip around the island and visit the **Faraglione della Canna** basalt stack, **Punta del Perciato, Grotta del Bue Marino** and **Capo Graziano**.

🏝 Alicudi
Road map D1.
This island was abandoned for the entire Middle Ages and was colonized again only in the Spanish period. Tourism is a relatively recent arrival, and there are no vehicles. The steps and paths are covered on foot, and accommodation can be found in private homes. There is no nightlife, making this an ideal spot for those in search of a peaceful, relaxing break.

Typical Aeolian landscape at Cala Junco, on Panarea

TRAVELLERS'
NEEDS

WHERE TO STAY

Sicily has a wide range of accommodation available, from simple campsites to refurbished mansions. Many hotels have been converted from old palazzi or farmhouses. You may find a room with a view of the Valle dei Templi in Agrigento or of the multicoloured roofs of the churches of Palermo. The place with the most varied accommodation, in all categories, is Taormina, for over a century a favourite with international clients. The coastline of Sicily is lined

Sign from a historic hotel *(see p206)*

with three- and four-star hotels, often with a pool or private beach. On the islands off the coast the hotels are often open only in the summer and half-board is obligatory. Alternatively you can stay in private homes or tourist villages. More adventurous visitors might opt for a farm holiday in the interior, which can be good value and often includes good local food. This section and the list of hotels on pages 198–207 provide further information on accommodation in Sicily.

The pool at Les Sables Noires on the island of Vulcano (see p207)

HOTEL GRADING AND FACILITIES

In common with the rest of Italy, Sicilian hotels are classified by a star-rating system – from one for family-run pensions with simple, basic facilities to five stars for luxury hotels. Among the best hotels in Sicily in this latter category are the **Villa Igiea** (*see p199*) in Palermo and the **San Domenico** and **Grand Hotel Timeo** in Taormina (*see p207*). All three are housed in historic buildings – the San Domenico is a former monastery – with spectacular views and beautiful gardens.

The four-star category offers first-class service without the very high prices of the luxury hotels. Four-star hotels include some lovely places, such as the **Baglio della Luna** in Agrigento (*see p201*), the **Villa Sant'Andrea** (*p207*) in

Taormina and the **Centrale Palace** in Palermo (*see p198*). Visitors are sometimes pleasantly surprised at finding good value for money in three-star hotels, such as the **Atelier** by the sea at Castel di Tusa (*see p199*), the **Domus Mariae** (*see p203*) in Syracuse or the **Baglio Santa Croce** (*see p201*) in Valderice.

In general, all Sicilian hotels have a restaurant, which is usually open to non-residents as well. Along the coast, all the four-star and most of the three-star hotels provide a swimming pool or a private beach. Facilities for the disabled and access for people in wheelchairs are usually available only in newer or recently renovated hotels.

HOTEL CHAINS

Besides such large international chains as **Best Western** and **Sheraton**, there are Sicilian hotel chains as well. One of these is **Framon Hotels**, which is based in Messina. Their 11 hotels, at different locations throughout Sicily, are known for their good restaurants, as well as other facilities.

PRICES

By law, every hotel room in Italy must carry, on the back of the door, the **Ente del Turismo** (Tourist Board) price for the room with the maximum charges during the year; these prices may not be exceeded. The displayed prices, or those quoted by the hotel when you book, usually include taxes and service. Breakfast is generally included as well, but you should check with the hotel beforehand. On the whole, you are expected to take half or full board in hotels on the coast.

Breakfast may be served outside in summer

◁ Shop window displaying baskets of marzipan fruits

A room at Kempinski Hotel Giardino di Costanza, Mazara del Vallo *(see p200)*

Extras are likely to include drinks taken with meals, room service, drinks and food taken from the minibar in your room, and telephone calls. Note, however, that hotel phone charges are usually extremely expensive.

In the off season you could try asking for a special bed and breakfast rate, rarely available in peak season.

TOURIST SEASON

Most of the hotels on the offshore islands are open seasonally, from April to October, so that visiting the Aeolian or Egadi islands in the winter months may be difficult. Hotels in the cities are open all year round.

BOOKING

Should you decide to go to Sicily in the summer, you need to book well in advance, especially for July and August and if you want to stay on the coast, as the island gets very busy in peak season. When you book, you will probably be asked to pay a deposit by international money order or by giving the hotel a credit card number.

TOURIST VILLAGES

Holiday villages give you the chance to enjoy a seaside holiday in a less formal atmosphere than in a hotel. Most villages are sited on the islands and along the Sicilian coast, and many offer inclusive package deals.

Accommodation may vary according to requirements, from rooms in a residence to small apartments with an outside terrace.

Each village offers a range of recreation and sports facilities. Besides one or more swimming pools, villages usually offer tennis courts and windsurfing, diving or sailing lessons. Some even provide baby-sitting. Among the best of these are **Kastalia** in Vittoria, the **Serenusa Village** in Licala and the **Villaggio Valtur Pollina** in the province of Palermo.

Some villages offer all-inclusive holidays where the price even includes drinks at the bar. Charges in tourist villages are always calculated on a weekly basis.

Alternatively, you may choose to rent an apartment and select and pay for any further recreation and sports facilities as you go along. This enables you to be independent, and at the same time provides a range of possible facilities. For full details concerning the main tourist villages, make enquiries at a travel agency, or contact the major tour operators who manage these villages, listed on page 197.

CAMPING

Spending your holiday on a camping site is a good way of keeping costs down. Almost all the camping sites in Sicily are on the coast, with direct access to a beach. In the interior there are only a few sites on the slopes of Mount Etna, well situated for excursions to the largest volcano in Europe. Camping outside official sites is prohibited, with camping on beaches particularly frowned upon. If you want to stay on private property you must ask the owner's permission.

In general, campsites are clean and well-managed. Besides an area for tents and/or caravans (trailers), most sites also provide bungalows with private bathrooms and a kitchen area. Facilities often include grocery shops, pizzerias (and, occasionally, restaurants), laundries and organized sports facilities.

For longer stays, book well ahead of time, and in high season, phone in advance even for a one- or two-night stop. If you are touring, start to look for a site by early afternoon. Most campsites are open from Easter to October. The main ones are listed on page 197.

The Hotel Grotta Azzurra in Ustica, built above the grotto *(see p201)*

HOSTELS, REFUGES, B&BS AND PRIVATE HOMES

There are very few youth hostels in Sicily, but they do offer very cheap accommodation (roughly €9 per night for a bed in a dormitory). A membership card is needed to use hostels affiliated with the **Associazione Italiana Alberghi della Gioventù** (Italian Youth Hostel Federation), listed on page 197.

There are also mountain refuges, most on Mount Etna, but the **Club Alpino Italiano** has two on the Madonie and Nebrodi mountains.

Bed & Breakfast Italia provides a selection of accommodation in Sicily, while on the Aeolian and Egadi islands, near Taormina and at Scopello, you can rent a room in a private home. You may see road signs indicating such rooms, but you can also ask at the local Pro Loco tourist bureaux or in the bars and cafés.

FARM HOLIDAYS

Spending your holiday on a working farm *(agriturismo)* can be both enjoyable and cheap. You may even be lucky enough to find accommodation in an orange grove with a view of Mount Etna or in a fortified farmstead in the vineyards around Marsala. This kind of holiday offers a good opportunity to become acquainted with local tradi-

The Baglio Santacroce in Valderice, with many original features *(see p201)*

tions. Farm holidays are not widely available in Sicily, but accommodation is well kept and hospitable, even if rooms are by no means as luxurious as the equivalent in Umbria or Tuscany. As well as rooms, usually with a private bathroom, some farms offer small apartments with a bathroom and kitchen area, perhaps in converted stables or buildings once used for wine-making.

Most of these farms offer half- or full-board and in the high season lodging is organized on a week-by-week basis. Meals consist of produce grown on the farm and standards are generally very good. Breakfast might include home-grown honey and jams made from the owners' fruit. Main meals may make use of vegetables from the kitchen garden, home-made cheese, or fish from local fishermen.

Meals are eaten at the owner's table together with the other guests, so if you are fussy about your privacy, this is not the type of holiday for you. But it is ideal for those who want to relax without the formalities of a hotel and for families with children, who will have space to play in. The owners will be only too happy to suggest the best excursions in the vicinity.

SELF-CATERING (EFFICIENCY APARTMENTS)

Renting an apartment for two weeks or a month is undoubtedly the cheapest solution for a family or group of friends who want

The tower at the Foresteria Baglio della Luna, Agrigento *(see p201)*

a reasonably priced holiday by the sea. If you have children, particularly small ones, self-catering is an excellent solution, as you are not tied in to formal meal-times. Renting an apartment for one week only is less advantageous economically, as cleaning costs can be high in proportion to the rent.

Self-catering options can be arranged through specialized agencies such as **Tailor-Made Tours, Individual Italy** and **Magic of Italy** before you leave for Italy, but be sure to book in advance as they can be booked up for months.

Another possibility, though more expensive, is to make enquiries through tour operators or travel agencies, who sometimes have lists of residential hotels. In these hotels charges are made on a weekly basis and a week's deposit is always required when making a booking.

If you decide to rent a private apartment, it is a good idea to find out the actual size of the property beforehand to make sure there is enough room. In some apartments, the living room is designed to double as a bedroom.

Before coming to an agreement on rental, be sure to ask whether electricity and gas are included in the rent or if they are extras. This also goes for other facilities such as swimming pools and use of gardens.

DIRECTORY

TOURIST INFORMATION

Assessorato Regionale del Turismo, delle Comunicazioni e dei Trasporti
Via Notarbartolo 9, Palermo. *Tel 091-707 82 01.* www.regione.sicilia.it/turismo/web_turismo

HOTEL CHAINS

Framon Hotels
Via Oratorio San Francesco 306, Messina.
Tel 090-228 22 66.
www.framon-hotels.com

TOURIST VILLAGES

Kastalia
Via Madrid 11, Ragusa.
Tel 0932-82 6095.
www.kastalia.it

Serenusa Village
SS 115, km 240, Licata.
Tel 085-836 97 77.
www.blueshotel.it

Valtur
Via Milano 46, Rome.
Tel 06-482 10 00.
www.valtur.it

CAMPING

Al Yag
Via Altarellazzo, Pozzillo, Acireale (Catania).
Tel 095-764 17 63.

Baia dei Coralli
Località Punta Braccetto, Santa Croce Camerina (Ragusa). *Tel 0932-918 192.*

Baia del Sole
Marina di Ragusa (Ragusa).
Tel 0932-230 344.
www.baiadelsole.it

Baia di Guidaloca
Scopello, Castellammare del Golfo (Trapani).
Tel 0924-541 262 (summer); 323 59 (winter).

Baia Macauda
Contrada Tranchina, Sciacca (Agrigento).
Tel 0925-997 001.

Baia Unci
Località Canneto, Lipari (Messina).
Tel 090-981 19 09.

Bazia
Contrada Bazia, Furnari (Messina).
Tel 0941-800 130.

Calanovella
Contrada Calanovella, SS 113, km 90 (Messina).
Tel 0941-585 258.
www.calanovella.it

Capo Passero
Contrada Vigne Vecchie, Portopalo di Capopassero (Syracuse).
Tel 0931-842 030.

Costa Ponente
Contrada Ogliastrillo, Cefalù (Palermo). *Tel 0921-420 085 (summer); 0921-421 354 (winter).*

El Bahira
Contrada MaKari, San Vito Lo Capo (Trapani).
Tel 0923-972 577 (summer); 0923-972 231 (winter). www.elbahira.it

Eurocamping Due Rocche
Contrada Faino, SS 115, km 241, Butera (Caltanissetta). *Tel 0934-349 006.*

Eurocamping Marmaruca
Via Leto 8, Letojanni (Messina).
Tel 0942-366 76.

Fontane Bianche
Località Fontane Bianche (Syracuse).
Tel 0931-790 333.

La Roccia
Località Cala Greca, Lampedusa (Agrigento).
Tel 0922-970 964.

Mareneve
Contrada Piano Grande, Milo (Catania).
Tel 095-708 21 63.

Miramare
Contrada Costicella, Favignana (Trapani).
Tel 0923-921 330.

Rais Gerbi
Contrada Rais Gerbi, Pollina Finale (Palermo).
Tel 0921-426 570.
www.raisgerbi.it

BED & BREAKFAST

Bed & Breakfast Italia
Tel 06-687 86 18.
www.bbitalia.it

FARM HOLIDAY ASSOCIATIONS

Terranostra
Tel 091-280 000.
www.terranostra.it

FARM HOLIDAYS

Agriturismo.com
Tel 0575-616 091.
www.agriturismo.com

Alcalà
Masseria Alcalà, Misterbianco (Catania).
Tel 095-713 00 29.

L'Antica Vigna
Contrada Montelaguardia, Randazzo (Catania). *Tel 095-924 003 or 922 766.*

Baglio Vajarassa
Contrada Spagnola 176, Marsala.
Tel 0923-968 628.

Borgo degli Olivi
Località Aielli, Tusa (Messina). *Tel 090-719 08.*

Casa dello Scirocco
Lentini (Syracuse).
Tel 095-44 77 09.
www.casadelloscirocco.it

Casa Migliaca
Località Migliaca, Pettineo (Messina).
Tel 0921-336 722.

Codavolpe
Località Trepunti, Giarre (Catania). *Tel 095-939 802.*
www.codavolpe.it

Feudo Tudia
Borgo Tudia, Castellana Sicula (Palermo).
Tel 0934-673 029.

Il Carrubbo
Contrade Bosco Grande Canalotti, Acate (Ragusa).
Tel 0932-989 038.
www.ilcarrubbo.it

Il Daino
San Piero Patti (Messina).
Tel 0941-660 362.
www.ildaino.com

Il Limoneto
Via Provinciale 195F, Acireale (Catania).
Tel 095-886 568.
www.illimoneto.it

Piccolo
Fattoria di Grenne, Ficarra (Messina). *Tel 0941-582 757.* www.grenne.com

Savoca
Contrada Polleri, Piazza Armerina (Enna).
Tel 0935-683 078.
www.agrisavoca.com

Tenuta di Roccadia
Carlentini (Syracuse).
Tel 095-990 362.
www.roccadia.com

Trinità
Via Trinità 34, Mascalucia (Catania).
Tel 095-727 21 56.
www.aziendatrinita.it

YOUTH HOSTELS

Associazione Italiana Alberghi della Gioventù
Via Cavour 44, Rome.
Tel 06-487 11 52.
www.ostellionline.org

Ostello Amodeo
2nd km on the Trapani–Erice provincial road.
Tel 0923-552 964.

Ostello delle Aquile
Salita Federico II d'Aragona, Castroreale (Messina). *Tel 090-974 63 98.*

Ostello Etna
Via della Quercia 7, Nicolosi (Catania).
Tel 095-791 46 86.

Ostello Lipari
Via Castello 17, Lipari (Messina). *Tel 090-981 15 40 or 981 25 27.*

SELF CATERING

Individual Italy
Tel 08700 772772.
www.individualtravellers.com

Magic of Italy
Tel 0870 888 02 28.
www.magicofitaly.co.uk

Tailor-Made Tours
Tel 020 8291 9736.
www.tailormadeinitaly.com

Choosing a Hotel

The hotels in this guide have been carefully selected across a wide price range for the quality of service, decor, location and value. They have been divided into five geographical areas and are listed by place and price category. The listings start with Palermo and continue with hotels further afield.

PRICE CATEGORIES
The following price ranges are for a standard double room and taxes per night during the high season. Breakfast is not included, unless specified.
€ up to €85
€€ €85–€150
€€€ €150–€250
€€€€ €250–€350
€€€€€ over €350

PALERMO

PALERMO Hotel Orientale   €

Via Maqueda 26, 90133 **Tel** *091-616 57 27 or 616 35 06* **Fax** *091-616 11 93* **Rooms** *24*   **Map** *2 D5*

The courtyard entrance speaks of the faded nobility that used to live in this 18th-century palazzo. The grand staircase leads to the "noble floor", with ceiling frescoes in the main salon (Mussolini once gave a speech from its balcony). A friendly, family-run hotel with pleasantly furnished rooms (not all are en suite). **www.albergoorientale.191.it**

PALERMO Villa Archirafi   €€

Via Lincoln 30, 91034 **Tel** *091-616 88 27* **Fax** *091-616 863* **Rooms** *37*   **Map** *2 E4*

Good for those who prefer a central location to size, the moderately priced Villa Archirafi is conveniently situated between Palermo's central train station and the botanical garden, and is a short walk from the Teatro Garibaldi, Santa Maria dello Spasimo and the museum of mineralogy. Comfortably furnished. **www.villaarchirafi.com**

PALERMO Ai Cavalieri Hotel   €€€

Via Sant'Oliva 8, 90141 **Tel** *091-583 282* **Fax** *091-612 65 89* **Rooms** *39*   **Map** *1 A2*

This classic 1891 hotel faces Piazza Sant'Oliva, with its good choice of neighbourhood restaurants, and is an easy walk to the Teatro Massimo, Teatro Politeama and Palazzo Abatellis. A Best Western hotel, Ai Cavalieri caters mainly to business travellers (it has two conference rooms). Daily parking costs €15. **www.aicavalierihotel.it**

PALERMO Centrale Palace   €€€

Corso Vittorio Emanuele 327, 90134 **Tel** *091-336 666* **Fax** *091-334 881* **Rooms** *104*   **Map** *1 C3*

On one of Palermo's lively main streets, this converted 18th-century noble palace is on all major transport routes, and a short walking distance to shops, museums, food markets and the Teatro Biondo. The hotel has a solarium and fitness centre, and in good weather guests can enjoy breakfast on the terrace. **www.centralepalacehotel.it**

PALERMO Excelsior Palace   €€€

Via Marchese Ugo 3, 90134 **Tel** *091-790 90 01* **Fax** *091-342 139* **Rooms** *123*

Built in 1891 and remodelled in 1987, this hotel is still a favourite of visiting aristocracy and has a loyal following. It features some lovely stairways and conversation spaces – a gracious throwback to a Palermo from genteel days gone by. Some rooms have antiques and high ceilings. **www.excelsiorpalermo.it**

PALERMO Grand Hotel et des Palmes   €€€

Via Roma 398, 90134 **Tel** *091-602 81 11* **Fax** *091-331 545* **Rooms** *180*   **Map** *1 C1*

On a central street that runs from the train station to Piazza Sturzo, this historic Ingham-Whitaker palazzo became a hotel in 1874. With its grand entrance and marble lobby, the Grand Hotel caters particularly to business travellers: it has conference rooms and services for meetings, conventions and banquets. **www.grandhoteletdespalmes.it**

PALERMO Hotel Principe di Villafranca   €€€

Via G. Turrisi Colonna 4, 90141 **Tel** *091-611 85 23* **Fax** *091-588 705* **Rooms** *34*   **Road Map** *C2*

This hotel is located in an upscale neighbourhood that offers good dining and shopping opportunities. The lobby has a small bar and in winter the fireplace adds a perfect touch of cosiness. Bathrooms are smallish, so request a room with a tub. The drinks in the room fridge are free. **www.principedivillafranca.it**

PALERMO Massimo Plaza Hotel   €€€

Via Maqueda 437, 90133 **Tel** *091-325 657* **Fax** *091-325 711* **Rooms** *15*   **Map** *1 B2*

Opened in 1999, the Massimo Plaza faces the Teatro Massimo. In the heart of the city, close to shops and restaurants and on public transport lines, this intimate hotel has only 15 rooms, so be sure to reserve well in advance. Bedrooms have damask covers and small writing desks; some also feature a balcony. **www.massimoplazahotel.com**

PALERMO Palazzo Conte Federico   €€€€

Via dei Biscottari 4, 90134 **Tel** *091-651 18 81* **Fax** *091-637 43 84* **Rooms** *4*   **Map** *1 B4*

Count and Countess Federico graciously welcome guests in their torch-lit noble palace with its 12th-century tower. They offer a complimentary drink on arrival, plus breakfast. The medieval bedroom has interconnecting chambers: ideal for accommodating additional family members who do not need private entrances. **www.contefederico.com**

Key to Symbols *see back cover flap*

FURTHER AFIELD Casena dei Colli

Via Villa Rosato 20, 90146 **Tel** 091-688 97 71 **Fax** 091-688 97 79 **Rooms** 93   **Road Map** C2

Once the home of Ferdinand of Bourbon's secretary, this residence is located near the Parco della Favorita and the Palazzina Cinese, and offers guests a patch of green in Palermo, away from the central bustle. In the summer months, breakfast is served in the garden. Rooms are comfortably furnished. **www.casenadeicolli.it**

FURTHER AFIELD Hotel Gallery House

Via Mariano Stabile 136, 90139 **Tel** 091-612 47 58 **Fax** 091-612 47 79 **Rooms** 12   **Road Map** C2

This hotel benefits from the charming personal touch of the family who runs it. Conveniently located a short walk from the historic centre, the Gallery House features nicely appointed guest rooms, plus two apartments that are handy for families with children. Garage service on request. **www.hotelgalleryhouse.com**

FURTHER AFIELD Splendid Hotel La Torre

Via Piano Gallo 11, Mondello, 90151 **Tel** 091-450 222 **Fax** 091-450 033 **Rooms** 168   **Road Map** C2

Mondello represents the centre of Palermo's beach action. This modern hotel is up above the crowd on a cliff with a luxuriant garden, tennis courts and sea-water swimming pool. Some rooms have a terrace with sea views for a slightly higher fee than a standard room. Large conference rooms host conventions. **www.latorre.com**

FURTHER AFIELD Villa d'Amato

Via Messina Marina 180, 90121 **Tel/Fax** 091-621 27 67 **Rooms** 37   **Road Map** C2

On the busy coastal road east of Palermo's port, this modern villa welcomes leisure and business travellers, plus meetings in its conference centre. Rooms are furnished in a modern style and some have a view of the sea. Breakfast is served on the terrace. A shuttle service operates on request. **www.hotelvilladamato.it**

FURTHER AFIELD Villa Esperia

Viale Margherita di Savoia 53, Mondello, 90151 **Tel** 091-684 07 17 **Fax** 091-684 15 08 **Rooms** 22   **Road Map** C2

The family atmosphere and smaller size of this hotel are draws if you seek a more intimate experience at the beach in Mondello. Rooms are attractively furnished, with rugs and iron-framed beds, some with canopies. Hedges around the hotel offer tranquillity in this busy area. The restaurant has garden dining. **www.hotelvillaesperia.it**

FURTHER AFIELD Astoria Palace

Via Montepellegrino 62, 90142 **Tel** 091-628 11 11 **Fax** 091-637 21 78 **Rooms** 326   **Road Map** C2

This modern hotel near the Fiera del Mediterraneo exhibition centre attracts a primarily business and convention clientele for the trade shows; it also hosts its own events in its conference centre. Rates tend to be lowest when the Fiera has no shows or events booked. Rooms are furnished in a standard modern style. **www.ghshotels.it**

FURTHER AFIELD Baglio di Pianetto

Santa Cristina Gela, Scorrimento Veloce, 90030 **Tel** 091-857 00 02 **Fax** 091-857 00 15 **Rooms** 13 **Road Map** B2

Count Marzotto produces high-quality wines, which inspired the countess to open an inn with views over the family vineyards, olive trees and nearby mountains. The chef's bounty comes from nearby fields and farms, and there is a wine tasting room as well as an outdoor swimming pool and a solarium. **www.bagliodipianetto.com**

FURTHER AFIELD Mondello Palace

Viale Principe di Scalea 2, Mondello, 90151 **Tel** 091-450 001 **Fax** 091-450 657 **Rooms** 83   **Road Map** C2

In the 1950s, this was the scene of dances and social events; now its main focus is conventions. The hotel has a historic bathhouse and retains a bygone allure. Some of the pleasantly furnished rooms have a sea view. There is also a private beach with a range of water sports, such as sailing and scuba diving. **www.mondellopalacehotel.it**

FURTHER AFIELD Grand Hotel Hilton Villa Igiea

Salita Belmonte 43, 90142 **Tel** 091-631 21 11 **Fax** 091-547 654 **Rooms** 113   **Road Map** C2

Set above the west end of Palermo's harbour, the city's most romantic and deluxe hotel is a favourite of the international and political elite. Elegantly furnished, Villa Igiea has a beautiful garden with pool and a classical temple overlooking the harbour. Facilities include a fitness centre and tennis courts. **www.villaigieapalermo.it**

NORTHWESTERN SICILY

CARINI Hotel Portorais

Via Piraineto 125, 90044 **Tel** 091-869 34 81 **Fax** 091-869 34 58 **Rooms** 55   **Road Map** B2

West of Palermo, on the coast near the airport, this modern hotel attracts guests with its fitness centre, swimming pool, beach and other facilities, such as table tennis and billiards. Its conference centre draws the business clientele. Rooms are furnished in a modern style and some have a view over the Gulf of Carini. **www.hotelportorais.com**

CASTEL DI TUSA L'Atelier sul Mare

Via Cesare Battisti 4, 98070 **Tel** 091-334 295 **Fax** 091-334 283 **Rooms** 40   **Road Map** D2

On the coast east of Cefalù, this hotel showcases the work of contemporary artists, turning itself into a sort of art gallery. The public areas have paintings and sculptures, as do some of the rooms. Those furnished by contemporary artists cost about €50 more than standard rooms. **www.ateliersulmare.com**

CASTELLAMMARE DEL GOLFO Hotel Al Madarig   🍴🗐🅿♿   €€

Piazza Petrolo 7, 91014 **Tel** *0924-33 533* **Fax** *0924-33 790* **Rooms** *38*   **Road Map** *B2*

In the town centre, facing a square by the harbour, this hotel was built into abandoned port warehouses. The steps (*al madarig* in Arabic) lead down to the beach. It's a good base for excursions to the Zingaro nature reserve, which is a short drive northwest along the coast. Modern, functional rooms, some with sea views. **www.almadarig.com**

CEFALÙ Baia del Capitano   🍴🏖🏃🗐🅿♿   €€

Contrada Mazzaforno, 90015 **Tel** *0921-420 003/5* **Fax** *0921-420 163* **Rooms** *52*   **Road Map** *D2*

Located near the beach, this pleasant, modern Mediterranean-style hotel has access to beach facilities as well as a swimming pool, tennis courts, bowling green, table tennis, windsurfing and a disco. Its two meeting rooms occasionally host small conferences. Dog-owners and their pets are welcome. **www.baiadelcapitano.it**

CEFALÙ Gli Alberi del Paradiso   🍴🏖🅿🗐🅿♿   €€€

Via dei Mulini 18–20, 90015 **Tel** *0921-423 900* **Fax** *0921-423 990* **Rooms** *55*   **Road Map** *D2*

A historic manor house on a small hill was converted to an inn, then expanded with a modern wing. It is run by a friendly family who will arrange tennis, golf, horse riding and a number of water sports for their guests. They are also particularly proud of their chef. Bedrooms are comfortable and pleasantly furnished. **www.alberidelparadiso.it**

ERICE Hotel Elimo   🍴🗐♿   €€

Via Vittorio Emanuele 75, 91016 **Tel** *0923-869 377* **Fax** *0923-869 252* **Rooms** *21*   **Road Map** *A2*

The lobby's warm colours, Oriental rugs and leather sofas are inviting, while in winter a fireplace becomes the room's focus. There is another large fireplace in the restaurant, which is an ideal spot for evening drinks. The rooms have red lacquer doors, nice drapes and comfortable furniture. Courtyard and terrace, too. **www.hotelelimo.it**

ERICE Hotel Moderno Erice   🍴🗐🅿♿   €€

Via Vittorio Emanuele 63, 91016 **Tel** *0923-869 300* **Fax** *0923-869 139* **Rooms** *40*   **Road Map** *A2*

The friendly family who runs this hotel is very present – you'll see them working at the reception desk, eating in the restaurant or relaxing in the lounge. Rooms are simply furnished (some are located across the street in the annexe); four have antique or handcrafted furniture. The small terrace has a lovely view. **www.hotelmodernoerice.it**

ERICE Torri Pepoli   🍴🗐   €€€

Giardini del Balio Viale Conte Pepoli, 91016 **Tel** *0923-860 117* **Fax** *0923-522 091* **Rooms** *7*   **Road Map** *A2*

Restored in 1870 by Count Pepoli, this Norman castle was reopened in 2005 by his descendants as a deluxe hotel. Rooms have commanding views of Erice's countryside and the Count's Room is one of the suites. Enjoy an apéritif or cappuccino in the restaurant bar. A grand, quiet hideaway with a charming lookout point. **www.torripepoli.it**

FAVIGNANA Aegusa   🍴🏃🗐♿   €€

Via Garibaldi 11–17, 91023 **Tel** *0923-922 430* **Fax** *0923-922 440* **Rooms** *28*   **Road Map** *A2*

A short hop on the ferry from Trapani is the island of Favignana. This small Mediterranean-style hotel, converted from an old palazzo, stands in the historic centre near the harbour. The lovely rooms are decorated simply and tastefully. The restaurant is open for lunch and dinner (except Tue lunch); alfresco dining is also available. **www.aegusahotel.it**

MARSALA Hotel Carmine   🗐🅿♿   €€

Piazza Carmine, 16, 91025 **Tel** *0923-711 907* **Fax** *0923-717 574* **Rooms** *28*   **Road Map** *A3*

This 17th-century former convent underwent a five-year renovation and is now a family-run hotel. All rooms have antique furniture, Oriental pattern rugs, good reading lights, pretty bath tiles and nice textiles; some also have a view of the square. A dining plan with three local restaurants can be arranged. **www.hotelcarmine.it**

MARSALA La Finestra sul Sale   🍽🗐🅿♿   €€

Contrada Ettore Infersa, 91025 **Tel** *0923-733 003* **Fax** *0923-733 142* **Rooms** *3*   **Road Map** *A3*

"Window over the Salt" bed and breakfast offers a unique immersion into the culture of sea salt in Sicily. All bedrooms have a view of Mozia, its salt flats, the bay and a windmill. Bedrooms have terracotta floors, ceilings of wooden beams and bricks, and wood furniture. Salt is harvested from May to June, but this hotel is lovely year-round.

MARSALA Agriturismo Baglio del Marchese   🍽🗐🅿♿   €€€

Lungomare Mediterraneo, 91025 **Tel/Fax** *0923-951 115 or 348 002 20 70* **Rooms** *10*   **Road Map** *A3*

This historic former manor house offers deluxe accommodation. Once a hunting reserve, the estate now cultivates vineyards, and wine tastings are available. Bedrooms have original antiques, marble floors, wood and volcanic-rock ceilings, and decorative tile baths. The beach and a nature reserve are nearby. **www.bagliodelmarchese.com**

MARSALA Agriturismo Tenute Montalto   🍽🏃🅿♿   €€€€

Lungomare Mediterraneo, Litoranea Sud, 91025 **Tel/Fax** *0923-951 115 or 348 002 20 70* **Rooms** *7*   **Road Map** *A3*

This historic estate produces wine (Nero d'Avola, Grillo), olive oil and citrus fruit. The accommodation consists of two villas: the larger one sleeps seven people; the smaller villa, four. Bedrooms have Sicilian furniture, plus some family antiques. The public spaces are decorated in Art Nouveau style. **www.tenutemontalto.com**

MAZARA DEL VALLO Kempinski Hotel Giardino di Costanza   🍴🏖🗐🅿♿   €€€€

Via Salemi, km 6.8, 91100 **Tel** *0923-675 000* **Fax** *0923-675 876* **Rooms** *8*   **Road Map** *A3*

Formerly known as Villa Fontanasalsa, this hotel was bought by the Kempinski chain, enlarged and transformed into a luxury resort with a beauty and wellness centre. Pool, sauna, gym and tennis are all available and the hotel has its own private beach. Bedrooms are luxurious and spacious, with all modern conveniences. **www.kempinski-sicily.com**

Key to Price Guide *see p198* **Key to Symbols** *see back cover flap*

SCOPELLO Albergo La Tavernetta
🍴 🗐 ♿ €€
Via Diaz 3, 90414 **Tel/Fax** *0924-541 129* **Rooms** *11* **Road Map** *B2*

This small hotel is situated at the southern end of the Zingaro nature reserve, between San Vito and Castellammare del Golfo. Once an Arab enclave, this simply furnished former residence is intimate in size and ideal for nature lovers who don't want to resort to camping. A restaurant is conveniently located on site.

SELINUNTE Hotel Miramare Selinunte
🍴 🗐 P €
Via Pigafetta 2, Marinella di Selinunte, 91022 **Tel** *0924-46 045* **Fax** *0924-46 744* **Rooms** *20* **Road Map** *B3*

Set in a peacefully quiet town, but with enough restaurants and beaches to keep you entertained, this hotel is a good choice. The terrace and some of the guest rooms have a view of the sea and of the archaeological ruins. There is a restaurant/pizzeria on the premises, and the hotel also has a private beach. **www.hotelmiramareselinunte.com**

TRAPANI Vittoria
🗐 €€
Via Crispi 4, 91100 **Tel** *0923-873 044* **Fax** *0923-29 870* **Rooms** *65* **Road Map** *A2*

The exterior will not win it any architectural awards, but this hotel is right in the centre of Trapani, so it is a popular choice with businesspeople. The rooms are furnished in a simple, basic style, but they are comfortable, and some have a view of the historic centre or of the sea. Helpful staff. **www.hotelvittoriatrapani.it**

TRAPANI Crystal Hotel
🍴 🗐 P ♿ €€€
Piazza Umberto 1, 91100 **Tel** *0923-20 000* **Fax** *0923-25 555* **Rooms** *68* **Road Map** *A2*

The modern white-and-glass exterior reflects the colour of the locally sourced sea salt. This hotel caters to the business traveller; its two meeting rooms often host conferences. Guest rooms are modern, most with a black-and-white colour scheme, and all have Wi-Fi Internet access. Located near the city centre. **www.framonhotels.com**

USTICA Grotta Azzurra
🍴 ≋ 🏃 🗐 P ♿ €€€
Contrada San Ferlicchio, 90010 **Tel** *0931-97 1018* **Fax** *0931-52 32 03* **Rooms** *52* **Road Map** *B1*

This white hotel stands out from the rocks and the natural blue cave in the hollow of the cliffs below. Most rooms face the sea and have a terrace. Lounge chairs are set out on platforms along the rocky shoreline. Facilities include a private beach, outside dining, a diving centre, windsurfing, boat taxi and boat rental. **www.framonhotels.com**

VALDERICE Baglio Santa Croce
🍴 ≋ 🏃 🗐 P ♿ €€€
Contrada Santa Croce, 91019 **Tel** *0923-891 111* **Fax** *0923-891 192* **Rooms** *67* **Road Map** *A2*

A new wing constructed in 2006 more than doubled this hotel's capacity. The original 1637 farm building has stone walls, terracotta floors, wood-beamed ceilings and rustic furniture. The new wing has lighter, larger rooms with oak doors, wooden furniture, tile floors, and larger beds and bathrooms. **www.bagliosantacroce.it**

VALDERICE Tonnara di Bonagia
🍴 ≋ 🏃 🗐 P ♿ €€€
Piazza Tonnara, 91019 **Tel** *0923-431 111* **Fax** *0923-592 177* **Rooms** *121* **Road Map** *A2*

The 17th-century maritime quarter of Valderice has been sympathetically converted and expanded into a hotel and convention centre. The *mattanza*, the ancient ritual of catching tuna, still takes place nearby in May and June. Facilities include a fitness centre, pool, diving centre, boat rental and tennis courts. **www.framonhotels.com**

SOUTHWESTERN SICILY

AGRIGENTO Hotel Kaos
🍴 ≋ 🏃 🗐 P ♿ €€
Villaggio Pirandello, 92100 **Tel** *0922-598 622* **Fax** *0922-589 770* **Rooms** *105* **Road Map** *C4*

Set above the beach, this restored aristocratic villa complex is delightful. The spacious pool curves graciously through the lovely garden, with its sea views and terrace dining. The interior is tastefully furnished and the staff are attentive. Tennis, soccer, bridge tournaments and cooking classes are all on offer. Beach shuttle. **www.athenahotels.com**

AGRIGENTO Foresteria Baglio della Luna
🍴 🗐 P ♿ €€€
Contrada Maddalusa Valle dei Templi, 92100 **Tel** *0922-511 061* **Fax** *0922-598 802* **Rooms** *24* **Road Map** *C4*

This former country estate with an ancient lookout tower offers a garden with a panorama of the countryside and Baroque art in some of the rooms. Bedrooms are comfortably furnished with modern conveniences; some have a view of the temples. The restaurant features local produce in traditional recipes. **www.bagliodellaluna.com**

AGRIGENTO Villa Athena
🍴 ≋ 🗐 P ♿ €€€
Via dei Templi 53, 92100 **Tel/Fax** *0922-402 180* **Rooms** *40* **Road Map** *C4*

Savour the view of the majestic Temple of Concord from the garden or head for the pool, set in a lovingly tended garden of luxuriant plants. Oriental carpets, antiques and tasteful art make for a pleasant stay in this lovely, well-managed hotel. **www.hotelvillaathena.com**

CALTANISSETTA Villa San Michele
🍴 🏃 🗐 P ♿ €€
Via Fasci Siciliani, 93100 **Tel** *0934-553 750* **Fax** *0934-598 791* **Rooms** *136* **Road Map** *D3*

Built to attract conventions in the hills of central Sicily, this modern hotel aims to keep abreast of business trends with its conference facilities, helipad and technical support. Guest rooms are large, with modern conveniences; some have a view of the hills. The restaurant is closed on Sunday and most of August. **www.hotelsanmichelesicilia.it**

ENNA Sicilia

☰☰P& €€

Piazza Colajanni 7, 94100 **Tel** *0935-500 850* **Fax** *0935-500 488* **Rooms** *80*   **Road Map** *D3*

This centrally located hotel in Enna is convenient for visits to the Castello di Lombardia, Duomo, Torre and other local sights. It is unexceptional in design or facilities, but serves the purpose for a brief stay for business or tourism. Rooms are furnished in a modern style and have all conveniences. **www.hotelsiciliaenna.it**

LAMPEDUSA I Dammusi di Borgo Cala Creta

⛄P& €

Contrada Cala Creta, 92010 **Tel** *0922-970 883* **Fax** *0922-970 590* **Rooms** *25*   **Road Map** *B5*

Traditional, Arab-inspired *dammusi* are stone houses with white cupolas and small windows to keep the interior cool. Here, each one has its own patio and garden. There is a shuttle service, plus optional excursions and boat trips. Half-board is available and weekly stays may be required in mid-August. **www.calacreta.com**

LAMPEDUSA Sirio

☰☰P €€

Via Antonello da Messina 5, 92010 **Tel/Fax** *0922-970 401* **Rooms** *10*   **Road Map** *B5*

This small hotel faces Lampedusa island's harbour. Bedrooms are furnished in typical blue and yellow seaside colours. During mid-August guests are requested to take the half-board option, which includes dinner in the hotel restaurant. Boat excursions can be arranged.

LAMPEDUSA Il Gattopardo

☰☰ €€€€€

Cala Creta, 92010 **Tel** *0922-970 051* **Fax** *0922-971 645* **Rooms** *12*   **Road Map** *B5*

Accommodation at Il Gattopardo is in *dammusi*, traditional stone houses, in a tranquil seaside setting. Two boats take guests out on daily excursions with lunch, and there are seven small cars available to explore the island's interior independently. The chef prepares a delicious dinner in the evening. Weekly stays only. **www.equinoxe.it**

PANTELLERIA Mursia

☰☰⛄☰P €€€

Mursia, 91017 **Tel** *0923-911 217* **Fax** *0923-911 026* **Rooms** *74*   **Road Map** *A5*

On the northwestern coast of Pantelleria, this hotel has two pools (salt- and freshwater), a children's pool, tennis courts and a piano bar. Bedrooms are furnished in handcrafted wood and neutral-colour fabrics, and they all have a terrace. Many rooms also have a vaulted ceiling with a cupola. **www.mursiahotel.it**

PIAZZA ARMERINA La Casa sulla Collina d'Oro

☰☰P& €

Via Mattarella snc, 94015 **Tel/Fax** *0935-89 680* **Rooms** *7*   **Road Map** *D4*

This 1872 house is the most historic building on the southern hill. Rooms are tastefully decorated in natural materials such as stone, wood, terracotta, linen and cotton, and the terrace has a view over the medieval village. The owners are passionate historians and offer tours in Italian or German. Dinner by request. **www.lacasasullacollinadoro.it**

PIAZZA ARMERINA Azienda Turistica Torre di Renda

☰☰⛄☰☰P& €€

Contrada Torre di Renda, 94015 **Tel** *0935-687 657* **Fax** *0935-687 821* **Rooms** *16*   **Road Map** *D4*

This cosy wooded mountainside inn, enlarged from a 17th-century residence, was once a bishop's summer home. Bedrooms are simply furnished in wood. The restaurant is open to public; the half-board option (with either lunch or dinner) costs an extra €18 a day. Horse riding is available nearby. **www.torrerenda.it**

PIAZZA ARMERINA Hotel Gangi

☰& €€€

Via Generale Ciancio 68, 94015 **Tel** *0935-682 737* **Fax** *0935-687 563* **Rooms** *18*   **Road Map** *D4*

This family-run hotel in the centre of Piazza Armerina offers a pleasant stay. Two rooms are decorated in a retro style. In nice weather, breakfast is served on the terrace. The staff are happy to arrange excursions nearby or across Sicily. Ideally located for walks into town, to the shops and restaurants. **www.hotelgangi.it**

SUTERA Piazza Bed & Breakfast

☰☰P €

Contrada Fosse, 93010 **Tel/Fax** *0934-954 125* **Rooms** *8*   **Road Map** *C3*

A family-run hotel in this unique town carved into a rock near picturesque mountains, ruins and valleys. The spotless bedrooms are simply furnished in wood, and one has a balcony with a view of faraway Etna. Hot, substantial English breakfasts are on offer, as well as guided walks. **www.bedandbreakfastpiazza.it**

SOUTHERN SICILY

CALTAGIRONE Grand Hotel Villa San Mauro

☰☰⛄☰P& €€€

Via Porto Salvo 10, 95041 **Tel** *0933-26 500* **Fax** *0933-31 661* **Rooms** *92*   **Road Map** *D4*

This hotel set among the hills aims to please both leisure and business travellers. It is decorated with beautiful local ceramics and most rooms have balconies with views of the surrounding countryside. The pool has a snack bar. The conference centre seats up to 160. One floor is reserved for non-smokers. **www.framonhotels.com**

MARINA DI RAGUSA Hotel Terracqua

☰☰⛄☰P& €€€

Via delle Sirene 35, 97010 **Tel** *0932-615 600* **Fax** *0932-615 580* **Rooms** *77*   **Road Map** *E5*

This hotel has a beautiful private beach across the road. The rooms are basic and few rooms have a sea view, but it continues to be a popular destination for receptions and conventions. Marina di Ragusa's continuing building boom might mean noise or unattractive surroundings. **www.shr.it**

Key to Price Guide *see p198* **Key to Symbols** *see back cover flap*

MODICA L'Orangerie

Vico de Naro 5, 97015 **Tel** *3470-674 698* **Fax** *0932-754 840* **Rooms** *7*   **Road Map** *F5*

This 19th-century neo-Renaissance palace in the heart of Modica is charming. Each room is decorated in a different elegant colour, and all have contemporary graphics. Enchanting period frescoes decorate some of the rooms and one of the halls. Breakfast is served in the traditional 19th-century kitchen. **www.lorangerie.it**

RAGUSA Hotel Locanda Don Serafino

Via XI Febbraio 15, Ragusa Ibla, 97100 **Tel** *0932-220 065* **Fax** *0932-663 186* **Rooms** *10*   **Road Map** *E5*

In the Baroque heart of town, this intimate hotel was constructed within an 18th-century palazzo. One room's Gothic arch dates to 1300, while another has a tub carved out of the rock. The furniture is handmade in early 19th-century style. The owners' restaurant a few blocks away also merits a visit. **www.locandadonserafino.it**

RAGUSA Mediterraneo Palace

Via Roma 189, 97100 **Tel** *0932-621 944* **Fax** *0932-623 799* **Rooms** *92*   **Road Map** *E5*

In the Baroque section of Ragusa, near the Museo Archeologico, is this hotel with comfortable, spacious rooms furnished in modern style with all conveniences. Baths are large, with marble floors, and some have a whirlpool, a good antidote to tired feet after a long day's sightseeing. **www.mediterraneopalace.it**

RAGUSA Eremo della Giubiliana

Contrada Giubiliana, 97100 **Tel** *0932-669 119* **Fax** *0932-669 129* **Rooms** *12*   **Road Map** *E5*

This 12th-century monastery is an elegant retreat and its plateau position offers superb panoramic views. This makes a more tranquil base for beach excursions than any hotel in Marina di Ragusa. Rooms are in former monks' cells, all elegantly furnished. **www.eremodellagiubiliana.it**

SYRACUSE Domus Mariae

Via Vittorio Veneto 76, 96100 **Tel** *0931-24 854* **Fax** *0931-24 858* **Rooms** *16*   **Road Map** *F4*

Ursuline nuns efficiently run this hotel with spacious rooms; a room with a sea view costs an additional €15. The hotel has a small library, where guests can dine during part of the year (the dining room is not open to outsiders). It all adds up to a pleasant and tranquil stay.

SYRACUSE Hotel Il Podere

Contrada Torre Landolina 11, 96100 **Tel** *0931-449 390* **Fax** *0931-723 006* **Rooms** *26*   **Road Map** *F4*

Inside the Fonte Ciane nature reserve, surrounded by citrus and olive groves, is this 19th-century farm complex, which has been elegantly converted to a hotel. Bedrooms are furnished with antiques and rugs. There are two pools, a play-ground, a private beach, horse riding and golf. Located near the Neapolis archaeological park. **www.ilpodere.it**

SYRACUSE L'Approdo delle Sirene

Riva Garibaldi 15, 96100 **Tel** *0931-24 857* **Fax** *0931-483 764* **Rooms** *8*   **Road Map** *F4*

This elegant historic two-storey building on the harbour channel has a roof terrace fragrant with jasmine and bougainvillea. Here you can have breakfast, admire the sunset or watch the action in the harbour. Some rooms have balconies overlooking the harbour. A light lunch is available on request. **www.apprododellesirene.com**

SYRACUSE Palazzo Giaracà

Via dei Mille 34, 96100 **Tel** *0931-464 907* **Fax** *0931-480 419* **Rooms** *27*   **Road Map** *F4*

This 1892 palace on the Ortygia harbour still has some original antiques. It is run by descendants of a noble family, whose personal touch creates a warm and inviting ambience. Floors are tiled or volcanic stone. The Count's Room has a fireplace, and there are down duvets. Some rooms have harbour views. **www.palazzogiaraca.it**

SYRACUSE Hotel des Etrangers et Miramare

Passaggio Adorno 10–12, 96100 **Tel** *0931-319 100* **Fax** *0931-319 100* **Rooms** *80*   **Road Map** *F4*

Reopened in 2005 after being closed for 30 years, this historic luxury hotel in central Ortygia faces a sandy beach. The hotel has two restaurants, one with a view of the coast and the other with a roof garden for alfresco dining. Sea-view rooms are more expensive. There is also a spa. **www.medeahotels.com**

SYRACUSE Villa Lucia

Trav. Mondello 1, Contrada Isola, 96100 **Tel** *0931-721 007* **Fax** *0931-721 587* **Rooms** *15*   **Road Map** *F4*

Once the summer home of the family who runs it, this patrician villa is set back among the trees and boasts a nicely landscaped pool. Inside, their furniture and mementos give the interior a personal, homely touch. Rooms are spacious; the carriage house nearby has budget-priced mini-apartments with kitchens. **www.siracusavillalucia.it**

NORTHEASTERN SICILY

ACITREZZA Hotel Eden Riviera

Via Litteri 57, 95026 **Tel** *095-277 760* **Fax** *095-277 761* **Rooms** *31*   **Road Map** *F3*

This family-run hotel in the hills above the sea has a terrace with views of Lachea Island and unique rock formations. Its small, enchanting garden has an impressive prickly pear cactus and other Mediterranean plants that surround the swimming pool. Dinner supplement. Discounts available (not in August). **www.hoteledenriviera.com**

CAPO D'ORLANDO La Tartaruga

Via Lido San Gregorio 70, 98071 **Tel** *0941-955 012* **Fax** *0941-955 056* **Rooms** *38*   **Road Map** *E2*

Halfway between Milazzo and Cefalù, this small seaside hotel attracts a business clientele during most of the year. In summer, families enjoy its beach facilities, pool, pizzeria and disco. Rooms are simply furnished in yellow, blue or green. Bedroom terraces and balconies face the sea, pool or inner courtyard. **www.hoteltartaruga.it**

CAPRILEONE Hotel Antica Filanda

Contrada da Raviola, 98070 **Tel** *0941-919 704* **Rooms** *16*   **Road Map** *E2*

The hilltop vista from the terrace is of the Aeolian Islands. Guest rooms are spacious and decorated in an antique style with cherrywood furniture. Two suites have a fireplace and Jacuzzi. Sip afternoon cocktails on the terrace or by the pool, and enjoy home-made jams at breakfast (flavours include peach, orange and lemon). **www.anticafilanda.it**

CATANIA Albergo Moderno

Via Alessi 9, 95124 **Tel** *095-326 250* **Fax** *095-326 674* **Rooms** *18*   **Road Map** *F3*

Opened in 1922 and run by the same family since 1955, the Moderno is an inexpensive option for those who prefer budget rates to chic or cutting-edge decor. Bedrooms have fluorescent lights and are rather spartan, but the hotel is clean and centrally located. **www.albergomoderno.it**

CATANIA Hotel Centrale Europa

Via Vittorio Emanuele, 167, 95124 **Tel** *095-311 309* **Fax** *095-317 531* **Rooms** *17*   **Road Map** *F3*

This historic hotel has an inviting exterior and the rooms are pleasant, simple, and with wooden furniture; most also have a terrific view of Piazza Duomo, so you can have fun watching the world go by. No lift (rooms are upstairs). The staff are very helpful. **www.hotelcentraleuropa.it**

CATANIA Garden

Trappeto, Via Madonna delle Lacrime, 95129 **Tel** *095-717 77 67* **Fax** *095-717 79 91* **Rooms** *95*   **Road Map** *F3*

The hotel's large Mediterranean garden with local and exotic plants is especially appreciated when the pool opens in summer. Rooms are comfortably furnished, many with walnut furniture in antique style, and there is a fitness centre and sauna. Located west of Catania, a short distance away from Etna's small towns. **www.gardenhotel.ct.it**

CATANIA Hotel del Duomo

Via Etnea 28, 95131 **Tel** *095-250 31 77* **Fax** *095-715 27 90* **Rooms** *12*   **Road Map** *F3*

Step into the courtyard and leave the bustle of the city behind. This hotel, near Piazza Duomo, is small, family run and quiet. Rooms are pleasantly furnished, some with rooftop views; one room (Brancati) has a balcony. The patisserie downstairs (not part of the hotel) is handy for a sweet snack. **www.hoteldelduomo.it**

CATANIA Castello di Xirumi-Serravale

Castello di Xirume, Frazione Lentini, 95129 **Tel** *095-447 987* **Fax** *095-504 553* **Rooms** *10*   **Road Map** *F3*

This 16th-century castle southwest of Catania, run by a noble family, is a link to Renaissance Sicily. The castle is furnished with antiques, and its atmosphere makes it a popular choice with locals for wedding receptions. A good base to see nearby Neolithic tombs, and the ceramics of Caltagirone are only half an hour away. **www.xirumi.com**

CATANIA Hotel Royal

Via A. Di Sangiuliano 337, 95124 **Tel** *095-250 33 47* **Fax** *095-250 33 60* **Rooms** *20*   **Road Map** *F3*

This trendy hotel, with its contemporary architectural design, has a wine bar, restaurant and tearoom. It is located near the top of the hill and the street leads to the harbour below – a good base for city walks. Room balconies face the street or the courtyard. Facilities include a solarium, Jacuzzi, gym, sauna and Turkish bath. **www.hotelroyalcatania.it**

CATANIA Il Principe Hotel

Via Alessi 24, 95124 **Tel** *095-250 03 45* **Fax** *095-325 799* **Rooms** *25*   **Road Map** *F3*

The flair of a contemporary architect shows in details like the lighting, wooden floors, luminous bathroom tiles and high-quality textiles in the guest rooms in this hotel. Services include a Turkish bath, Internet point, small bar and free parking. The Costanza Suite has a fireplace and skylight. **www.ilprincipehotel.com**

CATANIA Katane Palace Hotel

Via Finocchiaro Aprile 110, 95129 **Tel** *095-747 07 02* **Fax** *095-747 01 72* **Rooms** *58*   **Road Map** *F3*

This lovely hotel attracts a business and tourist clientele that enjoys modern conveniences and style. From the bellboy to the manager, the staff here take great pride in the details: the salon has travel books and a grand piano for guests to play, and the flower-filled patio expands the dining area, which is run by a capable chef. **www.katanepalace.it**

CATANIA Sheraton

Via Antonello da Messina 45, Acicastello, 95020 **Tel** *095-711 41 11* **Fax** *095-271 380* **Rooms** *170* **Road Map** *F3*

This modern hotel caters primarily to the business and conference clientele. Summer visitors can take the underpass directly to the private beach, and there is a fitness centre, beauty centre and spa. The management is placing extra emphasis on developing an innovative quality restaurant, Il Timo, to also attract locals. **www.sheratoncatania.com**

CATANIA Villa del Bosco Hotel

Via del Bosco 62, 95125 **Tel** *095-733 51 00* **Fax** *095-733 51 03* **Rooms** *45*   **Road Map** *F3*

This 19th-century villa is full of contemporary design. Rooms are furnished with subtle modern decor, and the roof terrace has a view of the city. The hotel has non-smoking rooms, is well equipped for business meetings and can arrange car rental. **www.hotelvilladelbosco.it**

Key to Price Guide *see p198* **Key to Symbols** *see back cover flap*

CATANIA Grand Hotel Baia Verde

Cannizaro, Via Musco 8–10, 95020 **Tel** *095-491 522* **Fax** *095-494 464* **Rooms** *162* **Road Map** *F3*

White-washed buildings at the sea's edge make this one of Catania's most attractive seaside resorts. The restaurant has a sea view and the terrace offers outdoor dining. The wellness centre is popular with locals too, who enjoy its many treatments and programmes. There is also a diving school. **www.baiaverde.it**

GIARDINI-NAXOS Arathena Rocks

Via Calcide Eubea 55, 98030 **Tel** *0942-51 349* **Fax** *0942-51 690* **Rooms** *50* **Road Map** *F3*

The sea-water swimming pool cut out of the rock is one of the main draws at this seaside hotel. Some bathrooms are decorated with Sicilian tiles. The hotel is open only during the warmer season, from April (sometimes earlier) to November. Half-board may be required during the month of August. **www.hotellarathena.com**

GIARDINI-NAXOS Nike

Via Calcide Eubea 27, 98030 **Tel** *0942-51 207* **Fax** *0942-56 315* **Rooms** *55* **Road Map** *F3*

Large terraces offer a panoramic view of the sea below. The hotel has a solarium, as well as its own private beach and a dock for pleasure boats. Some rooms do not have air conditioning, so specify which you prefer (the price difference is only a few euros). **www.hotelnike.it**

LIPARI Giardino sul Mare

Via Maddalena 65, 98055 **Tel** *090-981 10 04* **Fax** *090-988 01 50* **Rooms** *46* **Road Map** *E1*

This charming island hotel overlooks the sea and boasts its own private beach below. The terrace has magnificent views, and the garden has ancient plants and palm trees. All rooms are furnished in wood with blue and white floors and blue cotton bedcovers; most have sea views. **www.giardinosulmare.it**

LIPARI Hotel A Pinnata

Località Pignataro, 98055 **Tel** *090-981 16 97* **Fax** *090-981 47 82* **Rooms** *12* **Road Map** *E1*

From this hotel terrace the view to the island of Vulcano is breathtaking. Rooms are warm green or yellow, with mostly wooden furniture and iron beds. Guests have easy access to the beach. This hotel has no restaurant but there are many excellent eateries nearby. Closed Nov–Mar. **www.bernardigroup.it**

LIPARI Hotel Tritone

Via Mendolita, 98055 **Tel/Fax** *090-981 15 95* **Rooms** *39* **Road Map** *E1*

Volcanic spring water feeds the swimming pool at the Tritone; drinks and sandwiches are available pool-side. All rooms have a sea view, as does the breakfast room. The hotel, which has a health spa, is a short walk from the town centre and the sea. A shuttle service to the beach is provided. **http://tritone.hotelsinsicily.it**

LIPARI Villa Meligunis

Via Marte, 98055 **Tel** *090-981 24 26* **Fax** *090-988 01 49* **Rooms** *32* **Road Map** *E1*

Small and luxurious, this island hotel is located near Marina Corta in an 18th-century converted residence in a fishing village. The hotel has an established reputation for impeccable service, and facilities include a swimming pool and a Turkish bath. **www.villameligunis.it**

MESSINA Grand Hotel Liberty

Via I Settembre 15, 98122 **Tel** *090-640 94 36* **Fax** *090-640 93 40* **Rooms** *54* **Road Map** *F2*

Built in the Art Nouveau style, this classic hotel is located in the historic centre of Messina, near the train station and a short distance to the port for departures to the Aeolian Islands. In addition to the restaurant, services include tearoom, bar, conference rooms and Wi-Fi in the rooms, plus car and motorbike rentals. **www.framonhotels.com**

MESSINA Royal Palace

Via T. Cannizzaro 224, 98123 **Tel** *090-65 03* **Fax** *090-292 10 75* **Rooms** *116* **Road Map** *F2*

In the heart of Messina's shopping district and near the harbour, this hotel caters to both business and leisure travellers. The spacious rooms have plenty of light from big windows or terraces. Services include conference rooms and Wi-Fi in the guest rooms, plus car and motorbike rentals. **www.framonhotels.com**

MILAZZO Petit Hotel

Via dei Mille 37, 98057 **Tel** *090-928 67 84* **Fax** *090-928 50 42* **Rooms** *9* **Road Map** *F2*

Zen furnishings, handcrafted Bourbon-style ceramics and original paintings decorate this 19th-century building in Milazzo. The owners installed natural-fibre mattresses, a filtered and ionized air system that removes dust, climatized wall panels to regulate temperature and other environment-improving technology. **www.petithotel.it**

PANAREA Cincotta

Via San Pietro, 98050 **Tel** *090-983 014* **Fax** *090-983 211* **Rooms** *29* **Road Map** *E1*

Situated near Panarea's harbour and set into a cliff, this hotel offers a superb view of the sea from some of its rooms. The terrace has a sea-water swimming pool, and rooms are furnished in a warm Mediterranean style. From 7 to 27 August, the minimum stay is one week and half-board may be required. Closed Nov–Mar. **www.hotelcincotta.it**

PANAREA Hotel Quartara

Via San Pietro 15, 98050 **Tel** *090-983 027* **Fax** *090-983 621* **Rooms** *13* **Road Map** *E1*

White-washed Aeolian-style architecture shapes this hotel with a terrace overlooking the sea. The luminous rooms feature teak furniture, handmade bedcovers and verandas. The terrace restaurant is known as much for its food as for its view. Garden, Jacuzzi and massages are all nice extras. **www.quartarahotel.com**

PANAREA La Piazza
Via San Pietro, 98050 **Tel** *090-983 154* **Fax** *090-983 649* **Rooms** *33*   **Road Map** *E1*

Set above the Calette Bay on Panarea's eastern coast, in a lovely Mediterranean garden, is La Piazza. The sea-water swimming pool was supplemented by the island's only wellness centre. The season runs from April to October, but off-season a small annexe is open at bargain rates. **www.hotelpiazza.it**

PANAREA Raya
Panarea-Isole Eolie, 98050 **Tel** *090-983 013* **Fax** *090-983 103* **Rooms** *36*   **Road Map** *E1*

The Raya has traditional Aeolian style combined with some modern architecture to maximize use of the space above the sea. Bedrooms are simply furnished, in light or dark wood, with white textiles; mirrors expand the light and create a double sea vista. Plush down duvets on the beds add a touch of luxury. Closed Mar–Oct. **www.hotelraya.it**

SALINA L'Ariana
Via Rotabile 11, Rinella, 98050 **Tel** *090-980 90 75* **Fax** *090-980 92 50* **Rooms** *15*   **Road Map** *E1*

This early Liberty villa in Rinella's small harbour has a spectacular view of Lipari and Vulcano. Guest rooms are spacious, decorated in yellow and white, each with an antique family chest; some have a sea view. In the summer dinner is served on the terrace. Prices are very reasonable in low season. **www.hotelariana.it**

SALINA Hotel Signum
Via Scalo 15, Malfa, 98050 **Tel** *090-984 42 22* **Fax** *090-984 41 02* **Rooms** *30*   **Road Map** *E1*

An old hamlet of farmers' houses was entirely renovated to create this hotel complex. Three types of bedrooms are available, including some in the small houses among the gardens and vineyards. The outdoor swimming pool has a view of Stromboli. The restaurant serves traditional cuisine in a family atmosphere. **www.hotelsignum.it**

SAN GIOVANNI LA PUNTA Villa Paradiso dell'Etna
Via per Viagrande 37, 95030 **Tel** *095-751 24 09* **Fax** *095-741 38 61* **Rooms** *34*   **Road Map** *E3*

On the slopes of Etna, this 1927 villa has frescoed walls, *trompe-l'oeil* paintings, period furniture and fireplaces. The garden has trees that are centuries old and the swimming pool is heated. Non-smoking guest rooms. Services include a wellness centre, massages, tennis courts, bike rental and a private beach at Capomulini. **www.paradisoetna.it**

STROMBOLI La Sirenetta Park Hotel
Via Marina 33, 98050 **Tel** *090-986 025* **Fax** *090-986 124* **Rooms** *57*   **Road Map** *F1*

This white hotel's flower-filled patio connects to a flight of steps and tiny alleyways that wind uphill towards a magnificent amphitheatre carved out of volcanic rock. Services include a sea-water swimming pool, dive centre, and boat and bicycle rentals. The restaurant features local fish and vegetable dishes. Closed Nov–Mar. **www.lasirenetta.it**

TAORMINA Hotel Isabella
Corso Umberto 58, 98039 **Tel** *0942-23 153* **Fax** *0942-23 155* **Rooms** *32*   **Road Map** *F2*

Set in the town centre amid local shops and restaurants, the Isabella offers comfortable, reasonably priced, cheerful rooms. The roof terrace has views over the rooftops, gardens, the sea and Etna. Some rooms share a terrace above an ancient Roman aqueduct; floors above have sea or street views. There is a shuttle to a private beach. **www.gaishotels.com**

TAORMINA Hotel Villa Schuler
Piazzetta Bastione 16, 98039 **Tel** *0942-23 481* **Fax** *0942-23 522* **Rooms** *27*   **Road Map** *F2*

This no-frills 19th-century villa will appeal to the budget-minded traveller who still wants to enjoy a central, family-run hotel. Rooms are simply furnished in wood; a garden view is less expensive than a sea view or balconied room. The terrace has a lovely vista and there is a large private garden. Shuttle service to the beach. **www.hotelvillaschuler.com**

TAORMINA Hotel Villa Ducale
Via Leonardo da Vinci 60, 98039 **Tel** *0942-28 153* **Fax** *0942-28 710* **Rooms** *16*   **Road Map** *F2*

Flowers spill from everywhere here. The friendly owners and staff, who run this gem above Taormina, greet you with a welcome drink at check in. Rooms are cheerful, with tiles from Caltagirone, bright frescoes, wrought-iron beds and terraces that face Taormina, the sea or Calabria. Garden, Jacuzzi, spa and bar. **www.hotelvilladucale.com**

TAORMINA Hotel Villa Sirina
Via Crocifisso 30, 98039 **Tel** *0942-51 776* **Fax** *0942-51 671* **Rooms** *16*   **Road Map** *F2*

In the foothills below Taormina, surrounded by oleanders and citrus groves, is this early 20th-century family-run villa. Furnishings are homely and simple, with some antiques and crafts. Villa Sirina has a mountain and a sea view, and it is located only one kilometre from the Giardini (Taormina Gardens). **www.villasirina.com**

TAORMINA Park Hotel La Plage
Via Nazionale 107, Mazzarò, 98039 **Tel** *0942-626 095* **Fax** *0942-625 850* **Rooms** *66*   **Road Map** *F2*

Fifty stone bungalows set in a pine forest that descends to the sea at Isola Bella provide a simple and somewhat more economical option than the major beach hotels. Most bungalows are decorated in a rustic style; the nicer ones are the eight junior suites, some furnished with antiques. There is also a spa. Closed Dec–Jan. **www.laplage.it**

TAORMINA Residence Villa Giulia
Via Bagnoli Croce 75, 98039 **Tel** *0942-23 312* **Fax** *0942-23 391* **Rooms** *7*   **Road Map** *F2*

These small apartments with kitchens are ideal for families and those who want to peruse markets and create their own dishes with local ingredients. Each sunny apartment has a terrace, wooden tables and cheerful ceramics. You have the use of a pool at a nearby hotel, a beach/health club shuttle service and a restaurant. **www.gaishotels.com**

Key to Price Guide *see p198* **Key to Symbols** *see back cover flap*

TAORMINA Villa Carlotta
🏊 📋 🅿 ♿ €€€

Via Pirandello 81, 98039 **Tel** *0942-626 058* **Fax** *0942-23 732* **Rooms** *27* **Road Map** *F2*

This lovely stone villa, with its quirky tower, striped awnings and stained glass, is a real charmer. Spacious guest rooms have cherrywood furniture and a balcony. The bright top room is ideal for reading or for evening drinks. There is also a small swimming pool, hot tub and Internet point. Closed Jan & Feb. **www.hotelvillacarlottataormina.com**

TAORMINA Baia Taormina Hotel & Spa
🍴 🏊 📋 🅿 ♿ €€€€

Statale dello Ionio 39, Marina d'Agro, 98039 **Tel** *0942-756 292* **Fax** *0942-756 603* **Rooms** *60* **Road Map** *F2*

Set on a rocky slope above the bay a few kilometres north of Taormina, these villa-style buildings and terrace offer freshwater and saltwater swimming pools, private beach, gym, massages and a Turkish bath. Various sports can be arranged, including scuba diving, surfing, hang-gliding and tennis. Closed Nov–Mar. **www.baiataormina.com**

TAORMINA Hotel Caparena and Wellness Club
🍴 🏊 👤 📋 🅿 ♿ €€€€

Via Nazionale 189, Mazzarò, 98039 **Tel** *0942-652 033* **Fax** *0942-36 913* **Rooms** *88* **Road Map** *F2*

This tranquil beach hotel has its own garden for barbecues, a private beach, two rooftop restaurants, piano bar and year-round pool. The well-equipped wellness centre has massage therapists, gym, steam bath and various beauty treatments. The beach can be reached via an underground tunnel. Closed Nov–Mar. **www.gaishotels.com**

TAORMINA La Sciara Residence
🍴 🏊 €€€€

Via S. Cincotta, 98050 **Tel** *090-986 004* **Fax** *090-986 284* **Rooms** *62* **Road Map** *F1*

Set in a garden filled with bougainvillea, this hotel features guest rooms decorated with white interiors and hand-crafted furniture, which reflects the rustic style of the island. Bedrooms have either a view of the sea or of the volcano; some also have a terrace and there is a tennis court. Half-board is required 4–24 Aug. Closed Oct–Apr. **www.lasciara.it**

TAORMINA Grand Hotel Atlantis Bay
🍴 🏊 📋 ♿ €€€€

Via Nazionale 161, Mazzarò, 98039 **Tel** *0942-618 011* **Fax** *0942-23 194* **Rooms** *86* **Road Map** *F2*

Lavishly carved and decorated stone walls and a tropical aquarium give the impression of being in your own private grotto. The colour scheme is mostly white with natural fabrics; many rooms have sea views. Among the highlights are the pool, private beach and the wellness centre. Non-smoking rooms and Internet point. **www.atlantisbay.it**

TAORMINA Grand Hotel Mazzarò Sea Palace
🍴 🏊 📋 🅿 ♿ €€€€€

Via Nazionale 147, Mazzarò, 98039 **Tel** *0942-612 111* **Fax** *0942-626 237* **Rooms** *88* **Road Map** *F2*

Modern and comfortable, this hotel hosts business conferences but also welcomes leisure travellers who enjoy its pool, fitness centre and private beach. Most rooms have terraces with sea view, and the hotel also offers a piano bar, pay parking and non-smoking rooms. Various water sports can be arranged. Open Mar–Nov. **www.mazzaroseapalace.it**

TAORMINA Grand Hotel San Pietro
🍴 🏊 📋 🅿 ♿ €€€€€

Via Pirandello 50, 98039 **Tel** *0942-620 711* **Fax** *0942-620 770* **Rooms** *62* **Road Map** *F2*

This idyllic hotel harmonizes with Taormina's existing architecture and environment. Antiques adorn the lobby, while lovely prints and sumptuous textiles decorate the rooms; most have a sea view, some look towards Etna. The artist-in-residence gives painting lessons, and the chef prepares creative dishes. Shuttle to beach. **www.gaishotels.com**

TAORMINA Grand Hotel Timeo e Villa Flora
🍴 🏊 📋 🅿 ♿ €€€€€

Via Teatro Greco 59, 98039 **Tel** *0942-23 801* **Fax** *0942-628 501* **Rooms** *84* **Road Map** *F2*

Located next to the ancient Greek theatre, Taormina's first hotel (1850) exudes historic charm. The elegant salons have large windows and are ideal for conversation, reading or evening piano. The Literary Terrace looks over a splendid garden, the sea and Etna. Guest rooms also have terraces. Bar and tearoom. **www.framonhotels.com**

TAORMINA San Domenico Palace Hotel
🍴 📋 🅿 ♿ €€€€€

Piazza San Domenico 5, 98039 **Tel** *0942-613 111* **Fax** *0942-625 506* **Rooms** *111* **Road Map** *F2*

This former 15th-century Dominican convent matches its ancient grandeur with modern conveniences. The hotel has a lovely courtyard and inviting plush grand salons with some remaining frescoes. The garden terrace offers a sweeping vista of the sea and Etna. The stone fireplace is cosy and welcoming in winter. **www.sandomenico.thi.it**

TAORMINA Villa Sant'Andrea
🍴 📋 🅿 ♿ €€€€€

Via Nazionale 137, Mazzarò, 98039 **Tel** *0942-625 837* **Fax** *0942-24 838* **Rooms** *83* **Road Map** *F2*

An aristocratic British family built this villa in 1830. Set in a sub-tropical garden on the beach, it still maintains the charm of a private residence. Services include a private beach, wellness centre with sauna and massages and an entertaining piano bar. Staff can arrange for bicycles, scuba diving, windsurfing and other sports. **www.framonhotels.com**

VULCANO Hotel Conti
🍴 ♿ €€

Località Ponte di Ponente, 98050 **Tel** *090-985 20 12* **Fax** *090-985 20 64* **Rooms** *67* **Road Map** *E1*

A modest hotel in Aeolian style that offers peace and tranquillity near Vulcano's famous black-sand beach. The restaurant features various regional cuisines; half-board options are available and may be required in August. Closed Nov–Apr. **www.contivulcano.it**

VULCANO Les Sables Noires
🍴 🏊 📋 🅿 €€€

Ponte di Ponente, 98050 **Tel** *090-98 50* **Fax** *090-985 24 54* **Rooms** *48* **Road Map** *E1*

Named after the black volcanic sand on the beach, this hotel has modern, comfortable rooms – most with balconies. The interior colour scheme reflects the area's white-washed houses, while black accessories recall the island's sand. Most water sports can be arranged. Terrace restaurant. **www.framonhotels.com**

WHERE TO EAT

Sicilians love good food and like nothing better than joining family and friends around a restaurant table, especially if the food is genuinely home-made. Fish is one of the highlights of Sicilian cuisine. Almost all restaurants serve freshly caught fish, grilled or fried according to local recipes, and fish is often an ingredient for pasta sauces as well. Pasta is widely available and so is couscous, an Arab legacy.

A restaurant sign in a Sicilian village

Restaurant opening hours are typical of the southern Mediterranean: in general places open from 1–3:30pm for lunch and from 9 to midnight for dinner. Most restaurants generally close one day a week and may close for up to a month for annual holidays, so it is a good idea to check ahead to avoid disappointment. The restaurants listed on pages 212–21 have been selected from among the best on the island.

Buffet at the Azienda Agricola Trinità, in Mascalucia (see p168)

BREAKFAST AND SNACKS

Besides the traditional croissant, eaten with black coffee (espresso) or a milky coffee (cappuccino), Sicilians also enjoy croissants stuffed with ice cream and iced coffee and milk for breakfast. Bars and pastry shops (pasticcerie) stock a range of pastries, and Sicilian freshly squeezed fruit juices are excellent. If you are staying in a hotel where breakfast is included, it is likely to consist of coffee or tea with croissants and bread with fruit jam. More luxurious hotels will offer a buffet with yoghurt, breakfast cereal, fresh fruit, sliced ham and salami. For a mid-morning snack, or for lunch, you can go to a bar or rosticceria, where you will find a range of sandwiches (panini) and filled rolls (pezzi), arancini

(rice balls) and impanate (pies stuffed with aubergines (eggplant), spinach and cheese, or potatoes, cauliflower and onions). Favourite Palermo snacks are pane ca meusa (bread stuffed with spleen) or pane e panelle (chick pea fritters in a sandwich). Always ask for the price beforehand to avoid a surprise later on. These specialities are also sold in outdoor markets.

TYPES OF RESTAURANT

In Sicily, even the smallest village is likely to have a trattoria serving local specialities. There is not much difference (in terms of price, cuisine and decor) between a restaurant proper and a trattoria, especially along the coast, where even quite sophisticated establishments are decorated with maritime paraphernalia. Putie are typically simple trattorias with home cooking and a

set menu; they generally offer good value for money. Pizzerias are widespread and are ideal for cheap and fast meals. Another typical aspect of Sicilian tradition is the rosticceria, serving quick, hot meals from the roasting oven, and focacceria, where the Sicilian flat bread focaccia is used as a pizza base.

READING THE MENU

Printed menus are still rare in Sicily; it is the custom for the waiter to recite the day's list at your table. Good antipasti (see pp210–11) are vegetables (from aubergines to olives) in oil, seafood and fish salads and seafood soups (with mussels, clams, cuttlefish, squid). The first course is pasta, usually with vegetables or fish and often so hearty that it is as filling as a main course: try pasta con le sarde, with sardines (see p210); spaghetti alla Norma, with tomato, basil, aubergine and ricotta;

The terrace at I Mulini on the island of Pantelleria (see p216)

The renowned Wünderbar in Taormina *(see p178)*

cuscus alla trapanese, couscous with onion, spices and a fish sauce; *pasta n'casciata*, macaroni pie with meat sauce, sausage, cheese and hard-boiled eggs. The main course is often fish (typically tuna, swordfish, shrimp), freshly cooked and sold by weight (so ask for a rough price). Fresh fruit or dessert (*cannoli*, ricotta cheese and candied fruit rolls; *cassata*, cake with ricotta cheese, sugar, chocolate and candied fruit (*see p211*); ice cream) wind up the meal. For vegetarians there are excellent vegetables and a range of pasta dishes.

WINE

Most restaurants, even the average ones, have a wine list with a good selection of Sicilian wines. Trattorias on the other hand tend to offer their house wine, locally produced, and inexpensive table wine, usually served in a carafe.

FIXED-PRICE MENUS

Many Sicilian trattorias and restaurants offer fixed-price menus. You'll find them in larger cities and tourist hotspots.

PRICES AND PAYING

In trattorias a normal three-course meal will cost about €20–€25. In restaurants, a similar meal will cost upwards of €30. Even in a top restaurant you are unlikely to spend more than a maximum of €60 per person. Pizza is always good value, and rarely costs more than about €8–€10. Your bill may be a simple total, without the different courses being itemized. If you do have an itemized bill, the total will include a cover charge (€1–€3) and a service charge. Tipping is not obligatory, but if you decide to leave a tip, calculate 8–10 per cent. Italian law requires all eating establishments to issue a bona fide printed receipt (*ricevuta fiscale*) to clients when they pay. Anything else is illegal. Make sure you get a receipt as you may receive a hefty fine if you cannot produce a *ricevuta fiscale* if requested by a *finanziere* (the fiscal police).

Waiter with a tray of desserts

Most Sicilian restaurants and trattorias accept a range of credit cards, including Master-Card and Visa. Bars, cafés and smaller, family-run establishments may only accept cash, so check you have enough.

OPENING HOURS

All restaurants are closed one day during the week, with the possible exception of the high season, in July and August. This closing day is shown in the listings on pages 212–21. Restaurants and trattorias also close for about one month for annual holidays. In large cities like Palermo this usually occurs in August, whereas on the coast almost all restaurants are closed in the winter months. Island restaurants generally open according to the needs of the tourist season.

MAKING RESERVATIONS

In the evening, especially in the summer, restaurants often get very crowded and you may find it difficult to get a table. It is always a good idea to book a table in advance, even in trattorias. An alternative is to arrive early, about 8pm, to avoid standing in line.

Phoning ahead is also advisable if you want to make sure that a restaurant's specialities will be available.

CHILDREN

Children are always welcome in restaurants, particularly family-run places which are only too happy to prepare special dishes or half-portions for youngsters (although some places will charge you the full price for it). Sophisticated restaurants may be less geared for children, so telephone beforehand.

SMOKING

Smoking in restaurants is no longer allowed. Though many establishments might turn a blind eye, it is within your rights to ask someone not to smoke near you.

Sicilian ice cream, almost always locally made

The Flavours of Sicily

Sicilian cuisine is Italy's most varied and exotic, influenced by the different settlers who have grown flavourful ingredients in the lava-enriched soil and hot sunshine. Homer's *Odyssey* describes the island's bounty of apples, pomegranates and grapes. The Normans brought their way of curing fish with salt and the Spanish imported tomatoes and peppers. But it was the Arabs' introduction of almonds, aubergines (eggplants), saffron and sugar cane that defines much of Sicilian cooking. Their traditions of stuffing vegetables, making sweet pastries and using rice, couscous and sweet-sour combinations are still used today.

Fresh herbs

Local farmer with a basket of freshly made ricotta

NORTHWESTERN SICILY

Cooking in northwestern Sicily is often highly spiced, revealing a strong eastern influence, not least in the capital, Palermo, where the food markets have the feel of Arabian souks.

Blossom and fruits from the orange and lemon groves of La Conca d'Oro near Palermo perfume the air and feature in many dishes, while the vineyards around Marsala produce wines that are used in both savoury dishes and desserts. *Insalata d'arance* – orange salad – refreshingly combines oranges, mint and marsala.

Historically, villages along the northwest coast thrived on tuna fishing, and Mazara del Vallo has one of the Mediterranean's largest deep-sea fishing fleets.

SOUTHWESTERN SICILY

Inland the traditional fare is poultry, meat, offal and game. Liver is often cooked in a sweet-and-sour sauce while rabbit or goat is simmered with vegetables, herbs and spices. Fruits are made into preserves and pastes, almonds into marzipan treats. The speciality in Agrigento, where there is an almond festival each spring, is a sweet *cuscus*

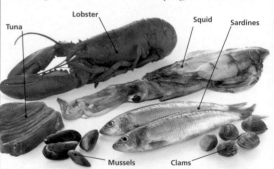

Lobster

Tuna

Squid

Sardines

Mussels

Clams

Selection of seafood from the clear waters of Sicily's coastline

SICILIAN DISHES AND SPECIALITIES

Antipasti include carpaccio of tuna or swordfish; *caponata* – aubergines (eggplant) in a rich sweet-and-sour tomato sauce with capers, olives, pine nuts and basil; and *frittedda* of artichokes, peas and broad (fava) beans. *Arancini* are small stuffed, fried balls of golden risotto rice, named for the little oranges they resemble. Fresh ricotta melds with aubergine and tomato as a sauce for *pasta alla norma*. Seafood and shellfish are also added to pasta, such as *pasta al nero di seppia* (with cuttlefish ink) and *pasta con aragosta* (with lobster). Sardines, squid and mullet are cooked in myriad ways, like *calamari in umido* (squid and anchovies in tomato sauce) and *triglie allo scoglio* (red mullet in a sweet-sour onion sauce).

Local figs

Maccheroncini con le sarde *is Sicilian macaroni with sardines, fennel, pine nuts, raisins, breadcrumbs and saffron.*

Farmer selling fruit from the back of his truck in Taormina, Sicily

aubergines (eggplants), courgettes (zucchini) and tomatoes are the basis for pasta sauces like *vermicelli alla siracusana* (of Syracuse), which also uses black olives, capers and anchovies.

Pork from the pigs farmed inland has the distinctive taste of the prickly pears on which they feed, and the local sausages are often flavoured with wild herbs.

Milk from cows, sheep and goats is made into cheeses such as pecorino, and is sometimes studded with peppercorns or olives. Ricotta is crumbled onto stews, pasta and rice dishes and is an essential ingredient in many desserts.

with chocolate, pistachios and almonds. A savoury *cuscus*, cooked with fish or chicken stock, cloves and nutmeg in a terracotta pot, is found on Pantelleria, the closest point to the North African coast.

NORTHEASTERN SICILY

Dominated by Mount Etna and its fertile slopes, the east has fields, orchards, citrus groves and vines. Local dishes use herbs rather than spices.

On the coast, Messina is known for swordfish, often served simply grilled with herbs and lemon, and Catania for *risotto nero* using dark cuttlefish ink (sometimes topped with tomato sauce to resemble an Etna eruption).

Mountain snow, mixed with sugar and flower essence or juice, began the Sicilian tradition of sorbets and ice creams.

SOUTHERN SICILY

In Ragusa province, vast greenhouses dot the landscape, enabling the year-round production and export of fruit and vegetables. Yellow peppers, plump

Freshly harvested olives ready to be pressed into rich oil

WHAT TO DRINK

High quality wines include Faro and Cerasuolo di Vittoria (both reds), Contea di Sclafari, Erice, Nero d'Avola and Etna wines from the slopes of the volcano (dry reds and whites).

Marsala, a fortified wine created by 18th-century English merchants, may be dry *(secco)* or sweet *(dolce)*.

Sweet *moscato* (muscat) comes from Noto, Syracuse and Pantelleria. Rare Malvasia from Lipari is known as "drinkable gold".

There are liqueurs made from almonds, lemon, prickly pears, and herbs and roots.

Pesce spada, *swordfish steak, may be cooked in an orange sauce, or pan-fried or grilled with lemon and herbs.*

Pollo alla marsala *is pan-fried chicken (veal may also be used) with marsala, lemon juice, capers and parsley.*

Cassata *is Sicily's famous sponge cake, with ricotta, nuts, marsala, chocolate, candied fruit and marzipan.*

Choosing a Restaurant

The restaurants in this chart have been selected across a wide price range for the high quality of their service, menu, decor and location. They have been divided into five areas and are listed by price category. See pp210–11 for more detailed information about types of cuisine and particular dishes.

PRICE CATEGORIES
The following price ranges are for a three-course meal, including beverage (except for wine), tax and service.

€ under €20
€€ €20–€30
€€€ €30–€40
€€€€ €40–€50
€€€€€ over €50

PALERMO

PALERMO Pasticceria Mazzara
€
Via Generale Magliocco 19, 90141 **Tel** *091-321 443*   **Map** *1 B2*

Located near the Teatro Massimo, this lovely patisserie with its attractive bars is known primarily for its sweets. However, they also serve a basic, economical lunch from 12:30pm to 3pm: it includes oven-baked pastas, salads and traditional Sicilian dishes. Try the pastries or the pistachio gelato for dessert. Opens at 7:30am.

PALERMO Ai Vecchietti
€€
Piazza S Oliva 10, 90141 **Tel** *091-585 606*   **Map** *1 A1*

The gregarious owner sets the friendly tone here. Mixed antipasti feature *pannella* (fried bread) and olives. Try the *pappardelle cantalupo* (wide pasta ribbons with cantaloupe melon and prawns) or the squid, which is fried expertly and lightly. The 18th-century *cassata* recipe was procured from cloistered nuns. Folk music plays in the background.

PALERMO Antica Focacceria San Francesco
€€
Via Alessandro Paternostro 58, 90133 **Tel** *091-320 264*   **Map** *2 D3*

Fragrant breads lure patrons into this historic, lively bakery opposite the church of San Francesco. Traditional dishes include *sfinciuni* (flat bread topped with tomatoes, anchovies and onions), *u pani ca' meusa* (stuffed bread) and lightly fried *panelle* (fritters made from chickpea flour). A good place to pick up a meal to take away. Closed Tue.

PALERMO Cin-Cin Ristorante
€€
Via Manin 22, 90139 **Tel** *091-612 40 95*

Vintage jazz plays softly in this restaurant where the elaborate 18th-century Baroque dishes have intriguing pungent notes. Try the fettucine with fresh oysters, and the perfectly cooked vegetables. Authentic Cajun meals can also be prepared (only on advance request) – the chef spent 20 years in Baton Rouge. Closed Sat lunch.

PALERMO Trattoria Il Maestro del Brodo
€€
Via Pannieri 7, 90133 **Tel** *091-329 523*   **Map** *1 C3*

At the entrance of the Vucciria market is this economical hole-in-the-wall eatery, where the "master of broth" specializes in boiled veal. The most popular pasta dish on the menu is made with swordfish, tiny shrimp and courgette (zucchini). Fish is served fried, grilled or poached in seawater. Closed dinner (except Fri & Sat); Mon.

PALERMO Capricci di Sicilia
€€€
Via Istituto Pignatelli 6, at Piazza Sturzo, 90139 **Tel** *091-327 777*   **Map** *1 B1*

Near the Politeama, this trattoria is handy for lunch after visiting the city or for dinner before or after a theatre performance. Most dishes revolve around meat and fish, and are traditionally Sicilian, sometimes with an elaborate, innovative twist. Closed Mon; 2 weeks Aug.

PALERMO Hanami
€€€
Via Alessandro Paternostro 56, 90133 **Tel** *091-320 264*   **Map** *2 D3*

At this stylish restaurant you can dine on sushi and other international food trends that inspire the chef. Interesting seating areas, nice lighting and stylish architectural details attract Palermo's smart set for drinks and nibbles at the bar, or for a complete meal. The tables outside have a view of San Francesco. Open for dinner only. Closed Tue.

PALERMO Mi Manda Picone
€€€
Via Alessandro Paternostro 59, 90133 **Tel** *091-616 06 60*   **Map** *2 D3*

When its neighbour Hanami is filled to overflowing, this restaurant is an easy back-up option. Mi Manda Picone does catering around Palermo, for large groups as well as private residences. One of its specialities is the *degustazione*, a wine-tasting menu that is matched to particular dishes on the menu. Closed Sun; Christmas.

PALERMO Osteria dei Vespri
€€€
Piazza Croce dei Vespri 6, 90133 **Tel** *091-617 16 31*   **Map** *2 D4*

Once the historic Gangi Palace stables, this cosy restaurant balances exceptional cuisine and lovely presentations with attentive service and a great wine list. Try the superb raw fish, the *anelletti* (pasta rings) with octopus and Nero d'Avola sauce, or the sublime desserts. There is also a generous selection of premium wines by the glass. Closed Sun.

Key to Symbols *see back cover flap*

PALERMO Santandrea

♿ 📶 📋   €€€

Piazza Sant'Andrea 4, 90133 **Tel** *091-334 999* — **Map** 1 C3

The interior of this restaurant near the Vucciria market is all calm, neutral tones and simple lines – a striking contrast to the Baroque square outside and the colours of the market. Focus is on traditional cuisine, from antipasti to pasta and fish. Santandrea attracts a well-dressed crowd. Closed lunch; Tue; Jan.

PALERMO Cucina Papoff

♿ 📋 🍷 📶   €€€€

Via Isidoro La Lumia 32, 90139 **Tel** *091-586 460*

This place is elegant through and through: from the ceiling's intricate woodwork to the well-dressed crowd of professionals and aristocrats that receive attentive service. Popular dishes include purée of fava beans, linguine with red mullet, risotto with citrus fruit, a casserole of tiny meatballs, plus meat or fish dishes. Closed Sat lunch; Sun; Aug.

FURTHER AFIELD Café Centro Città

🍴 ♿ 📶 📋   €

Via Archimede 184C, 90139 **Tel** *091-335 093* — **Road Map** *C2*

An ordinary coffee bar that expands between noon and 3:30pm to offer a no-frills lunch for local office workers. The choice includes pastas, rice moulds (either traditional, with tomato sauce, or in variations like courgette (zucchini) and Emmenthal), meat dishes or salads. Closed evening; Sun.

FURTHER AFIELD Caflisch

♿ 📶 📋 🍷   €

Mondello, 90151 **Tel** *091-684 04 44* — **Road Map** *C2*

Palermo's most outstanding patisserie is also one of Sicily's undisputed best. They also serve an informal express lunch, and diners can experience the pleasure of eating under the trees near Mondello beach. In the summer, don't miss the sublime *gel di melone* (watermelon gel). Extensive wine list. Closed Tue in winter.

FURTHER AFIELD Pasticceria Bar Aluia

♿ 📶 📋   €

Via Libertà 27, 90139 **Tel** *091-583 087* — **Road Map** *C2*

Sweets are this patisserie's primary business, but at lunchtime Aluia also offers hot meals of oven-baked pasta, vegetables and other options. Local office workers and shoppers come for the low prices and traditional fare. By late afternoon the pasta disappears, and it's back to the pastry-and-coffee clientele. Closed Mon.

FURTHER AFIELD Il Delfino

♿ 📶 📋   €€

Via Torretta 80, Sferracavallo, 90148 **Tel** *091-530 282* — **Road Map** *B2*

A short ride west of Mondello, this restaurant is known for its reasonable prices and its good fish and seafood menu. Specialities include pasta with sardines and fennel, seafood risotto or fettuccine with shrimp and clams. For the main course, indecisive diners are often directed towards the outstanding *sarde a beccaficu* (stuffed sardines).

FURTHER AFIELD La Dispensa dei Monsù

♿ 📶 📋 🍷   €€

Via Principe di Villafranca 59, 90141 **Tel** *091-609 04 65* — **Road Map** *C2*

A French chef (*monsù*) and a well-stocked pantry (*dispensa*) were obligatory in any Sicilian noble household. Here you will find excellent cheeses: fresh ricotta with pistachios, *caprino Robiola* (goat's cheese), *piacentu ennese* (with saffron and peppercorn), *pecorino ubriaco* (wine-aged), plus Sicilian prosciutto and salami. Open for dinner only; closed Sun.

FURTHER AFIELD La Tonnara

♿ 📶 📋   €€

Piazza Tonnara 18, Arenella, 90142 **Tel** *091-363 055* — **Road Map** *C2*

The name of this restaurant in the tiny Arenella harbour indicates that tuna is the main speciality, although other fish and seafood are also on the menu. Dishes such as ravioli filled with grouper or crabmeat are worth the trip out of town. Local wine is available by the carafe; other wines, by the bottle. Closed Wed; 2 weeks Aug.

FURTHER AFIELD Sapori di Mare

♿ 📶 📋   €€

Via Mondello 52, Mondello, 90151 **Tel** *091-684 06 23* — **Road Map** *C2*

Right in the midst of Mondello's beach scene, near the aquamarine sea, is this fish restaurant. Its signature dish is linguine with lobster, but other delicious specialities include ravioli stuffed with fish and topped with shrimp or lobster sauce, fish couscous, seafood risotto and spaghetti with sea urchins. Closed Tue in winter.

FURTHER AFIELD La Botte 1962

📋 🍷   €€€

SS186 km10, Contrada Lenzitti 20, Monreale, 90046 **Tel** *091-414 051* — **Road Map** *B2*

Plan your visit to this well-stocked wine shop in advance if you wish to dine here: they serve food only at lunchtime on Sunday and during the holidays. Regional fare, based on fish and meat, is highlighted. As you would expect, the wines are always superbly matched to the food on offer to enhance the flavours. Closed Mon–Thu; Jun–mid Sep.

FURTHER AFIELD U Sttrascinu

♿   €€€

2286 viale Regione Siciliana, 90125 **Tel** *091-401 292* — **Road Map** *C2*

This restaurant is a little distance from Palermo, but it is worth the trek. The interior is flamboyantly decorated with pieces harking back to Sicily's folklore, and the waiters are dressed in traditional costume. There is an all-you-can-eat starter buffet, then you can choose your own fish from the counter for your main meal. Closed 2 weeks Aug.

FURTHER AFIELD Bye Bye Blues

♿ 📋 🍷   €€€€

Via del Garofalo 23, Mondello, 90149 **Tel** *091-684 14 15* — **Road Map** *C2*

The excellent, refined food made here receives national attention. A main course may take the shape of pasta with sea urchins and puréed fava, potato and basil pie with fish soup, pork with onion marmalade, or snapper with lemon marmalade. Exquisite pistachio cake or ice cream. Closed lunch (except holidays); Tue; part of Nov.

FURTHER AFIELD Baglio di Pianetto
*Contrada Pianetto, Scorrimento Veloce, San Cristina Gela, 90030 **Tel** 091-857 00 02* **Road Map** *B2*

Surrounded by vineyards and olive groves, this eatery is perfectly located in the Baglio di Pianetto winery. The chef's cuisine comes from nearby fields and farms – lightly fried wild borage, lamb in delicate sauce, wild salad greens. You can sample the winery's excellent Merlot, Nero d'Avola, Viognier and others in the wine-tasting room. Book ahead.

FURTHER AFIELD Il Ristorantino
*Piazzale De Gasperi 19, 90146 **Tel** 091-670 2999* **Road Map** *C2*

Expect a new take on Sicilian cuisine in "the little restaurant" near the Parco della Favorita. Squid is served with salt and basil as an appetizer; *maltagliati* (irregularly shaped pasta) might have a sauce of bitter chocolate, aubergine (eggplant) and swordfish; fish might come in a potato crust with couscous on the side. Closed Mon; early Jan, Aug.

FURTHER AFIELD La Scuderia
*Via del Fante 9, 90146 **Tel** 091-520 323* **Road Map** *C2*

The light open room, wood panel walls and fireplace offer understated comfort in this haven for power brokers. Tradition reigns with some innovations, food presentations are lovely and there are 500 wines on the list. The stadium is next door, so make sure your arrival does not coincide with a game (the restaurant staff will advise). Closed Sun.

NORTHWESTERN SICILY

CASTELBUONO Nangalarruni Ristorante
*Via Alberghi 5 (formerly Via delle Confraternite), 90013 **Tel** 0921-671 428* **Road Map** *D2*

In the hills southeast of Cefalù, Nangalarruni is ideal for sampling wild mushrooms, including *basilisco*, the "king of mushrooms", which is prepared with tagliatelle. Wild herbs season the dishes, like Nebrodi pork with almonds and pistachios. Desserts include ricotta pastry and chocolate flan. About 600 international wines on the list. Closed Wed.

CASTELLAMMARE DEL GOLFO Torre Bennistra
*Via Natale di Roma 19, Località Scopello, 91014 **Tel** 0924-541 128* **Road Map** *B2*

Beautifully situated, Torre Bennistra has a homely family atmosphere. Antipasti include tuna *carpaccio* (thin, raw slices), shrimp with lemon and *sarde a beccafico* (stuffed sardines). The restaurant, which is part of a respected hotel, overlooks the village of Scopello and the rocks emerging from the ocean below.

CEFALÙ La Brace
*Via XXV Novembre 10, 90015 **Tel** 0921-423 570* **Road Map** *D2*

At this restaurant near the cathedral, one can enjoy local specialities like stuffed aubergines (eggplant). Ethnic theme nights on Wednesdays offer Spanish paella, while on Fridays the menu includes *cous cous mezzo Tunisino* (half-Tunisian), the other half being the chef's own interpretation. Mostly Sicilian wines. Closed Mon, Tue lunch; Christmas.

CEFALÙ Taverna del Presidente
*Via Lungomare G Giardina 163, 90015 **Tel** 0921-921 359* **Road Map** *D2*

On Cefalù's seafront, this restaurant offers views of the sea and the town, as well as terrace dining in warm weather. The fish, meat and vegetables are all locally sourced. Try the cod salad with citrus fruit, fish *carpaccio* (thin, raw slices), *pappardelle* (wide pasta ribbons) with rabbit and wild asparagus, tuna steak or braised pork. Closed Tue.

ENNA Centrale
*Piazza VI Dicembre 9, 94100 **Tel** 0935-500 963* **Road Map** *D3*

Try a 15th-century pasta dish made with wild fennel and fresh ricotta, or ravioli with lemon cream. Vegetarians will appreciate the wide assortment of seasonal vegetables, while meat eaters can turn to steak or local boiled beef with oranges or peaches, depending on the season. Two tasting menus and 49 Sicilian wines. Closed Sat lunch.

ERICE Monte San Giuliano
*Vicolo San Rocco 7, 91016 **Tel** 0923-869 595* **Road Map** *A2*

Located in the medieval centre, the menu here offers excellent seafood, veal roulades with prosciutto in Marsala and mushroom sauce, or pasta with fresh *pesto trapanese* (aubergine/eggplant, tomatoes, almonds, garlic, basil and breadcrumbs). Thirty Sicilian wines; the house red is a lovely Nero d'Avola. Closed Mon; Jan, 2 weeks Nov.

FAVIGNANA La Bettola
*Via Nicotera 47, 91023 **Tel** 0923-921 988* **Road Map** *A2*

Enjoy dining on the veranda or indoors at this small, informal trattoria. Regional specialities include couscous with various types of fish; fresh *busiati* pasta with swordfish and aubergine (eggplant); a cooked pesto of tuna, tomatoes, basil and anchovies; fish grilled over lava rocks; octopus salad and fried squid. Closed Thu; Dec.

FAVIGNANA Egadi
*Via Cristoforo Colombo 17, 91023 **Tel** 0923-921 232* **Road Map** *A2*

One of the best spots for dining in the Egadi Islands. Fresh fish is served grilled, poached or marinated, but the speciality is raw fish, including tuna *tartare*, or marinated in a variety of ways, including fresh herbs. Lobster soup is a signature dish, as is couscous with crustaceans. The cellar holds 50 different wines. Closed Oct–Apr.

Key to Price Guide *see p212* **Key to Symbols** *see back cover flap*

LEVANZO Paradiso   🖼 €€€
Via Lungomare 8, 91023 Tel 0923-924 080   **Road Map** A2

Paradiso cooks fish as it comes off the boats in the nearby port, views of which can be enjoyed from the veranda. Specialities include pasta with *pesto trapanese* (garlic, almonds, tomatoes, basil, olive oil), with tuna and fresh mint, or with mussels and sea urchins, and couscous with fish. There is a good list of Sicilian wines. Closed mid-Nov–Mar.

MARETTIMO Il Veliero   🖼 €€
Via Umberto 22, 91023 Tel 0923-923 274   **Road Map** A2

This trattoria on Marettimo, the westernmost of the Egadi Islands, offers diners a superb sea view. A dozen or so main courses include lobster served with pasta in its own broth and pasta with sardines. Tuna is especially popular, as is Trapani-style couscous. The list of wines is limited, with about ten regional labels on offer.

MARSALA Ristorante Mamma Laura   🍽 ♿ 🖼 €
Contrada Ettore Infersa, 91025 Tel 0923-966 036   **Road Map** A3

This cute rustic café at the edge of the salt flats offers a view of brilliant salt crystals and of the small boats that arrive and depart for Mozia. Outside, a thatched roof offers shady respite from the heat. No gourmet cuisine, but a few simple hot dishes and sandwiches at lunch. An ideal spot for a morning cappuccino or an apéritif while the sun sets.

MARSALA La Bottega del Carmine   ♿ 🖼 🗐 €€
Via Carturca 20, 91025 Tel 0923-719 055   **Road Map** A3

This hip newcomer sets the ambience with a dramatically lit courtyard, gauzy drapes and contemporary music. The fish roulades with rocket and cherry tomatoes are particularly delicious, and there is a good roast-meat platter. Bar snacks, like *arancini* (rice balls) or cheese bites, plus a glass of wine won't cost very much. Closed lunch.

MARSALA Tiburon Beach Lido Signorino   ♿ 🖼 P €€
Via Berbaro 278, 91025 Tel 0923-998 441   **Road Map** A3

This lively beach restaurant attracts everyone from wine executives and importers to teenagers who opt for pizza from their wood-burning oven. The antipasti plate, which includes *cannonichio* (a local mollusc), fried tiny octopus, shrimp in mayonnaise, sea urchins and other delights, can be a light summer meal on its own. Great value.

MARSALA Eubes   ♿ P 🍴 €€€
Contrada da Spagnola 228, 91025 Tel 0923-996 231   **Road Map** A3

A sandy lane across from Mozia's salt flats leads to Eubes's tempting variety of seafood dishes. Try the excellent smoked tuna, fried tuna with sweet-and-sour sauce or the fish balls. Pasta with shrimp is flavourful, as is the perfectly fried squid. The chef skilfully gives traditional dishes a delightfully inventive twist.

MARSALA Trattoria Garibaldi   ♿ 🖼 🗐 🍴 €€€
Piazza Addolorato 35, 91025 Tel 0923-953 006 or 989-100   **Road Map** A3

In summer the wooden tables expand into the lovely square. The generous antipasti buffet includes local fish, vegetables and meat. *Busiati* (sliced pasta tubes) with shellfish is particularly recommended. Select your fish from the display, and it will be cooked to order (fried, broiled or steamed). Closed Sat lunch, Sun dinner.

MARSALA Villa Favorita   ♿ 🖼 🗐 P 🍴 €€€
Via Favorita 27, 91025 Tel 0923-989 100   **Road Map** A3

Once a wine estate, this early 19th-century villa is a favourite of locals for its quality cuisine and the pretty setting. Its historic buildings and its Mediterranean garden are popular for wedding receptions and other important occasions. The fish dishes are particularly good, whether as antipasti, with pasta or as a main course.

MAZARA DEL VALLO Trattoria del Pescatore   ♿ 🗐 €€€
Via Lozzani 11, 91026 Tel 0923-947 580   **Road Map** A3

Fish is the star here. For starters, try the *arancini di mare* (seafood rice balls), a tasty variation on the traditional meat or cheese *arancini*. Much of the cuisine has a strong Tunisian influence, so look for fish couscous and other North African dishes. A tasting menu is also available. Closed Mon.

SAN VITO LO CAPO Gna Sara   €€
Via Duca degli Abruzzi 8, 91010 Tel 0923-972 100   **Road Map** B2

This busy trattoria has outside seating – some with sea view – and offers traditional fare with a twist. Popular dishes include couscous with fish; home-made pasta with Trapani-style pesto (tomatoes, aubergine/eggplant, almonds, pecorino cheese, basil); pasta with fish in lemon-wine sauce and pizza. About 120 wines on the list. Closed Nov–Dec.

SAN VITO LO CAPO Tha'am   ♿ 🖼 🗐 €€€
Via Abruzzi 32, 91010 Tel 0923-972 836   **Road Map** B2

Tha'am is Arabic for "food". In the local dialect, the word is also sometimes used to mean couscous. The speciality here is Tunisian cuisine, plus there is a good choice of local dishes. The list also features 40 Sicilian wines. The interior has some Arabic touches, and some outdoor tables have a view of the port. Closed Wed (except Jun–Sep); Jan.

TRAPANI Da Peppe   ♿ 🖼 €€
Via Spalti 50, 91100 Tel 0923-282 46   **Road Map** A2

Peppe's dishes place a special emphasis on fresh vegetables. *Pesto trapanese*, made with fresh tomato, almonds, basil and garlic, dresses pasta like *busiate* (sliced tubes), or you can try the fish couscous or fish soup. There is also much to satisfy vegetarians. The summer tasting menu is a bargain. Closed Mon in winter; Christmas mid-Jan.

TRAPANI Pocho   🅿🏨   €€€

Localita Isulidda, Makari, 91010 **Tel** *0923-972 525*   **Road Map** *B2*

Overlooking the splendid bay all the way to Monte Cofano, locals and visitors alike consider Pocho the best place for couscous. Never a standard menu, the owner prepares each day's dishes according to what's available at the market, serving classic Sicilian cuisine such as fish roulade. Children's menu available. Closed lunch; Tue in winter.

SOUTHWESTERN SICILY

AGRIGENTO Leon d'Oro   🅿🏨🍽🍷   €€€

Viale Emporium 102, San Leone, 92100 **Tel** *0922-414 400*   **Road Map** *C4*

On the road that links the Valle dei Templi to the sea, this local favourite offers meat and fish dishes. The popular antipasti platter includes mussels with lemon liqueur and fava purée. Those who need a break from seafood could try the filet steak with capers and olives. About 300 types of wine from Sicily and beyond. Closed Mon; mid-Oct–mid-Nov.

AGRIGENTO Trattoria del Pescatore   🅿🏨🍽🍷   €€€€

Via Lungomare 20, Lido di San Leone, 92100 **Tel** *0922-414 342*   **Road Map** *C4*

Fish, and only fish, is on the menu at this trattoria: raw, cooked or with pasta. The tranquil interior (no TVs, no family receptions or events) suits the clientele of local politicos, couples, businesspeople and tourists. The tables outside have a view of seaside amusement rides and the crowded seaside pavement in summer. Closed Mon in winter; Jan, Nov.

AGRIGENTO Villa Athena   🅿🏨🍽🅿   €€€€

Via dei Templi 53, 92100 **Tel** *0922-596 288*   **Road Map** *C4*

The view alone is reason enough to come here. Enjoy your dinner alfresco, in the carefully tended Mediterranean garden with its citrus trees, exotic flowers, pool and spectacular view of the Temple of Concord. Arrive in time for the sunset or in evening, when the temple is illuminated. The menu and wine list are somewhat limited.

CALTANISSETTA Cortese   🅿   €€

Viale Sicilia 166, 93100 **Tel** *0934-591 686*   **Road Map** *D3*

Regional cooking with a focus on meat and local vegetables is offered at this restaurant. *Ditalini* (small pasta tubes) with broad beans and salted, aged ricotta is a speciality, as is *cravatte* (pasta bow ties) served with aubergine (eggplant) and tomato. Don't miss the *cannoli* and other desserts. The wine list includes about 80 labels. Closed Mon; Aug.

LAMPEDUSA I Gemelli   🅿🏨🍷   €€

Via Cala Pisana 2, 92010 **Tel** *0922-970 699*   **Road Map** *B5*

The island of Lampedusa is close to the North African coast, so it is no surprise to learn that the fare here is influenced by the cuisine of Tunisia. Look for spicy dishes, including octopus, aubergine (eggplant) and sausage, and a Tunisian version of paella. Closed lunch; Nov–May.

LICATA La Madia   🅿🍽   €€€€

Via Filippo Re Capriata 22, 92027 **Tel** *0922-771 443*   **Road Map** *C4*

This elegant and tranquil restaurant is decorated with frescoes that show town scenes. The chef experiments with original recipes but maintains some traditional touches, like home-made pasta and bread. This is baked twice daily: first at lunch, then a new batch at dinner. The fishermen's catch determines the day's fish specials. Closed Tue.

PANTELLERIA I Mulini   🏨   €€

Contrada Tracino, 91017 **Tel** *0923-915 398*   **Road Map** *A5*

On the island of Pantelleria, near an old mill, is this restaurant in a traditional *dammuso* (a house with small windows to keep the interior cool). Dinner is served on the terrace, from which there is a splendid view. Look for dishes that feature locally grown capers, and finish with a *passito* wine, for which the island is famous. Closed Tue; Nov–Feb.

PANTELLERIA La Risacca   📝   €€

Via Milano 65, 91017 **Tel** *0923-912 975*   **Road Map** *A5*

Pantelleria's harbour is the backdrop for this restaurant that prepares island specialities. Start with *caponata* (aubergine stew), then, for your main course, choose between ravioli with ricotta and mint, and fish couscous. The menu also features various types of fish, including deep-water fish. They have about 15 local and Sicilian wines on the list. Closed Mon.

PIAZZA ARMERINA Al Fogher   🅿🏨🍽🅿🍷   €€€

Contrada Bellia, SS 117 bis (towards Aidone), 94015 **Tel** *0935-684 123*   **Road Map** *D4*

A rustic, cosy tavern with elegantly appointed tables and refined cuisine. *Gnocchetti* (tiny pasta dumplings) with porcini mushrooms, braised veal with truffles and mushrooms, or Nebrodi pork coated with pistachios and tuna *bottarga* (roe) are some of the divine flavour combinations. Closed Mon, Sun dinner; usually mid-Aug.

SCIACCA Hostaria del Vicolo   🅿🍽🍷   €€€

Vicolo Sammaritano, 92019 **Tel** *0925-230 71*   **Road Map** *B3*

Located in Sciacca's historic centre, this rustic eatery specializes in fish-based cuisine. Some dishes are traditional, while the chef has creatively reinterpreted others. Popular choices include fresh tagliatelle with prawns and courgette (zucchini), as well as angler fish in wine sauce. The cellar offers about 150 wines. Closed Sun, Mon.

Key to Price Guide *see p212* **Key to Symbols** *see back cover flap*

SCIACCA Villa Palocla
Contrada Raganella Ovest, 92019 **Tel** *0925-902 812*
Road Map *B3*

Set in an 18th-century villa, this restaurant specializes in fish, often grilled as a main course. Pasta like local *busiati* (sliced tubes) might be combined with sardines or with *bottarga* (roe), sea urchins and eggplant. At lunch or dinner, you can dine inside or in the garden, which has citrus trees and a view of the mountains. Closed lunch in winter.

SUTERA Ristorante Civiletto
Via San Giuseppe 7, 93010 **Tel** *0934-954 587*
Road Map *C3*

In the former Arab quarter, this beloved restaurant showcases local ingredients, all creatively transformed into new variations that show great international flair. There are two tasting menus available where you can sample a range of dishes. The chef-sommelier stocks 100 regional and national wines, plus international wines based on demand. Closed Mon.

SOUTHERN SICILY

AUGUSTA Donna Ina
Contrada Faro Santa Croce, 96011 **Tel** *0931-983 422*
Road Map *F4*

Diners at Donna Ina select fish from a market-style display to be grilled, steamed in seawater or poached with oranges. Antipasti include raw fish, grilled shrimp or classic mixed fried-fish platter. For main course, try the lasagne with swordfish sauce, the fish ravioli or the penne with vegetables. There are 70 Sicilian wines on the list. Closed lunch; Mon.

BUCCHERI U Locale
Via Dusmet 14, 96010 **Tel** *0931-873 923*
Road Map *E4*

A handy spot for sustenance for those who are visiting the Akrai or Pantalica archaeological sites, this family-run trattoria offers meals using seasonal produce and game typical of the hillside forests, like wild boar. *Pappardelle* (broad pasta ribbons) with roast peppers and tomatoes is another popular choice. Closed Tue; Jul.

CHIARAMONTE GULFI Il Tegamino
Contrada Ponte 35, 97010 **Tel** *0932-921 333*
Road Map *E4*

"The Casserole Pot" has a casual atmosphere and offers mainly fresh fish. The *tagliatelle all'astice* (pasta ribbons with lobster) is perfect, with just the prawns' own juices as pasta sauce to enhance the flavours. They also make a good mixed roast-fish and shellfish platter. Pizza serves as a hearty starter or a simple dinner. Closed Tue.

CHIARAMONTE GULFI Majore
Via Martiri Ungaresi 12, 97010 **Tel** *0932-928 019*
Road Map *E4*

Set up on the hill in the town of Chiaramonte Gulfi, this restaurant is unique in that, from appetizers to desserts, the main theme on the menu is pork in all its forms: as salami, in aspic, roasted and sliced, in sauces, in a risotto. No doubt, pork ends up as *strutto* (shortening) in dessert crusts or cookies, or as gelatin. Closed Mon.

MARINA DI RAGUSA Da Serafino
Lungomare Doria, 97010 **Tel** *0932-239 522*
Road Map *E5*

A beach restaurant since 1953, Da Serafino is a summer tradition in Marina di Ragusa. The restaurant has its own private beach facilities, so one can rent chairs and an umbrella for the day and enjoy some of the loveliest water in Sicily. The menu of fish-based courses is simple but expertly prepared. They also make pizza. Closed Oct–Mar.

MODICA Fattoria delle Torri
Vico Napolitano 14, 97015 **Tel** *0932-751 286*
Road Map *E5*

This former 18th-century warehouse is now a restaurant, wine bar and cellar offering dishes like terrine of aubergine (eggplant) with basil, ravioli with fava beans and herbed ricotta, and rabbit with truffles. Some desserts are based on the chocolate of Modica, a relative of Mexican chocolate. Extensive wine list. Closed Mon; late Jun–early Jul.

NOTO Del Carmine
Via Ducezio 1, 96017 **Tel** *0931-838 705*
Road Map *E5*

The menu in this simple family-run trattoria is based on the bounty of southern Sicily's hills. Pasta dishes include ricotta-filled ravioli with pork sauce, and *tagliatelle capricciose* (pasta with fresh vegetables). Rabbit *alla stimpirata* has sweet-and-sour sauce with seasonal vegetables. *Cannoli* and cake are two of the dessert options. Closed Mon.

PALAZZOLO ACREIDE Anapo da Nunzio
Corso Vittorio Emanuele **Tel** *0931-882 286*
Road Map *E4*

This trattoria in the centre of town is a handy stop after touring the archaeological excavations at Akrai. Cheese is a local speciality, so begin or end your meal with a cheese platter to sample *provola* and pecorino (sheep's cheese, fresh or aged). Ravioli filled with ricotta is an excellent menu staple. Closed Mon.

RAGUSA Baglio La Pergola
Piazza Luigi Sturzo 6, 97100 **Tel** *0932-686 430*
Road Map *E5*

This elegant restaurant in the Baroque part of town features traditional cuisine with some new twists, like antipasti of grilled cheese with peppers and cinnamon, or macaroni made from spelt flour, pistachios and shrimp. Fish might be served with lemon and mint, and accompanied by *caponata* (aubergine/eggplant stew). Closed Tue; mid-Aug.

RAGUSA IBLA Duomo

Via Capitano Bocchieri 31, 97100 **Tel** *0932-651 265*   **Road Map** *E5*

One of Italy's top restaurants is located in a Baroque palazzo near the Duomo. Tradition informs contemporary and innovative dishes with international flair: couscous with pistachios and mint paired with fish soup and harissa (a spicy North African sauce); or pork in a sauce of cocoa beans, legumes and spinach. Closed Mon, Sun eve; Oct.

RAGUSA IBLA Locanda Don Serafino

Via Orfanotrofio 39, 97100 **Tel** *0932-248 778*   **Road Map** *E5*

An 18th-century palazzo hosts one of Ragusa's best restaurants. Contemporary variations on traditional recipes include red mullet stuffed with courgette (zucchini), baked ricotta with fried chicory, and lasagne made with cocoa filled with ricotta. There are also elaborate desserts, flavourful mini-cookies and 1,000 wines on the list. Closed Tue.

ROSOLINI Locanda del Borgo

Via Controscieri 11, 97100 **Tel** *0931-850 514*   **Road Map** *E5*

This restaurant occupies the former offices of the 18th-century Prince of Platamone, with their two cupolas and original frescoes. The covered terrace offers a view of the hills, and the cuisine uses traditional ingredients that had almost been forgotten in new, imaginative ways. About 300 wines feature on the list. Closed Tue, some Sun.

SCOGLITTI Sakalleo

Piazza Cavour 12, 97019 **Tel** *0932-871 688*   **Road Map** *D5*

Sakalleo is the name of a boat that was used for sponge fishing. Recipes at this restaurant on the coast south of Gela maintain the old culinary traditions and are based on fish brought in from one of the owner's three boats. There is no menu as such, just what is caught that morning. The wine list includes about 80 labels. Closed Mon.

SYRACUSE La Medusa da Kamel

Via Santa Teresa 21, 96100 **Tel** *0931-614 03*   **Road Map** *F4*

Near the ancient spring of Fonte Aretusa, in Ortygia's historic centre, this restaurant specializes in Sicilian seafood. On Thursday evenings the Tunisian chef offers a menu that features fish or lamb couscous with other traditional North African accompaniments; there are also various fish pastas and mixed grilled fish. Closed Mon.

SYRACUSE La Spiaggetta

Viale del Lido 473, Fontane Bianche, 96010 **Tel** *0931-790 334*   **Road Map** *F4*

All dining rooms, terrace and garden have a magnificent view of the sea. Fish is prepared in various forms, and specialities include *zuppa di pesce* (fish soup), spaghetti with sea urchins, linguine with lobster, swordfish *involtini* (roulades) or fish with Syracuse-style sauce of tomatoes, capers, olives and garlic. Closed Tue Oct–Mar.

SYRACUSE Jonico 'a rutta 'e ciauli

Riviera Dionisio il Grande 194, 96100 **Tel** *0931-655 40*   **Road Map** *F4*

This restaurant is perched on a cliff and offers alfresco dining. One of their specialities comes from a humble tradition: *pasta ca muddica* is pasta mixed with olive oil, breadcrumbs, anchovies and red peppers – a tasty option today, but a necessity in days gone by, when no meat, cheese, eggs or other fish were easily available. Closed Tue.

SYRACUSE Don Camillo

Via Maestranza 46, 96100 **Tel** *0931-671 33*   **Road Map** *F4*

Barrel-vaulted ceilings and stone walls stacked with wine bottles set the stage for the refined cooking here. Soup of newborn red mullet in a delicate broth, spaghetti with sea urchins and shrimp, and grilled tuna encrusted with black pepper are some of the dishes on offer. Excellent selection of cheeses. Closed Sun; mid-Feb, mid-July, Christmas.

NORTHEASTERN SICILY

ACI CASTELLO Alioto

Via Mollica 24–26, 95021 **Tel** *095-494 444*   **Road Map** *E3*

This seaside village restaurant offers a wide selection of fresh fish and shellfish. Main courses include *risotto pescatore* (rice with fish and seafood); *linguine al cartoccio* (pasta and seafood steamed inside paper wrapping); and pasta with lobster. End your meal with a delicious strawberry cake or *cassata*. Closed Tue; 2 weeks Aug.

ACIREALE A'Cumarca

Via Timone Zaccanazzo 87, 95024 **Tel** *095-886 200*   **Road Map** *E3*

The main attraction here is the terrace with its view of Etna, the mountains and the sea. The food is traditional and reasonably priced, with antipasti, *caponata* (aubergine/eggplant stew), pizza and light snacks being the most popular fare. Open only for dinner, but until late (about 1am). Closed Mon.

ACIREALE La Grotta

Via Scalo Grande 46, 95024 **Tel** *095-764 81 53*   **Road Map** *E3*

Built inside a grotto by the sea, this small restaurant sits only 25 people inside, but the outside area more than doubles that number. Fish is the speciality and prices are reasonable. La Grotta's most popular dishes are the seafood salad and mixed grilled fish. There is also a limited selection of Sicilian wines. Closed Tue; mid-Oct–mid-Nov.

Key to Price Guide *see p212* **Key to Symbols** *see back cover flap*

ACI TREZZA Verga da Gaetano

Via Provinciale 119, 95021 **Tel** *095-276 342*

Road Map E3

Near a small harbour, this restaurant has walls hung with photographs from the Luchino Visconti film *La Terra Trema*, in which the owner's wife had a role. Outside, the view is of the sea, the Cyclops Island and a lighthouse. The small trattoria (70 seats) specializes in fish and offers 20 Sicilian and Italian wines. Closed Thu; Jan.

CAPRILEONE L'Antica Filanda

Contrada Raviola SS 157, 98070 **Tel** *0941-919 704*

Road Map E2

This elegant hillside restaurant offers excellent meat dishes as well as local cheeses. Nero dei Nebrodi pork is prepared in a variety of ways, as are lamb and goat. Local wild field greens and mushrooms are used liberally, and bread is made in their wood-burning oven. Impressive selection of cheeses and wines. Closed Mon.

CATANIA Al Gabbiano

Via Giordano Bruno 128, 95100 **Tel** *095-537 842*

Road Map E3

This economical classic trattoria features only fish. Antipasti include mixed fried fish, shrimp with rocket, and octopus salad, as well as potato fritters. Spaghetti with clams is a popular first course. Fish can be roasted, fried, baked in salt, poached in seawater or steamed in paper. Seventeen local wines appear on the list. Closed Sun; Aug.

CATANIA Antica Marina

Via Pardo 29 (Pescheria di Catania), 95100 **Tel** *095-348 197*

Road Map E3

This is the ideal place to come for those who want to dine in the midst of Catania's fish market. It is best at lunch when the action is in full swing (except Sunday, when the market is closed). Recommended dishes are the mixed seafood starter and the spaghetti with sea urchins, but check to see what is being offered on the day. Closed Wed; Aug.

CATANIA I Vicerè

Via Grotte Bianche 97, 95021 **Tel** *095-320 188*

Road Map E3

The chef at this restaurant close to the 11th-century Norman castle is fond of inventing his own recipes. As one would expect from a coastal village, seafood is strongly featured. Pasta with fish and pine nuts or with clams often appears on the menu. A good choice of meat is available too, including steak, pork, lamb and rabbit. Open dinner only.

CATANIA Menza

Viale Mario Rapisardi 143–153, 95100 **Tel** *095-350 606*

Road Map E3

This rotisserie is a good spot to try a variety of specialities from Catania, such as *arancini* (rice balls), which are usually eaten as an appetizer or snack, or *crispelle* (rice fritters) with honey for dessert. One can put a satisfying meal together here with baked pasta and roasted meats. Closed Mon.

CATANIA Sicilia in Bocca Piazza Pietro Lupo

Piazza Pietro Lupo 16, 95100 **Tel** *095-746 13 61*

Road Map E3

This trattoria dates back to the early 20th century. The speciality is seafood at reasonable prices. Try the fish-stuffed ravioli or one of the many pasta dishes with a fish sauce. Choose from the day's catch, which might be swordfish, snapper or grouper, and accompany it with one of the 50 wines on offer. Friendly service. Closed Mon, Wed; 2 weeks Aug.

CATANIA Dell'Hotel Poggio Ducale – Da Nino

Via Gaifami 7, 95100 **Tel** *095-330 016*

Road Map E3

This family-run restaurant attracts a business clientele who appreciate the personal attention, professional service and excellent fish preparations. The raw fish is served in a variety of interesting combinations, including with mandarin, garlic and olive oil. The refreshing lemon-mint sorbet provides a light finish. Closed Mon lunch, Sun eve; Aug.

CATANIA Le Tre Caravelle

Via Catania Savoca 2, San Gregorio, 95100 **Tel** *095-717 74 34*

Road Map E3

Since 1998 this restaurant has been serving traditional local food, well prepared and simple. One of the most popular dishes is spaghetti with clams and shrimp. For the main course, diners select fish from the display and have it cooked in one of several different ways. The wine list includes a vast selection of Sicilian wines.

CATANIA Sicilia in Bocca alla Marina

Via Dusmet 35, 95100 **Tel** *095-250 02 08*

Road Map E3

This atmospheric trattoria in a 14th-century palazzo attracts a young crowd. You can enjoy the pizza and lively outdoor dining scene downstairs, or dine on the terrace upstairs, which offers a great view of the cupola of the Duomo and the Museo Diocesano. Closed Mon.

CATANIA Azienda Vinicola Benanti

Via Garibaldi 475, Viagrande, 95029 **Tel** *095-789 35 33*

Road Map E3

The prestigious Benanti winery offers a tour of its wine cellar and vineyards followed by a wine tasting. By advance reservation only, a lunch with wine tasting will be prepared for a minimum of five (and a maximum of 100) people. Diners can finish with cigars and spirits from Benanti's select collection. Ask about dining outside during the summer.

CATANIA La Siciliana

Viale Marco Polo 52A, 95126 **Tel** *095-376 400*

Road Map E3

One of Catania's most popular restaurants. The food prepared includes some inventive dishes, as well as plenty of traditional favourites, like *pasta alla Norma* (pasta with fried aubergine (eggplant), aged ricotta and tomato sauce), cuttlefish risotto black from its ink, and local ricotta cheese. Closed Mon & Sun evening.

CATANIA Osteria Tre Bicchieri

Via San Giuseppe al Duomo, 31, 95100 Tel 095-715 35 40   **Road Map** E3

In a 19th-century palazzo, this wine bar is elegant to the last detail: Rosenthal porcelain, Riedel glasses and silver cutlery make dining here truly special. The selection of over 500 wines, good cheese and salami platters, and creative Mediterranean cuisine also contribute to the fine dining experience. Closed lunch; Sun, Mon; most of Jul–Aug.

FILICUDI Nino Santamaria

Filicudi Porto, 98050 Tel 090-988 99 84   **Road Map** E1

Here one can dine on a terrace that overlooks the brilliant, clear waters of the Tyrrhenian Sea. Specialities include octopus salad, fried calamari (squid) and pasta with swordfish, which you can accompany with some nice local wines. Prices offer some of the best value anywhere. Cash only. Closed Oct–Mar.

LETOJANNI Nino

Via Rizzo 29, Letojanni, 98037 Tel 0942-361 47   **Road Map** F2

Begin with the heavenly antipasti: small fish cakes, squid with artichokes, octopus with home-pickled garlic, blood orange stuffed with shrimp and wild fennel, large shrimp stuffed with mashed fennel potatoes. The main courses are equally delicious. If you are still hungry, end your meal with the home-made ice cream. Closed Tue in winter; Dec–Feb.

LIPARI E Pulera

Via Diana, 98055 Tel 090-981 11 58   **Road Map** E1

Considered one of Lipari's top restaurants. Here you can dine on a terrace surrounded by a lush garden; each table is covered with vividly coloured ceramic tiles that represent different islands in the Aeolian archipelago. The cuisine is traditional Aeolian prepared with a refined touch, and the atmosphere is elegant. Closed lunch; early Oct–early May.

LIPARI La Nassa

Via Franza 36, 98055 Tel 090-981 11 39   **Road Map** E1

Diners can reach La Nassa by walking up the hill. The reward for this effort is a meal on the lovely terrace, in the welcome shade of the garden. This restaurant specializes in traditional Aeolian cuisine, with the emphasis on fish. Try some of the Malvasia and other regional wines. Closed Thu in spring; Nov–Mar.

MESSINA Trattoria Anselmo

Via Lago Grande 29, Ganzirri, 98100 Tel 090-393 225   **Road Map** F2

Ganzirri is at the northeast tip of Sicily, where the island almost touches Calabria, in the windy Strait of Messina. Some say the strong sea currents make the fish taste even better, and this restaurant certainly provides ample proof of such outstanding quality. Located in a rebuilt area, Trattoria Anselmo specializes in shellfish. Closed Mon in winter.

MESSINA Da Piero

Via Ghibellina 119, 98100 Tel 090-718 365   **Road Map** F2

Locals, many of whom consider this to be Messina's best restaurant, come here for its classic local cuisine, which is a tradition since 1962. Seafood and meat dishes are featured, as well as some lighter vegetable or salad plates. Attentive, professional service is the norm. Open for dinner only, closed Sun; Aug.

MILAZZO Piccolo Casale

Via R D'Amico 12, 98057 Tel 090-922 479   **Road Map** F2

This former 19th-century country home is tastefully furnished and inviting. On the menu are mostly fresh local fish and vegetables, with some meat options, and imaginative pasta dishes like cocoa ravioli filled with ricotta and almonds. There are over 800 wines on the list. Summer terrace dining takes place among the rooftops of Milazzo. Closed Mon.

PANAREA Da Francesco

Via San Pietro (Porto), 98050 Tel 090-983 023   **Road Map** E1

This trattoria near the port serves reliable food at economical prices, and the terrace offers a lovely view. Main fare is fish, usually grilled, but there are also good vegetable options: *spaghetti alla disgraziata*, for example, with tomatoes, aubergine (eggplant), peppers, chilli peppers, capers and olives. The baby squid in Malvasia wine is very tasty.

PANAREA Da Pina

Via San Pietro 3, 98050 Tel 090-983 032   **Road Map** E1

Pina offers reliably good dining, which includes typical traditional dishes from the island as well as their own innovative specialities. Try the home-made *tagliolini* (thin pasta strands) with delicate lemon sauce, which marries happily with fish dishes like the swordfish *involtini* (lightly braised roulades).

PANAREA Hycesia

Via San Pietro, 98050 Tel 090-983 041   **Road Map** E1

This intimate restaurant is only minutes from the port and the menu reflects the daily catch. Scorpion fish *tartare* (raw), linguine with asparagus and shrimp, and crustaceans in a cream sauce are some favourites. Reserve ahead – even VIPs compete to score one of the 12 tables. Vast wine list and tastings of olive oil and spirits, too. Closed Nov–Mar.

SALINA Porto Bello

Via Bianchi 1, Santa Marina, 98050 Tel 090-984 31 25   **Road Map** E1

This restaurant is known as much for its gracious service as for its fine cuisine, which one can enjoy on the shaded terrace. Most dishes here are traditional, but there is also some innovative fare. Try the tuna in olive oil, sea perch baked with potatoes, or squid with onions and Malvasia wine. Closed Wed Oct–May; Nov.

Key to Price Guide *see p212* **Key to Symbols** *see back cover flap*

SAN GIOVANNI LA PUNTA Giardino di Bacco

Via Piave 3, 95037 **Tel** *095-751 27 27* **Road Map** *E3*

Dine on the southeast slope of Europe's largest volcano, Mount Etna. This cheerful, well-run restaurant is in the former gatehouse to a grand villa and makes for elegant dining in the evening. The emphasis is on local cuisine, which is prepared expertly. Closed lunch (except on holidays); Mon; Jan.

SANT'ALFIO Azienda Agricola Casa Perrotta

Via Andronico 2, 95010 **Tel** *095-968 928* **Road Map** *E3*

On Etna's slope, this 16th-century monastery offers views of the volcano and the sea. The menu offers more than 40 antipasti, meat or vegetable, hot or cold. Try the spicy pork with sweet-and-sour sauce or the beef *involtini* (roulades) in lemon leaves. Desserts include *Gelo di cannella*, a cinnamon-based sweet. Closed lunch (Mon–Fri); Mon in winter.

TAORMINA A'Zammara

Via Fratelli Bandiera 15, 98039 **Tel** *0942-244 08* **Road Map** *F2*

The rustic wooden furniture, nostalgic prints on the walls, and family atmosphere give diners a sense of stepping back into a Taormina of years ago. Unpretentious and hearty food includes meatballs wrapped in lemon leaves or veal *involtini* (roulades). Good selection of regional wines. Closed Wed in winter; early Jan–early Feb, mid-Nov–mid-Dec.

TAORMINA La Botte

Piazza San Domenico, 98039 **Tel** *0942-241 98* **Road Map** *F2*

One of Taormina's rare budget restaurants, La Botte is frequented by locals, as well as by tourists and the Hollywood set when it's in town (Woody Allen was a regular when filming in the area). There are lots of colourful ceramics and a sense of fun about this casual and cosy place, which is decorated with wooden wine barrels (*botti*). Closed Mon.

TAORMINA Al Duomo

Vico Ebrei 11, 98039 **Tel** *0942-625 656* **Road Map** *F2*

The owner of this intimate, friendly, colourful restaurant across from the cathedral takes pride in preserving historic recipes, some of which date back 1,000 years and reflect Arabic and French traditions. Some are staples of the *cucina povera* ("humble cuisine"), with wild field greens, bread and beans. Closed Wed; Feb.

TAORMINA Casa Grugno

Via Santa Maria dei Greci, 98039 **Tel** *0942-212 08* **Road Map** *F2*

In the heart of medieval Taormina, this 16th-century palazzo highlights its architectural features with modern decor and candlelight. Traditional and historic recipes are given modern interpretations by the chef, who keeps the flavours very Mediterranean in style. Excellent wine selection. Closed Sun; part of Feb and Nov.

TAORMINA La Baronessa

Corso Umberto, 98039 **Tel** *0942-620 163 or 628 191* **Road Map** *F2*

The lovely 19th-century decor creates an elegant Victorian ambience. Anchovy and wild mint *timballo* (soufflé), pasta with lobster, *canule* (roulades) with artichokes and broad beans, the signature *sformatino* (layered pie) with ricotta and aubergine (eggplant), or *millefoglie* (paper-thin layers) of swordfish are all good main courses. Closed lunch.

TAORMINA La Giara Ristorante e Pianobar

Vico La Floresta 1, 98039 **Tel** *0942-625 083 or 233 60* **Road Map** *F2*

A splendid example of that vanishing species of elegant supper and dancing club, La Giara draws an upmarket clientele for drinks, dining, music at the piano bar and dancing. Expect to see a well-heeled, traditional crowd with the occasional jet-setter stopping by. Closed winter (except for special events).

TAORMINA Maffei's

Via San Domenico de Guzman 1, 98039 **Tel** *0942-240 55* **Road Map** *F2*

This Taormina chef has an extraordinary refined, subtle touch – his sauces enhance flavours without ever being heavy or dominating. Try the fresh oysters from Messina, the light and flavourful spaghetti with sea urchins, or the delicious sea snails in tomato sauce. Great service and a superb wine selection. Closed Tue; early Jan–mid-Feb.

TAORMINA Ristorante Vicolo Stretto

Via Vicolo Stretto 6, 98039 **Tel** *0942-838 19* **Road Map** *F2*

This gem of a restaurant is tiny (30 seats inside) and features traditional Sicilian cuisine with creative variations. Start with raw fish, fish salads or delicious vegetable antipasti. *Gnocchi* (potato dumplings) with shrimp and pistachios are tasty. Fish couscous or grouper *involtini* (roulades) are popular. International wine selection. Closed Mon; Dec–Feb.

TAORMINA (BEACH) La Capinera

Via Nazionale (under Autostrada Spisone), 98039 **Tel** *0942-626 247* **Road Map** *F2*

Right on the beach, with a sea view as well as indoor dining, this place run by the chef and his sisters has something for everybody. The seafood menu changes by the season and there is also a good vegetarian selection. There are three tasting menus: meat, fish and the so-called Chef's Inspiration. Closed Mon.

TRECASTAGNI All'Angolo

Via Catania 37, 95039 **Tel** *095-780 69 88* **Road Map** *E3*

Set at the foot of Mount Etna, west of Acireale and north of Catania, this old farmhouse offers an Italian (rather than Sicilian) menu in an intimate setting with just 20 seats. The interior is furnished in part with antiques and you can dine in the garden in the summer. The list of 180 wines includes some international labels. Closed lunch (open by request only).

SHOPS AND MARKETS

All the most well-known fashion designer shops can be found in the larger Sicilian cities (such as Palermo, Catania and Syracuse), together with smart chain stores stocking household articles and furniture. In tourist resorts it is possible to find shops specializing in Sicilian handicrafts, in particular ceramics, although the best items are sold in the places where they are made. Sicilian pastry shops sell delicious cakes,

A decorated Sicilian terracotta dish

cannoli pastries, *cassata* cakes and *torroncini* (almond nougat). Keep an eye out for the delicatessens selling local specialities, such as spiced capers, *ventresca* (tuna in oil), tuna *(tonno)*, salted mullet roe *(bottarga)* and aubergine *caponata*. You can also buy excellent produce such as organic fruit, olive oil, honey and fruit jam at farmhouses offering accommodation for visitors. Another good and typically Sicilian purchase is salt.

A shop specializing in wrought-iron products

OPENING HOURS

Generally, shops, boutiques and department stores are open from 8 or 9am to 1pm, and in the afternoon opening hours are 4–8pm. In the summer these hours may be extended, particularly in tourist resorts. In the cities, most shops close for two or three weeks in August. Seaside resort towns, on the other hand, usually operate on a seasonal basis, opening only from June to September.

HOW TO PAY

In the larger cities, the leading shops and department stores accept major credit cards, especially Visa and MasterCard, whereas in the towns and villages many shops still prefer cash payment.

In Palermo, Catania and Syracuse, some top hotels have deals with shops and restaurants for discounts of up to 40 per cent. The concierge will be able to tell you if your hotel takes part in this scheme.

HANDICRAFTS

In Caltagirone, Sciacca, Santo Stefano di Camastra and Burgio, the main production centres for striking Sicilian ceramics, there are shops and workshops selling plates, jugs, tiles, vases, mugs and statuettes. The **Laboratorio Branciforti** in Caltagirone makes jugs, vases and dishes with traditional decorative motifs.

At Sciacca, stylish ceramics can be found in the studio of **Giuseppe Navarra**, who has exhibited his works in New York and Montreal. The **Artigianato del Sole** also has a good range: as well as dinner services, jugs and ornamental plates, they make furniture, such as tables made of lava stone, and majolica tiles. Many artisans work in wrought iron. Among the good workshops near Giarre and Giardini Naxos is the **Laboratorio Patanè** and in Cefalù, **A Lumera**.

Two traditional puppet-makers

still active in Palermo are **Piero Scalisi** and **Vincenzo Argento**, whose studios are open to the public.

Another typical gift is the *coppola*, the traditional Sicilian cap.

OPEN-AIR MARKETS

If you want to experience the atmosphere of the old quarters of Sicilian towns and buy local produce, you have to go to the outdoor markets. In Palermo, the **Vucciria** market, immortalized by artist Renato Guttuso, is at its most atmospheric when the fishermen are setting up their stalls. In Via Argenteria pause at the stall of **Antonino Giannusa**, who offers an amazing range of preserves as well as an excellent Palermo-style pesto sauce. Another market worth visiting is the **Ballarò**,

Renato Guttuso, *La Vucciria* (1974)

between Piazza del Carmine and Piazza Ballarò, which is busiest around noon. In Catania, by Piazza Duomo, there is a colourful **fish market** every morning (stalls selling vegetables and meat stay open until the evening). On Sundays Piazza Carlo Alberto fills with an **antiques market** with second-hand items as well as rare pieces of Sicilian craftsmanship. Every day, just by the Porta Uzeda, there is an **antiques market** where furniture sellers and second-hand dealers offer items costing from a few cents to thousands of euros.

ICE CREAM PARLOURS AND PASTRY SHOPS

Popular pastry shops include **Alba** and **Bar Massaro** in Palermo, **Castorina** in Acireale or **Colicchia** in Trapani, where you can enjoy coffee or an aperitif. Sicilian pastry shops are a delight for the

eye and tastebuds with their *cannoli, cassata* and almond paste cookies. Some cake shops offer their own specialities. These include the marzipan sweets with citron filling at the **Antica Pasticceria del Convento** in Erice; ricotta puff pastries at **Scivoli** in Caltagirone; vanilla- or cinnamon-flavoured chocolate at **Antica Dolceria Bonaluto** in Modica; ricotta and pistachio *cannoli* at **Savia** in Catania; chestnuts filled with citrus fruit jam and topped with dark chocolate at the **Caffè Sicilia** in Noto; and nougat at **Geraci**, in Caltanissetta. Sicily is a paradise for ice-cream buffs. The **Caffè del Corso**, in Acireale, sells traditional ice creams in all flavours, and the speciality at **Stancampiano** is frozen yoghurt with blackberries or nutella with whipped cream. In Taormina **Niny Bar** is the place to go, and in Catania it is **Saint Moritz**.

Marzipan figure, an Erice speciality

A stall with Sicilian cheese in the varied market in Catania

REGIONAL SPECIALITIES

Delicatessens and *agriturismo* are ideal places for regional specialities. Smoked swordfish and tuna in oil can be found at the **Casa del Pesce** in Syracuse; salted mullet roe at **Quartana** in Trapani; on Mount Etna the **Azienda Luigi Conti** sells olive oil, bottled olives, cream of artichoke, wild asparagus and pumpkin. The **Azienda Agricola Trinità** has tangerines, olive oil, honey and wine, and the **Azienda Agricola Alcalà** offers a mail order service for all products, including fresh fruit. **Fiasconaro** produces a green golden ice cream made with Bronte pistachios.

DIRECTORY

CERAMICS

A Lumera
Corso Re Ruggero 180, Cefalù. **Tel** 0924-921 801.

Artigianato del Sole
Via Santa Margherita 72, Misterbianco (Catania).
Tel 095-398 472.

Laboratorio Branciforti
Scala S. Maria del Monte 3, Caltagirone (Catania).
Tel 0933-244 27.

Studio Navarra
Corso Vittorio Emanuele 38, Sciacca (Agrigento).
Tel 0925-850 00.

WROUGHT IRON

Laboratorio Patanè
Via Regina Margherita 111, Giardini-Naxos (Messina).
Tel 0942-511 49.

PUPPETS

Piero Scalisi
Via Federico De Maria 30, Palermo.
Tel 091-488 898.

Vincenzo Argento
Corso Vittorio Emanuele 445, Palermo. **Map** 1 B4.
Tel 091-661 36 80.

PASTRY SHOPS

Alba
Piazza San Giovanni Bosco 7d, Palermo.
Tel 091-309 016.

Antica Dolceria Bonaiuto
Corso Umberto I 159, Modica (Ragusa).
Tel 0932-941 225.

Antica Pasticceria del Convento
Via Guarnotta Gian Filippo 1, Erice (Trapani).
Tel 0923-869 777.

Bar Massaro
Via Ernesto Basile 26, Palermo.
Tel 091-489 922.

Caffè Sicilia
Corso Vittorio Emanuele 125, Noto (Syracuse).
Tel 0931-835 013.

Castorina
Corso Savoia 109, Acireale.
Tel 095-601 546.

Colicchia
Via delle Arti 6, Trapani.
Tel 0923-547 612.

Geraci
Via Niscemi 253, Caltanissetta.
Tel 0934-581 570.

Savia
Via Etnea 302, Catania.
Tel 095-322 335.

Scivoli
Via Milazzo 123, Caltagirone (Catania).
Tel 0933-231 08.

ICE CREAM PARLOURS

Caffè del Corso
Corso Umberto 165, Acireale. **Tel** 095-604 626.

Niny Bar
Via Vittorio Emanuele 216, Letojanni-Taormina (Messina).
Tel 0942-361 04.

Saint Moritz
Viale Raffaello 10, Catania.
Tel 095-437282.

Stancampiano
Via Notarbartolo 51, Palermo.
Tel 091-681 7244.

REGIONAL SPECIALITIES

Azienda Alcalà
Statale 192, km 78, Misterbianco (Catania).
Tel 095-713 00 29.

Azienda Luigi Conti
Contrada Pozzillo, Biancavilla (Catania).
Tel 095-981 132.

Azienda Trinità
Via Trinità 34, Mascalucia (Catania).
Tel 095-727 21 56.
www.aziendatrinita.it

Fiasconaro
Piazza Margherita, Castelbuono.
Tel 0921-677 132.

Quartana
Via 30 Gennaio 17, Trapani. **Tel** 0923 206 86.

What to Buy in Sicily

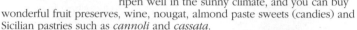

In general, Sicilian artisans now concentrate on ceramics and lava stone products. The prices are by no means low, but the objects are often beautifully handcrafted. However, historically, the most classic creations are the traditional Sicilian rod puppets and carts. They have become rarities because there are so few people left who know how to make and repair them. Some shops offer drab reproductions for tourists; but in the antique shops you can still find fine – if expensive – examples of these ancient crafts. When it comes to food and wine, Sicily excels: citrus fruit such as oranges, lemons and grapefruit ripen well in the sunny climate, and you can buy wonderful fruit preserves, wine, nougat, almond paste sweets (candies) and Sicilian pastries such as *cannoli* and *cassata*.

Rococo lamp made by Sicilian artisans in the 18th century

Marzipan fruit

Sicilian oranges

Sicilian confectionery *Buy* cannoli *and* cassata *just before going back home – they should be eaten within 12 hours. Marzipan fruit will last up to three months.*

Citrus fruit
Delicious tangerines, blood and navel oranges, grapefruit, lemons and mandarins – superior to those sold elsewhere in Italy – can be purchased in any market. You can also order them directly from the producer, who will send them to your home address.

Wine *Buy sweet Malvasia from Lipari, sweet Passito wine from Pantelleria, Nero d'Avola from Noto and dry red or white Corvo from Salaparuta or Bianco d'Alcamo. Buy directly from the producers or from wine shops, which also provide shipment to an onward destination.*

Wines from Pantelleria

Fillets of tuna

Tuna and vegetables in oil *Tuna fillets, salted tuna roe (bottarga), spiced capers in extra virgin olive oil, spiced black olives, aubergines (eggplant) in oil and chilli pepper are all regional specialities that can be purchased in leading Sicilian delicatessens.*

Olive oil *The best comes from the Valle del Belice; it is heavy, almost salty, with a peppery flavour. Ragusa oil is green and fragrant, and Taormina oil is more delicate.*

Preserves and honey *Organic fruit jams, prepared on the spot in the "agritourist" farms, have an unmistakable flavour. The fragrant and rare orange and lemon blossom honey also has therapeutic properties. The best is from the hills around Ragusa and Mount Etna.*

SICILIAN CERAMICS

This is probably the most highly appreciated handicrafts product of all. Light blue, yellow and green are the dominant colours in the lovely ceramics made in Caltagirone; they are richly decorated with volutes, flowers and geometric motifs. You can purchase vases, jugs, plates, mugs, jars and statuettes. Terracotta plaques with house numbers are also very much in demand. In the ceramics made in Sciacca – less famous but just as lovely as those from Caltagirone – the lemon is the prevailing decorative motif. Tiles also come in a variety of styles. The multicoloured majolica tiles bear 19th-century motifs and can be used for floors or simply as decorative objects to be set on an elegant table.

Elaborately decorated 19th-century tiles

Ceramic mask

Carts *Once used to transport heavy loads, traditional Sicilian carts – covered with paintings of religious or historical scenes – are now purely decorative objects. There are very few originals left, and sadly this ancient, noble craft is dying out.*

Jew's harp

Jew's harp *This typical musical instrument consists of an iron frame in the shape of a lyre around a thin flexible metal tongue that produces the sound.*

Sicilian cart

Sicilian puppets

Traditional Sicilian puppets *The armoured knights errant and the Saracens with round shields and turbans are characters from the puppet plays about Charlemagne. These small masterpieces can be purchased at the few puppet makers' workshops or in antique shops.*

Terracotta pieces *Simple and elegant Sicilian terracotta products – oil jars and huge water storage jars, dishes, jugs and oil cruets – are still made by local craftsmen and can be used as decorative objects for your home.*

Terracotta jar

ENTERTAINMENT IN SICILY

The entertainment on offer in Sicily is wide-ranging and varied, and the programmes for cultural, musical and theatrical events are particularly imaginative. In the cities, the theatres put on a long and eclectic winter season, while in the spring and summer the ancient sites become the venues for top-level ancient Greek theatre and symphony concerts. There are also many cultural events

Bar sign

connected with artists and personalities who have contributed to Sicily's colourful history. Added to this, there are numerous folk festivals and vibrant carnival celebrations. Far from being performed for the benefit of tourists, these are genuine expressions of the spirit of Sicily. The nightlife is lively in the main towns and the seaside resorts also stay active until the small hours.

PRACTICAL INFORMATION

Information in English about what is on in Sicily is difficult to find, but there are several excellent Italian-language websites that offer up to date details on events. The most informative for the island as a whole is www.lasicilia.com/eventi_sicilia.cfm, which lists events in all nine provinces for any particular day. For Palermo, www.palermoweb.com provides a comprehensive guide to entertainment in Sicily's largest city.

The site www.sicilycinema.it offers a complete guide to what is playing in all of the island's cinemas.

BOOKING TICKETS

There are several nationwide booking agencies operating in Sicily, including **Box Office** and **Ricordi Media Store**. Each of these has offices in the main Sicilian centres.

The more prominent theatres and music venues also have their own websites where you can book online.

OPERA, THEATRE, CLASSICAL MUSIC

Palermo's **Teatro Massimo** stages a year-long opera programme that includes favourites such as Verdi and Puccini alongside more contemporary composers, like Samuel Barber. The theatre's orchestra readily embraces an eclectic mix of music, including tribute bands to The Beatles. The **Politeama**, home to the Sicilian Symphony Orchestra, hosts classical music concerts throughout the year, as well as artists such as Paolo Conte.

Palermo's main playhouse is the **Teatro Biondo**, the repertoire of which ranges from popular Greek tragedies and Tennessee Williams to August Strindberg and Eduardo De Filippo.

Programme for a performance at the Teatro Greco in Syracuse

With its excellent acoustics, Catania's **Teatro Massimo Bellini** is a favourite with performers. The opera season lasts all year, while the Bellini Orchestra's concert season runs from October to June. The 477-seat **Teatro Sangiorgi**, owned by Teatro Bellini, stages contemporary music, chamber music, operetta, prose and experimental theatre. Catania's chief theatre is the **Teatro Stabile**, which presents mainstream drama by the likes of Shakespeare, Molière and Pirandello.

Sicily's ancient Greek and Roman outdoor theatres come into their own in the warmer months, providing spectacular settings for traditional and modern drama. One of the best known is the **Teatro Greco** in Syracuse, a large and well-preserved monument dating back to the 5th century BC. A classical theatre season is held here biennially in May and June (see p38).

Outdoor performances are always popular in the summer months

The **Ortygia Festival**, at the Archaeological Park and the Castello Maniace, showcases some of the most innovative Italian theatre and also attracts international artists.

In odd-numbered years, Segesta's temple is the atmospheric backdrop for both traditional and modern plays *(see p38)*, while Taormina's ancient Greek theatre plays host to music and drama during **Taormina Arte** *(see p39)*, a series of events running from April to October. In early June, the theatre stages La Kore, the fashion world's equivalent of the Academy Awards.

Each year Agrigento pays a double tribute to Luigi Pirandello. In summer, during the Rappresentazioni Pirandelliane *(see p39)*, plays are performed in front of the house where the great Sicilian novelist and playwright was born; and in December, the Rassegna di Studi Pirandelliani *(see p41)*, held at the **Centro Nazionale Studi Pirandelliani**, provides an opportunity for students to visit the places that inspired him.

You don't need to understand Italian to appreciate a good puppet show. Puppet theatre reached the height of its popularity in the mid-1800s,

A traditional Sicilian puppet in full armoured suit

The scenic setting of a classical production at the Teatro Greco in Syracuse

but there has been renewed interest in this traditional art. Based on local folklore and comedy and usually involving one of Charlemagne's knights, Orlando, fighting the Saracens, puppet theatre is performed throughout Sicily. In Palermo the **Museo delle Marionette** puts on tourist performances, but for a more authentic experience, visit the **Cuticchio Puppet Theatre**. Puppet shows can also be enjoyed in Acireale, Taormina and Syracuse.

CINEMA

At Taormina's annual **FilmFest**, movies are screened in the ancient Greek theatre, against the dramatic backdrop of Mount Etna. At over 50 years old, this is the longest lasting film festival in Italy after Venice. Today its focus is predominantly on new directors and films from developing countries.

Lipari, in the Aeolian Islands, hosts its own film festival, **Un Mare di Cinema**, in the first week of August. Since 1990, directors and actors have vied for the festival's prestigious Efesto d'Oro prize.

Sicily is also a popular film location *(see p24)*. Sicilian director Giuseppe Tornatore filmed his Academy Award-winning *Cinema Paradiso* (1989) around Palermo, and his wartime film *Malena* (2000) was also shot in various locations on the island, including Messina, Siracusa, Noto and Taormina. His latest

film, *Baaria* (2009), was about his hometown of Bagheria and its post-war history. Filmed almost completely on the Aeolian island of Salina, Michael Radford's poignant *Il Postino* (1994) features some splendid scenes shot around the village of Pollara.

CARNIVALS AND FOLK FESTIVALS

February is carnival time in Italy, and this period is also celebrated with enthusiasm in many Sicilian towns. One of the most spectacular events is the **Carnevale di Acireale** *(see p41)*, blending poetry, games and a procession of colourful floats through the town centre. The famous **Carnevale di Sciacca** *(see p41)* is symbolized by a huge puppet and a procession of floats through the town's streets. In the same month, the people of Catania worship the memory of **Sant'Agata** *(see p41)*, whose relics, including a veil that the faithful believe once shielded Catania from lava erupting out of nearby Mount Etna, are carried through the town.

In Agrigento, the imminent arrival of spring is celebrated each February with the **Sagra del Mandorlo in Fiore** *(see p41)*. As fragrant almond blossoms fill the air, a procession makes its way to the lovely Valle dei Templi. Coinciding with this is the **Folklore Festival** *(see p41)*, featuring dance, traditional costumes and music.

Carnival time in Sicily spells a week of crowds and colour

Noto also welcomes spring, but not until the third week in May, with **L'Infiorata** *(see p38)*, which sees the laying down of a carpet of flowers depicting religious or mythological themes.

Easter is an important time for religious festivals. In Caltanissetta, a week is given over to processions, including the Good Friday carrying of a crucifix made of black wood, which was found in a cave in 1625 *(see p38)*. A weeklong festival held in Enna culminates on Easter Sunday, when images of Christ and the Madonna are brought together in the Piazza Duomo *(see p38)*. Trapani's **Mystery Procession** *(see p38)* is almost 400 years old. Winding its way through the town, it showcases 20 wooden and fabric sculptures embellished with silver, and each one is carried on the shoulders of at least ten men.

Caltigirone produces a dazzling spectacle for the feast of its patron saint, the **Festa di San Giacomo** *(see p39)*, with 4,000 candles illuminating the 142 steps of the Scala di Santa Maria del Monte.

In July, the feast day of the patron saint of Palermo, **Santa Rosalia** *(see p39)*, involves actors and musicians recreating the arrival of the Flemish painter Antony van Dyck, who visited Palermo in 1624 and painted Saint Rosalia interceding to rescue the town from the plague.

In August, Piazza Armerina celebrates its French heritage with the **Palio dei Normanni** *(see p39)*. The three days of festivities begin with a re-enactment of Roger's entrance into the town and culminate in a medieval tournament.

Christmas is the occasion for a number of festivals. The town of Agira, near Enna, is the setting of the only **Presepe Vivente** (Nativity play) in Italy to take place on Christmas night. More than 100 players in period costume take part in the festival, which also features ancient crafts such as spinning, carpentry and pasta-making.

Another fascinating **Presepe Vivente** is played out in the northwestern town of Custonaci, in a cave called Grotta Mangiapane, named after the family that lived in it from the 1800s until 1945.

TRADITIONAL AND POPULAR MUSIC

Traditional Sicilian folk music has a loyal following. Among the best-known exponents are Carmelo Salemi and Giancarlo Parisi, players of the *zampogna* (bagpipes), *friscalettu* and other Sicilian wind instruments. They are regular performers at festivals such as Agrigento's **Folklore Festival** *(see p41)*, Taormina's **Womad**, Palermo's **World Festival on the Beach** and the **Ortygia Festival**.

Jazz also finds a dedicated audience. The Palermo-based Brass Group, an association that promotes this genre of music, has its headquarters in a historic building called **Lo Spasimo**, which is also home to the Sicilian Jazz Orchestra.

In Catania the best place for live music is **La Chiave**, where they play blues on Thursdays and jazz on Sundays.

NIGHTLIFE

Sicily's lively nightlife centres on the cities in winter and the tourist resorts in summer. Discos often charge a cover fee that can be as high as €20.

Palermo has its share of pubs, including **Mikalsa**, **Agricantus**, **Cambio Cavalli** and **Crazy Bull**, the latter offering live Italian, American, English and South American music. New musical talent is showcased at the **Biergarten**, **I Candelai** and **Malox**. Popular discos in the inner city are **Tonnara Florio**, in the ancient district of Arenella, the **Anticlea Pub** and the **Country Club**, whose large dance floors become open-air in summer. Outside central Palermo are well-known discos like **Il Moro** and **Kandinsky Florio**.

Located just out of Catania is **Banacher**, an outdoor club that attracts a mix of locals and tourists; here you can dance amid a maze of plants. **Il Bagatto** is a popular watering hole offering live music on the island of Ortygia, the ancient heart of Syracuse.

Buzzing Taormina caters for all tastes, from casual cafés to late night discos. **La Giara** is a popular apéritif and after-dinner drink spot that does not get crowded until after 10pm. **Bar Morgana** is for the young and fashionable and is open till late. In the seaside town of Giardini Naxos is **Marabù**, a beautiful open-air disco where you can dance until the early hours.

Catania boasts one of the most vivacious nightlife scenes in Sicily

DIRECTORY

BOOKINGS

Box Office
Via Cavour 133, Palermo.
Map 1 C2.
Tel 091-335 566.
Via G Leopardi 95, Catania.
Tel 095-722 53 40.

Ricordi Media Store
Via Sant'Euplio 38, Catania.

Ticket One
www.ticketone.it

OPERA, THEATRE, CLASSICAL MUSIC

Centro Nazionale Studi Pirandelliani
Via Santa Lucia 27,
Agrigento.
Tel 0922-290 52.
www.cnsp.it

Cuticchio Puppet Theatre
Via Bara all'Olivella 95,
Palermo. **Map** 1 B2.
Tel 091-323 400.
www.figlidartecuticchio.
com

Museo delle Marionette
Via Butera 1, Palermo.
Map 2 E3.
Tel 091-328 060.
www.museomarionette
palermo.it

Ortygia Festival
Via Agatocle 51, Syracuse.
Tel 0931-483 648.
www.ortigiafestival.it

Politeama
Piazza Ruggero Settimo,
Palermo. **Map** 1 A/B1.
Tel 091-605 34 21.

Taormina Arte
Tel 0942-211 42.
www.taormina-arte.com

Teatro Biondo
Via Teatro Biondo 11,
Palermo. **Map** 1 C3.
Tel 091-743 43 00.

Teatro delle Marionette
Via di Giovanni, Taormina.
Catania 195, Acireale.
Tel 095-764 80 35.

Teatro delle Marionette
Via Giudecca 5, Syracuse.
Tel 093-146 55 40.

Teatro delle Marionette
Via di Giovanni, Taormina.
Tel 0942-628 644.

Teatro Greco
Corso Gelone 103,
Syracuse.
Tel 0931-465 831
or 0931-674 15.
www.indafondazione.org

Teatro Massimo
Piazza Giuseppe Verdi,
Palermo. **Map** 1 B2.
Tel 091-605 31 11.
www.teatromassimo.it

Teatro Massimo Bellini
Via Perrota 12, Catania.
Tel 095-730 61 11.
www.teatromassimo
bellini.it

Teatro Sangiorgi
Via A di Sangiuliano 233,
Catania.
Tel 095-730 61 11.

Teatro Stabile
Via Fava 39, Catania.
Tel 095-354 466.
www.teatrostabile
catania.it

CINEMA

Taormina FilmFest
Tel 094-223 243.
www.taorminafilmfest.it

Un Mare di Cinema
Lipari.
Tel 090-981 29 87.

CARNIVALS AND FOLK FESTIVALS

Carnevale di Acireale
Acireale. *Tel 095-891 19
99.* www.carnevale
acireale.com

Carnevale di Sciacca
Sciacca.
Tel 0925-245 37.
www.carnevaledisciacca.it

Festa di San Giacomo
Caltagirone.
Tel 093-353 809.

Festa di Sant'Agata
Catania.
Tel 095-760 62 33.
www.comune.
catania.it/portale

Festa di Santa Rosalia
Palermo. *Tel 091-583 847.*
www.palermoweb.com/
santarosalia

Folklore Festival
Agrigento.
www.mandorloinfiore.net

L'Infiorata
Noto.
www.infioratadinoto.it

Mystery Procession
Trapani. *Tel 092-354 55 11.*
www.processione
misteritp.it

Palio dei Normanni
Piazza Armerina. *Tel 0935-
682 501 or 0935-686 063.*
www.paliodeinormanni.
com

Presepe Vivente
Agira. *Tel 0935-691 111.*

Presepe Vivente
Custonaci.
Tel 0923-973 553.
www.mcsystem.it/presepe

Sagra del Mandorlo in Fiore
Agrigento.
Tel 092-220 454.
www.mandorloinfiore.net

TRADITIONAL AND POPULAR MUSIC

La Chiave
Via Landolina, Catania.
Tel 347-948 09 10.
www.lachiave.it

Ortygia Festival
Syracuse.
www.ortigiafestival.it

Lo Spasimo
Via Giuseppe La Farina,
Palermo. *Tel 091-348 751.*
www.thebrassgroup.it

Womad
Taormina.
www.womad.org

World Festival on the Beach
Palermo.
www.wwfestival.com

NIGHTLIFE

Agricantus
Via XX Settembre 82,
Palermo.
Tel 091-487 117.

Anticlea Pub
Viale Galatea 6, Palermo.
Tel 091-346 772.

Il Bagatto
Piazza San Giuseppe,
Ortygia, Syracuse.
Tel 093-122 040.

Banacher
Via Vampolieri 2, Aci
Castello. *Tel 095-27 12 57.*

Bar Morgana
Scesa Morgana 4,
Taormina.
Tel 094-262 00 56.

Biergarten
Viale Regione Siciliana
6469, Palermo.
Tel 091-680 97 27.

Cambio Cavalli
Via Patania 54, Palermo.
Map 1 C2.
Tel 091-581 418.

I Candelai
Via Candelai 65, Palermo.
Map 1 B3.
Tel 091-327 151.

Country Club
Via dell'Olimpo 5,
Palermo.
Tel 091-453 782.

Crazy Bull
Via Atenasio 8a, Palermo.
Tel 091-685 05 27.

La Giara
Vico La Floresta 1,
Taormina.
Tel 094-223 360.

Kandinsky Florio
Via Discesa Tonnara,
Palermo.
Tel 091-637 38 51.

Malox
Piazzetta della Canna 8–9,
Palermo. **Map** 1 B3.
Tel 091-612 47 12.

Marabù
Via Iannuzzo,
Giardini Naxos, Taormina.
Tel 094-265 30 29.

Mikalsa Pub
Via Torremuzza 27,
Palermo.
Tel 348-973 2254.

Il Moro
Piazza Monsignore Poltino
3, Palermo.
Tel 091-546 213.

Tonnara Florio
Via Discesa Tonnara,
Palermo. *Tel 091-637
56 11.* www.tonnara
florio.com

SPECIALIST HOLIDAYS AND OUTDOOR ACTIVITIES

For most visitors to Sicily, sporting activities tend to be water-based: swimming, fishing, windsurfing and diving in the crystal-clear waters off the extensive coast and the many islands that dot the Tyrrhenian and Mediterranean seas. Sailing enthusiasts have a vast choice of enticing routes on a variety of charter craft. There are plenty of other outdoor activities to enjoy too, such as hiking along old pathways in the Madonie and Nebrodi mountains or on Mount Etna. In the winter, the snowy slopes of the imposing volcano provide good conditions for downhill as well as cross-country skiing. Horse riding, including organized programmes of long-distance trekking, is also becoming increasingly popular in Sicily. Visitors can embark on many of these activities under their own steam, though an ever-growing number of local and overseas agencies offer a good choice of all-inclusive outdoor and sporting holidays.

Sport fishing

Sailing has become an increasingly popular activity in Sicily

SAILING

The coastline and inlets of Sicily and the region's wonderful islands are a paradise for sailing aficionados, and the sport is especially popular along the island's northern coast. True to their name – derived from the Greek god of wind – the Aeolian Islands *(see pp188–91)* guarantee a constant stiff breeze, as does the distant Pelagie archipelago *(see pp124–5)* off the southwestern coast.

In 2005, the international races held in the waters off the coast of Trapani as part of the prestigious America's Cup trials represented a landmark event for Sicily. This, along with the coming and going of yachts from all over Europe, has had a very positive influence of late,

triggering a series of improvements in nautical tourism facilities in the many port towns along the coast.

Yachts of varying sizes and degrees of comfort are available for charter at ports all around the island through companies such as **Onda Eoliana**. Many nautical centres hold sailing courses for the uninitiated, including **Centro Vela** in Lampedusa, though qualified multilingual crews can always be requested to transport passengers who desire a thoroughly relaxing sailing experience. **Syracuse Sailing Team** offers a number of trips around Sicily's islands and **EtnaSail** can arrange an unusual trip in a traditional Turkish-style *caicco* boat.

The **Velalinks** website (www.velalinks.it) is helpful in locating charter companies and instructors. There are also several UK-based companies that organize all-inclusive sailing holidays.

WINDSURFING

This energetic sport can be practised at most Sicilian seaside resorts thanks to conditions that guarantee constant winds. Virtually every beach in Sicily offers rental facilities. Mondello beach *(see p72)*, just outside Palermo, is well-served by **Albaria Windsurfing Club**. However, expert windsurfers claim that the best places for the sport are the Aeolian Islands and the Capo Passero area *(see p148)* in the south where the Ionian and Mediterranean seas merge. This same area is also favoured by kitesurfers. The popular beach location of Pozzallo has rental facilities, and expert instruction for different abilities is also available. The **Kitesicilia** website (www.kitesicilia.it) offers suggestions on the island's hot spots and a list of local contacts.

Windsurfers can often be spotted in the waters around Sicily

DIVING

The sea beds around Sicily are the delight and joy of scuba- and free-divers, who head for the offshore islands – especially the Aeolians *(see pp188–91)*, which are of volcanic origin. The island of Ustica *(see p109)* has a marvellous marine reserve making it an ideal spot for underwater sports. Agencies here include **Alta Marea**, which offers diving courses for all levels of experience, and **Barracuda**. Almost in Tunisian waters, the Pelagie islands of Pantelleria *(see p124)* and Lampedusa *(see p125)* offer superb diving in brilliantly clear waters. As well as fish, you may spot some historical artifacts such as Roman amphorae from an ancient shipwreck on the sea bed. **Dibex Centro Subacqueo** has a particularly good range of diving trips from Pantelleria.

The rugged coastline in the Riserva dello Zingaro, ideal for hiking

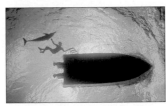
The crystalline waters around the Aeolian Islands favour snorkelling and scuba diving

Generally speaking, most seaside resorts offer at least basic diving facilities, including refills of your oxygen cylinder. The resort of Terrasini, on the coast west of Palermo, offers both instructors and facilities.

If you are planning to dive independently, always make sure that someone knows of your whereabouts and plans. The Italian website **Dive Italy** has useful information and a number of operators, such as **The Sicilian Experience**, can organize diving holidays.

WALKING & TREKKING

There is an impressive range of rewarding walking itineraries all over Sicily. The choice includes hills, mountains, coastal districts and fantastic limestone gorges such as the ones at Pantalica *(see p157)* and Cava d'Ispica *(see p149)* in the Monti Iblei (Hyblaei Hills). The protected park area around Mount Etna *(see pp170–73)* offers marvellous opportunities for high-altitude trips among the lava fields and grottoes. Qualified leaders from **Etna Guides** escort thrilling climbs to the smoking summit craters. To the east is the Alcantara River valley *(see p181)*, which offers easy routes through old settlements and a fascinating basalt ravine gouged out by the impetuous watercourse.

The rugged Madonie mountains and park feature spectacular panoramas, marked paths and rare vegetation in the Vallone Madonna degli Angeli, near Piano Battaglia *(see p94)* and the Pizzo Carbonara summit.

Highlights of the vast rolling Nebrodi mountain chain *(see p186)*, another protected area, include the Biviere di Cesarò, a pretty lake and important staging point for migratory birds. **Parco Regionale dei Monti Nebrodi** provides extensive and helpful information about the area. Close by, and towering over the village of Alcara Li Fusi, is the dramatic Rocche di Crasto, home to the griffon vulture. These impressive rock formations are accessible on clear paths. Other interesting areas for walkers include Piana degli Albanesi *(see p96)* and the divine coastline of the **Riserva dello Zingaro** *(see p97)*.

Several islands have unusual walking opportunities, such as the Aeolians *(see pp188–91)*, with ascents of volcanoes, both extinct and active, on Stromboli (where a guide is essential), Vulcano, Salina and Lipari. **Magma Trek's** tour leaders are particularly knowledgeable about the science and history of Stromboli's active volcano.

In both the interior and main cities of Sicily, visitors can find a number of sports associations and guesthouses offering trekking holidays and excursions. **Club Alpino Italiano** also organizes excursions on a regular basis as does **Explore Worldwide**.

The awesome ravine gouged out of the basalt rock by the course of the Alcantara River

A group of friends horse riding on a Sicilian beach

HORSE RIDING

This popular activity is gathering an increasingly loyal following, especially among local inhabitants. Sicily's rugged, mountainous interior is perfectly suited to horse riding enthusiasts, featuring numerous routes that are easily accessible from village centres.

One particularly interesting multi-day itinerary is the one that stretches for 70 km (43.5 miles) and runs east to west along the central ridge of the Nebrodi mountain range (see p186), following age-old droving routes. This region is home to 5,000 native horses, a pretty, dark variety known as San Fratellino. Believed to descend from an ancient breed known to the Greeks and Romans, the horses are left to graze freely.

Many *agriturismo* farms and some of the larger holiday villages have riding schools that cater to varying levels of ability. Tucked away in the divine Anapo Valley (see p157), near a wild gorge, **Pantalica Ranch** arranges horse riding trips. **Centro Ippico Amico del Cavallo** is an equestrian centre based in Misterbianco, close to Catania, which offers one-day trips as well as longer treks on horseback. There are also many establishments dotted around the slopes of Mount Etna offering various horse riding excursions.

For further information on the most important horse riding centres in Sicily, contact the **Associazione Nazionale Turismo Equestre** (ANTE) in Rome.

SKIING

If the weather is good, the panorama from the slopes of Mount Etna (see pp170–73) is simply awe-inspiring, with the sea at Taormina mirroring the sunlight and the volcano's fumes rising lazily above you.

However, do not expect to find state-of-the-art skiing facilities here. There is no artificial snow (the perennial drought in Sicily precludes anything of the kind), and the heat of the volcano tends to melt the snow in a hurry, so the skiing season is limited to a few months, from late December until March. Thanks to a cable-car and four ski lifts, you can ski up to 3,000 m (9,850 ft) above sea level on the runs around **Rifugio Sapienza** and the old Montagnola crater.

On the northern flank of the mountain, reconstruction of both facilities and runs continues in the wake of destructive 2002 eruptions that all but wiped out the small-scale resort of Piano Provenzana (see p172).

Perfect for all age groups, the thrill of tobogganing is another good, fun activity.

Mount Etna is not only for downhill-skiing enthusiasts, though their numbers continue to grow with each year. There is also a beaten track near the Grande Albergo, just below **Rifugio Sapienza**, which is ideal for cross-country skiing.

The volcano also attracts lovers of alpine techniques, telemarking and even the increasingly popular pursuit of snowshoeing; real off-the-beaten-track activities.

The wonderfully wild Nebrodi range (see p186) also gets a decent snow cover and offers many opportunities for exploration with cross-country skis and snowshoes.

Making the most of the brief skiing season on Mount Etna

Piano Battaglia (see p94), in the Madonie mountains, attracts weekenders from Palermo for its lovely, if limited, pistes and lifts.

Finally, thrill-seekers will enjoy the uniquely Sicilian sport of travelling down the black volcanoes of the Aeolian Islands (see pp188–91) on a snowboard. But be warned, the dry lava surface is much harder than snow.

Snowboarding on a lava field on Vulcano, one of the Aeolian Islands

DIRECTORY

SAILING

Centro Nautica
(charter & rental)
Baia Levante, Vulcano.
Tel 090-982 21 97.
www.baialevante.it

Centro Vela
(courses)
Lampedusa.
www.centrovelalam
pedusa.com

Etnasail
Catania
Tel 095-712 69 52.
www.etnasail.com

Gulliver
(rental & courses)
Favignana.
www.arteutile.net/gulliver

Harbour Office
Lipari.
Tel 090-981 32 22.
www.lipari.guardia
costiera.it

Harbour Office
Ustica.
Tel 091-844 96 52.

Nauta
(charter & rental)
Lipari.
Tel 090-982 23 05.

Nautica Levante
(charter & rental)
Salina.
Tel 090-984 30 83.
www.nauticalevante.it

Onda Eoliana
(rental)
Tel 090-984 40 10.
www.ondaeoliana.com

Rinauro
(charter & rental)
Stromboli.
Tel 090-986 156.

Sailing Information
www.lampedusa.to

Sopravvento
(rental & courses)
Pantelleria.
www.sopravvento.net

Syracuse Sailing Team
(charter)
Tel 0931-608 08.
www.sailingteam.biz

Trinacria Sailing
Tel 090-641 34 38.
www.trinacriasailing.com

Velalinks
www.velalinks.it

Vulcano Consult
Tel 800-090 541.
www.vulcanoconsult.it

WINDSURFING

Albaria Windsurfing Club
Tel 091-684 44 83.

Kitesicilia
www.kitesicilia.it

DIVING

Alta Marea
Ustica.
Tel 091-625 40 96.
www.altamareaustica.it

Barracuda
Ustica.
Tel 091-844 91 32.
www.barracudaustica.
com

Centro Immersioni Lo Verde
Lampedusa.
Tel 0922-970 181.

Dibex Centro Subacqueo
Pantelleria.
www.pantelleria.it/divex

Dive Italy
www.diveitaly.com

Diving Cala Levante
Tel 0923-915 463.
www.calalevante.
pantelleria.it

Diving Center Manta Sub
Lipari.
Tel 090-981 10 04

Green Divers
Tel 0923-918 209.
www.greendivers.it

Hospital
(hyperbaric chamber)
Tel 090-988 51

La Sirenetta Diving Center
Stromboli.
Tel 090-986 338.
www.lasirenettadiving.it

Lipari Diving Centre
Tel 339-647 22 72.

Profondo Blu
Tel 091-844 96 09.
www.ustica-diving.it

Ricarica ARA
Filicudi.
Tel 090-988 99 84.

Ricarica ARA
Diving Center La Gorgonia
Tel 090-981 26 16.
www.lagorgoniadiving.it
Salina.
Tel 090-984 30 92.

Ricarica ARA di Rosalia Ailara
Tel 091-844 96 05.
www.ustica.ara.it

Salina Diving
Tel 338-495 90 80.
www.salinadiving.com

Scubaland
Tel 091-844 96 36.
www.scubaland.it

The Sicilian Experience
6 Palace Street,
London SW1E 5HY.
Tel 020-7828 9171.
www.thesicilian
experience.co.uk

Sotto l'Acqua del Vulcano
Tel 090-986 025.

Terrasini Dive Center
Tel 091-868 76 95.
www.divecompanie.com

Vulcano Mare
Vulcano.
Tel 090-985 31 05.
www.vulcanomare.com

WALKING & TREKKING

Club Alpino Italiano
Catania.
Tel 095-715 35 15.
www.caicatania.it
Palermo.
Tel 091-329 407.
www.palermoweb.com/
caipalermo

Etna Guides
Tel 095-791 47 55.
www.etnaguide.com

Explore Worldwide
www.explore.co.uk

Magma Trek
Stromboli.
Tel 090-986 57 68.
www.magmatrek.it

Parco dell'Etna
Nicolosi. *Tel 095-821 111.*
www.parks.it/parco.etna

Parco Fluviale dell'Alcantara
Francavilla di Sicilia.
Tel 0942-98 99.
www.parcoalcantara.it

Parco delle Madonie
Petralia Sottana.
Tel 0921-923 327.
www.parcodelle
madonie.it

Parco Regionale dei Monti Nebrodi
Caronia.
Tel 0921-333 211.
www.parcodeinebrodi.it

Riserva dello Zingaro
Tel 0924-351 08.
www.riservazingaro.it

HORSE RIDING

Associazione Nazionale Turismo Equestre
Rome. *Tel 06-3265 0230.*
www.fiteec-ante.it

Centro Guide Equestri Ambientali Sanconese
Tel 0933-970 883.
www.geasanconese.it

Centro Ippico Amico del Cavallo
Misterbianco.
Tel 095-461 882.
www.amicodelcavallo.
com

Pantalica Ranch
Tel 0931-942 069.
www.pantalicaranch.it

Rifugio Villa Miraglia
Portella Femmina Morta,
Nebrodi.
Tel 095-773 21 33.
www.villamiraglia.it

SKIING

Funivia dell'Etna
Tel 095-911 158.
www.funiviaetna.com

Rifugio Ostello della Gioventù
Piano Battaglia.
Tel 0921-649 995.

Rifugio Sapienza
Tel 095-915 321.

SURVIVAL
GUIDE

PRACTICAL INFORMATION

In recent years, there has been renewed interest in caring for and revitalizing the unique historic, artistic and natural heritage of Sicily, and the island is no longer a destination solely for the adventurous. The Sicilian coastline, one of the most beautiful in Italy, attracts thousands of visitors every year. The island's long history and numerous monuments are as much an attraction – if not a greater one – than its marvellous landscape. Those who are interested in Sicilian history and culture

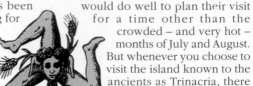

The Trinacria, ancient symbol of Sicily, now regional coat of arms

would do well to plan their visit for a time other than the crowded – and very hot – months of July and August. But whenever you choose to visit the island known to the ancients as Trinacria, there is always something exciting to explore. Everyone comes expecting to enjoy the island's food and wine, coastline and art treasures. But there are also inland areas to explore, including Mount Etna, the Madonie Mountains and Riserva dello Zingaro nature reserves, as well as sports activities and spas.

Ferry boats, connecting the island of Sicily with mainland Italy

OPENING HOURS

In Sicily shops are generally open from 8 or 9am until 1pm and then from 3:30 or 4pm (in the winter) or 5pm (in the summer) to 7 or even 8pm from Monday to Saturday. They are closed on Sundays and for one afternoon during the week.

Banks are open from 8:30am to 1:30pm and 3:30 to 4:30pm from Monday to Friday. Restaurants are closed one day a week and for annual holidays, usually in the winter. Off season most hotels, especially those along the coast, will be closed, so that if you travel in the winter months you should book accommodation ahead to avoid complications.

One of the special charac-teristics of Sicilian life is that people dine later than on the

mainland, particularly in the summer when the weather can be very hot. The midday meal may begin as late as 2pm, and evening meals may not be served until 10pm.

MUSEUMS AND MONUMENTS

Normally Sicilian museums and archaeological sites are open every day in the morning except for Monday. Many sites are also open in the afternoon. Opening hours tend to be longer during the summer. Apart from particularly important places such as Agrigento, admission to archaeological areas is free.

Entrance fees for museums vary from €1 to €5. Youngsters and senior citizens are usually either allowed a reduction or enter free of charge. Church opening hours can be erratic,

and you will need both luck and patience if you want to see every interior, especially in smaller villages. Most churches are open to the public during morning and evening mass. Should a church be closed, you can always try asking the priest or sacristan if he will let you in for a brief visit.

COMMUNICATIONS

It is easy enough to find a post office or phone booth in the larger towns, but they are rare, if not non-existent, in the interior and small villages. Reception on a mobile phone might not be good, especially on the islands. It is wise to carry an Italian phrasebook as English is not always spoken.

Telephone booths, quite rare in the interior of Sicily

◁ Horse riding in the hilly countryside

NEWSPAPERS

The leading local papers are *Il Mediterraneo* and *Giornale di Sicilia* in Palermo, *Gazzetta del Sud* in Messina, *Gazzettino di Sicilia* in Syracuse, and *La Sicilia* in Catania. All are useful for local events information. The leading Italian daily newspapers are sold in Sicily. English-language newspapers are sold in the larger towns.

Italian and foreign daily newspapers sold in Sicily

IMMIGRATION AND CUSTOMS

European Union (EU) residents and visitors from the United States, Canada, New Zealand and Australia, for example, need no visa for a stay of up to three months. Information concerning visas can be obtained in advance at your nearest Italian consulate. Non-EU citizens must carry a valid passport, while for EU citizens an ID will suffice. By law you must carry your ID with you at all times, as it may be needed – during a road block *(see p238)* for instance. Any customs formalities are completed at the first Italian arrival point (usually the mainland). Non-EU citizens can claim back sales tax (IVA) on purchases costing over €336.

TOURIST INFORMATION

The provincial capitals of Sicily have an official tourist board, the **Ente Provinciale per il Turismo** (it might also be called **Azienda Autonoma Provinciale per l'Incremento**

DIRECTORY

TOURIST BOARDS

Assessorato al Turismo Regione Sicilia
Via Notarbartolo 11, Palermo.
Tel 091-696 11 11.
www.regione.sicilia.it/turismo

Agrigento
AAPIT *Tel* 0922-401 352.
AAST *Tel* 0922-204 54.

Caltagirone
AAST *Tel* 0933-538 09.

Caltanissetta
AAPIT *Tel* 0934-530 411 or
530 403. www.aapit.cl.it

Catania
AAPIT *Tel* 095-730 62 22 or
730 62 33. www.apt.catania.it

Cefalù
AAST *Tel* 0921-921 990 or
421 458. www.cefalu-tour.pa.it

Enna
AAPIT *Tel* 800-221 188.
www.apt-enna.com
AAST *Tel* 0935-261 19/500 875.

Erice
AAST *Tel* 0923-869 388/522 021.

Gela
AAST *Tel* 0933-923 268.

Giardini Naxos
AAST *Tel* 0942-510 10.
www.aastgiardininaxos.it

Isole Egadi
Tel 0923-922 121.
www.isoleegadi.it

Lampedusa
www.enteturismolampedusa.it

Lipari
Tel 090-988 00 95.

Messina
AAPIT *Tel* 090-674 236.
AAST *Tel* 090-293 52 92.
www.azienturismomessina.it

Noto
APT *Tel* 0931-836 744/573 779.

Palermo
APT *Tel* 091-605 81 11.
Azienda Autonoma Turismo
Palermo e Monreale
Tel 091-540 122.
www.palermotourism.com

Ragusa
AAPIT *Tel* 0932-221 511 or
663 094. www.ragusaturismo.it

Sciacca
AAST *Tel* 0925-227 44.
www.aziendaturismosciacca.it

Syracuse
AAPIT *Tel* 0931-481 200.
www.apt-siracusa.it
AAST *Tel* 0931-652 01/464 255.

Taormina
AAST *Tel* 0942-232 43 or 239 12.
www.gate2taormina.com

Trapani
AAPIT *Tel* 0923-545 511.
www.apt.trapani.it
AAST *Tel* 0923-290 00.

UK TOURIST OFFICE

Italian State Tourist Office (ENIT) UK
1 Princes Street, London W1R 2AY.
Tel 020-7408 1254.
www.enit.it

ITALIAN EMBASSIES AND CONSULATES

United Kingdom
38 Eaton Place, London SW1.
Tel 020-7235 9371.
www.amblondraesteri.it

United States
690 Park Avenue, New York.
Tel 212-737 9100.
www.italyemb.org

Australia
6–9 Macquarie Street, Sydney 2000,
NSW. *Tel* 02-247 84 42.
www.ambitalia.org.au

Turistico or **Azienda Provinciale Turismo)**, where information and brochures are available. Larger towns have an **Azienda Autonoma di Soggiorno**. In the small towns and villages, make enquiries at the **Pro Loco** or the Town Hall. You can get the addresses and phone numbers of smaller bureaus at the **Azienda Provinciale Turismo**. You can obtain information on how to organize your trip from the **Enti Provinciali per il Turismo** or the **Assessorato al Turismo della Regione Sicilia** in Palermo. The web site www.sicilia.com is useful.

Personal Security and Health

On the whole, Sicily is safe for visitors. At busy tourist spots, such as the ferry ports and main stations, it is wise to keep a close eye on your belongings. Also, avoid leaving valuables in your car if the parking lot is unattended. However, in the smaller towns and villages, petty crime is rare. The rural areas are even safer, and if you speak a little Italian, getting to know people will increase your personal security. The summer heat can leave the countryside susceptible to fires. Visitors and residents alike are asked to do all they can to prevent fires from breaking out.

In the event of fire, follow the firemen's instructions carefully

A *carabinieri* patrol boat on duty off the coast of Sicily

PERSONAL PROPERTY

It is not really a good idea to carry large sums of money on you. Major credit cards such as Visa and MasterCard are accepted by most businesses throughout the island. There are automatic cash dispensers *(bancomat)* in all larger towns and you may choose to buy travellers' cheques in addition.

In general, parking is safe. However, in large cities it is best not to leave your car unattended for too long.

State policeman   City policeman

In the event of a theft, make sure you report it immediately to the local police or *carabinieri* stations (you have to do this in order to make an insurance claim).

ROADBLOCKS

Generally speaking, travelling on Sicilian roads poses few problems apart from some reckless drivers. However, because of the presence of the Mafia, you may be stopped at a police or army roadblock *(posto di blocco)*, particularly around the Palermo area. Officers usually check your ID and the vehicle, but it is possible that they might ask to search your car. Simply stay calm and cooperate with the police – there should be no cause for alarm.

IN THE EVENT OF FIRE

Sadly, fires are a scourge in Sicily – and in the rest of Southern Italy, for that matter. Some of them are natural occurrences, some are genuine accidents, but most are cases of arson. Fire can spread rapidly, especially in the dry summer vegetation, and the wind may carry the fire for long distances in a very short time. Firefighting is usually entrusted to the local fire departments and forest rangers, volunteers and specially equipped firefighting planes, which are located at strategic points around the island.

FIRE PREVENTION RULES

1. Do not throw cigarettes out of your car.
2. Never light a fire except in areas where this is explicitly permitted.
3. If you see a fire, call 1515 at once.
4. Do not stop or park your car to watch a fire; you may block the road and interfere with the firefighting operations.
5. Pay attention to the wind direction: it is extremely dangerous to be downwind of a fire, as it may spread rapidly and catch you unawares.

The coastguards at Lampedusa

HEALTH

Emergency medical care is free for all EU citizens in Italy, with a European Health Insurance Card (EHIC). The form is available from main post offices in the UK. Only emergencies are covered, and private medical insurance is needed for all other situations. Non-EU citizens should get comprehensive medical insur-

EMERGENCY NUMBERS

General Emergencies
Tel 113.

Police
Tel 112.

Fire Department
Tel 115.

Road Emergencies
Tel 116.

Telephone Information
Tel 12.

Nautical Information
Tel 196.

Ambulance & Mountain Emergencies
Tel 118.

Forest Fires
Tel 1515.

ance before their arrival. Sicily has a network of hospitals and first-aid stations *(pronto soccorso)*. All tourist resorts operate seasonal emergency treatment centres *(guardia medica)*. Pharmacies are normally open from Monday to Friday at 9am–1pm and 4–7pm and on Saturday morning. However, for emergencies, a list of the night and holiday opening rotas will always be posted on or near the shop door.

Italian pharmacy sign

Police car

Carabinieri car

Red Cross ambulance

SAFETY OUTDOORS

During your stay in Sicily, whether you go in the summer or winter, you will be spending a good deal of time outdoors, so you must be prepared for the various problems outdoor life can pose in the different seasons. In the summer, whether you are at the seaside or in the interior, do not overdo sunbathing, as it may cause

serious burns and sunstroke. The wind can be very deceptive, often making you think the temperature is lower than it actually is.

While exploring among the tumbled stones of the ancient cities of Magna Graecia, or during a hike in the mountains, be on the lookout for snakes, which can be quite common in the summer.

Although camping just anywhere is not allowed, you can make private arrangements with landowners to put up your tent outside an official camp site. Remember, however, that you must take away all rubbish and must not light fires. While on a walk or hiking, keep your distance from sheepdogs, because they are trained to chase away all intruders.

Sicilians are very hospitable but are also reserved, so out of respect you should always ask permission before you cross over private property, go through a gate or a fenced area. On unpaved roads or paths you may come across closed gates or fences. It is always a good idea to ask whether in fact you can go through. Having done so, remember to close the gate or fence so that any animals in the field cannot escape.

CURRENCY

Sixteen countries – Austria, Belgium, Cyprus, Finland, France, Germany, Greece, Ireland, Italy, Luxembourg, Malta, The Netherlands, Slovakia, Slovenia, Portugal and Spain – have replaced their traditional currencies, such as the Italian lire, with a single European currency, the euro, which came into circulation on 1 January 2002. All euro notes and coins can be used anywhere inside the participating member states. You can exchange currency when you arrive, at an automatic cash dispenser (ATM), at the airport or at a bank, but it is best to have some euros with you beforehand. The best exchange rates are offered by the banks, where commission charges are lower. Euro banknotes have seven denominations. The €5 note (grey in colour) is the smallest, followed by the €10 note (pink), €20 note (blue), €50 note (orange), €100 note (green), €200 note (yellow) and €500 note (purple). All notes show the stars of the European Union. The euro has eight coin denominations: €1 and €2 (silver and gold in colour), 50 cents, 20 cents, 10 cents (gold), 5 cents, 2 cents and 1 cent (bronze). If you prefer travellers' cheques, choose a well-known name or a bank. There is a minimum commission charge for each transaction, so avoid changing small amounts. Bureaux de change have the same opening hours as shops. Credit card holders can draw money directly from ATMs, found throughout Sicily.

An automatic cash dispenser (ATM)

Euro notes

TRAVEL INFORMATION

The two main airports in Sicily are at opposite ends of the island, one at Palermo and one at Catania. In the holiday season, charter flights may land directly at one of these, but the majority of travellers flying to Sicily will fly first to a mainland airport, usually Milan or Rome, before changing to a connecting flight. A good ferry service links Sicily with the mainland (connecting Reggio Calabria and Messina). The state railway, Ferrovie dello Stato, runs regular trains using this ferry link. The smaller offshore islands are also easy to reach by ferry and some of them, for example Lampedusa, even have a small airport. There are plans to build a road bridge connecting Sicily to the mainland across the Straits.

Riding a scooter

AIRPORTS

There are regular flights from the Italian mainland to Palermo and Catania. Direct charter flights from European cities operate all year round, linking, for example, London Gatwick to Catania or Palermo. The island's main airport is **Palermo Punta Raisi**. It handles domestic flights to and from Rome, Naples, Bologna, Milan, Pisa, Genoa, Turin, Verona, Cagliari, and the Sicilian islands Pantelleria and Lampedusa. **Catania Fontanarossa** serves the eastern side, with domestic flights to and from Rome, Milan, Turin, Naples, Verona, Genoa and Pisa. The small **Trapani Birgi** airport offers connections only to and from Palermo and the islands of **Pantelleria** and **Lampedusa** (the latter has a tiny airport linked to Rome, Milan and Verona). The airports on the islands all connect to Trapani and Palermo airports, and to other mainland towns.

FLIGHT CONNECTIONS

British Airways run a London–Catania service, while **Ryanair** flies daily between Stansted and Palermo. Italian state airline **Alitalia** has no direct London–Sicily flights.

Alitalia, Meridiana, Air One, Alpieagles and **Volare/Air Europe** offer frequent services from the Italian mainland. The latter company also offers flights to Sicily's neighbouring islands (especially in the summer).

American, Delta and **United Airlines** offer direct flights from the United States to Rome, where you can catch a connecting flight to Sicily.

TRAINS

The Italian state railway (FS) operates services throughout Italy, with regular links to Sicily. If you plan to travel to Sicily by train, reserve a seat (the trains are crowded in high season) and be prepared for a long journey.

The train station in Palermo

By way of compensation, the coastline as you travel south of Rome is stunningly beautiful. If possible, book a berth or couchette (sleeping compartment) before you travel.

BUS SERVICES

Given the varied and often mountainous topography of Sicily, not everywhere is accessible by train, and even where there are lines, services can be slow. In recent years local investment in infrastructure has focussed on developing the roads rather than the railway. An extensive network of local bus services connects even the smallest villages, and there are good long-distance bus links to the most important resorts.

FERRIES

Reggio Calabria is the principal mainland port with ferry connections to Sicily. In the summer there are also ferries between Palermo and Genoa, Livorno and Naples, and car ferries between Messina and Naples.

Catania airport, the main point of arrival for visitors to eastern Sicily

The hourly summer ferry service connecting Reggio Calabria and Messina

CONNECTIONS TO THE SMALLER ISLANDS

Ferry services to the Sicilian islands are well organized and operate regularly. Several ferry companies, such as **Siremar**, **Alilauro**, **Ustica**, **SNAV** and **Covemar**, operate on different routes (for more information visit www.ferries online.com). Ferries *(traghetti)* and hydrofoils *(aliscafi)* can get quite crowded in the summer, but services continue all year round. In the archipelagoes, such as the Aeolian Islands, local ferry companies operate services alongside the larger ones: information about these companies and timetables can be obtained from the local tourist information bureaux and Pro Loco offices.

DIRECTORY

AIRLINE INFORMATION

Air One (Italy)
Tel 199-207 080.
www.flyairone.it

Alitalia (UK)
Tel 0871-424 14 24.
www.alitalia.co.uk

Alitalia (US)
Tel 800-223 5730.
www.alitaliausa.com

Alpieagles (Italy)
Tel 899-500 058.
www.alpieagles.com

American Airlines (US)
Tel 800-433 73 00.
www.aa.com

British Airways (UK)
Tel 0844-493 0787.
www.britishairways.com

Delta Airlines (US)
Tel 800-241 41 41.
www.delta.com

Meridiana (Italy)
Tel 078-952 682.
www.meridiana.it

Ryanair
Tel 0871-246 00 00.
www.ryanair.com

United Airlines (US)
Tel 800-538 29 29.
www.united.com

Volare/Air Europe
Tel 899-65 65 45.
www.volareweb.com

AIRPORTS

Catania Fontanarossa
Tel 095-405 05.
www.aeroporto.catania.it

Lampedusa
Tel 0922-971 548.

Palermo Punta Raisi
Tel 091-702 07 18.
www.gesap.it

Pantelleria
Tel 0923-911 817.
www.pantelleriaairport.it

Trapani Birgi
Tel 0923-842 502.
www.airgest.com

TRAIN INFORMATION

Citalia (UK)
Tel (Italian State Railways)
0870-901 40 13
www.citalia.co.uk

Disabled Assistance
Tel Rome 06-6821 9168.

Trenitalia (Italy)
Tel (Italian State Railways)
892 021 (24-hr info line).
www.trenitalia.com
(timetables, info in English.)

MAINLAND CONNECTIONS

Caronte & Tourist
Tel Messina
090-572 65 04.
www.carontetourist.it

AEOLIAN ISLANDS CONNECTIONS

Blue Lines – Agenzia Chidas
Tel from Sant'Agata
(August only) Militello
0941-701 318.

Siremar
www.siremar.it
Tel Milazzo 090-928 32 42.
Tel Naples 081-551 90 96.

SNAV
www.snav.it
Tel Cefalù 0921-421 595.
Tel Messina 091-362 114.
Tel Naples 081-428 55 55.
Tel Palermo 091-362 114
Tel Reggio Calabria
0965-295 68.

EGADI ISLANDS CONNECTIONS

Siremar
Tel Favignana
0923-921 368.
Tel Levanzo
0923-924 128.
Tel Marettimo
0923-923 144.
Tel Trapani
0923-545 411.

PANTELLERIA CONNECTIONS

Siremar
Tel 0923-911 120.

Ustica Lines
Tel 0923-911 078.
www.usticalines.it

USTICA CONNECTIONS

Siremar
Tel Naples
081-580 03 40.
Tel Palermo
091-582 403.
Tel Ustica
091-844 90 02.

Ustica Lines
Tel Trapani 0923-222 00.
www.usticalines.it

Getting Around Sicily

No-parking sign

The heart of the largest island in the Mediterranean is rugged and mountainous. You will notice this as soon as you begin to travel around Sicily. Roads become steep and winding the further you go inland. What may look like a short journey on the map may in fact take quite a long time. Networks of railways and buses connect most towns and villages, but you may need a car for the more inaccessible areas. Sicily's rail network includes a full circuit of Mount Etna, a journey that takes five hours.

A fast, straight road crossing a valley in the interior of Sicily

GETTING AROUND BY TRAIN

The two major railway lines run south from Messina to Catania and Syracuse, and west in the direction of Palermo. A secondary route branches off from the Messina–Palermo line at Termini Imerese and goes – fairly slowly – to Agrigento.

Another line connects Palermo with Trapani, Marsala, Mazara, Castelvetrano and Ribera.

North of Catania, the privately run Ferrovia Circumetnea railway line *(see p166)*, describes a huge circle around Mount Etna through fertile lava fields filled with vines and fruit trees.

The state-run railway network (FS) offers frequent connections between Sicily and the mainland *(see p240)*, but the long-distance trains to and from the island win no prizes for quality and comfort.

GETTING AROUND BY CAR OR MOTORCYCLE

If you want to get to know the real Sicily, travelling around by car, or even by motorcycle if you are brave, is probably the best way. The main roads and motorways linking the major towns are generally in good condition. This includes the Messina–Palermo, Messina–Catania and Catania–Palermo roads.

When planning your trip, bear in mind that on some of these routes, including long stretches of the southern coast, the roads may be busy with traffic and therefore quite slow, and that the mountain roads may be even slower. As a precaution, it is a good idea to buy a good up-to-date road map, such as the ones published by the Touring Club Italiano with a 1:200,000 scale. A road map of Sicily is provided on the back endpaper of this guide.

ARRIVING BY CAR

Car ferries go regularly across the Straits of Messina *(see pp240–41)*, and taking a car to Sicily should not present any particular problems. You need a valid driving licence to drive anywhere in Italy, and it may be a good idea to carry a translation of your licence.

CAR HIRE

Almost all the major car hire companies have branch offices throughout Sicily, including the seaports of Palermo and Catania and the airports of Palermo Punta Raisi, Catania Fontanarossa and Trapani Birgi. You can also find an office in every provincial capital. If you choose a major firm such as Hertz or Rent a Car *(see*

The Ferrovia Circumetnea *(see p166)*, offering a scenic route around Europe's largest volcano

Directory), check the rental conditions in advance to see what is included and whether you need additional insurance. A number of holiday companies offer inclusive fly-drive deals, enabling you to pick up your car on arrival at the airport. This is normally cheaper than renting a car on the spot. On some of the offshore islands you can find scooters as well as motorcycles and cars for hire. Island roads are often in poor condition, and you may find travelling by two-wheeled transport is a more comfortable way of getting around.

ROAD REGULATIONS

The rules of the road are the same as in the rest of Italy, including driving on the right, speed limits (50 km/h, 30 mph in towns) and compulsory seat belts in cars and helmets for motorcyclists. Parking is a real problem in the larger cities (especially Palermo), and also in historic centres. Petrol *(benzina)* is generally expensive.

BICYCLES AND MOUNTAIN BIKES

The roads in the interior are fairly quiet and are therefore suitable for cycling and even for touring by bicycle. As a result, some travel agencies have begun to offer bike excursions, with the added convenience of vans to carry

Using a rented bicycle, the best way to see the small islands

Buses, the best way of getting around larger cities such as Palermo

your luggage for you from place to place. Sicilian drivers are not used to seeing cyclists on the road, however, so stay alert at all times.

Mountain biking is becoming more popular as a sport in Sicily, particularly in the Peloritani, Nebrodi and Madonie mountain areas.

Cycling with a group of mountain bike riders is increasingly popular, and it is not uncommon to see a cavalcade on the cattle tracks and paths that run through the various parks and nature reserves on the island.

GETTING AROUND IN THE CITIES

Public transport is quite reliable, and easy to use in the main cities in Sicily – Palermo, Catania and Messina. In other towns, such as Trapani, Syracuse and Agrigento, and in the smaller towns, the best way to get around is on foot. Public transport in Palermo is run by the **AMAT** (tel: 848-800 817). The service connects all the most interesting sights, including Monreale and Mondello. The 101 bus runs north to south.

Tickets can be purchased at tobacconists *(tabaccaio)* and newsagents *(giornalaio)*, or in the AMAT kiosks, which also provide transport maps. Tickets are valid for two hours and cost €1; all-day tickets are also available. Note that there is a fine for riding without a valid ticket.

A Palermo transport system tourist ticket

All of Catania's most interesting sights can be reached on foot. However, should you need a bus to go from the centre to the airport take the Alibus (no. 457). The network of buses that go between the train station and the centre is run by **AMT** (tel: 801-018 696). Tickets are valid for 90 minutes, but there is also a 24-hour tourist ticket available. In Messina, public transport is handy if you want to visit the Museo Regionale *(see pp182–3)*, which is 45 minutes' walking distance from the centre of town; the stops for buses going in this direction are in Piazza Castronovo, which is also the terminus for buses to Ganzirri (Nos. 78, 79 and 81). Tickets can be purchased from tobacconists.

DIRECTORY

CAR HIRE

Avis
Tel Palermo 091-591 684.
Tel Catania 095-340 500.
www.avisworld.com

Europcar
Tel Palermo 091-301 825.
Tel Catania 095-348 125.
www.europcar.com

Hertz
Tel Palermo 091-213 112.
Tel Catania 095-341 595.
www.hertz.com

Rent a Car (Maggiore)
Tel Palermo 091-591681.
Tel Catania 095-340 594.
Tel Syracuse 0931-66548.
www.maggiore.it

General Index

Acknowledgments

Dorling Kindersley would like to thank the following people, museums and organizations, whose contributions and assistance have made the preparation of this book possible. Dorling Kindersley would also like to thank all the people, organizations and businesses, too numerous to mention individually, for their kind permission to photograph their establishments.

Alessandra Arena; Ms Puleo, Assessorato al Turismo Regione Sicilia; AAPT Caltanissetta, Egidio Cacciola, AAST Acireale; Grazia Incorvaia, AAST Agrigento; AAST Caltagirone; AAST Capo D'Orlando; Ms Lidestri, AAST Catania and Acicastello; AAST Cefalù; Ms Petralia, AAST Enna; AAST Giardini Naxos; AAST Messina; AAST Milazzo; Salvatore Giuffrida, AAST Nicolosi; AAST Palermo and Monreale; AAST Patti; Ivana Taschetta, AAST Piazza Armerina; AAST Sciacca; AAST Syracuse; AAST Taormina; Mario Cavallaro, APT Syracuse; Ms Mocata, APT Trapani; Carlo Rigano, Associazione Culturale Sicilia '71 di Mascalucia, Paolo Mazzotta, Biblioteca "E Vittorietti", Palermo; Barbara Caccianì; Franco Conti, Carthera Aetna; Nicolò Longo; Prof Giorgio De Luca, Istituto Europeo di Scienze Antropologiche; Giorgia Conversi; EPT Agrigento; Nello Musumeci, EPT Catania; Dr Ragno, EPT Messina; Dr Majorca, EPT Palermo; Manilo Peri, Fondazione Culturale Mandralisca, Cefalù; Dr Rosano, Framon Hotels; Galleria Regionale di Sicilia – Palazzo Abatellis (Palermo); Domenico Calabrò, Gazzetta del Sud; Gisella Giarrusso; Ernesto Girardi; Salvo Amato, Giuliano Rotondi Freelance Studio, Acireale; Carmelo Guglielmino; Mr Altieri, Hotel Baglio della Luna; Hotel Baglio Santa Croce; Hotel La Tonnara di Bonagia; Col Girardi; Hotel Villa Paradiso dell'Etna; Luigi Lacagnina and his family; Maggiore Budget Autonoleggi; Prof Gaetano Maltese; Emma Marzullo; Meridiana; Museo Archeologico Regionale Paolo Orsi (Syracuse); Museo Etnostorico dei Nebrodi; Prof Iberia Medici, Museo-Laboratorio Village, Giarre; Ignazio Paternò Castello; Società Aerofotogrammetrica Siciliana (Palermo); Sandro Tranchina; Teatro Massimo (Palermo); Teatro Biondo (Palermo); Prof Amitrano Svarese, Faculty of Anthropological Sciences, University of Palermo; Mara Veneziani; Pia Vesin.

Additional Assistance
Emily Anderson, Claire Baranowski, Maria Carla Barra, Tessa Bindloss, Michelle Clark, Lucinda Cooke, Michelle Crane, Conrad van Dyk, Gadi Farfour, Emer FitzGerald, Rhiannon Furbear, Katharina Hahn, Gerard Hutching, Hayley Maher, Sonal Modha, Ellen Root, Giuliano Rotondi, Sands Publishing Solutions, Ellie Smith, Mary Sutherland, Conchita Vecchio, Stewart J Wild.

Picture Credits
Key: t = top; tl = top left; tlc = top left centre; tc = top centre; trc = top right centre; tr = top right; cla = centre left above; ca = centre above; cra = centre right above; cl = centre left; c = centre; cr = centre right; clb = centre left below; crb = centre right below; cb = centre below; bl = bottom left; br = bottom right; b = bottom; bc = bottom

centre; bcl = bottom centre left; bcr = bottom centre right. Every effort has been made to trace the copyright holders. The publisher apologizes for any unintentional omissions and would be pleased, in such cases, to add an acknowledgment in future editions.

All the photographs reproduced in this book are from the Image Bank, Milan, except for the following:

ALAMY IMAGES: Claudio H. Artman 10cl; CuboImages srl/Alfio Garozzo 11tl, 11bc; CuboImages srl/Enrico Fumagalli 10tc; CuboImages srl/Enzo Signorelli 227bl; David Norton Photography/David Norton 10br; nagelestock.com 11cr. FABRIZIO ARDITO: 2, 3, 17b, 83br, 84, 100tl, 102bl, 110, 113tl, 114tl, 115br, 116tr, 116cl, 117cr, 118tr, 118bl, 119cr, 120tl, 120br, 121br, 122t, 122c, 123tl, 123b, 126cl, 128bl, 129cl, 129clb, 130tl, 131bl, 143tl, 143br, 144bl, 149tl, 149br, 153tl, 153cr, 154tl, 156c, 156b, 157br, 166tl, 166cr, 196, 209c. ARCHIVIO APT SIRACUSA: 136tl, 137bl, 139br. ARCHIVIO APT TRAPANI: 86tl, 87b. ARCHIVIO EPT PALERMO: 109cr. ARCHIVIO FRAMON HOTELS: 194cl, 195tl, 195br. CEPHAS PICTURE LIBRARY: Lehmann 224br. CORBIS: Dave Bartruff 210cl; 211tl; Owen Franken 211c; Mimmo Jodice 227tr. FABIO DE ANGELIS: 48tl, 48cl, 48bl, 49cr, 50tl, 50bc, 53br, 55cr, 56tl, 60tr, 60b, 61tr, 61br, 63tr, 65br, 66cr, 67tl, 68br, 69br, 73bl, 74tl, 90c, 210br, 224cl, 236tc, 236br, 237tl, 238cl, 238crb, 238bl, 239tl, 239tr, 239cra, 239crb, 240tc, 240cr, 240br, 242tl. IL DAGHERROTIPO: 230br, 231tr. DK IMAGES: 20br, 29bl, 35tr, 35tl, 36–7c, 44tr, 46, 57br, 62, 72cr, 76–7, 146br, 192–3, Ian O'Leary 210-211. EUROPEAN COMMISSION: 239br. CRISTINA GAMBARO–GINO FRONGIA: 69bl, 85, 86bl, 90cl, 91b, 92b, 93tl, 94c, 95, 97bc, 98cl, 98bl, 102tl, 104, 106tl, 106b, 107tl, 117bl, 133, 146c, 177br, 208cr. LEONARDO MEDIA LTD: 195tl. NICOLÒ LONGO: 18crb, 19crb. RECULEZ: 210–11. RONALD GRANT ARCHIVE: 24cla/tr. MARKA, MILAN: Sante Malli 231br; Danilo Donadoni 232cr. GIULIANO ROTONDI: 3c, 17tr, 22tr, 22cl, 22bc, 23tr, 23cl, 23bc, 24, 25tl, 25tc, 25c, 26, 27tc, 28tr, 28c, 28bl, 29tl, 29tc, 29cl, 29br, 30tl, 30cl, 30cb, 30br, 31tl, 31cla, 31bla, 31bl, 32tl, 32ca, 32clb, 32bl, 32bc, 33cr, 33bc, 34tl, 34cl, 34br, 35cr, 35bl, 35br, 36ar, 36cl, 36cla, 36cb, 36bl, 36br, 36clb, 37cla, 37cra, 37tr, 37bl, 37br, 45tr, 51c, 51br, 54t, 66tr, 66cl, 67tc, 67cr, 69t, 72bl, 75tl, 92tc, 92c, 94tl, 99tr, 99cl, 102br, 103cr, 103br, 105cr, 106cl, 106cr, 128tr, 128br, 129tr, 129br, 134bc, 145bl, 150tr, 151cr, 152b, 154cl, 154br, 155tl, 156tl, 157cr, 160bl, 163tl, 164tl, 167t, 167bl, 169br, 172tr, 173tl, 175br, 176bl, 178cl, 183br, 185tr, 185bl, 210tr, 222tc, 224tl, 224tr, 225tr, 225cla, 225cra, 225clb, 225crb, 225b, 226cr, 226bl, 228br, 240cl, 242bl. SBRIGLIO: 137tl, 138, 142c, 144tl, 144cl, 144br, 145cr, 145bl, 146tl, 146tr, 147tr, 147cl, 147br, 148c, 148br, 160tr. MARCO SCAPAGNINI: 142tr, 145tr, 147cr, 208tc, 226tc.

JACKET
Front – PHOTOLIBRARY: Luis Alberto Aldonza. Back – AWL IMAGES: Walter Bibikow tl; Demetrio Carrasco cla; DORLING KINDERSLEY: Demetrio Carrasco bl, clb. Spine – PHOTOLIBRARY: Luis Alberto Aldonza t.

SPECIAL EDITIONS OF DK TRAVEL GUIDES

Phrase Book

In Emergency

Help!	Aiuto!	*eye-yoo-toh*
Stop!	Fermati!	*fair-mah-tee*
Call a doctor.	Chiama un medico.	*kee-ab-mah oon meb-dee-koh*
Call an ambulance.	Chiama un' ambulanza.	*kee-ab-mah oon am-boo-lan-tsa*
Call the police.	Chiama la polizia.	*kee-ab-mah lah pol-ee-tsee-ah*
Call the fire department.	Chiama i pompieri.	*kee-ab-mah ee pom-pee-air-ee*
Where is the telephone?	Dov'è il telefono?	*dov-eh eel teh-leb-foh-noh?*
The nearest hospital?	L'ospedale più vicino?	*loss-peb-dah-leh pee-oo vee-chee-noh?*

Communication Essentials

Yes/No	Sì/No	*see/noh*
Please	Per favore	*pair fab-vor-eb*
Thank you	Grazie	*grah-tsee-eb*
Excuse me	Mi scusi	*mee skoo-zee*
Hello	Buon giorno	*bwon jor-noh*
Goodbye	Arrivederci	*ah-ree-veh-dair-chee*
Good evening	Buona sera	*bwon-ah sair-ab*
morning	la mattina	*lab mab-tee-nah*
afternoon	il pomeriggio	*eel poh-meh-ree-joh*
evening	la sera	*lab sair-ah*
yesterday	ieri	*ee-air-ee*
today	oggi	*ob-jee*
tomorrow	domani	*doh-mah-nee*
here	qui	*kwee*
there	là	*lab*
What?	Quale?	*kwab-leh?*
When?	Quando?	*kwan-doh?*
Why?	Perchè?	*pair-keh?*
Where?	Dove?	*doh-veh?*

Useful Phrases

How are you?	Come sta?	*kob-meh stah?*
Very well, thank you.	Molto bene, grazie.	*moll-tob beb-neb grah tsee oh*
Pleased to meet you.	Piacere di conoscerla.	*pee-ab-chair-eb dee cob-noh-shair-lah*
See you later.	A più tardi.	*ah pee-oo tar-dee*
That's fine.	Va bene.	*va beb-neh*
Where is/are ...?	Dov'è/Dove sono...?	*dov-eh/doveh sob-noh?*
How long does it take to get to ...?	Quanto tempo ci vuole per andare a ...?	*kwan-tob tem-poh chee voo-ob-leh pair an-dar-eh ah ...?*
How do I get to ...?	Come faccio per arrivare a ...?	*kob-meh fab-choh pair arri-var-eb ah ...?*
Do you speak English?	Parla inglese?	*par-lah een-gleb-zeb?*
I don't understand.	Non capisco.	*non ka-pee-skoh*
Could you speak more slowly, please?	Può parlare più lentamente, per favore?	*pwoh par lah-reh pee-oo len-ta-men-teh pair fab-vor-eb?*
I'm sorry.	Mi dispiace.	*mee dee-spee-ab-cheh*

Useful Words

big	grande	*gran-deb*
small	piccolo	*pee-kob-lob*
hot	caldo	*kal-doh*
cold	freddo	*fred-doh*
good	buono	*bwob-noh*
bad	cattivo	*kat-tee-voh*
enough	basta	*bas-tah*
well	bene	*beb-neh*
open	aperto	*ah-pair-toh*
closed	chiuso	*kee-oo-zoh*
left	a sinistra	*ah see-nee-strah*
right	a destra	*ah dess-trah*
straight ahead	sempre dritto	*sem-preb dree-toh*
near	vicino	*vee-chee-noh*
far	lontano	*lon-tab-noh*
up	su	*soo*
down	giù	*joo*
early	presto	*press-toh*
late	tardi	*tar-dee*
entrance	entrata	*en-trab-tab*
exit	uscita	*oo-shee-ta*
toilet	il gabinetto	*eel gab-bee-net-toh*
free, unoccupied	libero	*lee-bair-oh*
free, no charge	gratuito	*grah-too-ee-toh*

Making a Telephone Call

I'd like to place a long-distance call.	Vorrei fare una interurbana.	*vor-ray far-eb oona in-tair-oor-bab-nah*
I'd like to make a reverse-charge call.	Vorrei fare una telefonata a carico del destinatario.	*vor-ray far-eb oona teb-leb-fon-ab-tah ah kar-ee-koh dell dess-tee-nah-tar-ree-oh*
Could I speak to...	Potrei parlare con...	*po-tray par-lab-reb con*
I'll try again later.	Ritelefono più tardi	*ree-teb-leb-foh-noh pee-oo tar-dee*
May I leave a message?	Posso lasciare un messaggio?	*poss-oh lash-ab-reb oon mess-sab-joh?*
Hold on.	Un attimo, per favore.	*oon ab-tee-moh, pair fab-vor-eh*
Could you speak up a little, please?	Può parlare più forte?	*pwoh par-lab-reh pee-oo for-teh?*
local call	telefonata locale	*te-leh-fon-ab-tah lob-cab-leb*

Shopping

How much does this cost?	Quant'è, per favore?	*kwan-teb pair fab-vor-eb?*
I would like ...	Vorrei ...	*vor-ray...*
Do you have ...?	Avete ...?	*ah-veb-teb...?*
I'm just looking.	Sto soltanto guardando	*stob sol-tan-tob gwar-dan-dob*
Do you take credit cards?	Accettate carte di credito?	*ab-chet-tab-teb kar-teb dee creb-dee-tob?*
What time do you open/close?	A che ora apre/ chiude?	*ah keb or-ah ab-preb/kee-oo-deb?*
this one	questo	*kweb-stob*
that one	quello	*kwell-oh*
expensive	caro	*kar-ob*
cheap	a buon prezzo	*ah bwon pret-sob*
size, clothes	la taglia	*lab tab-lee-ah*
size, shoes	il numero	*eel noo-mair-oh*
white	bianco	*bee-ang-koh*
black	nero	*neb-rob*
red	rosso	*ross-ob*
yellow	giallo	*jal-lob*
green	verde	*vair-deb*
blue	blu	*bloo*

Types of Shop

antique dealer	l'antiquario	*lan-tee-kwab-ree-oh*
bakery	il forno/ il panificio	*eel forn-ob/ eel pan-ee-fee-choh*
bank	la banca	*lab bang-kah*
bookstore	la libreria	*lah lee-breb-ree-ah*
butcher	la macelleria	*lah mah-chell-eh-ree-ah*
cake shop	la pasticceria	*lah pas-tee-chair-ee-ah*
delicatessen	la salumeria	*lah sab-loo-meh-ree-ah*
department store	il grande magazzino	*eel gran-deb mag-gad-zee-noh*
pharmacy	la farmacia	*lah far-mah-chee-ah*
fishseller	il pescivendolo	*eel pesh-ee-ven-doh-loh*
florist	il fioraio	*eel fee-or-eye-oh*
greengrocer	il fruttivendolo	*eel froo-tee-ven-doh-loh*
grocery	alimentari	*ab-lee-men-tab-ree*
hairdresser	il parrucchiere	*eel par-oo-kee-air-eb*
ice-cream parlour	la gelateria	*lab jel-lab-tair-ree-ah*
market	il mercato	*eel mair-kab-toh*
newsstand	l'edicola	*leb-dee-kob-lab*
post office	l'ufficio postale	*loo-fee-choh pos-tab-leh*
shoe shop	il negozio di scarpe	*eel neb-gob-tsioh dee skar-peh*
supermarket	il supermercato	*eel su-pair-mair-kab-tob*
tobacconist	il tabaccaio	*eel tab-bak-eye-ob*
travel agency	l'agenzia di viaggi	*lah-jen-tsee-ah dee vee-ad-jee*

Sightseeing

art gallery	la pinacoteca	*lab peena-koh-teb-kab*
bus stop	la fermata dell'autobus	*lab fair-mab-chee-ah dell ow-tob-booss*
church	la chiesa/ la basilica	*lab kee-eb-zah/ lah bab-seel-i-kah*
closed for holidays	chiuso per le ferie	*kee-oo-zob pair leh fair-ee-eb*
garden	il giardino	*eel jar-dee-no*
library	la biblioteca	*lah beeb-lee-oh-teb-kah*
museum	il museo	*eel moo-zeb-ob*
train station	la stazione	*lah stab-tsee-ob-neh*
tourist information	l'ufficio di turismo	*loo-fee-chob dee too-ree-smob*

Staying in a Hotel

Do you have any vacant rooms?	Avete camere libere?	ab-veb-teb kab-mair-eb lee-bair-eb?
double room	una camera doppia	oona kab-mair-ab dob-pee-ab
with double bed	con letto matrimoniale	kon let-tob mab-tree-moh-nee-ab-leb
twin room	una camera con due letti	oona kab-mair-ab kon doo-eb let-tee
single room	una camera singola	oona kab-mair-ab sing-gob-lab
room with a bath, shower	una camera con bagno, con doccia	oona kab-mair-ab kon ban-yob, kon dot-chab
porter	il facchino	eel fab-kee-nob
key	la chiave	lab kee-ab-veb
I have a reservation.	Ho fatto una prenotazione.	ob fat-tob oona preb-nob-tab-tsee-ob-neb

Eating Out

Do you have a table for …?	Avete una tavola per …?	ab-veb-teb oona tab-vob-lab pair …?
I'd like to reserve a table	Vorrei riservare una tavola	vor-ray ree-sair-vah-reb oona tab-vob-lab
breakfast	colazione	kob-lab-tsee-ob-neb
lunch	pranzo	pran-tsob
dinner	cena	cheb-nab
The bill, please	Il conto, per favore.	eel kon-tob pair fab-vor-eb
I am a vegetarian.	Sono vegetariano/a.	sob-nob veb-jeb-tar-ee-ab-noh/nab
waitress	cameriera	kab-mair-ee-air-ab
waiter	cameriere	kab-mair-ee-air-eb
fixed-price menu	il menù a prezzo fisso	eel meb-noo ab pret-sob fee-sob
dish of the day	piatto del giorno	pee-ab-tob dell jor-no
appetizer	antipasto	an-tee-pass-tob
first course	il primo	eel pree-mob
main course	il secondo	eel seb-kon-dob
vegetables	il contorno	eel kon-tor-nob
dessert	il dolce	eel doll-cheb
cover charge	il coperto	eel kob-pair-tob
wine list	la lista dei vini	lab lee-stab day-ee vee-nee
rare	al sangue	al sang-gweb
medium	al puntino	al poon-tee-nob
well done	ben cotto	ben kot-tob
glass	il bicchiere	eel bee-kee-air-eb
bottle	la bottiglia	lab bot-teel-yab
knife	il coltello	eel kol-tell-ob
fork	la forchetta	lab for-ket-tab
spoon	il cucchiaio	eel koo-kee-eye-ob

Menu Decoder

l'acqua minerale gassata/naturale	lab-kwah mee-nair-ab-leb gab-zab-tab/ nab-too-rab-leb	mineral water fizzy/still
aceto	ab-cheb-tob	vinegar
aglio	al-ee-ob	garlic
l'agnello	lab-niell-ob	lamb
al forno	al for-nob	baked/roasted
alla griglia	ab-lab greel-yab	grilled
l'aragosta	lab-rab-goss-tab	lobster
arrosto	ar-ross-tob	roast
basilico	bab-zee-lee-kob	basil
la birra	lab beer-rab	beer
la bistecca	lab bee-stek-kab	steak
il brodo	eel brob-dob	broth
il burro	eel boor-ob	butter
il caffè	eel kab-feb	coffee
i calamari	ee kab-lab-mab-ree	squid
i carciofi	ee kar-choff-ee	artichokes
la carne	la kar-neb	meat
la cipolla	la chip-ob-lab	onion
i contorni	ee kon-tor-nee	vegetables
le cozze	leb cob-tzeb	mussels
i fagioli	ee fab-job-lee	beans
il fegato	eel fay-gab-tob	liver
il finocchio	eel fee-nok-ee-ob	fennel
il formaggio	eel for-mad-job	cheese
le fragole	leb frab-gob-leb	strawberries
il fritto misto	eel freet-tob mees-tob	mixed fried dish
la frutta	la froot-tab	fruit
frutti di mare	froo-tee dee mab-reb	seafood
i funghi	ee foon-ghee	mushrooms
i gamberi	ee gam-bair-ee	shrimp
il gelato	eel jeb-lab-tob	ice cream
l'insalata	leen-sab-lab-tab	salad

il latte	eel labt-teb	milk
lesso	less-ob	boiled
la melanzana	lab meb-lan-tsab-nab	aubergine (eggplant)
la minestra	lab mee-ness-trab	soup
l'olio	lob-lee-ob	oil
il pane	eel pab-neb	bread
le patate	leb pab-tab-teb	potatoes
le patatine fritte	leb pab-tab-teen-eb free-teb	French fries
il pepe	eel peb-peb	pepper
la pesca	lab pess-kab	peach
il pesce	eel pesb-eb	fish
il polipo	eel pob-lee-pob	octopus
il pollo	eel poll-ob	chicken
il pomodoro	eel pob-mob-dor-ob	tomato
il prosciutto cotto/crudo	eel pro-sboo-tob kot-tob/kroo-dob	ham cooked/cured
il riso	eel ree-zob	rice
il sale	eel sab-leb	salt
la salsiccia	lab sal-see-chab	sausage
le seppie	leb sep-pee-eb	cuttlefish
secco	sek-kob	dry
la sogliola	lab soll-yob-lab	sole
i spinaci	ee spee-nab-chee	spinach
succo d'arancia/ di limone	soo-kob dab-ran-chah/ dee lee-mob-neb	orange/lemon juice
il tè	eel teb	tea
la tisana	lab tee-zab-nab	herbal tea
il tonno	eel ton-nob	tuna
la torta	lab tor-tab	cake/tart
l'uovo	loo-ob-vob	egg
vino bianco	vee-nob bee-ang-kob	white wine
vino rosso	vee-nob ross-ob	red wine
il vitello	eel vee-tell-ob	veal
le vongole	leb von-gob-leb	clams
lo zucchero	lob zoo-kair-ob	sugar
gli zucchini	lyee dzu-kee-nee	zucchini
la zuppa	lab tsoo-pab	soup

Numbers

1	uno	oo-nob
2	due	doo-eb
3	tre	treb
4	quattro	kwat-rob
5	cinque	ching-kweb
6	sei	say-ee
7	sette	set-teb
8	otto	ot-tob
9	nove	nob-veb
10	dieci	dee-eb-chee
11	undici	oon-dee-chee
12	dodici	dob-dee-chee
13	tredici	tray-dee-chee
14	quattordici	kwat-tor-dee-chee
15	quindici	kwin-dee-chee
16	sedici	say-dee-chee
17	diciassette	dee-chah-set-teb
18	diciotto	dee-chot-tob
19	diciannove	dee-chah-nob-veb
20	venti	ven-tee
30	trenta	tren-tab
40	quaranta	kwab-ran-tab
50	cinquanta	ching-kwan-tab
60	sessanta	sess-an-tab
70	settanta	set-tan-tab
80	ottanta	ot-tan-tab
90	novanta	nob-van-tab
100	cento	chen-tob
1,000	mille	mee-leb
2,000	duemila	doo-eb mee-lah
5,000	cinquemila	ching-kweb mee-lah
1,000,000	un milione	oon meel-yob-neb

Time

one minute	un minuto	oon mee-noo-tob
one hour	un'ora	oon or-ab
half an hour	mezz'ora	medz-or-ab
a day	un giorno	oon jor-nob
a week	una settimana	oona set-tee-mab-nab
Monday	lunedì	loo-neb-dee
Tuesday	martedì	mar-teb-dee
Wednesday	mercoledì	mair-kob-leb-dee
Thursday	giovedì	job-veb-dee
Friday	venerdì	ven-air-dee
Saturday	sabato	sab-bab-tob
Sunday	domenica	dob-meb-nee-kah

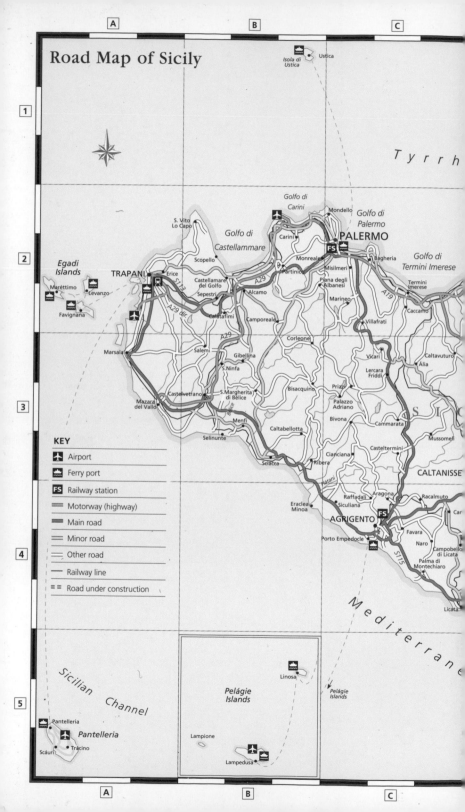